Quick Guide

M000100826

WRITE SOURCE

A BOOK FOR WRITING, THINKING, AND LEARNING

Written and Compiled by

**Dave Kemper, Patrick Sebranek,
and Verne Meyer**

Illustrated by

Chris Krenzke

WRITE SOURCE®

GREAT SOURCE EDUCATION GROUP
a division of Houghton Mifflin Company
Wilmington, Massachusetts

Reviewers

Marilyn Erbentraut
Randall Consolidated
Bassett, Wisconsin

Alberta Lantz
School District of Waukesha
Waukesha, Wisconsin

Tamara Jo Rhomberg
Rockwood School District
St. Louis, Missouri

Mary M. Fischer
Arlington Public Schools
Arlington, Massachusetts

Rita Martin
Jenks Public Schools
Jenks, Oklahoma

Michelle Gallagher
Pinellas County Schools
Largo, Florida

Inge Noa
Unified School District 475
Junction City, Kansas

Cullen Hemstreet
Jefferson Parish Schools
Metairie, Louisiana

Mary Osborne
Pinellas County Schools
Largo, Florida

Technology Connection for *Write Source*

Visit our Web site for additional student models, writing prompts, updates for citing sources, multimedia reports, information about submitting your writing, and more.

The Write Source Web site . . . www.thewritesource.com

Printed in the United States of America

International Standard Book Number: 0-669-51808-5 (hardcover)

1 2 3 4 5 6 7 8 9 10 -RRDC- 11 10 09 08 07 06 05

International Standard Book Number: 0-669-51812-3 (softcover)

1 2 3 4 5 6 7 8 9 10 -RRDC- 11 10 09 08 07 06 05

Using the *Write Source* Book

Your *Write Source* book is loaded with
information to help you learn about writing.
One section that will be especially helpful is
the "Proofreader's Guide" at the back of the book.
This section covers all of the rules for language
and grammar.

The book also includes four main units
covering the types of writing that you may have
to complete on district or state writing tests.
At the end of each unit, there are samples and
tips for writing in science, social studies, and math.

The *Write Source* book will help you with other
learning skills, too—study-reading, test taking,
note taking, and speaking. This makes the
Write Source book a valuable writing and
learning guide in all of your classes.

Your Write Source guide . . .

With practice, you will be able to find
information in this book quickly using the
guides explained below.

The **TABLE OF CONTENTS** (starting on the next page)
lists the six major sections in the book and the chapters found
in each section.

The **INDEX** (starting on page 607) lists the topics covered in the
book in alphabetical order. Use the index when you are interested
in a specific topic.

The **COLOR CODING** used for "The Basic Elements of Writing,"
"A Writer's Resource," and the "Proofreader's Guide" make these
important sections easy to find.

The **SPECIAL PAGE REFERENCES** in the book tell you where
to turn for additional information about a specific topic.

contents

The Writing Process

The Forms of Writing

PARAGRAPH WRITING

DESCRIPTIVE WRITING

RESPONSE TO LITERATURE

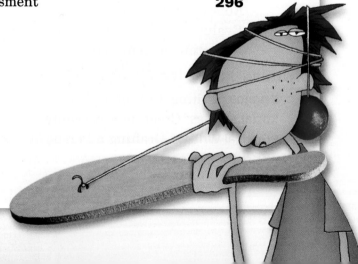

CREATIVE WRITING

RESEARCH WRITING

Speaking and Writing to Learn

SPEAKING TO LEARN

WRITING TO LEARN

The Basic Elements of Writing

WORKING WITH WORDS

A Writer's Resource

Proofreader's Guide

Why Write?

Writing won't help you become the star sprinter on the track team. And it won't give you a beautiful singing voice. But writing *will* help you in four very important ways.

Writing will help you . . .

- **become a better student.** Writing in a learning log about the subjects you are studying helps you understand and remember things better. Writing clear essays and paragraphs shows your teachers what you have learned.

- **understand your experiences.** Writing in a personal journal helps you sort out your thoughts about the everyday happenings in your life.

- **connect with others.** Writing e-mail messages and friendly letters keeps you in contact with the people that mean the most to you.

- **enjoy life.** Writing poems, stories, and plays allows you to be creative and have fun with the language.

Remember . . .

You can become a very good writer. All it takes is practice. That is why all of the writing that you do is important— no matter if you are writing for yourself or for an assignment.

Using the Writing Process

Understanding the
Writing Process

Baseball players have it tough, trying to hit an incoming fastball with a small, rounded bat. Even the best ballplayers usually get a hit only three out of ten times at bat.

Writers have it tough, too. They rarely come up with their best work in one try. In fact, writers may come to the plate many times before getting a "solid hit." That is why writing is often called a process. The best stories and essays have gone through a series of steps or stages before they are ready to share.

This chapter will explain the steps in the writing process and help you to build good writing habits along the way.

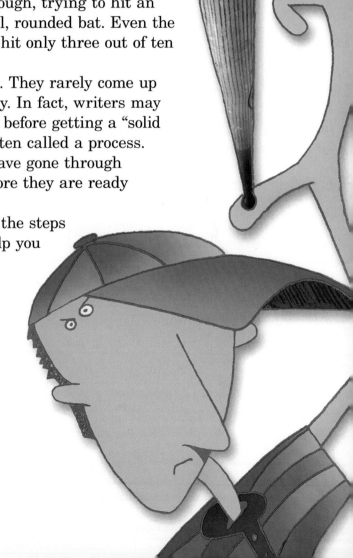

Mini Index

- Becoming a Writer
- The Writing Process
- The Process in Action
- Working with the Traits

Becoming a Writer

You can become a great writer, but you must work at it. The tips below will get you started.

Read! Read! Read!

Read books, magazines, and newspapers—and read them often! As you read, you will learn what the pros do, and how they do it.

> Read like a wolf eats.
> —Gary Paulsen

Write for yourself . . . and for other people.

Write in a personal journal. Also write stories, poems, . . . even plays! And make sure to share some of your writing with friends and family members.

> Write about what makes you want to write more.
> —Tamora Pierce

Celebrate the language!

Become aware of all the wonderful words in our language—and use them in your writing.

> Who could improve on splash, smash, ooze, shriek, slush, glide, squeak, coo?
> —Arville Schaleben

Write about a quotation. Write nonstop for 3 to 5 minutes about one of the quotations on this page. Consider what it means to you.

The Writing Process

If you work on your writing step-by-step, there's a good chance that you will be happy with the results. The steps in the writing process are described below.

The Steps in the Writing Process

 Prewrite The first step in the writing process is getting ready to write. You select a topic, collect details about it, and plan how to use them.

 Write During this step, you write a first draft. It is your first chance to get all your ideas down on paper.

 Revise You start the revising process by reviewing your first draft. Then you change the parts of the content that may be confusing or incomplete.

 Edit Next, you check your revised writing for errors and write a final copy.

 Publish In the last step, you share your final copy. This makes all of your work worth the effort.

 Think about writing. Suppose a student said, "Writing is easy. You just write everything down and then hand in your paper." What advice would you give to this student?

The Process in Action

What should you do during each step in the writing process? The next two pages will tell you.

 The gray arrows in the graphic below show that sometimes you have to repeat a step in the process. For example, after starting a first draft, you may need to do more prewriting.

Prewriting
Selecting a Topic

- Search for possible topics for the assignment.
- Select a specific topic that interests you.

Gathering Details

- Gather information about your topic.
- Think of a focus or main idea about the topic that you want to emphasize.
- Identify the details that support your focus. Also plan how to organize these details.

Writing
Developing the First Draft

- Use your prewriting as a guide.
- Get all of your ideas on paper.
- Include a beginning, a middle, and an ending.

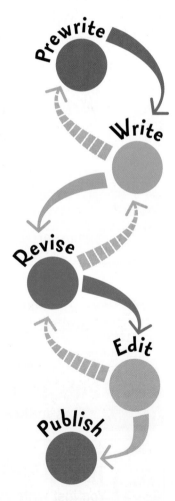

Revising Improving Your Writing

- Read your first draft once aloud and once silently.
- Also ask at least one other person to read your draft.
- Use these questions as a basic revising guide:
  - **Are my ideas clear and complete?**
  - **Does the beginning attract the reader?**
  - **Are the details in the middle easy to follow?**
  - **Does the ending say something important about the topic?**
  - **Do I sound interested in my topic?**
  - **Do I use specific words?**
  - **Are my sentences easy to read?**
- Add, cut, or rewrite parts as needed.

Editing Checking for Conventions

- Find and correct punctuation, capitalization, spelling, and grammar errors.
- Also ask someone else to check your writing for errors.
- Write a neat final copy and proofread this copy for errors.

The Writing Process

Writing is a step-by-step process.

Publishing Sharing Your Writing

- Share your finished writing with others.
- Decide if you will include the writing in your portfolio.

 Create a mini-poster. Design a writing-process poster on a piece of notebook or computer paper. Include a title, a short statement about the writing process, and an interesting graphic.

Working with the Traits

Because writing is a process, you don't have to think about everything at once. Instead, you can deal with the six traits of writing (shown below) when they become important. For example, *ideas* are important right away, while *word choice* becomes more important later on. Here are some of the key things you have to think about during your writing.

What main ideas should I include?
How should I organize my details?
Do I sound interested in my topic?
Have I used the best words?
Will readers enjoy my sentences?
Have I checked for errors?

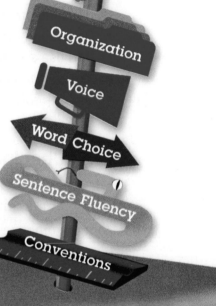

Ideas
Organization
Voice
Word Choice
Sentence Fluency
Conventions

Use the process. On your own paper, match each activity on the left to its proper place in the writing process on the right.

_____ **1.** Rewrite some of your sentences.

_____ **2.** Select an interesting topic.

_____ **3.** Post your story on your Web site.

_____ **4.** Double-check your writing for errors.

_____ **5.** Develop a creative beginning.

A. Prewriting

B. Writing

C. Revising

D. Editing

E. Publishing

One Writer's Process

Author James Howe says, "Writing is like digging in the sand for buried treasure: You have to be willing to do a lot of digging." Luckily, writing can be broken down into steps, which makes all of the "digging" more manageable. The steps in the writing process include *prewriting, writing, revising, editing,* and *publishing.*

This chapter shows you how Max Koski used the writing process to write an expository essay explaining the importance of friends. As Max worked step-by-step on his essay, it became more detailed, more interesting, and more accurate.

Mini Index

- **Previewing the Goals**
- **Prewriting**
- **Writing**
- **Revising**
- **Editing**
- **Assessing the Final Copy**
- **Reflecting on Your Writing**

Previewing the Goals

Before Max began writing, he read the goals for the assignment. These goals helped him to get started. He also reviewed the rubric for expository writing on pages 176–177.

Your goal is to . . .

Ideas — Select a topic that explores something important to you.

Organization — Make sure that your essay is easy to follow from beginning to end.

Voice — Let the reader know that you really care about the topic.

Word Choice — Use specific nouns, vivid verbs, and colorful adjectives.

Sentence Fluency — Write sentences that flow smoothly and clearly.

Conventions — Follow the rules for punctuation, capitalization, spelling, and grammar.

Answer these questions about Max's writing assignment.

1 What type of topic should Max select?

2 How should he sound in his essay?

3 What should he remember about his sentences?

Prewriting Selecting a Topic

Max was given the following assignment: *Write an expository essay that explains something that is very important to you.* To think of topics, Max freely wrote about the assignment.

Freewriting

> Many things are important to me. I love sports, especially soccer and baseball. Of course, my family is important to me. My mom helps me in all kinds of ways. And how could I live without all my friends? Steve is . . .

Max decided to write about the importance of friends. He knew his classmates could identify with this topic.

Gathering Details

Ms. Lee, Max's teacher, helped the class think of different strategies that help explain a topic. They could . . .

✔ 1. define the topic,
2. share a quotation related to the topic,
✔ 3. explain what the topic means to them,
✔ 4. share what other people think about the topic,
5. relate the topic to something they had read, or
✔ 6. show the topic in action.

Max checked four strategies that he would like to use. Then he gathered details for his essay. He looked up the word *friend* in a dictionary and in a thesaurus. He also thought about the importance of friends in his own life. And he asked others what they thought about friends. He took good notes along the way.

Writing **Completing Your First Draft**

When Max wrote his first draft, he included the ideas he gathered during his prewriting on page 11. He tried to get all his thoughts down on paper. (Naturally, there are some errors in Max's first draft.)

The beginning paragraph states the main idea of the essay (underlined).

The writer shares his own thoughts.

The writer also shares the thoughts of other people.

The dictionary says what the word friend means. A few synonyms for friend include companion and classmate. You may also call your friends "amigos!" That's cool. <u>A friend is one of the most important things you can have.</u>

To me, maybe a friend is like a trusted baseball glove. My glove never let's me down. It helps me play good most of the time. That's how I think a friend shoud be: dependable, great to be around, and helpful. I guess that knowing that having friends is a good thing, and it keep me going when I'm having a bad day.

Friends are different things to different people. My little sister thinks a friend shoud like to swim and ride bikes. My Mom's idea of a friend is Mrs. Milanovich who walks and talks a lot with my mom. My Dad's friends are neighbors who do projects with him.

The topic is shown in action.

Steve is definitely a best friend to me. We play soccer hang out and talk about sports. I broke my leg. He always came over to play video games. In school he carried my backpack and gets my lunch tray for me. I can always count on Steve. He knows that he can count on me.

A final idea about the topic is given.

Sum friends come and go in your life. Others will be there for a long time, maybe even forever I would hate to move, unless I coud take my friends with me. They are that important.

Practice

Review the goals for ideas, organization, and voice on page 10. Does Max meet these goals in his first draft? Explain.

Revising Improving Your Writing

After Max read through his first draft, he made the following changes to his essay.

A definition is added.

The dictionary says, ~~what~~ *that* the word friend "a person someone knows and likes well" means. A few synonyms for friend include companion and classmate. *If you speak Spanish,* You may also call ~~your~~ friends "amigos!" ~~That's cool.~~ *In any langauge* A friend is one of the most important things you can have.

Details are added and unneeded words are cut.

To me, ~~maybe~~ a friend is like a trusted baseball glove. My glove never lets me down. It helps me play good ~~most of the time~~. That's how I think a friend shoud be: dependable, great to be around, and helpful. ~~I guess that~~ having friends is a good thing, and it keep me going when . . .

Words are deleted to make the voice sound more confident.

Practice

Review Max's changes. Identify two changes that seem the most important. Explain your choices.

Revising Using a Peer Response

Using a classmate's comments, Max made more changes in his essay. These changes made his essay even better. (See pages **39–42**.)

The dictionary says that the word friend

means a person someone knows and likes well. A

Could you add more synonyms?

few synonyms for friend include companion ~~and~~
pal and buddy.
classmate.ₐIf you speak Spanish, you may call

friends "amigos!" In any langauge, a friend is one

of the most important things you can have.

Tell me more about how the glove helps you.

To me, a friend is like a trusted baseball
It feels comfortable on my hand and
glove. My glove never lets me down.ₐ~~It~~ helps me

play good. That's how I think a friend shoud be:

easy
dependable, ~~great~~ to be around, and helpful.

What do you mean by "great" and "a good thing"?

makes my life more fun,
Having friendsₐ~~is a good thing,~~ and it keep me

going when I'm having a bad day. . . .

Practice

Answer the following questions: Which comment by the classmate is most helpful? Explain. What comment would you like to add? Explain.

Editing Checking for Conventions

Before writing a final copy, Max checked his essay for spelling, punctuation, capitalization, and grammar. (See inside the back cover of this book for a list of editing and proofreading marks.)

Words being used in a special way are underlined.	The dictionary says that the word <u>friend</u> means "a person someone knows and likes well." A few synonyms for friend include <u>companion</u>,
Commas are placed between words in a series.	<u>classmate</u>, <u>pal</u>, and <u>buddy</u>. If you speak Spanish, you may call friends "amigos!" In any ~~langauge~~ language a friend is one of the most important things you can have.
Spelling and usage errors are corrected.	To me, a friend is like a trusted baseball glove. My glove never lets me down. It feels comfortable on my hand and helps me play ~~good~~ well. That's how I think a friend ~~shoud~~ should be: . . .

Practice

Review Max's editing. Then discuss these questions as a class: Do you make some of the same kinds of errors? Do you use editing marks? Do you check for errors in the same way each time you edit your writing?

Max's Final Copy

Max felt great about his final essay. It captured how important friends are in his life.

Max Koski

The Power of Friends

The dictionary says that the word *friend* means "a person someone knows and likes well." A few synonyms for friend include *companion, classmate, pal,* and *buddy*. If you speak Spanish, you may call friends "amigos!" In any language, a friend is one of the most important things you can have.

To me, a friend is like a trusted baseball glove. My glove never lets me down. It feels comfortable on my hand and helps me play well. That's how I think a friend should be: dependable, easy to be around, and helpful. Having friends makes my life more fun, and it keeps me going when I'm having a bad day.

Koski 2

Friends are different things to different people. To my little sister, a friend is someone who likes to swim and ride bikes. My mom's idea of a friend is Mrs. Milanovich, someone who walks (and talks) with my mom every morning. My dad's friends are neighbors who help him with projects like building sheds and planting trees.

Steve is my best friend. We play soccer, hang out, and talk about sports. When I broke my leg, he always came over to play video games. In school, he carried my backpack and got my lunch tray for me. I know I can always count on Steve, and he knows that he can count on me.

Some friends may be in your life for just a little while. Others will be there for a long time, maybe even forever. I would hate to move, unless I could take my friends with me. They are too important to leave behind.

Assessing the Final Copy

Max's teacher used the rubric on pages 176–177 to assess his final copy. A 6 is the very best score that a writer can receive for each trait. The teacher also included comments under each trait.

Ideas

6 Ideas
I especially liked the synonyms for friend that you included.

Organization

5 Organization
Each middle paragraph has a clear topic sentence and gives valuable information.

Voice

5 Voice
You sound very interested in your topic.

Word Choice

4 Word Choice
Your verbs could have been stronger. You use the verbs is and are a lot.

Sentence Fluency

5 Sentence Fluency
Your sentences are smooth and easy to read.

Conventions

6 Conventions
Your essay is free of careless errors.

Discuss the assessment. Do you agree with the scores and the comments made by Max's teacher? Why or why not? What do you really like in the essay? What would you have done differently?

Reflecting on Your Writing

Once Max finished his essay, he filled out a reflection sheet.

> Thinking about your writing makes you aware of ways to improve as a writer.

Max Koski

My Expository Essay

1. The best part of my essay is . . .
   how I explained the word <u>friend</u> with great examples.

2. The part that still needs work is . . .
   my word choice. I could have used more specific action verbs.

3. The main thing I learned about writing an expository essay is . . .
   that it can take a lot of thinking and even some research. Expository writing must include a lot of good information.

4. The next time I write an expository essay, I would like to . . .
   compare my two favorite sports, soccer and baseball.

Understanding the
Traits of Writing

To make a great pizza, you must work with the best ingredients: a homemade crust, tasty cheese, and fresh toppings. To write great stories or reports, you must also work with the best "ingredients." They include great ideas, specific details, colorful words, and smooth sentences.

This chapter reviews the traits found in all good writing. After learning how to use these traits, or ingredients, you'll be taking your writing from "bland" to "tasty" in no time.

Mini Index

- **Introducing the Traits**
- **Learning About the Traits**

Introducing the Traits

Keep the following traits in mind when you write. If you follow them, you will do your best work.

Ideas — The best writing has a clear message to share. It includes plenty of specific ideas and details.

Organization — Good writing has a clear beginning, middle, and ending. It is easy to follow from beginning to end.

Voice — In the best writing, you can hear the writer's voice. Voice is the special way a writer expresses ideas and feelings.

Word Choice — Good writing contains strong words, including specific nouns *(poodle, shack, mango)* and verbs *(fizzle, leap, squirt)* and colorful adjectives *(clumsy, brilliant, tender)*.

Sentence Fluency — Excellent writing flows from one sentence to the next. Sentences begin in different ways. They also vary in length.

Conventions — Good writing follows the rules for punctuation, capitalization, grammar, and spelling.

tip One additional trait to consider is the **presentation** of your writing. Good writing looks neat and follows guidelines for margins, spacing, and indenting. (See pages **44–46**.)

Understanding Ideas

It's simple. Good writing includes good ideas. Author Phoebe Gilman knows the value of writing ideas. She always records the best ones for future use: "It's very handy to scribble ideas down right away. Otherwise, they evaporate."

What is the key idea in a writing assignment?

The key idea in all writing assignments is the topic. Always choose a topic that is neither too broad nor too narrow.

Sample Assignment: Write an essay about a specific topic related to our study of the oceans.

Possible Topics

- The ocean contains a lot of food. (too broad)
- The ocean keeps our neighborhood cool. (too narrow)
- The ocean gives us salt. (just right)

Should I say everything about a topic?

No. Even though you may learn a lot about a topic, it's best to focus on a specific or certain part of it or a feeling you have about it. The statement below focuses on a specific part of the topic. It helps the writer know what details to include in the writing.

Focus statement: The salt from the ocean (topic) helps people in important ways (a specific part).

Writing that is not focused is unclear and hard to follow.

How should I collect ideas about a topic?

There are many ways to collect ideas about a topic. Some of the best ways are listed below.

1 **Find out what you already know about a topic.**

Once you select a topic, decide what you already know about it and write it down.

Listing ● Make a list of ideas that come to mind as you think of your topic.

Freewriting ● Write freely about your topic for 3 to 5 minutes.

Clustering ● Begin a cluster, or web, by writing your topic in the middle of your paper. Then write related words and ideas around it.

2 **Learn more about a topic.**

You will have to research some topics before you can write about them. Use the following strategies:

Reading ● Learn facts and details by reading about your subject in books, encyclopedias, and magazines.

Exploring the Internet ● Explore the Internet for up-to-date information. (See pages **323** and **398** for help.)

Interviewing ● Talk with an expert about your topic. You can meet in person, talk on the phone, or send e-mail messages.

Practice

Practice choosing a topic and writing a focus statement for the following assignment: *Write an essay about the value of some type of exercise.* Then list your first thoughts about the topic.

Understanding Organization

Writer Vicki Spandel states, "Effective organization keeps a piece of writing together and makes it easy to follow."

How important is the beginning part?

The beginning part is very important. It should get the reader's attention and share the focus or main idea of your writing.

Beginning Paragraph

Interesting opening

Focus (underlined)

Believe it or not, I once dove into water that was full of sharks. But I wasn't afraid. That's because I was inside an underwater craft with my dad and a guide. I had a chance to do this when I was visiting my grandparents in Florida. I'll never forget the underwater sights.

What should I include in the middle part?

The middle part of your writing should include specific details related to the focus of your topic. Here are some ways to do this.

Sample Middle Paragraph

Explain: Share information about your topic.

Define: Give the meaning of important terms.

Compare: Show how two things are alike and different.

Describe: Include sensory details about your topic.

Sensory details

It was dark as we dove down, and the lights on our craft lit up the sea. Brilliant-colored fish were darting in front of the thick glass window. A nurse shark bumped into the window with a thud. Lobsters skittered away. With the help of our guide, we listed the names of the creatures we saw.

How important is the ending part?

The ending of your writing is very important because it is the reader's last look at your ideas. You should spend as much or more time on the ending than you do on the beginning. An effective ending does one or more of these things:

- Reminds the reader of the main idea.
- Summarizes the key points.
- Emphasizes one point.
- Answers any final questions the reader may have.
- Keeps the reader thinking about the topic.

Ending Paragraph

Summary of key points

From our underwater craft, we saw a whole world of ocean creatures. There were strange kinds of animals and plants that most people never see. Some of the creatures were very weird and looked nothing like the fish we see in Lake Erie. I would recommend a visit under the ocean for anyone who gets a chance.

Practice

Review one or two of your last pieces of writing. Rewrite the ending in one of the pieces using the summary method or one of the other strategies listed above as a guide.

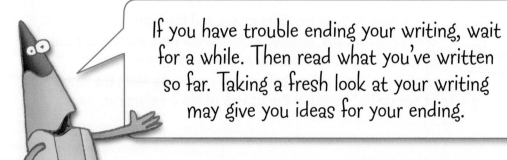

If you have trouble ending your writing, wait for a while. Then read what you've written so far. Taking a fresh look at your writing may give you ideas for your ending.

Understanding Voice

Developing your own special way of saying things may take time, but as Judy Blume states, "Eventually you'll come up with your own voice." Just read and write as much as you can.

Why is voice so important?

Writing that has voice interests readers. A strong voice helps bring the writer's thoughts and ideas to life and makes the reader say, "Hey, I like that."

WRITING THAT LACKS VOICE

I once got an autograph from a good tennis player. The player was Venus Williams. I was happy.

WRITING THAT HAS VOICE

Suddenly, there was Venus Williams listening to headphones. I had butterflies in my stomach when I asked her for an autograph. I actually felt numb when she signed my paper. As I made my way to my seat, I pinched myself to make sure I wasn't dreaming.

How can I write with voice?

Follow these suggestions to develop an effective writing voice:

- **Read a lot.** Reading shows you how others express themselves.
- **Write a lot.** Your voice will develop as you continue writing.
- **Select good topics.** Write about topics that truly interest you.

Practice

Write freely for 3 to 5 minutes about the most exciting thing that has ever happened to you. When you finish, underline words and phrases that sound like you.

Understanding Word Choice

Experienced writers love working with words. As author Seymour Simon states, "Putting together words is one of the most thrilling things that one can do."

What should I know about the words that I use?

Your goal is to use the best words to express your ideas.

Choose Specific Nouns

Some nouns are general—*car, animal, house*—and give the reader only a fuzzy picture. Other nouns are specific—*convertible, llama, igloo*—and give the reader a much clearer, more detailed picture.

Use Strong Action Verbs

Use strong action verbs like *glared* and *stared*. For example, the statement "Mr. Brown *glared* at the two tardy boys" is much more interesting than "Mr. Brown *looked* at the two tardy boys."

Select Effective Modifiers

Use colorful **adjectives** in your writing. When you say, "The Thunderbolt is a *screaming* roller coaster," you are describing the ride in a colorful way.

Use **adverbs** to make the action in the sentence more specific. The statement "Mugsy barked *wildly* when the doorbell rang" is more specific than "Mugsy barked when the doorbell rang."

Practice

In one of your stories or essays, circle your strongest nouns, verbs, and modifiers. Then change at least three words that could be more specific.

Understanding Sentence Fluency

Make sure that your sentences read smoothly from one to the next. Smooth sentences are enjoyable to read.

How can I make my sentences flow smoothly?

Vary Your Sentence Beginnings If you start too many sentences in the same way, your writing will sound boring.

TOO MANY SENTENCES BEGINNING IN THE SAME WAY

The McKinley girls' soccer team made history last night. The soccer team became the first city team to win a state soccer title. The team beat Milton 2–0 in the finals.

VARIED BEGINNINGS

The McKinley girls' soccer team made history last night. The Panthers became the first city team to win a state soccer title. In the finals, they beat Milton 2–0.

Combine Short, Choppy Sentences If you combine short, choppy sentences, your writing will be easier to read. (See pages **445–447**.)

SHORT, CHOPPY SENTENCES

We're having a family contest. Who can plan the best trip? I want to go camping. My sister wants to visit New York City.

COMBINED SENTENCES

We're having a family contest to see who can plan the best trip. I want to go camping, but my sister wants to visit New York City.

Practice

Using the index, find some more information about sentence combining in this book. List two new things that you learn.

Understanding Conventions

Conventions cover the rules of punctuation, capitalization, grammar, and spelling. When you follow these rules, your writing will be clear and easy to understand.

How can I make sure my writing follows the rules?

A conventions checklist like the one below can guide you as you edit and proofread your writing. When you are not sure about a rule, check the "Proofreader's Guide." (See pages **478–605**.)

Conventions

PUNCTUATION

_____ **1.** Do I use end punctuation after every sentence?

_____ **2.** Do I use commas correctly in compound sentences?

_____ **3.** Do I use apostrophes to show possession
(*the girl's backpack*)?

CAPITALIZATION

_____ **4.** Do I start every sentence with a capital letter?

_____ **5.** Do I capitalize the names of people and places?

SPELLING

_____ **6.** Have I checked my spelling?

GRAMMAR

_____ **7.** Do I use the correct forms of verbs
(*had seen*, not *had saw*)?

_____ **8.** Do I use the right words (*to, too, two*)?

Always have at least one other person check your writing for conventions. You could ask a classmate, a teacher, or a family member for help.

Using a Rubric

Car mechanics are lucky. They can use a diagnostic machine to evaluate the overall performance of an engine. If the machine finds a problem, the mechanic knows what to repair.

As a writer, you must use a rubric, instead of a machine, to evaluate your stories and essays. A rubric is a chart that lists the main traits for a form of writing. This chapter explains how to use rubrics to rate and "repair" your writing.

Mini Index

Understanding Rubrics

Many of your writing assignments are rated, most often with a rubric. The rubrics in this book use the following scale.

6	5	4	3	2	1
Amazing	Strong	Good	Okay	Poor	Incomplete

tip The rubrics are arranged according to the traits of writing—*ideas, organization, voice, word choice, sentence fluency*, and *conventions*. (For more information about the traits, see pages 21–30.)

Rating Guide

This guide will help you understand the rating scale.

A **6** means that the writing is truly amazing.
It far exceeds the main requirements for a trait.

A **5** means that the writing is very strong.
It meets the main requirements for a trait.

A **4** means that the writing is good.
It meets most of the requirements for a trait.

A **3** means that the writing is okay.
It needs work to meet the main requirements.

A **2** means that the writing is poor.
It needs a lot of work.

A **1** means that the writing is incomplete.
It is not yet ready to assess, or evaluate.

Reading a Rubric

The rubrics in this book are color coded for the six main traits (green for *ideas*, pink for *organization*, and so on). Each trait includes six rating numbers and a description for each number. The description will help you evaluate your writing for a certain trait.

Rubric for Narrative Writing

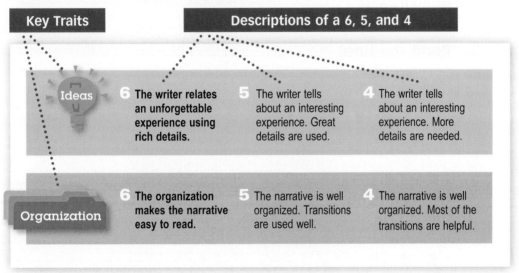

Key Traits	Descriptions of a 6, 5, and 4

Ideas

6 The writer relates an unforgettable experience using rich details.

5 The writer tells about an interesting experience. Great details are used.

4 The writer tells about an interesting experience. More details are needed.

Organization

6 The organization makes the narrative easy to read.

5 The narrative is well organized. Transitions are used well.

4 The narrative is well organized. Most of the transitions are helpful.

A Closer Look

When you read a rubric for each trait, follow these four steps:

1. First, read the 5 description. (*Remember:* A 5 is very strong writing that meets the main requirements for that trait.)

2. Decide if your writing should get a 5 for that trait.

3. If not, check the descriptions for 6, 4, 3, 2, and 1 until you find the rating that best fits your paper.

4. If you are still revising and your rating is a 4 or lower, make the changes needed to improve the rating for that trait.

Review the complete narrative rubric. Review the rubric on pages 120–121. Which traits will be the hardest for you to achieve a 5 or 6 rating? Which will be the easiest? Explain.

Assessing with a Rubric

When you assess or evaluate a piece of writing with a rubric—like the one on page 35—follow these four steps.

1. Make an assessment sheet. Use this sample as a guide.

2. Read the final copy. Get an overall feeling for the writing before you evaluate it.

3. Assess the writing using the rubric. For each trait, decide which rating (1–6) best fits the writing and put that number on your assessment sheet.

```
ASSESSMENT SHEET    Title: _____

____  IDEAS
      1.
      2.

____  ORGANIZATION
      1.
      2.

____  VOICE
      1.
      2.

____  WORD CHOICE
      1.
      2.

____  SENTENCE FLUENCY
      1.
      2.

____  CONVENTIONS
      1.
      2.

              Evaluator: _____
```

4. Make comments for each trait. Write one strength (1.) and one weakness (2.) beneath each trait. (See page **37**.)

Make an assessment sheet. Create an assessment sheet like the one shown above. You will use this sheet to complete an assessment for the narrative on page 38.

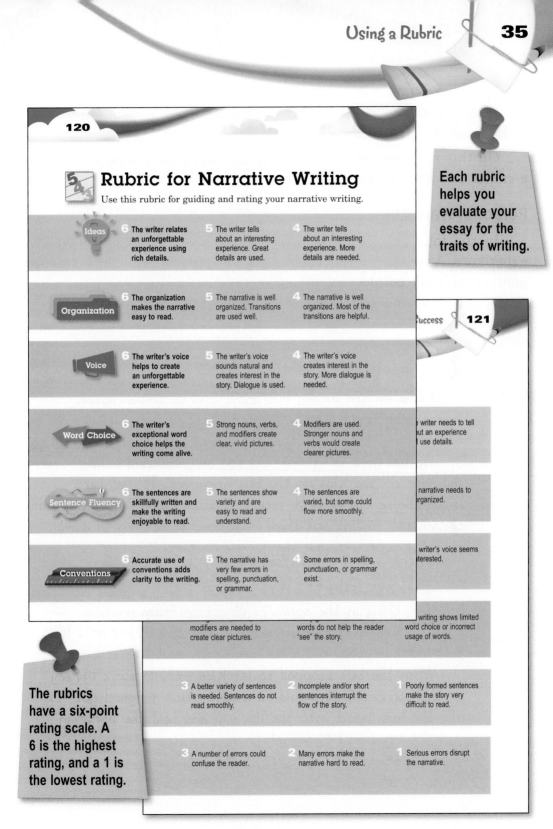

120

Rubric for Narrative Writing

Use this rubric for guiding and rating your narrative writing.

Each rubric helps you evaluate your essay for the traits of writing.

Ideas
- **6** The writer relates an unforgettable experience using rich details.
- **5** The writer tells about an interesting experience. Great details are used.
- **4** The writer tells about an interesting experience. More details are needed.

Organization
- **6** The organization makes the narrative easy to read.
- **5** The narrative is well organized. Transitions are used well.
- **4** The narrative is well organized. Most of the transitions are helpful.

Success   121

Voice
- **6** The writer's voice helps to create an unforgettable experience.
- **5** The writer's voice sounds natural and creates interest in the story. Dialogue is used.
- **4** The writer's voice creates interest in the story. More dialogue is needed.

Word Choice
- **6** The writer's exceptional word choice helps the writing come alive.
- **5** Strong nouns, verbs, and modifiers create clear, vivid pictures.
- **4** Modifiers are used. Stronger nouns and verbs would create clearer pictures.

e writer needs to tell ut an experience use details.

Sentence Fluency
- **6** The sentences are skillfully written and make the writing enjoyable to read.
- **5** The sentences show variety and are easy to read and understand.
- **4** The sentences are varied, but some could flow more smoothly.

narrative needs to organized.

Conventions
- **6** Accurate use of conventions adds clarity to the writing.
- **5** The narrative has very few errors in spelling, punctuation, or grammar.
- **4** Some errors in spelling, punctuation, or grammar exist.

writer's voice seems terested.

modifiers are needed to create clear pictures.

words do not help the reader "see" the story.

writing shows limited word choice or incorrect usage of words.

The rubrics have a six-point rating scale. A 6 is the highest rating, and a 1 is the lowest rating.

- **3** A better variety of sentences is needed. Sentences do not read smoothly.
- **2** Incomplete and/or short sentences interrupt the flow of the story.
- **1** Poorly formed sentences make the story very difficult to read.

- **3** A number of errors could confuse the reader.
- **2** Many errors make the narrative hard to read.
- **1** Serious errors disrupt the narrative.

Reviewing an Assessment

On this page and on page 37, you can see how one student used a rubric and an assessment sheet to evaluate her writing.

Personal Narrative

In the following narrative, the writer shares an embarrassing experience. As you read this sample, pay special attention to its strong points and weak points.

New Kid Lost

I was on the wrong bus and I was so embarrassed. It was supposed to be bus three but I was on bus eight. What an end to my first day at a new school!

We had lived in Springfield for only about a week, and none of the kids on the bus knew me. It was hard enough being the newest fourth grader. I didn't need my classmates finding out that I had done something so dumb. Getting on the wrong school bus was something a first grader might do!

Nothing on the streets looked familiar. We were probably going in the opposite direction from my new house. I felt like crying. My face was all red and hot. I felt like everybody must be looking at me.

When the bus stopped to let kids off, I saw a library on the corner. That would be a safe place to go. I got off the bus, went into the library, and told the librarian my mistake. She let me call home.

Mom said I made a good decision.

Sample Self-Assessment

The student who wrote "New Kid Lost" used the rubric on pages 120–121 to evaluate her narrative. Beneath each trait, she named one strength (1.) and one weakness (2.) in her writing.

ASSESSMENT SHEET   Title: "New Kid Lost"

__4__   IDEAS
1. My background details are clear.
2. More details about the ride are needed.

__4__   ORGANIZATION
1. My beginning introduces the topic.
2. My ending could say more.

__4__   VOICE
1. I shared real feelings.
2. Dialogue would help.

__4__   WORD CHOICE
1. Red and hot are strong words.
2. Some words could be more interesting.

__5__   SENTENCE FLUENCY
1. My sentences are easy to read.
2. Some of the sentences in paragraph three could be combined.

__5__   CONVENTIONS
1. My spelling is perfect!
2. I forgot to use commas in my compound sentences.

Evaluator: __Sonia Lee__

Review the self-assessment. Read through the assessment sheet above. Then list one strength and one weakness (for any trait) that the writer may have missed.

Assessing a Narrative

As you read through the personal narrative below, pay special attention to the strengths and weaknesses in the writing. Then follow the directions at the bottom of the page.

Cousin Jake

"Do I have to go to the family reunion?" I asked my mom. Every summer, everything is the same.

"Yes, you have to go," Mom answered. So we packed up the car, and off we went to Montana.

When we arrived at Uncle Billy's house, I saw a new kid hanging around. He was about my age, but he didn't look like he belonged in our family. Most of us are tall, and have red hair. This kid was short, and he had curly, black hair. His name was Jake, and he was my new cousin! Uncle Billy had gotten married, and Jake was his new wife's son.

Through the whole reunion, Jake and I had fun. He let me fly his Japanese kite. We built a skateboard ramp, rode our bikes, and played baseball. One night, Jake and some of his friends and I slept outside in a big tent. Jake was a nice kid, and I was happy that he was a part of my family.

When it was time to go home, I felt sad. I'm already looking forward to next year. With Jake around, family reunions will be a lot more fun.

Use a narrative rubric. Assess the narrative you have just read using the rubric on pages 120–121 as a guide. Record your ratings and comments on the assessment sheet you made on page 34.

Peer Responding

Sooner or later, writers need someone to read what they've written. At school, you might say, "LaKisha, please read my report." At home, you might ask for a parent's opinion. If you do, you are acting like a real author.

Getting someone else's response can help you improve a first draft. This chapter explains how to organize a peer-editing session.

Mini Index

- **Peer-Responding Guidelines**
- **Making Helpful Responses**
- **Peer Response Sheet**

Peer Respons

Writer: Curtis Davis .... Resp

Title: "Flying Fish, Ocean Acroba

What I liked about your writing:

* Your opening is full of action.

* The details really helped me learn

* The story about the fisherman is

Questions I have . . .

* What do you know about their ener

* What different ways could you begir

sentences?

Peer-Responding Guidelines

When you first do a peer response, you may work with one classmate. Later, you may have a chance to work with a small group of classmates. Either way, you need to know how to share and respond to a piece of writing.

The Author's Role

As an author, share a piece of writing that you are working on. If possible, make a copy for each member of the group.

- **Introduce your writing,** but don't say too much about it.
- **Read your writing out loud,** or ask group members to read it silently.
- **Ask group members what they think.** Listen carefully.
- **Take notes** to help you remember what was said.
- **Ask for help** with any specific problems.

The Responder's Role

As a responder, make sure to show the writer the proper respect. Also follow these guidelines:

- **Listen (or read) carefully.** Take notes to help you remember what you want to say.
- **Tell what works** well in the writing.
- **Ask questions** if you are unsure about something or find a part that could be improved.

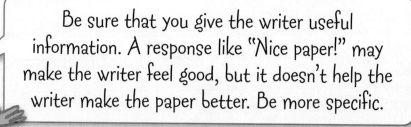

Be sure that you give the writer useful information. A response like "Nice paper!" may make the writer feel good, but it doesn't help the writer make the paper better. Be more specific.

Making Helpful Responses

Responses from your classmates are very important when you are ready to revise your writing. Responders can help you find parts that work well, as well as parts that don't work so well.

Be Specific

The most useful responses help a writer improve his or her writing. Try to state your responses in the form of a question.

INSTEAD OF . . .	TRY SOMETHING LIKE . . .
✗ Your writing is dull.	✔ What different ways could you begin some of your sentences?
✗ Some of your facts are wrong.	✔ Do flying fish really "fly"?
✗ The third paragraph doesn't say anything new.	✔ What do you know about their enemies?

Ask Good Questions

The best questions cannot be answered with a simple yes or no. Instead, they ask the writer to think.

- What got you interested in your topic?
- What is your most important point?
- How do you want the reader to feel about your topic?

Practice

As a class or small group, discuss the types of comments that are most helpful to authors during peer-responding sessions. Make a chart of helpful comments or questions to post in the classroom.

Peer Response Sheet

Your teacher may want you to complete a response sheet like the one below. (Sample comments are included.)

Peer Response Sheet

Writer: Curtis Davis   Responder: Kim Lee

Title: "Flying Fish, Ocean Acrobats"

What I liked about your writing:

* Your opening is full of action.

* The details really helped me learn about flying fish.

* The story about the fisherman is interesting.

Questions I have . . .

* What do you know about their enemies?

* What different ways could you begin some of your sentences?

Practice

Exchange an essay or a story with a classmate. Then fill out a response sheet like the one above for each other's writing.

Publishing and Portfolios

Publishing is the important final step in the writing process. It makes all of your prewriting, drafting, and revising worth the effort. Your writing is ready to publish once it says exactly what you want it to say.

This chapter will help you prepare your writing for publishing. It will show you how to design a great-looking final copy and how to assemble a classroom portfolio.

Mini Index

- Designing Your Writing
- Types of Portfolios
- Parts of a Portfolio
- Sample Portfolio Reflections

Designing Your Writing

Once your writing is complete, think about how you want your paper to look. The guidelines below, and the example on pages 45–46, will help you design and publish your writing using a computer.

Typography

- Use a clear and easy-to-read font for the body and any headings.
- Keep the title and any headings short. Follow the rules for capitalizing titles and headings. (See pages **45–46**.)

Spacing and Margins

- Double-space your writing.
- Indent the first line of every paragraph.
- Use one space after every period.
- Avoid odd breaks between pages. For example, don't leave a heading or the first line of a paragraph alone at the bottom of a page.

Graphics

- Use numbered or bulleted lists to set off important points.
- Include a table, a chart, or an illustration if it helps make an idea clearer. Make sure that there is plenty of space for any graphics you use.

Practice

Find a page in one of your textbooks (including this one) that you feel is well designed. Share the page with your classmates and point out at least three features that you like.

Great-Looking Design in Action

Roy Wilson

Saving a Vanishing Falcon

The font is easy to read.

Imagine a bird dropping out of the sky at 200 miles an hour. That is what makes the peregrine falcon such a successful bird of prey. In fact, the Air Force Academy has made the falcon its official mascot. The peregrine falcon was placed on the Endangered Species list until 1999. A well-planned reintroduction effort has saved these amazing birds.

Why were falcons endangered?

Although a falcon pair may raise as many as four chicks, only two usually survive past their first year. The loss of these chicks from a variety of causes threatened the survival of the species. The main problems are listed here.

A bulleted list helps organize the essay.

- **Hunting and egg removal:** Before 1950, hunters shot falcons. Eggs were often taken from nests for falconry or food.
- **Pesticides:** Falcons ate birds that had eaten poisoned insects. The main poison, DDT, affected the thickness of eggshells. Eggs cracked, and the chicks died before hatching.

What did falcons need?

The peregrine falcons needed a chance to raise enough chicks to replace their numbers. They also needed pesticide-free food.

How were falcons saved?

Several wildlife organizations and government programs worked to restore the peregrine population.

1. Falcons were placed on the Endangered Species list.
2. Pesticides such as DDT, which could last a long time in nature, were banned.
3. Safer pesticides were developed.
4. Eggs were taken from captive birds.
5. Newly hatched birds were fed and protected.

More than 6,000 falcons have been bred and released. They are successfully living in wild areas as well as in cities with tall buildings. This recovery of the fastest birds of the air shows what can be done if people become involved.

Margins are at least one inch all around.

A numbered list makes ideas easy to follow.

An illustration is added.

Types of Portfolios

A portfolio is a collection of your writing that you put together for a specific reason. There are four basic types of portfolios.

Showcase Portfolio

A showcase portfolio shows off your best writing for a grading period. This is the most common type of portfolio. (See page **48**.)

Growth Portfolio

A growth portfolio shows your progress as a writer. It contains writing assignments that show how your writing skills are developing throughout the year.

Personal Portfolio

A personal portfolio contains writing that you want to save and share with others. You can include different types of writing—poetry, stories, reports, essays. You can have different themes—friends, animals, hobbies, sports.

Electronic Portfolio

An electronic portfolio is presented on a Web site or saved on a disk. In addition to your writing, you may include graphics and sound. Electronic portfolios make your writing available to many people.

Practice

Write a brief paragraph about your experience with portfolios. When did you put one together? How did you feel about it when you finished?

Parts of a Portfolio

You may be asked to keep a showcase portfolio. It should contain the parts listed below, but check with your teacher to be sure.

- **A table of contents** lists the writing samples you have included in your portfolio.

- **A short essay or letter** introduces your portfolio. It tells how you put it together and how you feel about it.

- **The writing samples** present your best work. Your teacher may ask you to include all of your work—from prewriting through editing—for one or two samples.

- **Reflection sheets or checklists** identify the writing skills that you have mastered and the ones that you still need to work on.

- **A creative cover for your portfolio** may include graphics and sketches that say something about you as a writer.

GATHERING TIPS

- **Date and save all your work,** including prewriting notes, first drafts, and revisions for each writing assignment.
- **Store your writing in a pocket folder.** Then you will have everything that you need in one place.
- **Take pride in your work.** Prepare a portfolio that shows you at your best.

Practice

Plan a showcase portfolio cover. Include your name and a title. Then add your own sketches and graphics.

Sample Portfolio Reflections

To reflect on your writing, think about the process that you used to develop it. The samples below will help you get started.

Student Reflections

My story called "Two Faces of Thanksgiving" taught me an important lesson about life. People change from year to year, and we can't do anything about it.
—Tina Sung

"Floating or Fishing?" was really hard to write because it was a comparison essay. I had to figure out how to organize the details about my two topics, Lake Superior and Great Salt Lake.
—Jon Worthy

Professional Reflections

"As I began writing what became my first book, *The Moves Make the Man,* I found that I loved writing in Jerome's voice about basketball."
—Bruce Brooks

"By the time I wrote *Catherine, Called Birdy,* I already knew a great deal about the Middle Ages, and when I wanted to learn more, I was able to find lots of books about everyday life during those times."
—Karen Cushman

50

Paragraph Writing

Writing Paragraphs

A paragraph is a group of sentences sharing details about one specific topic. The first sentence in a paragraph usually identifies the topic, or main idea, and the other sentences give details and facts about it.

Here are four main reasons to write a paragraph.

1. **Describe** someone or something.
2. **Share** an event or an experience.
3. **Explain** or give information about a topic.
4. **Give your opinion** about something.

Mini Index

- **The Parts of a Paragraph**
- **Writing Strong Topic Sentences**
- **Using Different Levels of Detail**
- **Organizing Your Paragraph**
- **Writing Guidelines**
- **Test Prep for Paragraphs**

The Parts of a Paragraph

A paragraph has three main parts. (1) It begins with a **topic sentence** that states the main idea. (2) The sentences in the **body** share details about the main idea. (3) The **closing sentence** sums up the paragraph's message.

Topic sentence
•••••••••••••

Body

Closing sentence
••••••••••••

Roughing It

During the winter, the Korth family in Alaska lives almost totally off the land. Much of their time is spent setting trap lines for pelts. They also hunt caribou and moose for meat. Meat is stored outside because the temperature stays below freezing. In addition, the family members either break through the ice on a river for water, or they melt snow. They live in a small, one-room cabin that is heated by wood that they cut. If there is an emergency, someone in the family will write a huge message in the snow, in hopes that an airplane pilot will see it. Few people are able to live the way this family does.

Respond to the reading. (1) What is the main idea of this paragraph? (2) Which details stand out the most for you? (3) How does the title fit the paragraph?

A Closer Look at the Parts

The Topic Sentence

The **topic sentence** tells the reader what the paragraph is about. An effective topic sentence (1) names the topic and (2) states an important detail or feeling about it.

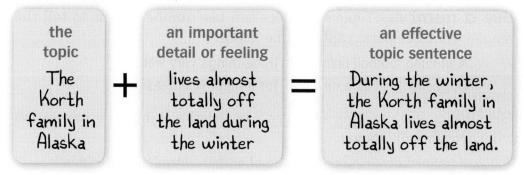

the topic		an important detail or feeling		an effective topic sentence
The Korth family in Alaska	**+**	lives almost totally off the land during the winter	**=**	During the winter, the Korth family in Alaska lives almost totally off the land.

The Body

The sentences in the **body** include the information the reader needs in order to understand the topic.

- **Use specific details.** The following sentences include specific details (in blue):

  Much of their time is spent setting trap lines for pelts. They also hunt caribou and moose for meat. Meat is stored outside because the temperature stays below freezing. In addition, the family members either break through the ice on a river for water, or they melt snow.

- **Organize the sentences.** The sentences in the paragraph on page 52 are organized according to logical order. (See pages 56–57 for other methods of organization.)

The Closing Sentence

The **closing sentence** sums up the information in the paragraph or reminds the reader of the topic.

Few people are able to live the way this family does.

Writing Strong Topic Sentences

An effective paragraph starts with a strong topic sentence. Remember that a topic sentence should (1) name the topic and (2) state an important detail or feeling about it. Use the following strategies to help you write topic sentences. (See page **460** for more strategies.)

Use a number. Topic sentences can use number words to tell the reader what the paragraph will be about.

- A winning football team does three things very well.
- Our school needs a new gym for a number of reasons.

Create a list. A topic sentence can list the things the paragraph will cover or talk about.

- Unrefined rice is a good source of protein, vitamins, and minerals.
- Before any test, review your assignments, re-read any handouts, and study your notes.

Start with "to" and a verb. A topic sentence that starts with "to" and a verb clearly introduces the paragraph's topic.

- To guard a great shooter, a defender must keep totally focused.
- To appreciate what immigrants went through, visit Ellis Island.

Join two ideas. A topic sentence can combine two ideas by using a comma and a coordinating conjunction: *and, but, or, for, so, nor, yet.*

- Our coach wants morning practices, but many players don't like the idea.
- Lewis and Clark did reach the Pacific Ocean, yet their trip was not easy.

Practice

Reread the topic sentence information above and write a topic sentence for each of the four strategies listed.

Using Different Levels of Detail

The sentences in the body, or middle part, of a well-written paragraph usually contain at least three levels of details.

Level 1: Topic Sentence The topic sentence controls the paragraph and tells what the paragraph will be about.

> Ms. Burke taught me how to plant lettuce and radish seeds early in the year.

Level 2: Supporting Sentences The second level of detail supports the topic sentence or makes it clearer.

> The key is to plant the seeds just below the surface.

Level 3: Completing Sentence The third level of detail completes the supporting idea.

> That way, they will be warmed by the sun.

tip The graphic below shows you how the different levels of details would be arranged in an effective paragraph.

> Ms. Burke taught me how to plant lettuce and radish seeds early in the year. **The key is to plant the seeds just below the surface. That way, they will be warmed by the sun.** Also, Ms. Burke used some fast-growing seeds and some slow-growing seeds. She said this would make the garden come up sooner and last longer. Ms. Burke and I can't wait to taste our first salads!

The **topic sentence** is restated in the **closing sentence.**

Practice

Write a level-1 sentence (topic sentence) about one of the following topics: *a pet, earning money, music,* or *school life.* Then write at least one level-2 sentence that supports the topic and one or two level-3 sentences that complete the supporting idea.

Organizing Your Paragraph

The sentences in your paragraph must be organized so that the reader can follow your ideas. Some common organization patterns are *logical order, time order, order of location,* and *order of importance.*

LOGICAL ORDER

Use a "logical order" in expository paragraphs to organize your details in a way that makes the best sense. The following paragraph from page 52 is organized in this way.

> During the winter, the Korth family in Alaska lives almost totally off the land. Much of their time is spent setting trap lines for pelts. They also hunt caribou and moose for meat. Meat is stored outside because the temperature stays below freezing. In addition, the family members either break through the ice on a river for water, or . . .

Transitions to use with logical order

also   for this reason   in fact   in addition   another   for example

TIME ORDER

Use "time order" in narrative or expository paragraphs to organize details in the order in which they happened.

> Our class play about the Aztecs came to a surprise ending. During the big moment, Cortés and his soldiers were waiting for Montezuma II. Then the Aztec leader arrived. After the two leaders exchanged greetings, Cortés suddenly drew his sword.

Transitions to use with time order

during   next   second   then   soon   third   after   first   finally

ORDER OF LOCATION

Use "order of location" in descriptive paragraphs to arrange details in an order that best describes the topic. The details can be arranged from left to right, top to bottom, front to back, and so on.

> In the old photograph, my great-great-grandmother's dark hair is twisted high on top of her head. Under it, her face looks very serious, with dark eyes and no smile. She is wearing a long black dress. Beneath the hem of the dress appear her narrow black boots.

Transitions to use with order of location
on top of   beside   inside   beneath   under   in front of   between   over

ORDER OF IMPORTANCE

Use "order of importance" when writing persuasive and expository paragraphs. Arrange the details from the most important to the least important—or the other way around.

> Students should be able to choose their school clothes rather than wear uniforms. For one reason, allowing students to wear regular clothes saves money. For another reason, giving students a choice says, "We trust you." Most importantly, having a choice makes students more responsible.

Transitions to use with order of importance
for one reason   for another reason   most importantly   in addition

Practice

Write a paragraph using one of the organizational patterns shown on these two pages. Try to use some of the transitions for that type of organization.

Writing Guidelines

Prewriting Selecting a Topic

Often, your teacher will give you a *general subject* area to write about. Then it will be your job to select a *specific topic* for your paragraph. Always select a topic that truly interests you. (See page **455** for topic ideas.) Below are the ideas Julio came up with.

General subject area	Specific topic
an unforgettable experience	winning an art contest
the circulation system	measuring your heart rate
the Oregon Trail	guide Jim Bridger
a health issue	people should stop smoking
a natural wonder	the Grand Canyon

Gathering and Organizing the Details

Collect details about your topic using the information that follows as a guide.

For a . . .	you'll need . . .
descriptive paragraph	details showing how the topic looks, sounds, feels, tastes, and smells.
narrative paragraph	details about an experience—how it began, continued, and ended.
expository paragraph	details that give information or explain the topic.
persuasive paragraph	facts and examples that support your opinion.

After you've gathered your details, write a topic sentence that states the main idea of your paragraph. (See pages **53–54**.) Also decide on the best way to organize the details. (See pages **56–57**.)

Writing Creating Your First Draft

When you write your first draft, your goal is to get all your ideas and details on paper. Start with your topic sentence. Then write the supporting and completing sentences in the body of your paragraph. Make sure to organize these sentences in the best order. End with a closing sentence that sums up the paragraph's message.

Revising Improving Your Paragraph

Use the following questions as a guide when you begin revising your paragraph.

1 Is my topic sentence clear?
2 Have I included the important details in the best order?
3 Do I sound interested in the topic?
4 Do I use specific nouns and action verbs?
5 Do I use varied sentence lengths?
6 Do my sentences read smoothly?

Editing Checking for Conventions

Carefully edit your revised paragraph for conventions using these questions as a guide.

1 Do I use correct punctuation and capitalization?
2 Do I use the correct word (to, too, or two)?
3 Do I spell words correctly? Have I used my spell-checker?

Practice

Plan and write a paragraph that explains something about a remarkable person or family. Refer to the sample paragraph on page 52 and the guidelines on this page and on page 58 for help.

Test Prep for Paragraphs

On many writing assessments, you may be asked to write a brief paragraph summarizing a reading selection. Use the tips below.

WRITING TIPS

Before you write . . .

- **Read the selection at least twice.** Read it once for the general meaning. Then read it again to understand all the details.
- **Plan your paragraph.** Write a topic sentence that sums up the main idea. Decide which details to use in the middle of the paragraph.
- **Use your time wisely.** Spend a few minutes planning your writing and the last few minutes reviewing your writing.

During your writing . . .

- **Be brief**. A summary paragraph for a short reading selection should probably be four to six sentences long.
- **Use your own words to summarize.** Include words from the selection only when necessary.

After your writing . . .

- **Review your work.** Change any ideas that are unclear or incorrect.

Practice

Write a brief summary paragraph of the expository essay on page 182 in your book. Use the tips above and the sample summary on the next page as a guide for your writing.

Original Reading Selection

The Underlying Causes of War

The Stamp Act and other tax laws certainly led to the American fight for independence. And the first shots fired at Lexington and Concord actually started the Revolutionary War. But taxes and shooting were only part of the story. By the late 1700s, the American colonists were simply ready to separate from Great Britain.

The "English" way of life that was in place in the 1600s had slowly, but surely, developed into an "American" way of doing things by the mid-1700s. The Americans had begun to realize that they could govern themselves better than the British could do it.

Certain ongoing practices didn't help the situation. The British sent many of their prisoners to live in the American colonies. They also stopped some of the colonies from limiting the African slave trade. In addition, the royal governors and officers often looked down upon the colonists as inferiors, which strained the relationship between the two sides. Because of these circumstances, the colonists were ready to control their own destiny by 1775.

Sample Summary

Topic sentence

Body

Closing sentence

The American Way

By 1775, the American colonists wanted their independence. The Stamp Act and other tax laws may have led to the Revolutionary War. But by the time the first shots were fired, the colonists already had their own way of doing things. They didn't like the fact that the British had been shipping prisoners to the colonies. The Americans knew that they no longer wanted to be part of Great Britain.

Descriptive Writing

Descriptive Writing

Descriptive Paragraph

No two people are exactly the same. Each person has a special personality, a special look, and a one-of-a-kind mind. One of the best ways to capture a person's individual qualities is by writing a description.

In this chapter, you will write a paragraph describing a person. Your goal is to help your reader "see" the person you have chosen and understand something special about him or her.

Writing Guidelines

Subject: A person you see often
Form: Descriptive paragraph
Purpose: To describe a person
Audience: Classmates

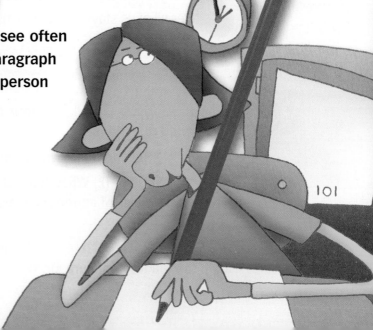

Descriptive Paragraph

A descriptive paragraph gives a detailed picture of a person, a place, a thing, or an event. It begins with a **topic sentence** that tells what the paragraph is about. The sentences in the **body** give all the details about the topic. In Juanita's paragraph below, many sensory details are used to describe a special school janitor. The **closing sentence** wraps up the paragraph.

Topic sentence

Body

Closing sentence

Squeaky Clean

Mr. Wolfe, our school janitor, looks just like Mr. Clean. At six feet three inches tall, he towers over everyone at school. His round, bald head shines under the hallway lights. His wide smile welcomes us each day. A crisp blue work shirt fits snugly across his broad shoulders. A gold, jingly key ring is attached to a belt loop of his khaki pants. His polished work shoes squeak as he cleans up our messy lunchroom. I wonder how someone who cleans up after all of us stays so clean himself.

Respond to the reading. On your own paper, answer each of the following questions.

- **Ideas** **(1) How does the writer introduce the topic?**
- **Organization** **(2) What method of organization does the writer use—order of importance, order of location, or time order? Explain.**
- **Voice & Word Choice** **(3) List three details that help the reader to picture Mr. Wolfe.**

Prewriting **selecting a Topic**

First, you need to choose a person to write about. You can use a "people chart" like the one Juanita used for the paragraph on page 64.

People Chart

Neighbors	School Staff	Relatives	Friends
Harold (Duke)	Mrs. Isley	Uncle Ray	Shannon
Mrs. Heck	Mr. Wolfe	Cousin Marsha	Freddy
Soo and Jin		Grandpa John	

Select a topic. Create a chart listing some people you know. Then circle the name of the person you would like to describe in your paragraph.

Gathering Details

When you write your descriptive paragraph, your goal is to create a true-to-life picture for the reader. A cluster, like the one below, can help you gather details about the person you plan to describe.

Gathering Cluster

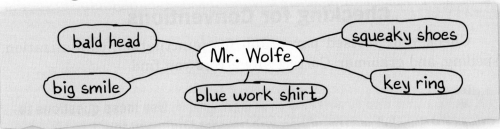

Make a cluster. Write the person's name in the center of your paper and circle it. Then write details about the person and connect them to the center circle.

Writing Creating Your First Draft

The first draft of your paragraph is your chance to put all of your ideas on paper. Start with a topic sentence that catches the reader's interest. Then arrange the body sentences (details) by location, head to toe. End with a personal comment that wraps up your paragraph.

Write your first draft. Be sure to include the most important details about your person.

Revising Improving Your Paragraph

As you revise, you can add or rearrange details. You should cut details that don't help the reader see the person you are describing.

Revise your paragraph. You can use the following questions.
1. Does my topic sentence get the reader's attention?
2. Have I used order of location to organize my details?
3. Do I sound like I care about the person I am describing?
4. Do I use specific words to describe my subject?
5. Are my sentences complete? Do they flow smoothly?

Editing Checking for Conventions

Check your revised paragraph for punctuation, capitalization, spelling, and grammar. Correct any errors you find.

Edit and proofread your paragraph. Use these questions to check for errors. Then write a neat final copy to share.
1. Do I use punctuation and capitalization correctly?
2. Are all my words spelled correctly?
3. Do I use the right words (then, than)?

Descriptive Writing

Describing a Person

Look around your classroom. Some of your classmates might have straight brown hair or curly black hair, some might wear glasses or earrings, some might be smiling or daydreaming. . . . No two classmates are exactly alike.

In this chapter, you will write an essay describing a person you admire. Besides physical characteristics, you'll describe something this person does that makes you admire him or her. All of these details will help the reader "see" the person and understand his or her personality.

Writing Guidelines

Subject: A person you admire
Form: Descriptive essay
Purpose: To describe a person
Audience: Classmates

Descriptive Essay

In the following essay, Natalia describes one of her favorite relatives. The notes on the side will help you to understand the different parts of this essay.

Aunt Frankie

BEGINNING

The writer gets the reader's attention and names the subject of the essay.

Have you ever eaten pieces of warm pie crust sprinkled with cinnamon and sugar? Well, if you ever come to visit my favorite aunt, you will. Aunt Frankie is a fun, busy, and caring lady!

The thing I like best about Aunt Frankie is that she is always ready to have fun. After a long day at work, she usually comes in the door singing some tune from the '80s. Sometimes she has a new dance step to share. Other times, she has a good story to tell as she hurries to change out of her work clothes.

MIDDLE

Each middle paragraph describes something different about Aunt Frankie.

Aunt Frankie is a woman who likes to be comfortable. At five foot three, she bounces out of her room with her shiny dark brown hair pulled into a ponytail. She tucks the loose ends behind her tiny ears and smiles at me with sparkly blue eyes and a little mouth that looks just right on her small face. She almost always wears a big white T-shirt, old pink shorts, and no shoes. Purple nail polish glows from her bare toes.

Aunt Frankie's favorite pastime is baking. She's a genius with eggs, flour, milk, and salt. It's something she learned from her mom, and she promises to teach me someday. After gathering her baking supplies, she quickly mixes up some dough and rolls out the crust. Soon the smell of cinnamon and sugar fills the air.

ENDING

The ending adds one final thought about Aunt Frankie.

Finally, she flops down next to me at the table. She puts her sticky hands on mine and asks me how my day was, how my classes are going, and what new friends I've made. Aunt Frankie always has time and treats to share at the end of the day.

Respond to the reading. After reading the essay, answer the following questions.

- **Ideas** (1) What details in the beginning get the reader's attention?

- **Organization** (2) In paragraph three, how does the writer organize the information—by order of importance or by order of location?

- **Voice & Word Choice** (3) List three words from the three middle paragraphs that show how the writer feels about Aunt Frankie.

Prewriting Selecting a Topic

For your descriptive essay, you need to choose a person you know and admire. A chart like the one below can help.

Topic Chart

Person	Qualities I Admire
Ms. Grossman, grocery store owner	generous nice to customers keeps store clean and neat
Uncle Alex, Mom's brother who is a carpenter	smart plays catch with me builds houses
Raymond, our mail carrier*	positive attitude likes his job cares about people

Make a topic chart. Create a chart that lists at least three people and the qualities you admire about them. Put a star (✱) next to the person you choose for your essay.

Gathering Details

Think about the personality, the physical appearance, and the good qualities of the person you chose.

Gather details. Answer the following questions.

1 What one word best describes the person's personality? Why?

2 How would you describe the person from head to toe?

3 What does the person do that makes you admire him or her?

Using Sensory Details

A chart covering the five senses can help you gather specific details about your subject.

Sensory Chart

See	Hear	Smell	Taste	Touch
curly black hair	whistles	cologne	cool water	heavy bag
eagle patch	cheerful		cookies	
blue shirt	stories			

Create a sensory chart. Using the chart above as a guide, create your own sensory chart.

Organizing Your Details

Each paragraph in your essay has a different job to do. A list like the one below can help you organize the details for your paragraphs.

Directions   **Organized List**

Name your subject.   Raymond, our mail carrier

List personality traits.   1. cheerful, friendly

Describe appearance.   2. curly black hair, blue shirt
                                         with patch, kneesocks

Name something you   3. cares about people, checks
admire about the person.   on Mrs. Jordan

Create an organized list. Follow the directions above to create an organized list for your description.

Writing Starting Your Essay

Your beginning paragraph should get the reader's attention and introduce the person you will describe. Here are two ways you could begin your description.

> Beginning
> Middle
> Ending

Beginning Paragraph

■ **Make a connection with the reader.**

> Everybody dreams of doing something important. Raymond dreamed of being a big-time drummer. He once played in the Narly Trees Band. When that band broke up, he had to find other work. Now Raymond is our mail carrier, and he's important to our whole neighborhood.

■ **Begin with a familiar saying.**

> Raymond lives by the saying "If you can't live the life you love, love the life you live." As a boy, Raymond dreamed of being a drummer in a band. Now he's living a different dream as the best mail carrier we've ever had.

Write

Write your beginning paragraph. You can choose one of the approaches above to get you started.

Focus on the Traits

Voice The special way you express your ideas is called *voice*. The voice in your essay should show that you know and care about the person you are describing.

Developing the Middle Part

The middle part of your essay should have three paragraphs that follow your organized list (from page 71). See the side notes below.

Beginning

Middle

Ending

Middle Paragraphs

The person's personality is described.

Raymond is always cheerful. He greets everyone with a big smile and a friendly "Hi, how are you?" Best of all, he really wants to know! It's hard to be gloomy when we hear him whistling up and down the street.

The person's appearance is described.

Our mail carrier makes sure he always looks his best. Raymond wears a gray golfer's cap on his curly black hair, and silvery sunglasses hang on a chain around his neck. His blue postal shirt has a patch like a Boy Scout badge on the top of the left sleeve. It shows an eagle with a United States flag behind it. Blue suspenders hold up his gray shorts, and black kneesocks and shoes cover his legs and feet.

The writer shares a story about the person.

Raymond cares a lot about the people on his route. Every day, he knocks on Mrs. Jordan's door to ask for a drink of cool water. He's not really thirsty. Mrs. Jordan is old, and he just wants to make sure she's okay.

Write

Write your middle paragraphs. Follow your organized list (from page 71) as you write your three middle paragraphs.

Writing **Ending Your Essay**

The ending paragraph in your essay should share an interesting final thought with the reader.

Beginning
Middle
Ending

Ending Paragraph

> **The writer gives a final thought about the person.**
>
> The U.S. Postal Service got a great employee when they hired Raymond. People depend on him for their mail, and they look forward to his friendly daily visits. In our neighborhood, Raymond is much more than just a mail carrier.

Write

Write your ending paragraph. Try to leave the reader with an interesting final thought about the person.

Revising and Editing

Revise

Revise your description. Use the questions below as a guide when you revise your essay.

- **Ideas** Do I include sensory details?
- **Organization** Do I have a clear beginning, middle, and ending?
- **Voice** Does my voice show that I care about my topic?
- **Word Choice** Have I carefully chosen descriptive words?
- **Sentence Fluency** Do my sentences flow smoothly?

Edit

Edit your description. Use the checklist on page 30 to guide your editing. Then prepare a neat final copy and have a trusted classmate or parent help you proofread it one more time.

Descriptive Writing

Across the Curriculum

"Tell me all about it!" Friends want to know what you did over the weekend or what happened at the game. They want to know what things looked like, sounded like, and tasted like. So it's important to be able to describe things well.

You'll also be asked to describe things in your school subjects. You may need to write a description of a historical figure in social studies or a description of how a science topic relates to your everyday life. This chapter will help you sharpen your description skills.

Writing Guidelines

- **Social Studies:** Describing a Person from History
- **Science:** Describing a Chemical Change
- **Assessment:** Writing for Assessment

Social Studies:
Describing a Person from History

Your teacher may ask you to write about a famous person from history. Notice how descriptive writing is used in the sample below.

Molly Pitcher

The **beginning** tells why the person is important.

During the Revolutionary War, Mary Hays McCauly earned the name "Molly Pitcher" at the Battle of Monmouth in 1778. She was a brave woman, and George Washington and his troops respected her.

Mary dressed like any other young woman of her time. She piled her long blond hair on top of her head and covered it with a dust cap. She often wore a white blouse and rust-colored skirt. That's what she wore on the day of the battle at Monmouth, New Jersey.

The **middle** describes the person and what she did.

June 18 was a hot, hot day. Soldiers were roasting in their heavy wool uniforms, and they were very thirsty. The metal gun barrels got so hot that the soldiers couldn't touch them. Mary helped the troops by carrying pitcher after pitcher of cool water to them. She raced back and forth across the battlefield with her skirt fluttering like a flag. Although she choked on the smoky air and bullets whizzed by her, Mary kept running.

The **ending** includes a final thought about the person.

Suddenly Mary dropped her pitcher. Her husband had fallen from heat stroke, so she took his place and helped his crew fire the cannon. She helped fire the cannon at the enemy again and again. Mary's strength and courage inspired the soldiers. From that day on, she was known as Molly Pitcher.

WRITING TIPS

Before you write . . .

- **Choose a person from history.**
  Select a person from a time you have studied.
- **Do your research.**
  Find information and pictures about the person and what he or she did to earn a place in history.
- **Take notes.**
  Focus on the person's appearance and actions.

During your writing . . .

- **Organize your details.**
  Introduce your topic in the beginning. In the middle, give details about the person. End with a final thought about the person.
- **Show, don't tell.**
  Use descriptive details that help the reader see the person and understand why he or she is important.
- **Sound excited.**
  Use specific words that show you know a lot about this person.

After you've written a first draft . . .

- **Check for completeness.**
  Make sure to give the reader a clear picture of the person.
- **Check for correctness.**
  Proofread your essay for errors in punctuation, capitalization, spelling, or grammar.

Plan and write an essay. Choose a person from history, and write a detailed description of the person following these writing tips.

Science: Describing a Chemical Change

Your science teacher may ask you to describe how science affects your everyday life. In the sample below, Ravi uses descriptive writing to tell what part science played at a family campfire.

The beginning introduces a science topic.

The middle relates personal experience to the topic.

The ending summarizes the topic with a final thought.

S'more Changes

Last Tuesday our science teacher told us about chemical changes. A chemical change makes a new substance that has different properties. Burning is an example of a chemical change. For example, when you burn wood, you change the properties of wood into the properties found in smoke, gases, and ashes.

This weekend my family built a campfire, and we made s'mores. To make a s'more, you have to heat a marshmallow on a pointed stick over a fire. If you take your time, the marshmallow will get soft and gooey. When you press it between two graham crackers along with some chocolate, the whole thing is sweet and crunchy. If you would let the s'more cool off, you could carefully separate the parts again.

However, I was in too much of a hurry. I put my marshmallow too close to the heat. It caught on fire and turned black like charcoal. Instead of being soft and gooey, it was crackly and dry. It didn't smell sweet anymore. It tasted like ashes.

So I learned that a chemical change doesn't happen when I slowly heat a marshmallow. Its properties are not permanently changed. A burned marshmallow, though, is the result of a chemical change because it will never be soft, sweet, and gooey again.

WRITING TIPS

Before you write . . .

- **Choose a topic that interests you.**
  Select something you have both studied in science class and experienced in your everyday life.
- **List the main ideas you want to include.**
  Consider what you know about your topic and how you experienced it.

During your writing . . .

- **Write a clear beginning, middle, and ending.**
  Introduce the topic in the beginning, describe the experience in the middle, and end with a summary of your findings.
- **Organize your details.**
  Choose the best organization for your description— order of location, time order, or order of importance.
- **Use specific words.**
  Select specific nouns, action verbs, and adjectives.

After you've written a first draft . . .

- **Check for completeness.**
  Add details to make your topic clearer.
- **Check for correctness.**
  Proofread your description for errors in punctuation, capitalization, spelling, and grammar.

Describe a science-related experience.
Use these tips to guide your writing.

Writing for Assessment

Some writing tests may contain a descriptive writing prompt. Study the following prompt and the student response to it.

Descriptive Prompt

Write a paragraph describing a perfect picnic lunch. Think of the person you would like to have a picnic with, where it would be, and what you would eat.

The **topic sentence** uses key words from the prompt. (underlined)

Descriptive details fill the **body** sentences.

The **closing sentence** makes a personal comment.

> <u>My cousin Julie and I often have a great picnic lunch in our old tree house.</u> It's full of spiderwebs and smells like old wood, but it's a perfect place for a picnic. I sometimes bring leftover spaghetti. It's good when it is hot, but when it's cold, the pasta is chewier and the sauce is sweeter. Julie brings crusty French bread, cheddar cheese, and juicy apple slices. Julie's mom sends a dessert, usually German chocolate cake with coconut frosting. Julie and I are lucky to have each other and to have a special place for a picnic.

Respond to the reading. Answer the following questions about the response paragraph.

- **Ideas** (1) What sensory details stand out? Name two.
- **Organization** (2) How does the topic sentence relate to the prompt?
- **Voice & Word Choice** (3) What words show that the writer cares about the topic?

WRITING TIPS

Before you write . . .

- **Understand the prompt.**
  Be sure you understand what you need to describe.
- **Use your time wisely.**
  Spend several minutes of your time planning and making some notes. After writing, use the last few minutes to proofread and correct any errors you find.

During your writing . . .

- **Write an effective topic sentence.**
  Use a key word or words from the prompt to form a topic sentence.
- **Be selective.**
  Choose sensory details that describe your topic.
- **End in a meaningful way.**
  Close with a comment that makes a personal connection to the topic.

After you've written a first draft . . .

- **Check for completeness and correctness.**
  Make sure your ideas make sense, and correct any errors.

Descriptive Prompts

- One of your friends is moving to another city. Write a paragraph describing this friend to your cousin who lives in that city.
- Think of a fun place. Write a paragraph describing that place.

 Plan and write a response. Respond to one of these two prompts. Finish your writing in the amount of time your teacher gives you. Afterward, list one part you like and one part that could be better.

Narrative Writing

Narrative Writing

Narrative Paragraph

Every time you finish a challenging job, you experience success. Think about some of your successes. Maybe you remembered all your lines in the school play, played your trombone solo well, or got a perfect score on a math test. It's successes like these that make you feel good about yourself.

You can share your success stories with others by writing about them. The following pages will help you write a narrative paragraph about a time when you succeeded at doing something you thought was challenging.

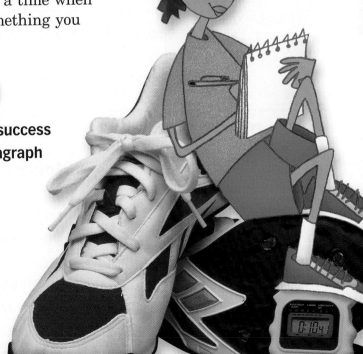

Writing Guidelines

Subject: Experiencing success
Form: Narrative paragraph
Purpose: To entertain
Audience: Classmates

Narrative Paragraph

A narrative paragraph shares a personal experience. It begins with a **topic sentence** that introduces the main idea. The **body** of the paragraph contains details about what happened, and the **closing sentence** gives the reader something to think about. In the paragraph below, Tameeka shares an unexpected moment of success in gym class.

Topic sentence

Body

Closing sentence

A Successful Run

I never thought I was a good runner, until the day in gym class when I won the mile race. The course was marked with colorful flags, and the sight of the flags seemed to fire me up. When Ms. Holt, our gym teacher, blew her whistle, I charged ahead. To my surprise, I was one of the leaders right away. About halfway around the course, I noticed a few kids grabbing their sides. Some kids even started walking. I felt tired, too, but I kept running. Ms. Holt congratulated me when I was the first runner across the finish line. I thanked her and grinned. Now I think about running all the time. Maybe someday I'll even get the chance to run in the Olympics.

Respond to the reading. Answer the following questions on your own paper.

- **Ideas** (1) What is the main idea of this paragraph?
- **Organization** (2) Does the writer organize the details by time or by location?
- **Voice & Word Choice** (3) What words show the writer's personal feelings? Name two or three.

Prewriting Selecting a Topic

The writer of "A Successful Run" used a topic chart to record some of her unexpected successes.

Topic Chart

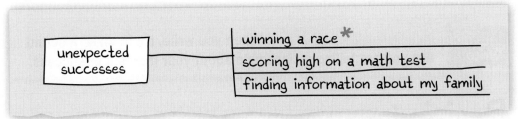

unexpected successes	winning a race *
	scoring high on a math test
	finding information about my family

Make a chart like the one above. First, write "unexpected successes" in a box. Then, on the lines, write three examples. Put a star (✳) next to the one you want to write about.

Gathering Details

Next, Tameeka used a grid to gather details. She listed her moment of success, the events leading up to it, and how she felt afterward.

Gathering Grid

My moment of success	Events in the order they happened	How I felt afterward
• won a race	• mile run in gym class • flags marked the course • kept on running and passed other kids • finished first	• happy • wanted to run more races • dreamed about being in the Olympics someday

Make an gathering grid. Write down your moment of success, the events that led you to it, and how you felt afterward.

Writing Developing the First Draft

Your narrative paragraph should include a topic sentence, a body, and a closing sentence. The topic sentence introduces the main idea, the body tells what happened, and the closing sentence gives the reader something to think about.

Write your first draft. When you write, try to make it sound like you are telling a classmate about your moment of success.

Revising Improving Your Paragraph

The tips that follow will help you revise your first draft.

- **Show, don't tell.** Instead of writing "I was happy," write "I threw my glove in the air."
- **Use time order.** Be sure the actions or details are arranged in the order in which they happened.
- **Choose the best words.** Use strong nouns and vivid verbs. Keep your sentences flowing smoothly from one to the next.

Revise your paragraph. Use the tips above to help you improve the first draft of your narrative paragraph.

Editing Checking for Conventions

It's important to check your writing for punctuation, capitalization, spelling, and grammar errors.

Edit and proofread your work. Use the following questions as a guide when you edit. Then make a clean copy and give it a final proofreading.

1 Have I used capital letters and end punctuation marks?

2 Have I checked for grammar and spelling errors?

Narrative Writing

Sharing a Personal Success

How would you complete the following sentence? "I felt really proud when I . . . " Whenever you succeed at something, big or small, you should feel proud.

This chapter will help you recall times when you succeeded at something. Then it will guide you as you share your success story in a personal narrative.

Writing Guidelines

Subject: A time when you succeeded
Form: Personal narrative
Purpose: To share a true experience
Audience: Classmates

Understanding Your Goal

Your goal in this chapter is to write an essay about a personal success. The traits listed in the chart below will help you understand how to meet that goal.

Your goal is to . . .

Ideas — Use specific details to write about an important achievement. Make the reader want to know what happens next.

Organization — Start with an interesting beginning that pulls the reader into the story. Then present the details in the order in which they happened.

Voice — Use a strong voice, one that sounds like you are telling your story to a friend.

Word Choice — Use specific nouns, vivid verbs, and colorful adjectives.

Sentence Fluency — Use clear sentences that flow smoothly from one idea to the next.

Conventions — Be sure that your punctuation, capitalization, spelling, and grammar are correct.

Get the big picture. Look at the rubric on pages 120–121. It will help you to stay on track as you write your essay.

Personal Narrative

In this narrative, Jamaal shares an important personal success—winning an award in an art contest.

What Is It?

BEGINNING

The beginning sets the scene.

When I paint, I love splashing bright colors and wild designs across the paper. That's my style. Last month, Ms. Robertson, my art teacher, told me about the school's art contest. She said, "Jamaal, entering this contest would be a good experience for you."

"Why?" I asked. "Most people think my art is weird."

"Well, I don't," Ms. Robertson replied.

The contest's theme was "The World: Its Continents and Countries." I immediately thought of Africa. Bright sunsets and patterns of wild animal hides rushed through my brain. Right then, I decided to enter the contest.

MIDDLE

The middle includes colorful details.

I sketched out my idea and worked hard on my painting. Streaks of red, orange, gold, and yellow spread across my paper. I zigzagged zebra stripes, made giant giraffe spots, and added gray ridges of elephant skin. Between the colors and patterns, I hid the letters A-F-R-I-C-A. After hours and hours of work, I stood back and took one last look. I saw Africa.

The very next day I took my painting to school. Ms. Robertson looked at it and said, "Well, Jamaal, I'm not at all surprised by your painting."

"Is that good or bad?" I asked.

Instead of answering me, she just took my painting and hung it up next to all of the other ones.

During the day, I kept wondering what the judges thought of my painting. Then in the afternoon, I received an envelope. My heart pounded as I opened it. The first three judges wrote about how they liked my colors and my bold designs. As I unfolded the final sheet, my eyes shot to words in bright orange ink. "Africa! I can just see the sun setting on the Serengeti Plains." I was so surprised.

I won a red ribbon for second place! But I almost felt like I had won first place because someone actually saw my Africa. After that, I felt more excited about painting. Now if people ask, "What is it?" I proudly tell them.

Respond to the reading. Answer the following questions about the narrative.

- **Ideas** (1) What specific success does the author write about?

- **Organization** (2) How is the middle part organized— by time order or by order of importance?

- **Voice & Word Choice** (3) What words and phrases reveal the writer's personal feelings? Name two or three.

Prewriting

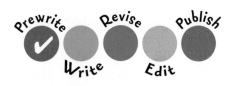

To get started, you need to choose a personal experience to write about. After that, you need to gather plenty of details.

Keys to Prewriting

1. **Think** of several personal successes you have had.

2. **Choose** one that will make a great story.

3. **Use** a time line to organize your story.

4. **Gather** sensory details about the experience.

5. **Think** about dialogue to include.

Prewriting **Selecting a Topic**

Completing a sentence starter is a great way to think of possible topics. Anna, the writer of the essay on pages 99–102, used the sentence starter "I was proud when I . . . " to think of successes in her life.

Sentence Starter

Personal Successes

<u>I was proud when I . . .</u>

    learned to play the guitar.

* made tacos all by myself.

    improved my grade in science.

    finished a walkathon.

> You will do your best writing if you choose a topic you truly care about.

Brainstorm for topics. On your own paper, complete the sentence starter "I was proud when I . . . ." List four or five different personal successes. Put a star (*) next to the experience that would make the best story.

Reflecting on Your Topic

Thinking about your topic is an important part of prewriting. One way to think is to write freely about your success. Begin by explaining why the experience is special to you. Continue writing down whatever thoughts come to mind about it.

Reflect on your topic. Write freely for 5 minutes about your topic, using the information above as a guide.

Finding the Basics

A 5 W's chart can help you gather basic details for your story. You may add H (*How?*) to your chart for even better coverage. Anna used the chart below to gather her details.

> Using graphic organizers will help you collect the best details for your story.

5 W's Chart

Topic: Making tacos by myself

Who?	My mom, my sister, and me
What?	I made supper when my mom sprained her ankle.
When?	Around supper time
Where?	At my house
Why?	I wanted to cook by myself and help my mom.

Prewrite

Make a chart. Create a 5 W's chart like the one above for your narrative.

Focus on the Traits

Ideas A strong narrative includes (1) the *basic details* of what happened; (2) *sensory details* about what you saw, felt, and heard; and (3) *dialogue* to show what people said.

Prewriting Putting Things in Order

Just as a 5 W's chart works well for gathering basic details, a time line is handy for listing specific details in the order in which they happened.

Time Line

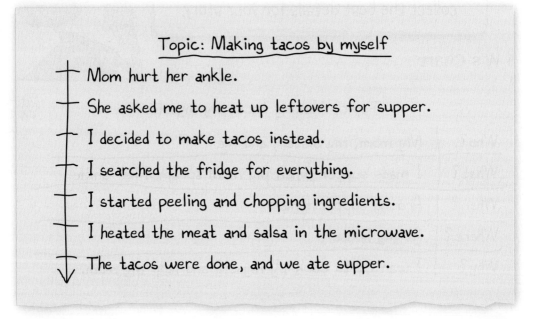

Topic: Making tacos by myself

Mom hurt her ankle.

She asked me to heat up leftovers for supper.

I decided to make tacos instead.

I searched the fridge for everything.

I started peeling and chopping ingredients.

I heated the meat and salsa in the microwave.

The tacos were done, and we ate supper.

Prewrite

Create your time line. On your own paper, make a time line like the one above. List the main details in time order.

Focus on the Traits

Organization For a narrative, you should arrange the details in time order, the order in which they happened. Ever since you heard your first story, you've been learning how to use this basic method of organization.

Collecting Sensory Details

There is more to writing a narrative than just telling what happens first, second, and third. A narrative needs **sensory details** that help the reader see, feel, smell, and hear an experience.

Sentences with effective sensory details:

Using a dull table knife, I sawed into the tomato. Splat—red juice squirted onto my new white T-shirt!

The writer of the narrative on pages 99–102 used a sensory circle chart to collect sensory details for her narrative.

Sensory Circle Chart

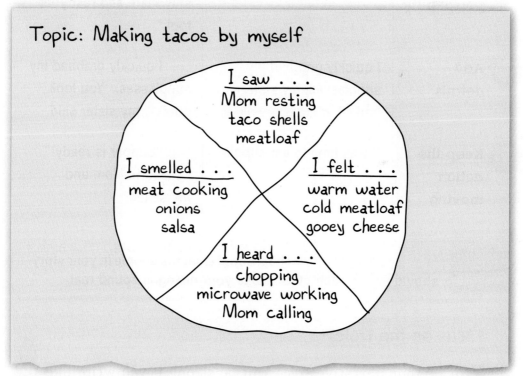

Topic: Making tacos by myself

I saw . . .
Mom resting
taco shells
meatloaf

I smelled . . .
meat cooking
onions
salsa

I felt . . .
warm water
cold meatloaf
gooey cheese

I heard . . .
chopping
microwave working
Mom calling

Prewrite

List sensory details. Draw a circle chart and label it with the same headings shown in the example above. Then list the sensory details connected with your own experience.

Prewriting **Thinking About Dialogue**

Dialogue makes an experience come alive for the reader. The chart below shows the three main things that dialogue can do.

		Without dialogue	With dialogue
1	Show something about a speaker's personality.	Mother sat in her chair while I worked in the kitchen. I told my mother to stay in her chair.	"How are things going in there?" she called from the other room. "Fine!" I said. "Just stay there and rest your foot."
2	Add details.	I quickly grabbed my sunglasses. My sister looked at me.	I quickly grabbed my sunglasses. "You look goofy!" my sister said.
3	Keep the action moving.	It was time to eat supper.	"Supper is ready!" I called to Mom and my sister.

Prewrite

Plan some dialogue. Think about what the people in your story should say to each other. Make your dialogue sound real.

Focus on the Traits

Voice Your narrative voice will be strong if you write like you know the topic well and are truly interested in it. Also, using dialogue can make your voice sound more natural.

Writing

Now that you have gathered details for your narrative, you are ready to write your first draft. Your goal is to get all of your thoughts about the topic down on paper.

Keys to Writing

1. **Use** the details you have collected as a guide.

2. **Write** a strong beginning paragraph to get the reader's attention.

3. **Use** sensory details and dialogue to tell your story.

4. **Think** about dialogue to include.

5. **Share** how you felt or what you learned in the ending paragraph.

Writing **Getting the Big Picture**

The chart below shows how the parts of a personal narrative fit together. (The examples are from the narrative on pages 99–102.) You are ready to write your essay when you have . . .

- put the events of your story in time order and
- gathered enough details.

Beginning

The **beginning** catches the reader's attention.

Opening Sentence
One day, my mom sprained her ankle and had to stay off her feet.

Middle

The **middle** part gives details about what happened during the experience.

- We had everything I needed.
- First, I washed my hands. . . .
- In our kitchen, kids can't . . .
- Carefully, I started peeling . . .
- Then I only had to prepare . . .
- Finally, it was time to eat. . . .

Ending

The **ending** tells how you felt about the experience.

Closing Sentence
I felt great about doing something special for Mom, and she was proud of me for making supper all by myself.

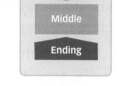

Starting Your Personal Narrative

In the first paragraph, you should get the reader's attention and introduce your personal experience. Here are three ways to begin your paragraph.

- **Start with dialogue.**

  "I sprained my ankle," Mom said. "You will have to make supper tonight."

- **Begin with an interesting statement or fact.**

  One day, my mom sprained her ankle and couldn't walk.

- **Put yourself in the middle of the action.**

  When Mom asked me to heat up leftovers for supper, I had another idea. I decided to surprise her with tacos!

Beginning Paragraph

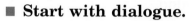

The writer begins with an interesting statement.

One day, my mom sprained her ankle and had to stay off her feet. She asked me to make supper. Mom said I could microwave the leftover meatloaf, but I wanted to surprise her with her favorite meal—tacos!

Remember to sound interested in your topic when you write.

Write your beginning paragraph. Use the ideas on this page to write two or three beginnings for your first paragraph. Choose the best one and finish the paragraph.

Writing Developing the Middle Part

The middle part of a narrative tells the story. It should be organized chronologically, or in time order. Here are some other things to keep in mind.

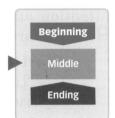

- **Include sensory details.**
- **Use dialogue.**
- **Share the feelings you experienced.**

Middle Paragraphs

> **The writer immediately gets the story moving.**

We had everything I needed. I'd seen a box of taco shells in the cabinet. In the fridge, there was leftover meatloaf. We had plenty of fresh tomatoes, onions, lettuce, and salsa, too. I also found a box of cheese, the kind that melts on cheeseburgers. So I couldn't wait to get started!

> **Transition words (blue) help put the story in time order.**

First, I washed my hands. Then I crumbled the cold meatloaf into little pieces. I planned on zapping the meat and the salsa when it was time to eat. Next, I shredded the lettuce into little pieces and piled it in a bowl.

In our kitchen, kids can't use sharp knives or the stove unless Mom is there to supervise. No problem. Using a dull table knife, I sawed into the tomato. Splat—red juice squirted onto my new white T-shirt! I hoped Mom didn't hear me groaning.

"How are things going in there?" she called from the other room.

"Fine!" I said. "Just stay there and rest your foot."

> Dialogue makes the characters real.

Carefully, I started peeling the onion. Ouch! The fumes burned my eyes. Big tears streamed down my cheeks like a waterfall. I quickly grabbed my sunglasses. "You look goofy!" my sister said. I realized the glasses didn't help.

Then I only had to prepare the cheese. I thought this would be the easy part. I tried to grate it, but it was too soft. Soon I had cheese goo all over my hands, and the grater was all clogged. I ended up using the knife on the cheese, too. It took forever to cut it into itty-bitty pieces.

> Sensory details help the reader "see" and "feel" the experience.

Finally, it was time to eat. I microwaved the meat and salsa, and then I put the tacos together. At the last minute, I remembered to grab the sour cream. Mom loves a big spoonful on her taco.

"Supper is ready!" I called to Mom and my sister.

Write your middle paragraphs. Before you start, review your details to make sure that you don't forget anything.

Writing **Ending Your Personal Narrative**

The final paragraph should bring your narrative to a close. Here are three strategies you can use to end your story.

Beginning
Middle
Ending

- **Tell what you learned from the experience.**

    My tacos tasted great, and Mom loved her surprise. In the beginning, I wasn't sure I could make tacos all by myself. But I learned that if I try, I can make supper for my family.

- **Explain how the experience changed you.**

    Mom said they were the best tacos she ever ate! That made me grin from ear to ear. I showed her that I'm a responsible kid. Now I want to help make meals more often.

- **Tell how you felt about the experience.**

Ending Paragraph

The writer tells how she felt.

> Mom smiled when she saw my tacos. They didn't look like Mom's tacos, but she said they were a wonderful surprise. I felt great about doing something special for Mom, and she was proud of me for making supper all by myself.

Write your ending. Use one of the three strategies listed above to end your narrative. If you're not happy with your first attempt, try another idea.

Revising

Revising may be the most important step in the writing process. During this step, you can improve your narrative by adding details and by changing parts that sound confusing.

Keys to Revising

1. **Read** your narrative once to see how you feel about it.

2. **Review** each part carefully— the beginning, the middle, and the ending.

3. **Ask** a classmate to read your first draft, too.

4. **Change** any parts that need to be improved.

Revising for Ideas

6 My details work together, which gives my narrative a strong sense of focus.

5 My narrative tells about one experience. I use effective sensory details.

4 My narrative tells about one experience. More details would make it better.

When you revise for *ideas*, make sure that you have shared just one experience. Also make sure that you have used plenty of effective details. The rubric above will guide you as you improve your ideas.

Do my details move the story along?

Every detail should help you tell your story from beginning to end. Together, the details should answer any important questions a reader may have about your experience. Any detail that doesn't add to your story should be cut.

Practice

Read the following paragraph. Then identify the two sentences (details) that should be cut because they don't add to the story.

1 Dad said he would take me camping if I improved my math
2 grade. I really wanted to go, so I decided to work harder on my
3 math homework. After supper every night, I went to my room and
4 got right to work. Sometimes we have cheeseburgers for supper,
5 which I like a lot. Right away I started to understand things better.
6 At parent-teacher conferences, Mr. Black told my parents I had
7 raised my grade to a B. Mr. Black is a new teacher. The next
8 weekend my dad took me camping.

Revise

Check the details in your narrative. Does each detail add something important to your story? Delete any details that don't.

3 I need to focus on one experience. Some of my details don't relate to the topic.

 2 I need to focus on one experience and add details.

 1 My main topic is still unclear.

Do my details make the story seem real?

Your story will seem real if you include sensory details. Sensory details help a reader see, hear, feel, taste, or smell an experience.

Practice

From the following paragraph, list one detail for each of these senses—seeing, hearing, feeling, and smelling.

1   My mom finally let me take the subway by myself. The seat
2 feels cold on my legs. Everything looks and feels a little dirty. The
3 air smells of perfume and sweat. Across from me, a homeless
4 man is talking to himself. He looks like a bundle of rags. The train
5 suddenly screeches to a stop.

 Review your details. Have you used sensory details in your narrative? If not, make sure to add some.

Revising in Action

In the sample below, a sensory detail is added and an unneeded detail is cut.

Carefully, I started peeling the onion. Ouch! The fumes burned my eyes. Big tears streamed down my cheeks like a waterfall. ~~I hated it.~~ I quickly . . .

Revising for Organization

6		5		4	
	My organization makes my narrative enjoyable and very easy to read.		My events are in time order, and I use transitions well. I have a strong beginning, middle, and ending.		My events are in time order. Most of my transitions are helpful. I have a beginning, a middle, and an ending.

When you revise for *organization*, make sure that the beginning, middle, and ending work well together. The rubric above can help you.

How do I know if my beginning is strong?

Your beginning works well if it gets the reader's interest and introduces the story. Remember these three different ways to start your narrative. (See page **99** for examples.)

1. Start with some dialogue.

2. Begin with an interesting statement or fact.

3. Put yourself in the middle of the action.

Check your beginning. Does your beginning work well? If not, rewrite it. Use one of the three suggestions above.

How do I know if the middle is well organized?

The middle is well organized if the details are in the same order in which they happened. Transition words and phrases help connect events. The following sets of transitions work well in narratives.

first then next	before after finally
now then soon	as soon as at last in the end

Review the middle part. Make sure that all your ideas and details are arranged in time order. Use transition words to help you connect your details.

Some of my events are out of order. I need more transitions. My beginning or ending is weak.

 I need to use time order and transitions to create a clear beginning, middle, and ending.

 My writing is confusing. I need to put my events in time order.

How do I know if my ending is strong?

Your ending will be strong if it does the following two things:

- It comes right after the most important moment or detail.
- It explains how you felt about the experience or how it changed you. (See page **102** for more information.)

Check your ending. Does your ending work well? If not, try one or two new versions.

Revising in Action

In the sample narrative below, Anna added a sentence to show how she felt about her experience—and how her mom felt as well.

Mom smiled when she saw my tacos. They didn't
look like Mom's tacos, but she said they were a
I felt great about doing something special for Mom, and
wonderful surprise. ʌShe was proud of me for making
supper all by myself.

Revising for Voice

6 My writer's voice creates a memorable experience for the reader.	**5** My writer's voice shows excitement, and the dialogue works well.	**4** My voice shows excitement. I need to make the dialogue help tell my story.

When you revise for *voice*, be sure your writing sounds natural—as if you were telling your story to a classmate. Use the rubric strip above as a guide when you revise for voice.

Does my narrative have "voice"?

Your narrative will have voice if (1) you are excited about the experience and (2) you want to share it with your classmates.

WRITING WITH VOICE

> Just then I felt a rush of wind, and I hit the ground facedown. But Bo pulled me right up by the T-shirt. He pointed his flashlight toward a big branch. Then I saw it. A huge great horned owl swiveled its head toward us. Wow! I was staring into a very spooky pair of yellow-gold eyes.

Practice

Freewrite for 4 minutes, starting with the following idea:

My friend and I . . .

After you finish your writing, underline parts that sound exciting or just like you.

 Check for voice. Review your narrative to see if you sound excited and interested. Change any parts that sound dull.

Sometimes my voice shows excitement. I need to use dialogue help to tell my story.

 My writer's voice shows very little excitement. I need to use some dialogue.

 My voice shows that I'm not excited about this writing.

Does my dialogue work well?

Your dialogue works well if it makes the people seem real and helps you tell your story.

Sample Dialogue

We had climbed into a tree house, about 20 feet off the ground. "Whoa! Is it safe up here?" I exclaimed.

"Safer than on the streets," Bo laughed.

Then I heard some bird squawking. "What's his problem?" I asked.

Bo whispered, "A raven has spotted an owl."

Revise

Check the dialogue. Does the dialogue work well in your narrative? If not, rewrite it to make it sound more real.

Revising in Action

Dialogue adds personality and voice in the sample below.

I quickly grabbed my sunglasses. "You look goofy!" my sister said. ~~My sister said I looked silly.~~ I realized the glasses didn't help.

Revising for Word Choice

| 6 | My original word choice creates a true-to-life picture for the reader. | 5 | I create a clear picture with specific nouns, vivid verbs, and colorful adjectives. | 4 | Most of my nouns are specific. I use a number of vivid verbs and colorful adjectives. |

When you revise for *word choice*, check to see if you have used specific nouns, vivid verbs, and colorful adjectives in your narrative. The rubric above can help you.

Have I used the best nouns?

The best nouns are specific. The chart below shows the difference between general and specific nouns. Using specific nouns will make your story clear to the reader. (Also see pages **410–411**.)

GENERAL NOUNS	boy	fish	lake	bait
SPECIFIC NOUNS	Najib	king salmon	Pine Lake	minnow

Sentence with general nouns:
   The boy caught a fish on the lake using bait.

Sentence with specific nouns:
   Najib caught a king salmon on Pine Lake using a minnow.

Practice

List the following general nouns on a piece of paper. Next to each one, list a more specific noun.

school	coat	song	bike	movie
dessert	friend	chore	building	dog

Revise

Review the nouns in your draft. If you find any nouns that are too general, use a more specific noun instead.

3 I need to add more specific nouns, verbs, and adjectives.

 2 I use general nouns, verbs, and adjectives. My writing needs more specific words.

 1 I need to improve my word choice.

Have I used colorful adjectives?

You have used colorful adjectives if they are specific and help readers create clear word pictures in their minds. Notice how the specific adjectives below create a clearer picture. (See page **425**.)

- cuddly, black-eared **kitten**
- scratchy wool **sweater**
- saggy blue **jeans**
- sour **lemonade**

 tip   Avoid overused adjectives like *neat, big, small, bad, nice, good,* and *funny.*

 Revise   **Review the adjectives in your draft.** Change any adjectives that don't help readers picture things in their minds.

Revising in Action

In the sample below, one overused adjective and two general nouns are replaced.

> meatloaf
> Then I crumbled the cold ∧meat into little pieces. I
>
> salsa
> planned on zapping the meat and the ∧sauce when . . .
>
> sharp
> In our kitchen, kids can't use ∧good knives or the
>
> stove unless Mom is there to supervise. No problem. . . .

Revising for Sentence Fluency

6 My sentences are skillfully written and keep the reader's interest from start to finish.	**5** I use a variety of sentences that are easy to read. My sentence beginnings also vary.	**4** I include a variety of sentences, but I need to vary more of my sentence beginnings.

When you revise for *sentence fluency,* make sure that you have varied your sentence beginnings and lengths. Also try to use different kinds of sentences. The rubric strip above will guide you.

How can I make my sentences more interesting?

Interesting sentences begin in different ways. The easiest way to change some of your sentence beginnings is to move or add words.

SENTENCES BEGINNING WITH THE SUBJECT	VARIED BEGINNINGS
I quietly closed the door.	Quietly, I closed the door.
We heard a siren during recess.	During recess, we heard a siren.
Ms. Lee runs five miles.	On Saturday mornings, Ms. Lee runs five miles.

Practice

To make the paragraph below sound more interesting, change the beginnings of two sentences.

(1) I won my first wrestling match last year. (2) I wrestled someone from the next town. (3) I was really nervous before I got started. (4) I planned my first moves in my mind. (5) I scored a takedown during the first minute.

Revise

Check your sentences. Make sure that you have used a variety of sentence beginnings.

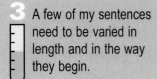

3 A few of my sentences need to be varied in length and in the way they begin.

2 I need to use different kinds of sentences and vary their beginnings.

1 Most of my sentences start the same way. I need to vary their beginnings.

How can I add variety to my sentences?

You can add variety to your writing by using different kinds of sentences. (See page **441** for more information.)

KINDS OF SENTENCES

Declarative	I want to make the volleyball team.
Interrogative	Who will practice with me?
Imperative	Practice your serves.
Exclamatory	I scored the winning point!

Revise

Check for sentence variety. If you have used all declarative sentences, consider changing a few of them to questions, commands, or exclamations.

Revising in Action

In the sample below, changes are made to improve the sentences.

In the fridge,
∧There was leftover meatloaf⊙ ~~in the fridge⊙~~ We had ~~There were~~

plenty of fresh tomatoes, onions, lettuce, and salsa,

too. I also found a box of cheese, the kind that melts

So I couldn't wait to get started!
on cheeseburgers.∧ ~~It was time to get started.~~

Revising Using a Checklist

Check your revising. Number a piece of paper from 1 to 10. If you can answer "yes" to a question, put a check mark after that number. If not, continue to work on that part of your essay.

Ideas

_____ 1. Do I include sensory details?

_____ 2. Do all my details add something to my narrative?

Organization

_____ 3. Do my beginning, middle, and ending work well?

_____ 4. Have I reorganized parts that were out of place?

Voice

_____ 5. Does my voice show my interest or excitement?

_____ 6. Does my dialogue sound real?

Word Choice

_____ 7. Have I used specific nouns?

_____ 8. Have I used colorful adjectives?

Sentence Fluency

_____ 9. Have I varied my sentence beginnings and lengths?

_____ 10. Have I used different kinds of sentences?

Make a clean copy. When you've finished revising your essay, make a clean copy for editing.

Editing

Editing is the next step in the writing process. When you edit, you make sure that you have followed the rules for punctuation, capitalization, spelling, and grammar. These rules are called the "conventions" of writing.

Keys to Editing

1. **Use** a dictionary, a thesaurus, and the "Proofreader's Guide" in the back of this book for help.

2. **Edit** on a printed copy if you use a computer. Then make your changes on the computer.

3. **Use** the editing marks shown inside the back cover of this book.

4. **Ask** someone else to check your writing for errors, too.

Editing for Conventions

6 I accurately use conventions, which adds clarity and style to my writing.

5 I have a few minor errors in punctuation, spelling, capitalization, or grammar.

4 I need to correct some errors in punctuation, spelling, capitalization, or grammar.

When you edit for *conventions*, you check your writing for errors. The rubric strip above will help you edit your work.

Is my dialogue punctuated correctly?

Your dialogue will be easy to follow if it is punctuated correctly. Follow the basic rules listed below. (Also see page **494**.)

■ In most sentences, use commas to set off the speaker's words from the rest of the sentence.

    "We are having pizza for lunch," said Anna, "so let's get in line."

■ Sometimes an exclamation point or a question mark is used to set off the speaker's words from the rest of the sentence.

    "Do you like mushrooms on pizza?" Guerdy asked.

■ Place the speaker's exact words within quotation marks.

    "I hate mushrooms!" Anna burst out.

Practice

Copy and correctly punctuate the following examples of dialogue.

1. Watch me do a backflip Justin called.
2. Awesome Carlo exclaimed.
3. Did you see my cannonball Justin asked.
4. For a guy my size he added I make a big splash.

Edit your dialogue. Use the rules and examples above to check your dialogue for correct punctuation.

3 Some errors may distract the reader. I need to punctuate my dialogue correctly.

2 Many errors make my narrative and dialogue hard to read. I need to correct them.

1 I need to correct numerous errors in my writing.

Is my dialogue indented correctly?

Begin a new paragraph each time a different person speaks.

DIALOGUE THAT RUNS TOGETHER

“Everyone line up,” barked Mr. Brown. “It’s time for physical fitness tests.” “Do we have to do push-ups or chin-ups?” asked Sam. “You’ll be doing chin-ups,” Mr. Brown answered.

DIALOGUE INDENTED FOR EACH NEW SPEAKER

“Everyone line up,” barked Mr. Brown. “It’s time for physical fitness tests.”

“Do we have to do push-ups or chin-ups?” asked Sam.

“You’ll be doing chin-ups,” Mr. Brown answered.

Edit **Check your dialogue for proper form.** Make sure that you start a new paragraph each time a different person speaks.

Editing in Action

Dialogue is corrected below. (¶ means “start a new paragraph.”)

“How are things going in there, ?” she called from the other room. ¶ “Fine!” I said. “Just stay there and rest your foot.”

Editing **Using a Checklist**

Check your editing. Number a piece of paper from 1 to 9. If you can answer "yes" to a question, put a check mark after that number. If not, continue to edit for that convention.

Conventions

PUNCTUATION

_____ **1.** Do I use end punctuation after all my sentences?

_____ **2.** In dialogue, do I place the speaker's words within quotation marks?

_____ **3.** Do I use a comma, a question mark, or an exclamation point to separate the speaker's words from the rest of the sentence?

CAPITALIZATION

_____ **4.** Do I start all my sentences with capital letters?

_____ **5.** Do I capitalize all proper nouns?

SPELLING

_____ **6.** Have I spelled all my words correctly?

_____ **7.** Have I double-checked the words my spell-checker might have missed?

GRAMMAR

_____ **8.** Do my subjects and verbs agree?
(He and I _were_ running, not He and I _was_ running.)

_____ **9.** Do I use the right words (_your_ or _you're_)?

Adding a Title

- Use strong, colorful words: **My Recipe for Success**
- Give the words rhythm: **Mom's Supper Surprise**
- Be imaginative: **Tasty Tacos, Anyone?**

Publishing

After you finish proofreading your story, make a neat final copy to share. You may also share your story in the form of a poster, an interview, or an oral reading. (See the suggestions below.)

Presentation

- Use blue or black ink and write neatly.
- Write your name in the upper left corner of page 1.
- Skip a line and center your title; skip another line and start writing.
- Indent every paragraph and leave a one-inch margin on all sides.
- Write your last name and the page number in the upper right corner of every page after the first one.

Share an Interview
Videotape a partner interviewing with you about your successful experience. Show the tape to your class.

Make a Poster
Title your poster "A Personal Success." Draw a picture that captures the high point of your success story.

Read Your Story to Others
Read your story to a younger class. Explain why your success experience was important.

Publish

Make a final copy. Follow your teacher's instructions or use the guidelines above. (If you are using a computer, see pages 44–46.) Write a final copy of your narrative and proofread it.

Rubric for Narrative Writing

Use this rubric for guiding and rating your narrative writing.

Ideas

6 The writer relates an unforgettable experience using rich details.

5 The writer tells about an interesting experience. Great details are used.

4 The writer tells about an interesting experience. More details are needed.

Organization

6 The organization makes the narrative easy to read.

5 The narrative is well organized. Transitions are used well.

4 The narrative is well organized. Most of the transitions are helpful.

Voice

6 The writer's voice helps to create an unforgettable experience.

5 The writer's voice sounds natural and creates interest in the story. Dialogue is used.

4 The writer's voice creates interest in the story. More dialogue is needed.

Word Choice

6 The writer's exceptional word choice helps the writing come alive.

5 Strong nouns, verbs, and modifiers create clear, vivid pictures.

4 Modifiers are used. Stronger nouns and verbs would create clearer pictures.

Sentence Fluency

6 The sentences are skillfully written and make the writing enjoyable to read.

5 The sentences show variety and are easy to read and understand.

4 The sentences are varied, but some could flow more smoothly.

Conventions

6 Accurate use of conventions adds clarity to the writing.

5 The narrative has very few errors in spelling, punctuation, or grammar.

4 Some errors in spelling, punctuation, or grammar exist.

3 The writer needs to focus on one experience. Some details do not relate to the story.

2 The writer needs to focus on one experience. Details are needed.

1 The writer needs to tell about an experience and use details.

3 The order of events needs to be corrected. More helpful transitions are needed.

2 The beginning, middle, and ending all run together. The order is unclear.

1 The narrative needs to be organized.

3 The writer's voice can be heard. More dialogue is needed.

2 The voice is weak. Dialogue is needed.

1 The writer's voice seems uninterested.

3 Strong nouns, verbs, and modifiers are needed to create clear pictures.

2 Many general and overused words do not help the reader "see" the story.

1 The writing shows limited word choice or incorrect usage of words.

3 A better variety of sentences is needed. Sentences do not read smoothly.

2 Incomplete and/or short sentences interrupt the flow of the story.

1 Poorly formed sentences make the story very difficult to read.

3 A number of errors could confuse the reader.

2 Many errors make the narrative hard to read.

1 Serious errors disrupt the narrative.

Evaluating a Narrative

As you read through Kim's narrative below, focus on the strengths and weaknesses in her writing. (The narrative contains some errors.)

Call Me Betsy

My sister, Marisa, says I'm too dramatic. I guess it's true. I'm always showing my feelings. Last fall I tried out for our school play.

The play was about the American Revolution. Betsy Ross was the main caracter. Our teacher, Mrs. Guzman, said that Betsy's part will take a lot of practice. I really wanted the part.

Marisa helped me a lot. She's been in plays before. She's a good actor. Every night, after supper she listened to me say my lines. When I got to a part about Paul Revere I shouted, "The British are coming!" Marisa put her hands over her ears. I was being too loud. This time she was right. Betsy wouldn't have yelled like that.

At tryouts, I was scarred. Mrs. Guzman asked me to begin. I sat in a rocking chair. I pretended to sew and said my lines. When tryouts were over, Mrs. Guzman read the names of the kids who would play each part. I held my breath as she said the names for the parts of Benjamin Franklin, Sam Adams, and George Washington. Then I heard my name. I was Betsy Ross!

My dramatic personality got me the part of Betsy.

Student Self-Assessment

Kim wrote a positive comment under each trait. Then she wrote about an improvement she could make. (She used the rubric and the number scale on pages 120–121.)

Ideas

5 Ideas
1. I think my story is interesting.
2. I could have included more sensory details.

Organization

3 Organization
1. I organized the events using time order.
2. My ending needs to tell more about how I felt or what I learned.

Voice

5 Voice
1. The way I told the story sounds like me.
2. Dialogue would make my speakers more real.

Word Choice

4 Word Choice
1. I think my title is good.
2. I could have used more words that show instead of tell.

Sentence Fluency

4 Sentence Fluency
1. I tried some new sentence beginnings.
2. I still have too many short sentences.

Conventions

4 Conventions
1. I did a pretty good job with punctuation.
2. I spelled a few words wrong.

Use the rubric. Assess your narrative using the rubric on pages 120–121. On your own paper, list the six traits. Leave room after each trait to write one strength and one weakness. Then choose a number (from 1 to 6) that shows how well each trait was used.

Reflecting on Your Writing

You've put a lot of time and effort into writing a good personal narrative. Now take some time to think about your writing. On your own paper, finish each sentence starter below.

When you reflect on your writing, you will see how you are growing as a writer.

My Narrative Essay

1. The best part of my essay is . . .

2. The part that still needs work is . . .

3. The main thing I learned about writing a personal narrative is . . .

4. The next time I write a narrative essay, I would like to . . .

Narrative Writing

Across the Curriculum

The world is full of stories, and narrative writing can help you tell them. For example, you can write a narrative that shares an important event in history. You can also write about your personal experiences with a challenging subject like math. You can even write an e-mail message to tell an absent classmate what happened in class.

On the following pages, you'll learn how you can use narrative writing in social studies class and math class. You will also learn how to take class minutes and answer a narrative prompt on a writing test.

Mini Index

- **Social Studies:** Sharing a Moment in History
- **Math:** Sharing a Personal Experience
- **Practical Writing:** Creating an E-Mail Message
- **Assessment:** Writing for Assessment

Social Studies:
Sharing a Moment in History

In the following narrative, Dominic shares the moment when two explorers, Lewis and Clark, finally reached the Pacific Ocean. Dominic writes his narrative from the point of view of William Clark.

BEGINNING

The main characters are introduced.

MIDDLE

Action and dialogue move the story along.

ENDING

A surprising twist in the story adds interest.

Lewis and Clark Reach the Pacific

I wipe the pouring rain off my face. Most explorers hope to find land, but Meriwether Lewis and I, William Clark, came all the way from St. Louis to reach the Pacific Ocean. I turn around and face the rest of our crew, the Corps of Discovery.

"We did it!" I shout. Everyone cheers as loudly as the sound of the huge waves crashing on the rocky shore. "We've paddled upstream, hiked over snowy mountains, and faced hunger and many other dangers."

Out of the corner of my eye, I see Sacagawea. She is calm, as usual. "Of course, without the help of our Indian friend, Sacagawea, we wouldn't have made it. Thank you, Sacagawea." The men cheer again, and Sacagawea smiles shyly.

I look back at the Pacific and notice that Meriwether looks unhappy. I truly can understand why. We had hoped to spot Asian trading ships at sea, but there are no ships anywhere. We planned to sail home by sea. Maybe the ships will come soon. If not, we'll have to go back the same way we came.

Prewriting **Selecting a Topic**

To find a topic, you can skim your social studies book for interesting historical events. Dominic wrote the following list.

Topics List

-Thomas Jefferson writes <u>Declaration of Independence</u>
-George Washington elected first president
-Meriwether Lewis and William Clark reach Pacific*

List topic ideas. Skim your social studies book and list three or four important events and the people involved. Put a star (✳) next to the event you would like to write about.

Gathering Details

To gather details about your topic, check your social studies book and the Internet for help. Dominic used the 5 W's to guide him.

5 W's Chart

Who? Meriwether Lewis, William Clark, Sacagawea,
      Corps of Discovery
What? Reached Pacific
Where? At the mouth of the Columbia River
When? November 1805
Why? President Jefferson wanted them to find an
      easy route to the Pacific.

Gather details. Answer the 5 W's for your topic. Review the names you have listed after "who." Choose one that you would like to be as you write your story.

Prewriting Bringing Your Story to Life

Next, you need to think of details that can help bring to life the people in your story. To do this, Dominic made the following cluster.

Details Cluster

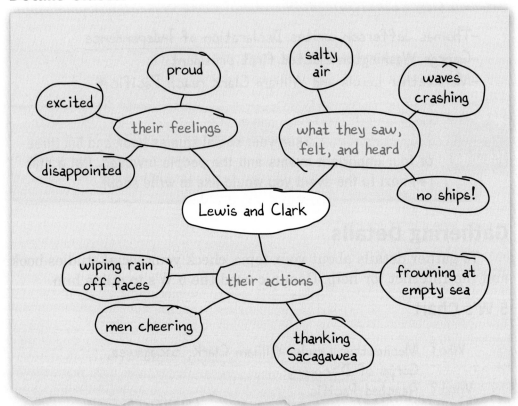

Create a cluster. Follow these instructions:

1 Write the main person or people at the center of your paper and circle it.

2 Create circles for "their feelings," "what they saw, felt, and heard," and "their actions." Connect the circles.

3 List three or four details for each new circle.

Writing **Creating Your First Draft**

Imagine being one of the people in your story and begin writing. In the first paragraph, introduce the people and the event. In the middle paragraphs, include feelings, sensory details, and actions to make the story interesting. In the last paragraph, include a final thought.

Write your first draft. Use your prewriting as a guide to help you bring the event to life.

Revising **Improving Your Writing**

Keep the following traits in mind as you revise your narrative.

- **Ideas** Do I focus on one event? Do I include enough details?
- **Organization** Does my story have an effective beginning, middle, and ending?
- **Voice** Does my voice sound like the person who's telling the story?
- **Word Choice** Have I chosen words that fit the event?
- **Sentence Fluency** Do my sentences read smoothly?

Revise your writing. Ask yourself the questions above as you review your story. Make any revisions needed.

Editing **Checking for Conventions**

When you are done revising, edit for conventions.

- **Conventions** Have I checked for errors in punctuation, capitalization, spelling, and grammar?

Edit your work. Also have someone else check your work. Then make a neat final copy and proofread it.

Math: Sharing a Personal Experience

A math narrative shares an adventure—or a misadventure—you've had with math. In the following narrative, Winona writes about a time she used math in her everyday life.

The **beginning** sets the scene.

The **middle** gives details about the experience.

The **ending** shows what the student has learned.

Math Memory

I use addition and subtraction a lot in my everyday life, but now I'm learning harder things like multiplying fractions. When would I ever use that? Well, last week our school had a bake sale, and I wanted to help my mom bake my favorite cookies. That's when I found out how important it is to know how to multiply fractions.

Mom said we needed to make a double batch of cookies. First, we multiplied the measurements for each ingredient by two. Next, we reduced the measurements to the lowest denominator. For example, 1/4 multiplied by two equals 2/4. Then 2/4 can be reduced to 1/2. Mom showed me how the 1/4 cup of brown sugar fit into the 1/2 cup twice. We knew we did it right. The cookies were delicious.

When I use math in my everyday life, it makes my homework easier to understand. I can remember what I learned and get the right answer. Math can be tough at first, but once I understand it, I don't forget it.

WRITING TIPS

Before you write . . .

- **Think of how you use math in everyday life.**
  List times outside of school when you've used math.
- **Pick a specific event for your narrative.**
  Choose a time that sticks out in your memory. It may be a time when you first understood a math concept. Think about how the experience made you feel.

During your writing . . .

- **Set the scene.**
  In the first paragraph, give the important background information to introduce the experience.
- **Focus on the details.**
  In the middle part, provide details about how you used math.
- **Share your feelings.**
  In the closing, reflect on how the experience changed your thinking.

After you've written a first draft . . .

- **Revise your writing.**
  Add any important details that are missing.
- **Check your organization.**
  Make sure that you have arranged the details in the best order.
- **Edit for conventions.**
  Check for errors in punctuation, capitalization, spelling, and grammar.

Write your math narrative. Focus on a specific time that you used math in your everyday life.

Practical Writing:
Creating an E-Mail Message

E-mail is one of the fastest ways to communicate. Kayla sent an e-mail to tell a friend about a class he had missed.

The **heading** gives information about the message.

The **beginning** tells why the writer is writing.

The **middle** tells what happened.

The **ending** closes politely.

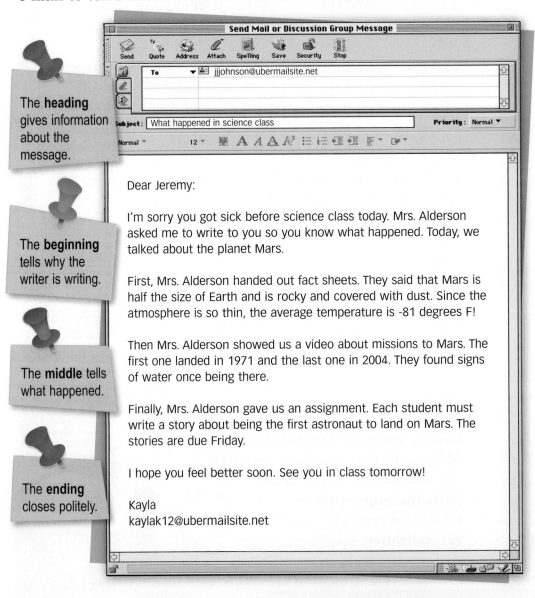

Send Mail or Discussion Group Message

Send | Quote | Address | Attach | Spelling | Save | Security | Stop

To ▼ jjjohnson@ubermailsite.net

Subject: What happened in science class   Priority: Normal ▼

Normal ▼   12 ▼

Dear Jeremy:

I'm sorry you got sick before science class today. Mrs. Alderson asked me to write to you so you know what happened. Today, we talked about the planet Mars.

First, Mrs. Alderson handed out fact sheets. They said that Mars is half the size of Earth and is rocky and covered with dust. Since the atmosphere is so thin, the average temperature is -81 degrees F!

Then Mrs. Alderson showed us a video about missions to Mars. The first one landed in 1971 and the last one in 2004. They found signs of water once being there.

Finally, Mrs. Alderson gave us an assignment. Each student must write a story about being the first astronaut to land on Mars. The stories are due Friday.

I hope you feel better soon. See you in class tomorrow!

Kayla
kaylak12@ubermailsite.net

WRITING TIPS

Before you write . . .

- **Know your goal.**
  Think about your reason for writing and what your reader needs to know.

During your writing . . .

- **Fill in the heading.**
  Make sure to write a subject line that is clear.

- **Greet the reader.**
  Politely say hello and tell why you are writing.

- **Organize your details.**
  Make sure your reader can understand the information.

- **Close politely.**
  Let the reader know what to do and politely include your name.

After you've written a first draft . . .

- **Read your message carefully.**
  Make sure your writing is complete and correct before hitting *Send.*

Write an e-mail message. Write to a friend, telling about the best thing that happened today during school.

Writing for Assessment

Some writing tests contain narrative prompts. A narrative prompt asks you to share an experience in your life.

Narrative Prompt

One part of growing up is learning to show responsibility. Think about a time when you showed responsibility. Write a narrative about that experience and include what you learned from it.

Sammy
—Let out
—Feed
—Fill water bowl
—Walk

The **beginning** introduces the focus (underlined).

Last summer I had a golden opportunity when our neighbors, the Hargroves, asked me to be their dog sitter while they were on vacation. I always wanted a dog, so I thought it would be fun. Mrs. Hargrove gave me the house key and instructions for taking care of Sammy, a golden retriever. <u>Taking care of Sammy would be a big responsibility, but I knew I could handle it.</u>

The **middle** paragraphs tell about the experience.

Every morning I let Sammy out into the Hargrove's backyard. After I let him back in, I gave him two cups of dry food just like the instructions said. Then I filled his water bowl, brushed him, patted him on the head, and locked

The middle part is organized by time.

the door. Whenever I could, I went over after lunch to play fetch with Sammy.

The last thing I did each day was walk Sammy around the neighborhood. He liked to stop and sniff the ground like crazy. Maybe he smelled a rabbit trail. After we got back to his house, I gave him one cup of food and filled his water bowl before I left. I double-checked that the door was locked.

The ending tells what the writer learned.

My two weeks with Sammy went quickly, even though it was hard work. It helped that Mrs. Hargrove paid me for my work. I hope I get to take care of Sammy the next time they go on vacation. I learned that being responsible means that people and pets can count on me!

Respond to the reading. Answer the following questions about the student response.

- **Ideas** (1) What is the topic of the response?
  (2) What key words in the prompt appear in the essay?
- **Organization** (3) How does the writer organize the details of the narrative?
- **Voice & Word Choice** (4) What words or phrases help make the writer sound responsible?

WRITING TIPS

Before you write . . .

- **Understand the prompt.**
  Make sure you understand the type of experience you are supposed to write about.
- **Use your time wisely.**
  Plan your narrative before you begin to write.

During your writing . . .

- **Find key words.**
  Use words from the prompt to introduce the experience.
- **Choose carefully.**
  Select details that will keep your story focused.
- **Write a strong ending.**
  Explain the importance of this experience to you.

After you've written a first draft . . .

- **Check your essay against the prompt.**
  Make sure you have done what the prompt asks.
- **Check for conventions.**
  Correct any errors you find.

Narrative Prompts

- Write about the most memorable experience you've had with a friend. Tell what happened at the beginning, in the middle, and at the end.
- Think about a time you helped someone. Write a narrative about that experience.

 Plan and write a response. Respond to one of the narrative prompts above. Complete your writing within the amount of time that your teacher gives you.

Narrative Writing in Review

In narrative writing, you tell a story about something that has happened. You may write about your own personal experiences.

Select a topic from your life that will interest your reader. (See page **92**.)

Gather important details about the people and events in your narrative. Use a graphic organizer. (See pages **93–95**.)

In the beginning part, give background information and introduce your topic. (See page **99**.)

In the middle part, tell your story using dialogue and specific details. (See pages **100–101**.)

In the ending part, tell why the event was important, how it changed you, or how your story might connect with the reader. (See page **102**.)

First, check the ideas, organization, and **voice** in your writing. Then review for **word choice** and **sentence fluency**. Make changes to improve your first draft. (See pages **104–114**.)

Also check your writing for conventions. Have a trusted classmate edit your writing as well. (See pages **116–118**.)

Make a final copy and proofread it for errors before sharing it. (See page **119**.)

Use the narrative rubric to assess your finished writing. (See pages **120–121**.)

Expository Writing

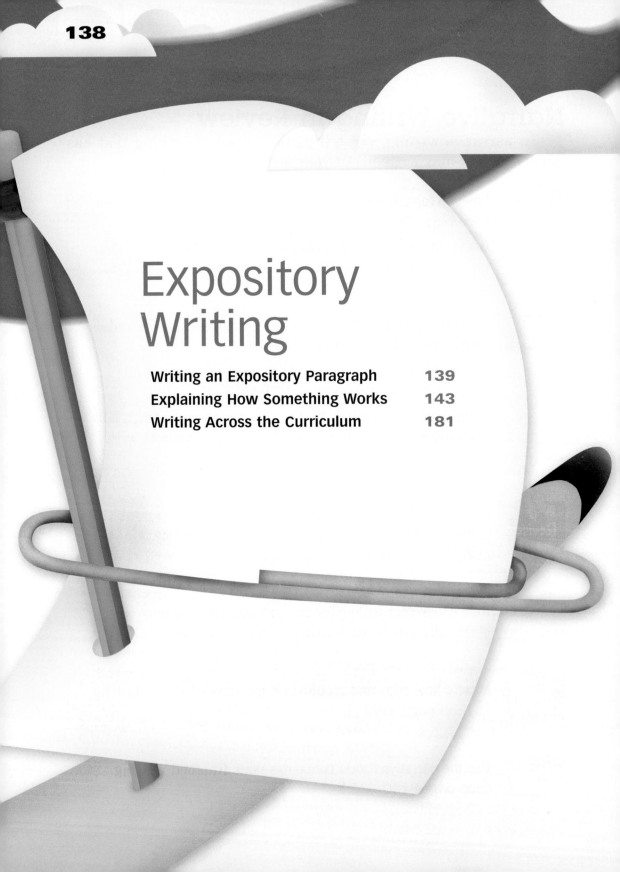

Expository Writing

Expository Paragraph

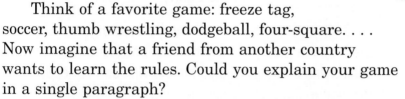

Think of a favorite game: freeze tag, soccer, thumb wrestling, dodgeball, four-square. . . . Now imagine that a friend from another country wants to learn the rules. Could you explain your game in a single paragraph?

An expository paragraph provides plenty of information in a small space. In the following chapter, you'll write an expository paragraph about a favorite game.

Writing Guidelines

Subject: A favorite game
Form: Expository paragraph
Purpose: To explain the rules
Audience: Classmates

Expository Paragraph

An expository paragraph starts with a **topic sentence**, which contains the main idea and explains what the paragraph will be about. The sentences in the **body** support the topic sentence, and the **closing sentence** completes the explanation. In the following paragraph, Marco tells about his favorite game back in Chile.

Topic sentence

Body

Closing sentence

Hit the Penny

Back in Chile, my friends and I played a game called "hit the penny." The game requires just a few pennies and a stick or broom handle with one flat end. First, set up the stick by pushing one end into the ground. Then lay a penny on the flat top end of the stick. Around the stick, draw a circle about six feet wide. Next, have each player stand outside the circle and take turns throwing another penny to knock the penny off the stick. If the knocked-off penny falls in the circle, the player gets one point, and if it falls outside, the player gets two points. Hit the penny takes only a couple minutes to learn, but a long time to master!

Respond to the reading. On your own paper, answer each of the following questions.

- **Ideas** (1) What things are needed to play the game?
- **Organization** (2) What transition words connect the sentences in the body of the paragraph? List two.
- **Voice & Word Choice** (3) What verbs does the writer use to give instructions? List two.

Prewriting **Selecting a Topic**

A cluster can help you think about your topic. Marco created the following cluster about his favorite games.

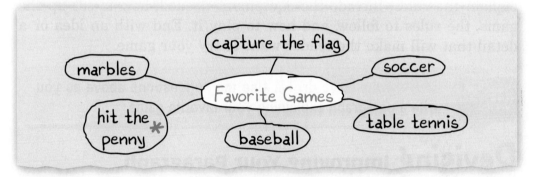

Create a cluster. Make a cluster like the one above. In it, list your favorite games. Put a star (✳) next to the game you want to write about. Be sure to choose one you can explain completely in a paragraph. (For example, baseball has too many rules to explain in a single paragraph.)

Writing a Topic Sentence

The topic sentence of your paragraph has two jobs. It should name the game you will explain and tell something interesting about it.

Write your topic sentence. Follow the pattern above to write the topic sentence for your paragraph. Try two or three different versions until the sentence sounds just right.

Writing Creating Your First Draft

Your first draft should sound as if you were explaining the rules of your favorite game to a friend. Start with your topic sentence. Then explain the rules. Include the equipment needed, how to set up the game, the rules to follow, and how to play it. End with an idea or a detail that will make the reader want to try your game.

Write your first draft. Use the suggestions above as you write a paragraph explaining your favorite game.

Revising Improving Your Paragraph

When you revise, consider the *ideas, organization, voice, word choice,* and *sentence fluency* of your paragraph.

Revise your paragraph. Let the questions below guide you.

1. Does my topic sentence clearly state my main idea?
2. Have I used transitions to connect the details in the body?
3. Does my voice show my interest in the topic?
4. Have I used specific nouns and verbs?
5. Are my sentences clear and complete?

Editing Checking for Conventions

Review your paragraph one last time. Focus on *conventions.*

Edit your work. Answer the following questions.

1. Does each sentence begin with a capital letter and include end punctuation?
2. Have I checked my spelling?
3. Have I used words correctly *(to, too, two)*?

Expository Writing

Explaining How Something Works

Do you know how a seed grows? How leaves make food for trees? How flowers turn into fruit? When you tell how something works, you are explaining a process.

In this chapter, you will write an expository essay that explains how something works. Your goal is to share interesting information with the reader. And you may just learn something yourself!

Writing Guidelines

Subject: A process (how something works)

Form: Expository essay

Purpose: To inform

Audience: Classmates

Understanding Your Goal

Your goal in this chapter is to write an essay that clearly explains a process (how something works). The traits listed in the chart below will help you reach your goal.

Your goal is to . . .

Ideas
Select an interesting topic, write a clear focus statement, and include supporting details.

Organization
Capture the reader's attention in the beginning. Then, in the middle, explain the process. In your ending, make sure you support your main idea.

Voice
Use a voice that fits your audience and shows that you know your topic well.

Word Choice
Use specialized words to help explain your topic.

Sentence Fluency
Write a variety of short, medium, and long sentences. Make sure each sentence is complete.

Conventions
Create an essay that has correct punctuation, capitalization, spelling, and grammar.

Get the big picture. Look at the rubric on pages 176–177. This rubric can help you measure your progress as you write.

Expository Essay

In the following expository essay, Terrell explains how the process of photosynthesis works.

Food for Everybody

BEGINNING

The beginning captures the reader's attention and gives the main idea in a focus statement (underlined).

Kids are always saying "I'm starving!" They probably hope to get some potato chips or oatmeal cookies. Moms may give them apples or oranges. All of these foods come from plants, but where do plants get their food? Plants actually make their own food through a process called photosynthesis.

Photosynthesis begins when a plant takes in water and carbon dioxide. The plant gets water from the ground through its roots. It gets carbon dioxide from the air through its leaves. Carbon dioxide is a gas that animals breathe out but that plants breathe in.

MIDDLE

Each middle paragraph tells about a different part of the process.

In the next part of the process, the water and carbon dioxide are changed into sugar in the leaves. Each leaf has cells full of a green substance called chlorophyll. Chlorophyll uses sunlight first to break down the water and carbon dioxide. It then combines these two elements into sugar.

Transitions (in blue) help organize the writer's thoughts by tying them together.

ENDING

The ending supports the main idea.

In the end, photosynthesis supports all life on earth. It creates the sugar that lets all green plants live. It also feeds the plant-eating animals, and eventually the animals that eat the plant eaters. When photosynthesis breaks down carbon dioxide, it releases oxygen. Without photosynthesis, humans and animals couldn't even breathe!

Bite into an apple and taste the sweetness. That taste comes from photosynthesis. Take a deep breath of fresh air. That freshness comes from photosynthesis, too. Next time you say, "I'm starving," remember that photosynthesis is the process that makes food for everybody.

Respond to the reading. Answer the following questions about the sample essay.

- **Ideas** (1) How does the writer introduce the topic?

- **Organization** (2) What transitions help connect the middle paragraphs?

- **Voice & Word Choice** (3) What words or phrases show that the writer understands and cares about the topic? Find two.

Prewriting

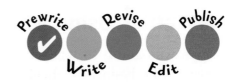

The writing process begins with prewriting. Prewriting starts when you think of possible writing topics and ends when you are ready to write your first draft.

Keys to Prewriting

1. **Select** a topic to write about.

2. **Gather** facts and details about the topic.

3. **Find** a few special details to include.

4. **Write** a focus statement and topic sentences.

5. **Create** an organized list of your facts and details.

Prewriting Using a "Basics-of-Life" List

Latonya was going to write an essay about a process (how something works). She began by checking a "Basics-of-Life" list. From the list, she chose two categories that interested her: food and environment.

"Basics-of-Life" List

agriculture	education	food *	love
animals	energy	freedom	machines
art/music	environment *	friends	money
books	exercise	health	plants
clothing	faith	housing	science/technology
community	family	laws	work/play

Choose two categories. Look at the "Basics-of-Life" list above and choose two general categories that interest you.

Selecting a Topic

Next, Latonya needed a specific topic to explain. She wrote down her two chosen categories and listed possible topics under each of them.

Topic List

Food	Environment
popcorn popper	global warming
the stomach	water cycle *
an ice-cream maker	hurricanes
the food chain	rock cycle

Select a topic. Write down the two categories you have chosen. Under each, list specific topics (things you can explain by telling how they work). Put a star (*) next to the topic you like the best.

Gathering Details

Latonya continued her prewriting by gathering details about her chosen topic. She created a KWL chart, which lists what a person **K**nows, **W**onders, and **L**earns about a topic. Latonya's science book and the Internet helped her fill in the last column.

KWL Chart

How the Water Cycle Works

K – What do I know?	W – What do I wonder about?	L – What did I learn?
• Water can be solid ice or a cloud.	1. Does the earth lose any water?	1. The earth just recycles water.
• Temperature makes the form of water change.	2. What words describe how water changes?	2. "evaporation," "condensation," and "precipitation"
• Water is in lakes, rivers, and oceans, under the ground, and in the air.	3. How much of the earth's water is in the oceans?	3. Oceans contain 97% of earth's water.

Prewrite

Create a KWL chart. Make a KWL chart about your topic. Check books, magazines, or the Internet to find answers.

1 In the first column, list what you already know.

2 In the second column, list what you wonder about.

3 In the third column, write new information you learn.

Prewriting Including Amazing Details

Every *reader* would like to tell every *writer,* "Tell me something I don't already know!" One way to keep the reader interested in your essay is to include amazing details.

Practice

Choose the most amazing detail below and tell why you like it.

1. Clouds hold water.
2. Water freezes at 32 degrees Fahrenheit.
3. The water that humans drink was once drunk by Tyrannosaurus rex.
4. Underwater volcanoes help make the sea salty.
5. Water runs downhill to reach the ocean.
6. The average American uses 100 gallons of water per day.

Prewrite

Check your details. Review the details you have gathered on your "KWL Chart" (from page 149). Did you find some amazing details to include? If you didn't, keep looking.

Focus on the Traits

Ideas Amazing details show that you are excited about your topic and want the reader to be excited about it, too.

Writing Your Focus Statement

Your focus statement appears at the end of your first paragraph. The focus statement names your topic and focuses on one part of it.

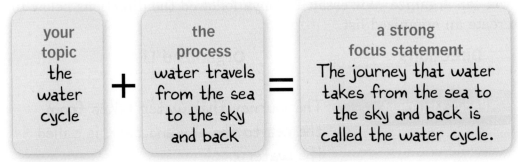

your topic		the process		a strong focus statement
the water cycle	**+**	water travels from the sea to the sky and back	**=**	The journey that water takes from the sea to the sky and back is called the water cycle.

Prewrite

Write your focus statement. Use the pattern above and try different versions until you are satisfied.

Writing Topic Sentences

Once you have a clear focus statement, you are ready to write topic sentences for your essay. Each topic sentence covers a specific part of the process. Here are some sentence starters to help you write your topic sentences.

To start,	In the first stage,	The process begins when . . .
Next,	During the next stage,	The next step in the process . . .
Finally,	In the last stage,	The end of the process comes when . . .

You may also use Latonya's topic sentences as models.

The water cycle begins with evaporation.

The next step in the water cycle is condensation.

When droplets in a cloud get big enough, precipitation begins.

Prewrite

Write topic sentences. Complete three of the sentence starters above. You can use Latonya's sentences as models, or try your own strategy.

Prewriting Organizing Your Ideas

Now that you have written a focus statement and topic sentences, you can organize your essay. Latonya followed the directions below to create an organized list.

Directions	Organized List

Focus statement

The journey that water takes from the sea to the sky and back is called the water cycle.

First topic sentence

1. The water cycle begins with evaporation.

List of details
- One trillion tons each day
- Gets rid of salt
- No water lost

Second topic sentence

2. The next step in the water cycle is condensation.

List of details
- Cools off/sticks to dust
- Cloud, fog, dew, frost
- Lemonade glass, mirror

Third topic sentence

3. When droplets in a cloud get big enough, precipitation begins.

List of details
- Rain, sleet, snow
- Falls in ocean or flows to ocean
- Oceans contain 97 percent

Prewrite

Make an organized list. Follow the model above to create your own organized list of topic sentences and details.

Writing

Once you have gathered and organized your details, you are ready to write your first draft. When you write your first draft, you put all your ideas on paper or on the computer.

Keys to Writing

1. **Write** a strong beginning paragraph that ends with a focus statement.

2. **Begin** each middle paragraph with a clear topic sentence.

3. **Organize** the supporting details in each middle paragraph.

4. **Write** a thoughtful ending paragraph.

Writing Getting the Big Picture

The chart below shows how the parts of an expository essay fit together. (The examples are from the sample essay on pages 155–158.) You are ready to begin writing your essay when you have . . .

- gathered enough details,
- written your focus statement and topic sentences, and
- created an organized list or outline.

Beginning

The **beginning** introduces the topic and gives the focus statement.

Focus Statement

The journey that water takes from the sea to the sky and back is called the water cycle.

Middle

Each **middle** paragraph explains one part of the process.

Topic Sentences

- The water cycle begins with evaporation.
- The next step in the water cycle is condensation.
- When droplets in a cloud get big enough, precipitation begins.

Ending

The **ending** summarizes your thoughts and supports the main idea.

Closing Sentence

Better yet, just take a sip from a drinking fountain and think of the journey that this water has taken!

Starting Your Essay

The first thing you want to do in your essay is catch your reader's attention. Here are some strategies.

| Beginning |
| Middle |
| Ending |

- **Ask a question.**
  How many gallons of water do you use each day?

- **Give a surprising fact.**
  People drink the same water dinosaurs once drank.

- **Create a picture in the reader's mind.**
  The world is like a giant terrarium.

- **Tell a one- or two-sentence anecdote.**
  Once I went sledding on a mountain and swimming in the ocean—on the same day.

Beginning Paragraph

The first sentence catches the reader's attention.

Once I went sledding on a mountain and swimming in the ocean—on the same day. That was an amazing journey, but water makes that journey all the time. After all, the snow that fell on the mountain once was in the sea! The journey that water takes from the sea to the sky and back is called the water cycle.

The focus statement is stated clearly (underlined).

Write

Write your beginning paragraph.
Use one of the four strategies above to write a sentence that grabs the reader's attention. Then write sentences that lead up to your focus statement.

Writing **Developing the Middle Part**

The middle paragraphs of your expository essay explain how your topic works. Each paragraph should cover a different part of the process.

Beginning
▶ Middle
Ending

Connecting Your Sentences

One way to connect ideas is to use transition words or phrases. Another way is to fit sentences together like the pieces of a puzzle. Notice how the words in italics connect the sentences.

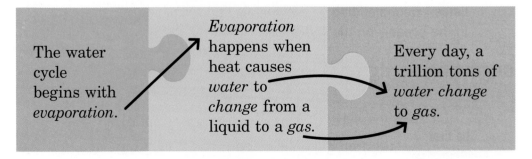

The water cycle begins with *evaporation*.

Evaporation happens when heat causes *water* to *change* from a liquid to a *gas*.

Every day, a trillion tons of *water change* to *gas*.

Middle Paragraphs

Topic sentence 1

Sentences are connected with repeated words.

The water cycle begins with evaporation. Evaporation happens when heat causes water to change from a liquid to a gas. Every day, a trillion tons of water change to gas. When water evaporates, it leaves its salt behind, so evaporation gives the world its freshwater. If water only evaporated, though, the oceans would eventually dry up, as they did on Mars. But earth's water cycle doesn't end with evaporation.

Topic sentence 2

The next step in the water cycle is condensation. Condensation is water vapor (evaporated water) turning back into drops of liquid. This happens if water vapor cools or water molecules stick to dust particles in the air. When water condenses in the air, it forms clouds or fog. When it condenses on the ground, it forms dew or frost. Water can also condense onto a cold lemonade glass or a cool bathroom mirror.

Details from the organized list are included.

Topic sentence 3

When droplets in a cloud get big enough, precipitation begins. Precipitation is just falling water. Different temperatures create different kinds of precipitation. Rain, sleet, and snow are forms of precipitation. Most precipitation ends up back in the ocean. That's where 97 percent of the earth's water is. Then the water cycle is ready to begin again!

A different part of the cycle is covered in each paragraph.

Write your middle paragraphs. Use the organized list you created on page 152 as you write your middle paragraphs. Try connecting some of your sentences with repeated words.

Writing **Ending Your Essay**

Now it's time to wrap up your explanation and give your reader something to think about. Here are four strategies for creating a strong ending.

- ■ **Connect with the reader.**
  Better yet, just take a sip from a drinking fountain and think of the journey that this water has taken!

- ■ **Add a final surprising detail.**
  Water makes up 60 percent of the human body, so everyone is part of the water cycle.

- ■ **Tell why the topic is important.**
  Without the water cycle, nothing could live on land—and that means all of us.

- ■ **Use the strategy you used in your beginning.**
  So, get out and enjoy the water cycle. Try sledding on a mountain or swimming in the sea.

Ending Paragraph

The writer used two of the strategies above.

So, get out and enjoy the water cycle. Try sledding on a mountain or swimming in the sea. Better yet, just take a sip from a drinking fountain and think of the journey that this water has taken!

Write your ending. Create a strong ending for your essay. Use one or more of the strategies above, or invent your own!

Form a complete first draft. Write your first draft on every other line so you have room to revise.

Revising

Revising may be the most important step in the writing process. When you revise, you check your essay for *ideas, organization, voice, word choice,* and *sentence fluency.*

Keys to Revising

1. **Read** your essay once to see how you feel about it.

2. **Review** each part: the beginning, the middle, and the ending.

3. **Ask** a classmate to read your first draft, too.

4. **Change** any parts that need to be improved.

Revising for Ideas

6 My topic, focus, and supporting details make my essay truly memorable.

5 My essay is informative with a clear focus. I include enough supporting details.

4 My essay is informative with a clear focus. I need a few more supporting details.

When you revise for *ideas*, you check each of your details. The rubric strip above can help guide your revision.

How do I know if I included enough details?

You know you have included enough details if your essay answers all the main questions. Here is a list of those questions.

1. What process am I explaining?
2. How does the process begin?
3. How does the process continue?
4. How does the process end?
5. Why do I think the process is interesting?

Practice

Read the paragraph below and then answer the five questions above.

Snails have a one-of-a-kind way to get around. First, a gland on the snail's belly releases slime. It makes the ground slick and also protects the snail's soft body. Then the motion begins. Rows of muscles on the snail's belly start to flex. These ripples push the snail over the slimy ground. The snail's belly is actually a foot, and the snail's scientific name, *gastropod,* means "belly foot." After the snail moves on, the slime trail dries. Often snails leave trails in gardens. A snail can move only two or three inches in a minute—but during a year, it could go 17 miles!

Revise

Check your details. Read your essay and then answer the five questions above. If you can't find an answer to a question, add supporting details to your essay to provide an answer.

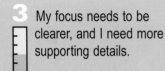

3 My focus needs to be clearer, and I need more supporting details.

2 I need a focus, and I need many more supporting details.

1 My topic is unclear.

How do I know if my details are interesting?

One way to find out whether your details are interesting is to ask a classmate or another reader.

Partner Conference Sheet

My favorite detail is _gastropod means "belly foot."_
An amazing detail is _snails can travel 17 miles a year!_
What I wonder is _how do snails crawl up walls?_

Hold a partner conference. Trade essays with a partner and read each other's work. Then, on your own paper, write your favorite detail, an amazing detail, and what you wonder. Discuss your answers.

Revising in Action

Notice in the sample below that an unneeded detail is taken out, and an important detail is added.

> Most precipitation ends up back in the ocean.
> That's where 97 percent of the earth's water is.
> ∧ ~~Only 1 percent of all water on earth is drinkable~~. . .

Revising for Organization

6 My essay is clear and easy to read, with every detail in just the right place.

5 I have a strong beginning, a middle that supports the focus, and a thoughtful ending.

4 My essay has a clear beginning, a middle, and an ending.

When you revise for *organization*, you check to make sure your beginning and ending work well. The rubric strip above can guide you.

How do I know if my beginning works well?

You know your beginning works well if it captures the reader's attention. Remember the strategies below. (Also see page 155.)

- Ask a question.
- Give a surprising fact.
- Create a picture in the reader's mind.
- Tell a short story or anecdote.

Practice

Replace each beginning sentence below with a new sentence that grabs the reader's attention. Use a different strategy for each sentence beginning.

1. A hurricane is a storm that goes in a circle.
2. One process that people care about is how a volcano works.
3. If cream is churned, it will turn into butter.
4. Sometimes snow on a mountainside comes loose.

Revise

Review your beginning. Does your first sentence capture the reader's attention? If not, rewrite it using one of the strategies above.

3 Most details are in order. My beginning and/or ending is weak.

 2 Many details are not in any order. My beginning, middle, and ending run together.

1 I need to organize my essay better.

How do I know if my ending works well?

You know your ending works well if it's interesting to read or gives the reader something to think about.

> On earth, 95 percent of all animal species are insects, and all of them go through metamorphosis. You might not want to be born as a worm, but wouldn't it be great to grow wings and fly?

Did you connect with the reader, add a surprising detail, or tell why the topic is important?

 Revise **Check your ending.** Do you leave your reader with something to think about? If not, try one of the strategies on page 158.

Revising in Action

In the sample below, a weak ending is revised.

So, get out and enjoy the water cycle. ~~There's not much else to say.~~ Try sledding on a mountain or swimming in the sea. Better yet, Just take a sip from a drinking fountain and think of the ~~water.~~ journey that this water has taken.

Revising for Voice

6 My voice is strong and lively. I sound confident, enthusiastic, and knowledgeable.

5 I sound well informed and confident. My voice fits my topic and audience.

4 I sound well informed, and my voice fits my topic and audience most of the time.

When you revise for *voice*, you make sure your writing voice fits your audience. The rubric strip above can help you.

Does my writing voice fit my audience?

Your writing voice works best if it sounds lively and interesting. However, be sure your voice is also suitable for the classroom.

TOO CASUAL FOR AN ESSAY

C'mon. Don't you know what double dribbling is? You can't just dribble and stop and dribble again. It's our ball. Give it here.

MORE FORMAL FOR AN ESSAY

The rules of basketball don't allow "double dribbling." Double dribbling happens when a player dribbles the ball, holds it, and then begins dribbling again. A player who double dribbles gets called for a foul, and the ball is given to the other team.

When you talk to friends, you sound very casual. An expository essay should have a more formal voice.

3 Sometimes I sound unsure. My voice needs to fit my topic and audience consistently.

2 I sound unsure. My voice needs to fit my topic and audience.

1 I need to think about my audience.

How can I make my voice suitable for an essay?

You can make your voice suitable for an essay by changing words or phrases that sound too casual.

Practice

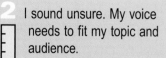

The paragraph below is too casual for an expository essay. Find three words, phrases, or clauses that make the voice too casual.

The baler goes rolling over a bunch of hay and gobbles up the stuff and squeezes it into a block. Some balers make wimpy little bales, but others make these huge ones that could crush a guy! The baler wraps the hay up, and you have got yourself a bale.

Review your voice. Read your essay. Replace overly casual words, phrases, or clauses with more suitable language.

Revising in Action

Casual words, phrases, and clauses are replaced in the sample below. The changes make the writing more informative.

When droplets in a cloud get big enough, ~~they go~~ precipitation begins.

~~Precipitation is just falling water.~~

~~"Hasta la vista!"~~ Different temperatures create . . .

Revising for Word Choice

| 6 | The words I use make my essay very clear, informative, and fun to read. | 5 | I avoid wordiness and use specialized words in my essay. | 4 | I avoid wordiness but could use a few more specialized words. |

When you revise for *word choice*, you fix wordy sentences and add specialized words that fit your subject. The rubric strip above will help you revise for word choice.

How can I remove wordiness from my essay?

You can fix wordiness by taking out words that don't mean much and just take up space. Here are some wordy words and phrases.

kind of	really	There is . . .
sort of	very	There are . . .
a little bit	totally	It is . . .

Practice

On your own paper, remove the wordiness from each sentence.

1. It is true that the human heart is really really important.
2. When blood needs a little bit of oxygen, it turns sort of a little dark red.
3. Blood that is totally full of oxygen is really very bright red.
4. It is interesting that the heart and the lungs sort of work as a kind of team.

Revise

Remove wordiness. Read your writing and watch for the wordy words and phrases above. Remove any you find.

3	I need to fix the wordiness in spots and add more specialized words.	2	My essay is wordy, and I need to use specialized words.	1	I need to improve the word choice in my essay.

How can specialized words improve my writing?

Specialized words can improve your writing by making it more exact. Notice how the specialized words relate to each subject below.

SUBJECT	SPECIALIZED WORDS
The human heart	arteries, veins, pulse, valves, atrium, ventricle
Basketball	dribble, foul, tip-off, jump shot, traveling
The sun	hydrogen, helium, fusion, mantle, sunspots

Revise

Use specialized words. Review your prewriting (pages 148–152). Circle any specialized words you discovered as you gathered information. Then look for places where such words could make your essay clearer or more exact.

Revising in Action

Notice how specialized words in the following paragraph make the meaning of the writing more exact.

> The next step in the water cycle is ^condensation. Condensation is water vapor (evaporated water)^ turning back into drops of liquid. This happens if water vapor cools or ~~it~~ water molecules sticks to dust ^particles~ in the air.

Revising for Sentence Fluency

| **6** My sentences are well crafted and flow smoothly. People will enjoy reading them. | **5** My sentences flow smoothly and have a variety of lengths. | **4** Most of my sentences flow smoothly, but I need to include more variety of lengths. |

When you revise for *sentence fluency*, you check for complete sentences and different sentence lengths to make your writing flow smoothly. The rubric strip above can help you revise.

How can I fix fragments in my writing?

You can fix fragments by making sure each sentence has a subject and a predicate and expresses a complete thought. If a group of words is missing a subject, a predicate, or both, it is not a complete sentence. It is a fragment. (See also page **436**.)

Practice

Read the following fragments. On your own paper, write the part or parts that are missing: subject, predicate, or both subject and predicate. Then choose three of the fragments and add words to make them into complete sentences.

1. Old-fashioned push lawn mowers.
2. Quieter than power mowers.
3. A whirling set of blades.
4. Spins and cuts the grass.
5. Grass clippings.
6. Is a good way to earn extra cash.

Revise

Revise any fragments. Check your essay for fragments. Fix any fragments you find by adding a subject, a predicate, or both so that each sentence expresses a complete thought.

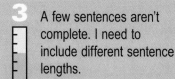

3 A few sentences aren't complete. I need to include different sentence lengths.

2 My sentences are all about the same length, and I have a number of sentence fragments.

1 I need to check for complete sentences.

How can I check the lengths of my sentences?

You can check sentence lengths by counting words in each sentence.

Practice

Count the words in each sentence below. How many sentences are short (up to 8 words), medium (8 to 12 words), and long (more than 12)?

(1) The team unrolls the hot-air balloon on the ground. **(2)** The burner and the basket are attached. **(3)** A big fan starts blowing air into the balloon. **(4)** Once it is partly full, the pilot uses the burner to heat up the air. **(5)** After the balloon is upright, the crew climbs aboard.

Check your sentence lengths. Count the number of words in each sentence of one paragraph in your essay. Make changes as needed to create a variety of sentence lengths.

Revising in Action

In the sample below, three short sentences are combined.

Once I went sledding on a mountain. Then I went swimming in the ocean. This happened on the same day. That was an amazing journey, but water . . .

Revising Using a Checklist

Check your revising. Number a piece of paper from 1 to 10. If you can answer "yes" to a question, put a check mark after that number. If not, continue to work with that part of your essay.

Ideas

_____ **1.** Do I focus on an interesting topic?

_____ **2.** Have I included enough details?

_____ **3.** Are my details interesting?

Organization

_____ **4.** Does my beginning capture the reader's attention?

_____ **5.** Does the ending make the reader think?

Voice

_____ **6.** Does my voice fit my audience?

Word Choice

_____ **7.** Have I avoided wordiness in my essay?

_____ **8.** Have I used specialized words?

Sentence Fluency

_____ **9.** Are all my sentences complete?

_____ **10.** Do I use a variety of sentence lengths?

Make a clean copy. When you've finished revising your essay, make a clean copy if necessary before you begin to edit.

Editing

Editing becomes important after you've revised your first draft. When you edit, you make sure you have followed the rules for using punctuation, capitalization, spelling, and grammar.

Keys to Editing

1. **Use** a dictionary, a thesaurus, and the "Proofreader's Guide" in the back of this book for help.

2. **Edit** on a printed copy if you use a computer. Then make your changes on the computer.

3. **Use** the editing marks shown inside the back cover of this book.

4. **Ask** someone else to check your writing for errors, too.

Editing for Conventions

6	I accurately use conventions that add style to my writing.	5	I may have a few minor errors in punctuation, spelling, or grammar.	4	I need to correct a few errors in punctuation, spelling, or grammar.

When you edit for *conventions*, you check for errors in spelling, punctuation, and grammar. The rubric strip above can help you.

Am I using the right words?

To use the *right* words listed below, you must pay attention to the apostrophe. If the word has an apostrophe, it is a contraction. Otherwise, it shows possession. (See pages **536–559**.)

Misused Words	What They Mean
it's/its	*It's* means "it is." *Its* means "belonging to it."
you're/your	*You're* means "you are." *Your* means "belonging to you."
they're/their	*They're* means "they are." *Their* means "belonging to them."

Practice

> **For each of the sentences below, two words are shown in parentheses. Choose the correct one for each sentence.**
>
> 1. A submarine floats when *(it's, its)* lighter than water.
> 2. To dive, the submarine takes water into *(it's, its)* tanks.
> 3. *(They're, Their)* pumped out when it's time to surface.
> 4. Submarines carry compressed air in *(they're, their)* tanks.
> 5. Maybe *(you're, your)* wondering if fish do the same.
> 6. *(You're, Your)* guess is right: Fish use swim bladders to dive.

Edit

Use the right word. Read your essay. Look for commonly misused words. Make sure you have used the right word.

My errors may confuse the reader. I need to fix them.

 Many errors make my essay hard to read. I need to carefully correct them.

 I need to correct numerous errors in my writing.

Do my pronouns agree with their antecedents?

Pronouns agree with their antecedents if they agree in number. Number agreement means that a singular antecedent needs a singular pronoun, and a plural antecedent needs a plural pronoun.

Singular Antecedent   *Singular Pronoun*
The ship's captain **always keeps** his **cabin in order.**

Plural Antecedent   *Plural Pronoun*
The crew members **must keep** their **lockers clean.**

Don't use the word **they** or **their** to refer to a singular noun!

 Check for agreement. Make sure the pronouns in your essay agree with the nouns they refer to.

Editing in Action

A pronoun-agreement problem is fixed in the sample below.

Every day, a trillion tons of water change to gas.
                          it leaves its
When water evaporates, ~~they leave their~~ salt behind,

so evaporation gives the world its freshwater. If . . .

Editing **Using a Checklist**

Edit

Check your editing. Number a piece of paper from 1 to 10. If you can answer "yes" to a question, put a check mark after that number. If not, continue to edit for that convention.

Conventions

PUNCTUATION

_____ 1. Do I use end punctuation after all my sentences?

_____ 2. Do I use commas after introductory word groups?

_____ 3. Do I use commas in all my compound sentences?

CAPITALIZATION

_____ 4. Do I start all my sentences with capital letters?

_____ 5. Do I capitalize all names (proper nouns)?

SPELLING

_____ 6. Have I spelled all my words correctly?

_____ 7. Have I looked for words my spell-checker might miss?

GRAMMAR

_____ 8. Do I use correct forms of verbs (*had gone*, not *had went*)?

_____ 9. Do my pronouns agree with their antecedents?

_____ 10. Have I watched for commonly misused words such as *our* and *you're*?

Adding a Title

Here are some ideas for writing a title.

■ Repeat a sound: **Wet, Wild, and Wonderful**

■ Use a common expression: **Water, Water, Everywhere**

■ Find a phrase from your essay: **From the Sea to the Sky**

Publishing

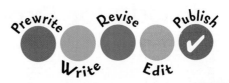

It's time to proofread your essay and make a neat copy to share. You could also turn your writing into a diagram, a speech, or a Web page. (See the suggestions below.)

Presentation

- Use blue or black ink and write neatly.
- Write your name in the upper left corner of page 1.
- Skip a line and center your title; skip another line and start writing.
- Indent every paragraph and leave a one-inch margin on all sides.
- Write your last name and the page number in the upper right corner of every page after the first one.

Create a Diagram

Make an illustration to show how your process works. You might model your diagram on one you find in a book, in a magazine, or on a Web site.

Give a Speech

Present your essay to the class as a speech. (See pages **373–378** for more about giving a speech.)

Design a Web Page

Create a Web page. Provide links to other sites where you found information about your topic.

Publish

Make a final copy. Follow your teacher's instructions or use the presentation guidelines above. (If you are using a computer, see pages **44–46**.) Create a clean final copy of your essay.

Rubric for Expository Writing

Use this rubric for writing and assessing expository essays.

Ideas

6 The topic, focus, and details make the essay truly memorable.

5 The essay is informative, with a clear focus and supporting details.

4 The essay is informative, with a clear focus. More supporting details are needed.

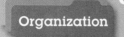
Organization

6 The organization makes the essay easy to read.

5 The beginning, middle, and ending work well. Transitions are used.

4 The essay's beginning, middle, and ending use some transitions.

Voice

6 The writer's voice sounds confident, knowledgeable, and enthusiastic.

5 The writer's voice sounds informative and confident. It fits the audience.

4 The writer's voice sounds well-informed most of the time and fits the audience.

Word Choice

6 The word choice makes the essay clear, informative, and interesting.

5 Specific nouns and action verbs make the essay clear and informative.

4 Some nouns and verbs could be more specific.

Sentence Fluency

6 The sentences flow smoothly and will hold the reader's interest.

5 The sentences flow smoothly and read well aloud.

4 Most of the sentences read smoothly, but some are short and choppy.

Conventions

6 Mastery of conventions adds style to the essay.

5 The essay has few errors in punctuation, spelling, or grammar.

4 The essay has several errors in punctuation, spelling, or grammar.

3 The focus of the essay needs to be clearer, and more supporting details are needed.

2 The topic needs to be narrowed or expanded. Many more supporting details are needed.

1 The topic is unclear.

3 The middle needs transitions and a paragraph for each main point.

2 The beginning, middle, and ending all run together. Paragraphs are needed.

1 The lack of organization is confusing.

3 The writer sometimes sounds unsure, and the voice needs to fit the audience better.

2 The writer sounds unsure. The voice needs to fit the audience.

1 The writer needs to be aware of the audience.

3 Too many general words are used. Specific nouns and verbs are needed.

2 General or missing words make this essay hard to understand.

1 The writer needs help finding specific words.

3 Many short, choppy sentences need to be rewritten to make the essay read smoothly.

2 Many sentences are choppy or incomplete and need to be rewritten.

1 Most sentences are difficult to follow.

3 Some errors confuse the reader.

2 Many errors make the essay confusing and hard to read.

1 Numerous errors need to be corrected.

Evaluating an Expository Essay

As you read through Miranda's essay below, focus on the strengths and weaknesses in the writing. (The essay contains several errors.)

Blowing Its Top!

In 1980, Mount Saint Helens in Washington State erupted with the force of a nuclear bomb. An explosion like that doesn't just happen. An eruption of Mount Saint Helens results from a long process.

The process begins out at sea. That's where the Pacific plate gets shoved under the North American plate. This movement is called subduction. The plate that is pushed down melts in the mantle and bubbles up as magma.

Next, the magma pushes up through cracks, trying to escape. The magma under Mount Saint Helens has a lot of air trapped in it. Its like soda in a bottle. As long as the pressure is on. The air is dissolved, and the magma stays put.

The last step in the process is removing the pressure. In 1980, an earthquake caused a huge landslide on one side of the mountain. With all that weight gone. The magma underneath shot out like soda out of a bottle. It totally rocked!

When Mount Saint Helens blew it's top, it destroyed lakes and forests. However, volcanoes can also make new land. They created one of the 50 states—Hawaii.

Student Self-Assessment

Miranda first writes a positive comment under each trait and then something she could improve on. (She used the rubric and the number scale on pages 176–177.)

Ideas

5 Ideas
1. I have a specific focus for my essay.
2. A few more details would make this essay even better.

Organization

4 Organization
1. I have a pretty good beginning, middle, and ending.
2. I should have used more transitions.

Voice

4 Voice
1. My voice is about right for an essay.
2. I should have cut out "It totally rocked."

Word Choice

4 Word Choice
1. I used specialized words like <u>magma</u> and <u>mantle</u>.
2. I didn't explain my specialized words.

Sentence Fluency

3 Sentence Fluency
1. I have different lengths of sentences.
2. I'm still having trouble with fragments.

Conventions

3 Conventions
1. I checked spelling closely.
2. I have a couple misused words.

Use the rubric. Rate your essay using the rubric shown on pages 176–177. On your own paper, list the six traits. Leave room after each trait to write one strength and one weakness. Then choose a number (from 1 to 6) that shows how well you used each trait.

Reflecting on Your Writing

You're done! If you can, set your essay aside for a few days. Then, on your own paper, complete each sentence starter below.

Come back to your essay and take a moment to reflect on your experience of writing an expository essay.

My Expository Essay

1. The best part of my essay is . . .

2. The part that still needs work is . . .

3. The main thing I learned about writing an expository essay is . . .

4. The next time I write an expository essay, I would like to . . .

Expository Writing
Across the Curriculum

Expository writing is useful in all your classes. For example, the expository writing in your math book explains how a pie chart or circle graph is divided up, and the expository writing in your history book helps you understand actual events. Expository writing could even help you on a writing test!

On the following pages, you'll get the chance to try four different types of expository writing.

Mini Index

- **Social Studies**: Writing a Comparison-Contrast Essay
- **Math**: Creating a Circle Graph
- **Practical Writing**: Taking Notes
- **Assessment**: Writing for Assessment

Social Studies:
Writing a Comparison-Contrast Essay

In the following essay, Anna showed how George Washington and King George III were alike and different.

Worlds Apart

BEGINNING

The beginning introduces the two leaders and gives a focus statement (underlined).

During the American Revolutionary War, King George III led Great Britain, while George Washington led the 13 colonies. Could these enemies have anything in common besides their first names? Though the two Georges private lives were very similar, they disagreed about governing the colonies.

MIDDLE
One paragraph explains how the two men were alike.

At home, the Georges could have been friends. Both were the oldest sons in their families and were young when their fathers died. They each were tutored and worked hard on their schoolwork. As they got older, they enjoyed math, science, and farming. King George III was nicknamed "Farmer George," and Washington loved to work at his farm called Mount Vernon.

The other paragraph explains how the two men were different.

When it came to politics, these leaders were very different. Washington wanted freedom for the colonies, but King George III wanted them to be taxed and ruled by Great Britain. George III turned out to be unpopular after losing the war. Washington's victory led to his becoming one of the most popular presidents ever.

ENDING

The ending gives the reader something to think about.

George Washington and King George III grew up in different worlds, but if they could have talked, they might have become good friends. Maybe if they had been neighbors, they could have given each other farming tips.

Prewriting **Selecting a Topic**

First, you need to find two people from history to compare and contrast. Anna began by listing historical leaders she knew about.

List

Leaders

Clara Barton	Thomas Jefferson	John Adams
George Washington	Abraham Lincoln	King George III

List historical people. Choose a type of historical person (explorers, inventors, artists) and list names. Then choose two people who have some similarities and some differences.

Gathering Details

You can gather information about your subjects from your history book, on the Internet, and at the library. Anna used a T-chart to write down what she learned.

T-Chart

George Washington	King George III
Voted first president	Oldest son *
Was young when father died *	Called "Farmer George" *
Liked math and science *	Liked math, agriculture, science *
Liked farming *	Was young when father died *
Wanted independence for colonies	Inherited throne
Popular president	Wanted British rule of colonies
Defeated Great Britain	Lost against colonies
Oldest son *	Unpopular king after the war

Create a T-chart. Under each name, write things you find out. Put a star (*) next to the similarities.

Prewriting **Writing a Focus Statement**

In a comparison-contrast essay, your focus statement should tell how the subjects are alike and different. Anna used this formula.

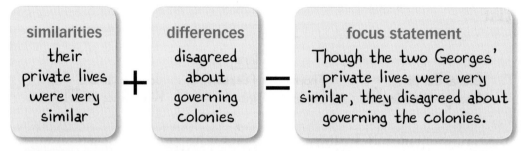

similarities		differences		focus statement
their private lives were very similar	**+**	disagreed about governing colonies	**=**	Though the two Georges' private lives were very similar, they disagreed about governing the colonies.

Prewrite

Write your focus statement. Sum up the similarities and differences. Then write a focus statement like the one above.

Organizing Your Ideas

An organized list can help you put your details in order. Anna created the organized list below.

Directions   **Organized List**

Focus statement ▶ Though the two Georges private lives were very similar, they disagreed about governing the colonies.

Similarities ▶ • At home, the Georges were similar.

Details ▶ – oldest sons, young when dads died
– liked to farm, enjoyed math and science

Differences ▶ • Politically they were different.

Details ▶ – King rules vs. colonies rule
– King loses/Washington wins
– King unpopular/president popular

Prewrite

Create an organized list. Refer to the sample above as you write an organized list for your comparison-contrast essay.

Writing Creating Your First Draft

Now you are ready to write your first draft. First, introduce your topic and give your focus statement. Then focus on similarities in one paragraph and differences in another. Start each paragraph with a topic sentence. In the end, sum up the similarities and differences.

Write your first draft. Use your organized list from page 184 as a guide as you create your first draft.

Revising Improving Your Writing

Next, you need to revise your work using the following traits.

- **Ideas** Do I have a clear focus and supporting details?
- **Organization** Do I have one middle paragraph for similarities and one for differences?
- **Voice** Does my voice show my interest in the topic?
- **Word Choice** Do I use specific nouns and active verbs?
- **Sentence Fluency** Do my sentences flow well?

Revise your work. Use the checklist above to revise your first draft. Then make a clean copy for editing.

Editing Checking for Conventions

Check to make sure you have followed the rules of English.

- **Conventions** Have I checked for punctuation, capitalization, spelling, and grammar errors?

Edit your work. Edit your essay using the questions above. Have someone else check your work, too. Then make a final copy and proofread it.

Math: Creating a Circle Graph

A circle graph can make writing about percentages much easier. Tamika created the circle graph below to show the different sources used to make electricity.

Making Electricity

Turning on a light or a TV is easy because of electricity. But where does all that electricity come from? Most power plants produce electricity by using energy sources like coal, oil, natural gas, and nuclear energy. Other plants make electricity by using sources such as sunlight, wind, water, or even heat from underground! That means there are eight different sources of electricity in use today.

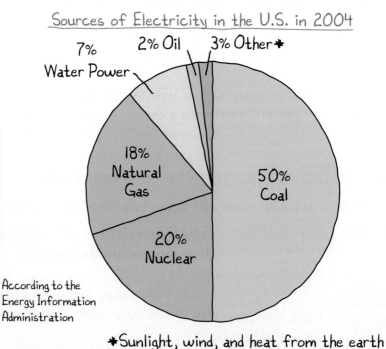

Sources of Electricity in the U.S. in 2004

7% Water Power

2% Oil

3% Other ✱

18% Natural Gas

50% Coal

20% Nuclear

According to the Energy Information Administration

✱Sunlight, wind, and heat from the earth

WRITING TIPS

Before you write . . .

- **Select a topic.**
  Choose a topic that focuses on different percentages of a whole, such as surveys or statistics.
- **Research your topic carefully.**
  Add up your percentages to make sure they equal 100%.
- **Do the math.**
  Figure out the right size for each piece of the pie. Multiply 360 (the number of degrees in a circle) by the percentage. For example, to draw a piece of pie to show 20 percent, your equation would be $360° \times .20 = 72°$.

During your writing . . .

- **Introduce your topic.**
  Write a paragraph to explain your topic.
- **Draw your circle using a compass.**
  Create each segment using a protractor to measure the number of degrees.
- **Color-code your graph.**
  Use colors to make your graph clear.
- **List your source.**
  Tell where you got your information.

Create a circle graph. Follow the directions above and look at the sample graph on page 186 as you make your own circle graph.

After you've written a first draft . . .

- **Check your layout.**
  Make sure that your numbers are correct.
- **Make a final version of your graph.**
  Remember to proofread your work.

Practical Writing:
Taking Two-Column Notes

Two-column notes can help you remember what you've learned. In the following example, a student takes notes about water molecules.

Len Hankavara   February 19
                    Water Molecules

Made of   – 2 hydrogen atoms
three atoms   – 1 oxygen atom

Always moving   – atoms move faster when
                   heated

Solid   – vibrate but can't move around
                    • Ice

Liquid   – vibrate and can move around
                    • Water

Gas   – vibrate and move very fast
                 – particles escape
                 – free to move anywhere
                    • Steam

Why do the particles escape?

WRITING TIPS

Before you write . . .

- **Create a heading.**
  Write your name, the date, and a topic heading at the top of your paper.
- **Divide your paper into two columns.**
  Create a narrower column on the left.

During your writing . . .

- **Write the main ideas on the left side.**
  Leave room between each main idea so that you have plenty of room to fit the details on the right side.
- **Write the details on the right side.**
  Use words and phrases instead of complete sentences.
- **Use drawings.**
  Illustrate your notes to make information clear.

After you've written . . .

- **Review for completeness and correctness.**
  Be sure important facts are correctly written down.
- **Write any questions you still have.**
  Jot down questions in your notes. Then check your book or ask your teacher for help to find answers.
- **Use your notes to help you study.**
  Read over your notes before a test. Have a friend or family member ask you questions from your notes.

Take notes. Use the tips above as you take notes in one of your classes. Afterward, review your notes.

Writing for Assessment

The next time you take a writing test, you may be asked to respond to an expository prompt. That means that you'll need to explain something or share information based on the prompt. A graphic organizer like the one below can help you plan your response.

Expository Prompt

Most people have a favorite place to be. Perhaps you enjoy a park in your town or a quiet room in your home. Maybe you love the downtown zoo or a faraway place you have visited. Write an essay about your favorite place and explain why it is your favorite.

Favorite Place: Holiday Camp

Activities	People
swim, climb	counselors
ropes	new friends
campfires	Tanya
store, games	

The **beginning** introduces the topic and the focus (underlined).

Most kids have a favorite spot. Some people like a quiet place to be alone. Others like a loud place to be with friends. For me, the best place of all is Holiday Camp.

Each **middle** paragraph focuses on a different part of the topic.

One of the best parts about Holiday Camp is that there's always something to do. Swimming in Potter Pond, rock climbing on Old Crag, or doing the ropes course challenge are just a few of the daytime activities. At night we have campfires, or the camp store is open so we can buy snacks while we play games.

The other great thing about Holiday Camp is the people. The counselors are all college students, and they are like big brothers and sisters. They keep us in line, but they let us have a lot of fun. I also make new friends with the other girls in my cabin. In fact, one of my best friends is Tanya, a girl that I met at camp three years ago.

Holiday Camp is set up to give city kids a break. We get to meet new people and have fun in the fresh, country air. I wish I could stay all summer. Maybe someday I will be a camp counselor so my wish will come true.

The **ending** sums up the topic and restates the main idea.

Respond to the reading. Answer the questions below to learn more about the response you just read.

- **Ideas** (1) What is the focus of the writer's response? (2) What details support the focus?

- **Organization** (3) How does the writer introduce the topic? (4) How does she restate the topic in the ending?

- **Voice & Word Choice** (5) What sentences show the writer's strong feelings? (6) What key words from the prompt also appear in the essay?

WRITING TIPS

Planning your response . . .
- **Understand the prompt.**
  Read the prompt carefully and look for key words that will help keep you on track.
- **Gather your ideas.**
  Make a list or simple graphic organizer.
- **Form a focus statement.**
  Write your main point in a single sentence.
- **Use your time wisely.**
  Plan time at the end to check your work.

Writing your response . . .
- **Begin with a strong opening paragraph.**
  Clearly state your main idea.
- **Organize your details.**
  Put your details into well-organized paragraphs.
- **End effectively.**
  Leave the reader with something to think about.

Checking your response . . .
- **Check for clarity and conventions.**
  Rewrite any confusing ideas and correct any errors.

Expository Prompts

- Your class has been asked to choose a classroom pet. What pet would you recommend? Explain why your choice would be a good one.
- What is your favorite time of the year? Write an essay explaining why it is your favorite.

 Respond to an expository prompt. Using the writing tips, write a response to one of the two prompts above. Finish writing within the amount of time that your teacher gives you.

Expository Writing in Review

In expository writing, you explain something to readers.

Prewrite

Select a topic that truly interests you and will also interest your reader. (See page 148.)

Gather and organize details about your topic using a graphic organizer. (See pages 149–150.)

Write a focus (thesis) statement, identifying an important part of the topic that you plan to cover. (See page 151.)

Write

In the beginning part, introduce your topic and state your focus. (See page 155.)

In the middle part, give the details that explain or support the focus. (See pages 156–157.)

In the ending part, summarize your main points and make a final comment about the topic. (See page 158.)

Revise

Review the ideas, organization, and **voice** of your writing first. Then review for **word choice** and **sentence fluency**. Make changes to improve your first draft. (See pages 160–170.)

Edit

Check your writing for conventions. Also have a trusted classmate edit your writing. (See pages 171–174.)

Publish

Make a final copy and proofread it for errors before sharing it. (See page 175.)

Use the expository rubric to assess your finished writing. (See pages 176–177.)

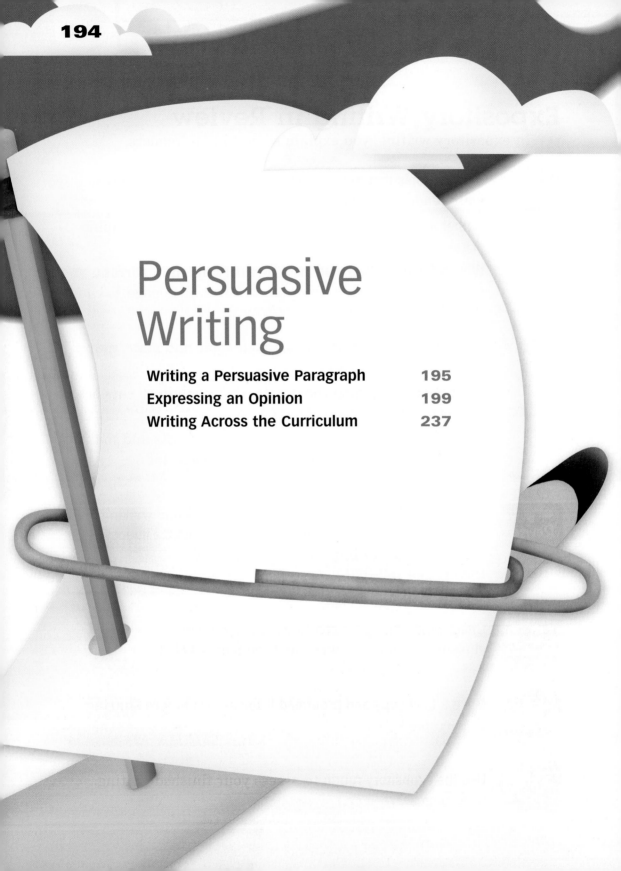

Persuasive Writing

Persuasive Writing

Persuasive Paragraph

Commercials on TV advertise all kinds of health-related products. The problem is that some of those products may do nothing at all—and some may even do harm.

What truly healthy habit would you suggest to your friends? In this chapter, you will write a persuasive paragraph that gives your opinion about a healthy habit. Think of it as a short commercial for a habit that is good for you.

Writing Guidelines

Subject: A healthy habit
Form: Persuasive paragraph
Purpose: To express an opinion
Audience: Classmates

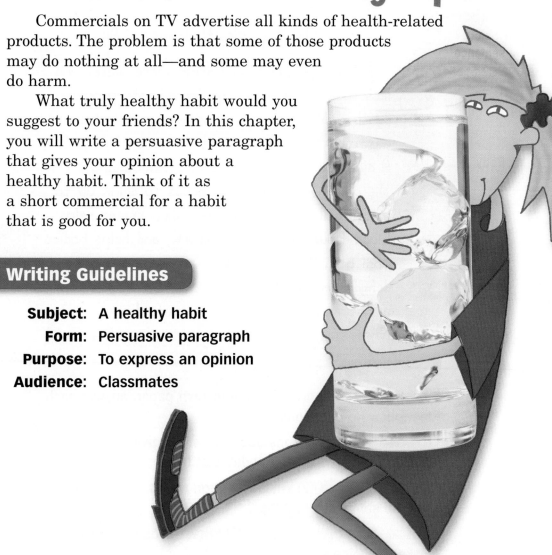

Persuasive Paragraph

A persuasive paragraph starts with a **topic sentence** that gives the writer's opinion. The sentences in the **body** support the topic sentence, and the **closing sentence** restates the writer's opinion. The following paragraph expresses an opinion about a healthy habit.

Topic sentence

Body

Closing sentence

The Best Health Drink of All

Young people should drink more water and less soda. Soda is full of ingredients people don't need. For example, a regular soda has caffeine and about nine teaspoons of sugar! A diet soda is full of weird chemicals. On the other hand, everyone needs to drink up to half a gallon of water every day. Water helps blood flow, helps brains work, and helps bodies cool off. Without water, a person can get dehydrated or have heatstroke. So do your body a favor and drink plenty of water!

Respond to the reading. On your own paper, answer each of the following questions.

- **Ideas** (1) What reasons does the writer give for drinking water instead of soda? List two.
- **Organization** (2) What transition words or phrases link the sentences together?
- **Voice & Word Choice** (3) What words or phrases make the voice sound convincing?

Prewriting Selecting a Topic

First, you need to find a health-related topic to write about. The writer of the sample paragraph on page 196 used freewriting to think about what she did to be healthy.

> What I do for my health. Hmm. Well, I try to eat good things, and I walk to school. That's good, except when I get caught in the rain and get sick. I also drink lots of water. That's a good thing. Most people don't even think about drinking water as a healthy habit. That would be a good topic.

Freewrite. Write freely about things you do to be healthy. Keep going until you find a topic you can write a paragraph about.

Gathering Reasons

Now that you have chosen a topic, you need to write an opinion about it and give reasons that support your opinion. The writer of the sample paragraph used a table diagram.

Table Diagram

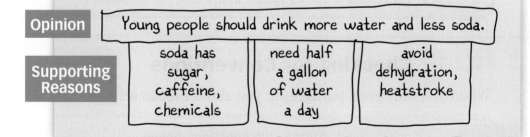

Opinion	Young people should drink more water and less soda.		
Supporting Reasons	soda has sugar, caffeine, chemicals	need half a gallon of water a day	avoid dehydration, heatstroke

Gather supporting reasons. Make a table diagram like the one above. In the tabletop, write your opinion using the word *should*. Then write reasons that support your opinion in the table legs.

Writing Creating Your First Draft

The following guidelines can help you persuade your reader. Start with a sentence that states your opinion. Remember to use the word *should*. Write body sentences that include your supporting reasons. End with a sentence that restates your opinion as a command or *call to action,* such as "drink plenty of water."

Write your first draft. Use the guidelines above to write your paragraph. Connect your ideas with transition words and phrases.

Revising Improving Your Paragraph

When you revise, check your paragraph for *ideas, organization, voice, word choice,* and *sentence fluency.*

Revise your paragraph. Ask yourself the following questions.

1. Is my topic sentence clear and interesting?
2. Do I use the word *should* in my topic sentence?
3. Do I use transitions to connect my ideas?
4. Does my voice sound convincing?
5. Do I make a call to action in my closing sentence?

Editing Checking for Conventions

When you edit your paragraph, you should focus on *conventions.*

Edit your work. Answer the questions below.

1. Does each sentence begin with a capital letter and include end punctuation?
2. Have I checked my spelling?
3. Have I watched for frequently misused words *(to, too, two)*?

Persuasive Writing

Expressing an Opinion

George Washington knew how to fight for independence, but he didn't know how to fight cavities. Nobody back then did. Washington was one of many people in those days who lost all his teeth.

People nowadays know more about being healthy. In this chapter, you will write about a health-related issue. Of course, no matter how persuasive you are, you'll be too late to save President Washington's teeth!

Writing Guidelines

Subject: A health-related issue
Form: Persuasive essay
Purpose: To express an opinion
Audience: Classmates

Understanding Your Goal

Your goal in this chapter is to write a persuasive essay opinion about a health-related issue. The traits in the chart below will help you reach your goal.

Your goal is to . . .

Ideas
Express an opinion about a health-related issue and use details to support your opinion.

Organization
Create a beginning that states your opinion, a middle that supports your opinion with reasons, and an ending that asks the reader to do something.

Voice
Use a voice that expresses your opinion and shows that you are serious about this issue.

Word Choice
Use specific words that have the right feeling or connotation.

Sentence Fluency
Write smooth-flowing sentences and avoid careless sentence errors.

Conventions
Check your essay for correct punctuation, capitalization, spelling, and grammar.

Get the big picture. Look at the rubric on pages 232–233. This rubric can help you assess your progress. Your goal is to write an effective persuasive essay about a health-related issue.

Persuasive Essay

The following persuasive essay expresses Elizabeth's opinion about dental hygiene. The side notes point out what each part of the essay does.

Polishing Your Pearly Whites

BEGINNING

The beginning gets the reader's attention and states the opinion (underlined).

George Washington had many great successes in his life, but he didn't succeed in keeping his own teeth! Back then, many people lost their teeth. They didn't understand dental hygiene the way people do now. For the sake of their teeth, modern people should brush, floss, and eat right every day.

The most important thing people should do for their teeth is brush. Brushing removes pieces of food that can feed bacteria. Brushing also helps get rid of plaque, which is where bacteria live. Some toothpastes can even help stop tartar, or minerals that build up on teeth. A person should brush after every meal to keep cavities from starting.

MIDDLE

Each middle paragraph supports the opinion statement with reasons.

In addition, people should floss to clean their teeth. Flossing helps get rid of food and plaque. It prevents tartar from developing between teeth. It also helps keep the gums clean so that they don't bleed or become diseased. People should floss at least once a day.

One other important thing people should do to keep teeth strong is to eat a healthy diet. For example, milk and cheese give teeth calcium, which they need to be strong. Fruits and vegetables also help by providing vitamins A and D. On the other hand, sugary foods rot teeth. People who want strong teeth should eat right.

So brush, floss, and eat right. If you do these things, you'll be able to have excellent teeth for your whole life. That's one success that even George Washington didn't have!

Respond to the reading. On your own paper, answer the following questions about the sample essay.

■ **Ideas** (1) How does the writer get the reader's attention?

■ **Organization** (2) What transition words or phrases in the topic sentences help to show the importance of each reason?

■ **Voice & Word Choice** (3) Find at least four places where the word *should* is used. How does it help the writer sound persuasive?

Prewriting

The writing process begins with the prewriting steps that are listed below. Prewriting starts when you consider what to write about. It ends when you are ready to create your first draft.

Keys to Prewriting

1. **Select** a topic that you have an opinion about.

2. **Gather** reasons to support your opinion.

3. **Think** about the order in which you will present your reasons.

4. **Write** an opinion statement and topic sentences.

5. **Create** an organized list of reasons and details.

Prewriting Selecting a Topic

First, you'll need to select a health-related topic. For her essay, Joelle used a line diagram to discover a health-related topic that she wanted to write about.

Line Diagram

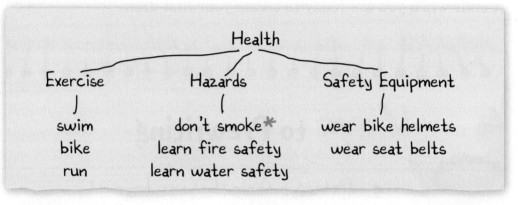

Health

Exercise   Hazards   Safety Equipment

swim   don't smoke*   wear bike helmets
bike   learn fire safety   wear seat belts
run   learn water safety

Prewrite

Create a line diagram. Use the sample above as a model to create your own line diagram. Follow the steps below.

1 Write "Health" at the top of the diagram.

2 Next, write three categories of health issues. You can use the categories above or ones such as these: "Diets," "Hygiene," "Safety Rules," "Diseases," or "Emotions."

3 Then write specific things people should do to be healthier. Put a star (*) next to the topic you'd like to write about.

Focus on the Traits

Ideas Your topic must be something people should do to be healthier. The word *should* makes this statement an opinion. Choose a topic you think you can support with at least three good reasons.

Gathering Details

It's time to think about your opinion and gather reasons to support it. Joelle used a T-chart to write down her opinion and her reasons.

T-Chart

Opinion	Reasons
I think . . . people who don't smoke <u>should</u> never start, and people who do smoke <u>should</u> quit.	Because . . . —smoking causes cancer. —smoking can be rude. —my grandpa got emphysema. —cigarettes cost a lot.

Create a T-chart. Use the sample above as a model.

1 Write "Opinion" in the left column. Then write "I think . . ." and give your opinion using the word *should*.

2 Write "Reasons" in the right column. Under it, write "Because . . ." and then list reasons that support your opinion. (Do additional research if necessary.)

Selecting Main Reasons

A well-organized persuasive essay provides at least three main reasons to support the opinion. Joelle reviewed her reasons and noticed that some of them belonged together.

smoking is unhealthy (cancer, emphysema)
smoking bothers people (bad smell and rudeness)
smoking is expensive (cigarettes and doctor bills)

Group your reasons. Review your T-chart and try to group your reasons into three or four main reasons.

Prewriting
Understanding Order of Importance

Think of the last time you tried to persuade someone:

> Our family should go to Fun Land this June for three reasons.
> First of all, we can get cheap tickets through the school.
> Secondly, we all enjoy Fun Land.
> Most importantly, my birthday is in June!

These three sentences try to persuade by building up to the most important reason. The transition words help show the organization: "First of all, . . . Secondly, . . . Most importantly, . . ."

Practice

Read the opinion below. Then match each transition on the left with a reason on the right. Afterward, write one sentence that tells why you chose a particular reason as the most important.

Opinion: Families should hold fire drills at home.

Transitions:	Reasons:
1. First of all,	a. Smoke from a fire makes a house very dark.
2. Also,	b. Practice can prevent terrible injuries.
3. Most importantly,	c. The whole family needs to follow the same plan.

Organizing your reasons by order of importance can make your writing more persuasive.

Find your most important reason.
Review your three or four main reasons from the bottom of page 205. Put a star next to the reason that you think is most important. Then arrange your other reasons in the best possible order.

Writing an Opinion Statement

Next, you need to write an opinion statement, which names your topic and gives your opinion about it. For this assignment, the opinion statement will appear at the end of your beginning paragraph.

name the topic		give your opinion		a strong opinion statement
smoking	**+**	people shouldn't, for many reasons	**=**	People shouldn't smoke for many important reasons.

Prewrite   Write your opinion statement. **Use the pattern above to write your opinion statement. Be clear, but also be creative.**

Writing Topic Sentences

Now is a good time to write topic sentences. Each one should focus on one main reason that supports your opinion. Transition words can help you arrange your topic sentences by order of importance.

TRANSITIONS: LEAST TO MOST IMPORTANT

To begin with,	One reason	For one thing,
Another reason	A second reason	In addition,
Most importantly,	The main reason	The biggest reason

To begin with, smoking costs a lot of money.

Another reason not to smoke is that it bothers people.

Most importantly, smoking causes major health problems.

Prewrite   Write your topic sentences. **Review your main reasons from page 205. Then write a topic sentence for each one. Remember to use transition words and phrases to show order of importance.**

Prewriting Organizing Your Ideas

Now you can organize your whole essay. Following the directions below, Joelle created an organized list. Notice that the topic sentences are written as complete sentences, but the details are not.

Directions   **Organized List**

Opinion statement

People shouldn't smoke for many important reasons.

First topic sentence

1. To begin with, smoking costs a lot of money.

List of details
   - over $1,000 each year
   - medicine/doctor visits
   - hospitals

Second topic sentence

2. Another reason not to smoke is that it bothers people.

List of details
   - secondhand smoke
   - rude in closed places
   - makes things smell bad

Third topic sentence

3. Most importantly, smoking causes major health problems.

List of details
   - cancer, emphysema
   - heart attack, stroke
   - asthma, trouble breathing

Prewrite

Organize your essay. Follow the directions above to make your own organized list. Include details about each main reason.

Writing

In the next part of the process, you will follow the steps below to write your first draft. When you write your first draft, you put all your ideas on paper (or enter them in the computer).

Keys to Writing

1. **Create** a beginning that introduces your topic and gives your opinion statement.

2. **Start** each middle paragraph with a topic sentence and include supporting details.

3. **Write** an ending that asks the reader to do something.

Writing **Getting the Big Picture**

The chart below shows how the parts of a persuasive essay fit together. (The examples are from the sample essay on pages 211–214.) You are ready to write your essay when you have . . .

- gathered enough details,
- written an opinion statement and topic sentences, and
- created an organized list.

Beginning

The **beginning** introduces the topic and gives the opinion statement.

Opinion Statement

People shouldn't smoke for many important reasons.

Middle

Each **middle** paragraph gives one main reason for the opinion and details to support it.

Topic Sentences

To begin with, smoking costs a lot of money.

Another important reason not to smoke is that it bothers people.

Most importantly, smoking causes major health problems.

Ending

The **ending** summarizes your opinion and calls the reader to action.

Call to Action

So if you don't smoke, don't start. If you do smoke, it's time to quit.

Starting Your Essay

The first paragraph in your essay should grab the reader's attention and give the opinion statement. Here are four ways to get your reader's attention.

- **Give surprising information.**
  Every year, smoking kills more Americans than any war in the last century did.

- **Refer to an expert.**
  Researchers say that people who start smoking as teenagers have a hard time quitting later.

- **Ask a question.**
  Can you think of one good reason to smoke?

- **Be creative.**
  The package calls them cigarettes, but many people call them "cancer sticks."

Beginning Paragraph

The topic is introduced.

The last sentence shares the opinion statement (underlined).

Have you ever had trouble breathing? If so, remember how scared you felt? Now imagine if you felt that way all the time. That's how my grandpa describes his emphysema. He says he wishes he had never started smoking. <u>People shouldn't smoke for many important reasons.</u>

Write

Write your beginning paragraph. **Try one of the strategies listed above to get the reader's attention. Then introduce your topic and write your opinion statement.**

Writing **Developing the Middle Part**

Now you are ready to write your middle paragraphs. Each middle paragraph begins with a topic sentence. The sentences after it support the topic sentence with details. Your organized list can guide you.

Connecting Your Sentences

Use transition words and phrases to connect the body sentences in your paragraphs. Here are the transitions Joelle used within her middle paragraphs.

| For example, also Of course, | → | To start, just as In addition, | ↗ | For instance, also As a result, |

Middle Paragraphs

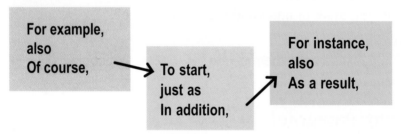

Topic sentence 1	To begin with, smoking costs a lot of money. <u>For example</u>, a person who smokes a
Supporting details are added.	pack of cigarettes every day spends more than $1,000 a year on smoking. Smokers <u>also</u> have to spend more on medicine and doctor visits.
Transitions (underlined) connect the sentences.	<u>Of course</u>, if smokers get sick more often, they also miss more work. That can cost them pay!
Topic sentence 2	Another important reason not to smoke is that it bothers people. <u>To start</u>, secondhand

Additional details support the second reason.

smoke is irritating and dangerous. It isn't polite for a person to smoke in front of a nonsmoker. It's <u>just as</u> impolite for the smoker to leave a friend and go have a cigarette. <u>In addition</u>, nonsmokers don't like the smell that cigarettes leave in rooms and cars—or on a smoker's clothing!

Topic sentence 3

The most important reason is given last.

Most importantly, smoking causes major health problems. <u>For instance</u>, smoking makes it harder to breathe if a person has asthma, bronchitis, or pneumonia. Smoking can even destroy a person's lungs, causing diseases like emphysema and cancer. The American Heart Association says that smoking <u>also</u> makes a person's blood thicker. <u>As a result</u>, smokers have more strokes and heart attacks.

Arrange your paragraphs by order of importance and include strong supporting details.

Write

Write middle paragraphs. Follow your organized list from page 208. Try to use transition words and phrases to connect sentences within your paragraphs.

Writing **Ending Your Essay: A Call to Action**

The ending of your essay should restate your opinion. Your ending should also ask the reader to do something. This is known as a *call to action*. A call to action uses a command verb such as "listen," "throw out" or "say no." Here are three sample calls to action.

- Listen to your wallet, your friends, your lungs, and your common sense—don't smoke!

- If every cigarette takes fifteen minutes off your life, throw out that pack and gain almost five hours!

- Say no to cigarettes so that your life doesn't go up in smoke!

For her ending paragraph, Joelle includes a strong call to action. She also connects with the reader through a personal comment.

Ending Paragraph

A call to action is given.

The reader is given something to think about.

So if you don't smoke, don't start. If you do smoke, it's time to quit. I'm glad my grandpa quit smoking, but I'm sad he did it after his lungs were already damaged. At least his smoking has had one good result. It has convinced me never to start!

Write your ending. Create a call to action and give your reader a final interesting thought.

Form a complete first draft. If necessary, write a complete copy of your essay. Write on every other line to make room for your revising changes.

Revising

Prewrite Write Revise Edit Publish

In this part of the process, you will revise your work following the steps listed below. When you revise, you check your essay for *ideas, organization, voice, word choice,* and *sentence fluency.*

Keys to Revising

1. **Read** your essay out loud.

2. **Ask** a classmate to respond to your first draft.

3. **Decide** what changes are needed.

4. **Revise** your essay for the traits.

Revising for Ideas

6 The ideas in my essay inform and convince my reader.

5 I convince my reader with just the right number of supporting details.

4 The details I use support my topic sentences, but I could add a few more to sound more convincing.

When you revise for *ideas*, you carefully check your details. You want to make sure you've used just the right details to support your topic sentences. The rubric strip above can guide your revision.

Do all my details support my topic sentences?

Details support the topic sentence if they answer the question "How?" or "Why?"

First of all, swimming is great for overall health. [How?] It gives the swimmer's heart and lungs a workout. That's called cardiovascular exercise. [Why?] Swimming is also good for the joints. Other sports may damage feet, knees, and hips, but swimming doesn't hurt them. [How?] Finally, swimming strengthens all the major muscles of the body—legs, back, stomach, and arms.

Practice

Which details answer "How?" or "Why?" Which two details do not?

Topic sentence: **Learning to swim can help prevent bad accidents.**

Detail 1: **Experienced swimmers know not to swim alone.**

Detail 2: **Swimming pools require much maintenance.**

Detail 3: **Strong swimmers understand their limits and don't go too deep.**

Detail 4: **Chlorine kills bacteria in the water.**

Revise

Review your details. Read your topic sentence. Then make sure that each detail answers "How?" or "Why?"

3 I use a few details that support my topic sentences. More details are needed.

2 My details are unclear and don't support my topic sentences.

1 My ideas and details are unclear and confusing

Do I need more supporting details in some places?

Just as a table needs at least three legs to stand up, a topic sentence needs at least three supporting details to be convincing.

Practice

Read the following paragraph. Decide whether the topic sentence is well supported. If not, think of other details that could give it more support.

The most important reason people should swim is to have fun together. Young kids enjoy playing Marco Polo. Older kids join swim teams and compete in meets.

Check your supporting details. Review each of your body paragraphs. Do you have at least three strong details to support each topic sentence? If not, add some more supporting details.

Revising in Action

In the sample below, supporting details are improved.

For example, a person who smokes a pack of

cigarettes every day spends more than $1,000 a year

have to spend more on medicine and doctor visits.

on smoking. Smokers also cough a lot more.

Revising for Organization

6 My organization makes my essay logical and convincing.

5 My paragraphs work well. Transitions connect the flow between and within paragraphs.

4 My essay has good paragraphs, but different transitions would improve the organization of my sentences.

When you revise for *organization*, you check the order of your paragraphs and sentences. The rubric strip above can help.

How can I check the organization of my paragraphs?

You can check the organization of your paragraphs by making sure that each part of your essay has a clear sense of direction. The questions below can help you find out.

Beginning Paragraph

1. Does my first sentence grab the reader's attention?

2. Does the last sentence in my beginning paragraph give my opinion statement?

Middle Paragraphs

3. Does each middle paragraph start with a clear topic sentence?

4. Do the middle paragraphs appear in order of importance?

Ending Paragraph

5. Does the ending paragraph contain a call to action?

6. Does the ending leave the reader with something to think about?

Revise

Check the organization of your paragraphs. Ask yourself the six questions listed above. Revise until you can answer "yes" to each question.

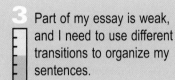

3 Part of my essay is weak, and I need to use different transitions to organize my sentences.

2 My essay has an unclear sense of direction. I need to use transitions to improve my writing.

1 There is no clear direction in my writing.

How can transitions help organize my paragraphs?

Carefully chosen transitions help improve the overall organization of a paragraph. (See also pages **472–473**.)

Practice

Find places where transitions could improve the following paragraph. Here are some transitions: *also, for example, finally, most importantly*.

Seat belts provide protection in different situations. Child seats keep toddlers in place instead of climbing all over the driver. Riders wearing seat belts are protected on bumpy roads and during quick stops. Seat belts often keep people in accidents from hitting their heads. If a car rolls over, seat belts keep riders from being thrown out.

Check your transitions. Read your essay and then add any transitions needed to connect your ideas.

Revising in Action

Notice how transitions connect the ideas in the sentences below.

Another important reason not to smoke is that it
                    To start,
bothers people.∧Secondhand smoke is irritating . . .

Revising for Voice

6 My voice is confident, serious, and convincing throughout the essay.	**5** My voice is serious and persuasive, showing that I want to convince the reader.	**4** My voice is persuasive, though I need to be sure to keep a serious voice throughout the essay.

When you revise for *voice*, you focus on how your writing sounds. These pages will help you create a persuasive voice in your writing. The rubric strip above can guide you.

Do I use the right voice in my writing?

The voice of your writing shows how you feel about your topic. A persuasive essay should have a serious voice.

Words such as silly, serious, angry, confused, worried, and excited describe voice.

Practice

Match each sentence below with the word that best describes the voice of the writing. Then, for each sentence, identify the words that help create the voice.

1. I can't stand it when people don't wash their hands.
2. Hand washing prevents serious diseases.
3. Just squirt the soap, splash the water, and off you go!
4. Fine, don't wash your hands. You might as well eat your lunch off the floor.
5. Even Rufus Raccoon washes his hands before he eats.

a. cutesy
b. careless
c. disgusted
d. serious
e. sarcastic

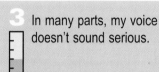

3 In many parts, my voice doesn't sound serious.

2 My voice sounds unconvincing for a persuasive essay.

1 My opinion is not evident.

How can I create a more serious voice?

You can create a more serious voice by showing that you believe in your opinion and want your reader to agree with you. Carefully chosen words and phrases can help you create a serious voice.

Practice

Find three words or phrases below that help create a serious voice.

Hand washing can prevent sickness. However, one person out of every three doesn't wash his or her hands after using the bathroom! When that person shakes hands with someone else, germs are likely to get passed. Just 30 seconds at the sink can help people stay healthy.

 Revise — **Check your voice.** Revise your work to create a serious voice.

Revising in Action

In the sentences below, a careless voice is made more serious.

Now imagine if you felt that way all the time. That's

how my grandpa describes his emphysema. He says

~~he wishes he had never started smoking.~~
∧ starting to smoke was as dumb as dumb could be. 6

Revising for Word Choice

6 The words I use in my essay are strong and help convince the reader.

5 I use specific words, and I avoid loaded words.

4 I use specific words, but I may have included a few loaded words.

When you revise for *word choice,* you look for specific words that fit your topic. You also avoid using loaded words—words that are too emotional or negative. The rubric strip above can help you revise.

How can I find specific words about my topic?

You can find specific words by reading books, magazine articles, or Web sites about your topic.

Practice

Read the following paragraph and find at least three specific words that you could use in an essay.

A person's attitude can shape his or her overall health. Optimists expect good things to happen, and their expectations often come true as well. Why is this? It's because people usually find what they are looking for. Most people have heard that laughter is the best medicine, but doctors have proven it. They have found that patients who laugh more also heal more quickly. Therefore, everyone should work hard to be more optimistic.

Revise

Search for specific words for your essay. Read an article or a Web site about your topic. Write down words that you could use in your essay.

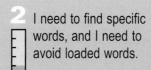

3 I should find a few more specific words and remove some loaded words.

2 I need to find specific words, and I need to avoid loaded words.

1 My word choice does not fit a persuasive essay.

Do my words have the right connotation?

Be sure to check your words to see that they have the right feeling, or connotation. Avoid loaded words, which are too emotional or negative. They may make the reader angry. (See pages **411** and **422**.)

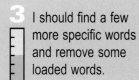

Practice

Choose the word in each pair that sounds more positive.

1. skinny, slender   5. sweat, perspire
2. sloppy, messy   6. gulp, drink
3. disagree, argue   7. medicine, drugs
4. dislike, hate   8. curious, nosy

Remove loaded words. Read your essay and look for words that are too emotional or negative. Replace any that you find.

Revising in Action

Loaded words have been replaced in the sentences below.

The American Heart Association says that~~this stinky~~ ^smoking

~~addiction~~ also makes a person's blood~~, like sludge.~~ ^thicker.

Revising for Sentence Fluency

6 My sentences flow smoothly, and people will enjoy reading them.

5 My sentences flow smoothly and are well written.

4 I need to expand some short, choppy sentences and check for other sentence errors.

When you revise for *sentence fluency,* you need to expand choppy sentences and correct sentence errors such as run-ons. The rubric strip above can guide your revision.

How can I expand a choppy sentence?

A choppy sentence is a short sentence that doesn't say much. One way to expand a choppy sentence is to ask the 5 W questions *(who, what, when, where, why)* and add details to answer them.

Bike riders should learn the rules.

When? **Before heading out,** bike riders should learn the rules.

Where? Before heading out, bike riders should learn the rules **at bike camp**.

Why? Before heading out, bike riders should learn the rules at bike camp, **so they can be safe.**

Practice

Expand each of the following choppy sentences by adding details.

1. Bikes need maintenance.
2. Rules are important.
3. Riders should use signals.
4. Reflectors help visibility.
5. Bikers should wear safety gear.

Revise

Expand choppy sentences. Answer some of the 5 W's to expand any choppy sentences in your essay.

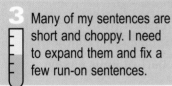

3 Many of my sentences are short and choppy. I need to expand them and fix a few run-on sentences.

2 Choppy sentences and run-on sentences make my writing hard to read.

1 My essay is hard to read. I need to rewrite most of my sentences.

How can I fix run-on sentences?

A run-on sentence is two sentences written together without the correct punctuation or a conjunction: (Also see page **437**.)

Reflectors make bike riders visible wearing bright clothes helps, too.

You can fix a run-on by turning it into two sentences.

Reflectors make bike riders visible. Wearing bright clothes helps, too.

You can also turn a run-on into a compound sentence.

Reflectors make bike riders visible, **and** wearing bright clothes helps, too.

Practice

Make each run-on below into two sentences. Then make it a compound sentence. (See page 600 for a list of coordinating conjunctions.)

1. Hand signals are easy to learn they alert drivers.
2. Bikes have the right of way riders should watch traffic.

Revise

Correct run-ons. Read your essay and watch for run-on sentences. Fix any you find by using one of the methods above.

Revising in Action

The run-on sentence below has been corrected.

So,
If you don't smoke, don't start͜if you do quit.
                                  smoke, it's time to

Revising Using a Checklist

Revise

Check your revising. Number a piece of paper from 1 to 10. If you can answer "yes" to a question, put a check mark after that number. If not, continue to work on that part of your essay.

Ideas

____ **1.** Do all my details support my topic sentences?

____ **2.** Have I used enough supporting details?

Organization

____ **3.** Do my beginning and ending work well?

____ **4.** Are the middle paragraphs organized by order of importance?

____ **5.** Have I used transitions to organize my sentences?

Voice

____ **6.** Have I used a serious voice?

Word Choice

____ **7.** Have I used specific words that fit my topic?

____ **8.** Have I avoided loaded words?

Sentence Fluency

____ **9.** Have I expanded some short, choppy sentences?

____ **10.** Have I fixed any run-on sentences?

Revise

Make a clean copy. When you've finished revising your essay, make a clean copy before you begin to edit.

Editing

Editing becomes important after you've revised your first draft. When you edit, you make sure you have followed the rules for using punctuation, capitalization, spelling, and grammar.

Keys to Editing

1. **Use** a dictionary, a thesaurus, and the "Proofreader's Guide" in the back of this book for help.

2. **Edit** on a printed copy if you use a computer. Then make your changes on the computer.

3. **Use** the editing marks shown inside the back cover of this book.

4. **Ask** someone else to check your writing for errors, too.

Editing for Conventions

6 I have strong control of conventions that add style to any writing.

5 I have a few minor errors in punctuation, spelling, or grammar.

4 I need to correct some errors in punctuation, spelling, and grammar.

When you edit for *conventions*, you need to check your essay for errors. These two pages will show you two ways to use commas. The rubric strip above can help you edit.

Have I used commas to set off introductory words?

You should put a comma after a phrase or clause that begins a sentence. Sometimes these introductory word groups are transitions.

According to some diets**,** people should eat no meat. (phrase)

On the other hand**,** some diets say people should eat only meat. (phrase)

When a diet focuses on one kind of food**,** it isn't well balanced. (clause)

Practice

Correctly punctuate the introductory word groups in the following sentences.

1. In fact each food group has something to offer.
2. Though too much fat is bad people need some fat to be healthy.
3. For example some vitamins need fat to be absorbed.
4. As the old saying goes a good diet includes "all things in moderation."

Edit

Add commas after introductory word groups. Read your essay and watch for phrases or clauses at the beginning of sentences. Make sure you have used a comma after each one.

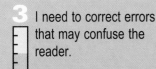

3 I need to correct errors that may confuse the reader.

2 My errors make my essay difficult to read. I need to correct them.

1 I need to correct numerous errors in my writing.

Have I used commas in a series?

When you list a series of three or more things, you should use commas after each item except the last one. A series can be made up of words, phrases, or clauses.

- **Words:** Fish, nuts, and beans all contain protein.
- **Phrases:** Eating right, drinking water, and taking vitamins help a person stay healthy.
- **Clauses:** Parents should limit sweets, schools should offer healthful foods, and kids should try to eat well.

Check commas in a series. Read your essay and watch for lists of words, phrases, or clauses. Make sure a comma appears after every item except the last.

Editing in Action

In the sentences below, commas punctuate an introductory group and a series.

Most importantly, smoking causes major health problems. For instance, smoking makes it harder to breathe if a person has asthma, bronchitis, or pneumonia.

Editing **Using a Checklist**

Check your editing. On a piece of paper, write the numbers 1 to 10. If you can answer "yes" to a question, put a check mark after that number. If not, continue to edit for that convention.

Conventions

PUNCTUATION

_____ **1.** Do I use end punctuation after all my sentences?

_____ **2.** Do I use commas after introductory word groups?

_____ **3.** Do I use commas in a series?

CAPITALIZATION

_____ **4.** Do I start all my sentences with capital letters?

_____ **5.** Do I capitalize all names (proper nouns)?

SPELLING

_____ **6.** Have I spelled all my words correctly?

_____ **7.** Have I checked for words my spell-checker might miss?

GRAMMAR

_____ **8.** Do I use correct forms of verbs (*had gone*, not *had went*)?

_____ **9.** Do my pronouns agree with their antecedents?

_____ **10.** Do I use the right word (*to, too, two*)?

Adding a Title

Write a title using one of these suggestions.

■ Use a common saying: **If You Don't Smoke, Don't Start!**

■ Use rhythm: **To Smoke or Not to Smoke**

■ Be creative: **Smoke Signal Warning**

Publishing

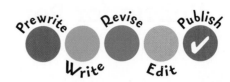

Prewrite · Write · Revise · Edit · Publish ✓

Now that you have finished editing your essay, it's time to make a final copy to share. You may also want to include a copy in your portfolio, create a poster, or send your essay to your school newsletter.

Presentation

- Use blue or black ink and write neatly.
- Write your name in the upper left corner of page 1.
- Skip a line and center your title; skip another line and start writing.
- Indent every paragraph and leave a one-inch margin on all sides.
- Write your last name and the page number in the upper right corner of every page after the first one.

Create a Poster

Turn your call to action into a slogan and design a poster around it.

Submit to a Class Newspaper

Include a letter about your opinion essay.

Add to Your Portfolio

Make a clean final copy of your essay for your writing portfolio. Include a reflection page. (See page **236**.)

Publish

Make a final copy. Follow your teacher's instructions or use the guidelines above to format your essay. (If you are using a computer, see pages **44–46**.) Create a clean final copy.

Rubric for Persuasive Writing

Use the following rubric for rating your persuasive writing.

Ideas

6 The clear reasoning informs and convinces the reader.

5 The essay has a clear opinion statement. Logical reasons support the writer's opinion.

4 The opinion statement is clear, and most reasons support the writer's opinion.

Organization

6 The organization is logical, and ideas flow smoothly from beginning to end.

5 An opening opinion statement is clearly supported in the middle. Transitions connect ideas.

4 The opening has an opinion statement. The middle adds support. Most transitions work.

Voice

6 The writer's voice is confident, positive, and very convincing.

5 The writer's voice is confident and helps persuade the reader.

4 The writer's voice is confident. It needs to persuade the reader.

Word Choice

6 Strong, engaging, positive words add to the main message. Every word counts.

5 Strong, positive words help make the message clear.

4 Strong words are used, but some may be too negative.

Sentence Fluency

6 The sentences flow smoothly, and people will enjoy reading the variety of sentences.

5 Variety is seen in both the types of sentences and their beginnings.

4 Sentence beginnings are varied. Sentence variety would make the essay more interesting.

Conventions

6 Mastery of conventions adds style to the essay.

5 A few grammar and punctuation errors do not distract the reader.

4 Grammar and punctuation errors in a few sentences may distract the reader.

3 The opinion statement is clear. Reasons and details are not as complete as they need to be.

2 The opinion statement is unclear. Reasons and details are needed.

1 An opinion statement, reasons, and details are needed.

3 There is a beginning, a middle, and an ending. Transitions are needed.

2 The beginning, middle, and ending run together.

1 The organization is unclear. The reader is easily lost.

3 The writer's voice needs to be more confident and to persuade the reader.

2 The writer's voice sounds unsure.

1 The writer needs to learn about voice.

3 Many words need to be stronger and more positive.

2 The same weak words are used throughout the essay.

1 Word choice does not communicate the main message.

3 Varied sentence beginnings are needed. Sentence variety would make the essay more interesting.

2 Too many sentences begin the same way. Compound and complex sentences are needed.

1 Sentences are choppy. Ideas do not flow smoothly.

3 There are enough errors to confuse the reader.

2 Frequent errors make the essay difficult to read.

1 Nearly every sentence contains errors.

Evaluating a Persuasive Essay

As you read through the persuasive essay below, focus on the strengths and weaknesses in the writing. (The essay contains several errors.) Then read the student self-assessment on the next page.

Take Five to Stretch

When I started jogging with my mom, she made me stretch before we ran. "How come I have to waste time stretching?" I asked. Mom told me that stretching makes me a better runner. For performance and for health, athletes should stretch.

People should stretch to get their bodies ready to move. Stretching warms up tendons and gets blood going. It makes joints more flexible.

Another important reason to stretch is to keep from getting hurt. Muscles that are cold can cramp up. That's no fun. For another thing joints that aren't ready to move get strains or sprains.

The most convincing reason to stretch is that it can help a person do better! That's because when one muscle flexes, the other has to stretch. If it doesn't, the muscles fight against each other. Stretching can help a person run faster and lift more!

When I first started running with Mom I just didn't like stretching. I thought pro runners were great because of their special shoes. Really they're great because of their training, which always includes stretching. So, remember to stretch. It'll help you feel good, avoid getting hurt, and perform better.

Student Self-Assessment

The writer of the essay on page 234 assessed his own work. First, Tomu wrote one positive comment and one possible improvement. Then he rated each trait using the rubric on pages 232–233.

Ideas

4 Ideas
1. I think I have a good topic.
2. I could use more details to support my topic sentences.

Organization

4 Organization
1. I have a really good beginning, middle, and ending.
2. I could have used more transitions.

Voice

5 Voice
1. I have a persuasive tone.
2. My call to action could have been stronger.

Word Choice

4 Word Choice
1. I don't use loaded words.
2. I could have found more words that fit my subject.

Sentence Fluency

4 Sentence Fluency
1. I fixed my choppy sentences.
2. I could have smoothed out a few parts.

Conventions

5 Conventions
1. I used the checklist and my dictionary.
2. I missed a comma after introductory words.

Use the rubric. Assess your essay using the rubric shown on pages 232–233. List the six traits and leave room after each trait to write one strength and one weakness. Then choose a number (from 1 to 6) that shows how well you used each trait.

Reflecting on Your Writing

Now that you've finished your persuasive essay, take a moment to reflect on the job you have done. On your own paper, complete each sentence starter below.

Thinking about your essay will help you be even more persuasive next time.

My Persuasive Essay

1. The best part of my essay is . . .

2. The part that still needs work is . . .

3. The main thing I learned about persuasive writing is . . .

4. The next time I write a persuasive essay, I would like to . . .

Persuasive Writing
Across the Curriculum

Most newspapers feature an editorial page, a page where opinions about current events or issues are expressed.

In this section, you will write an opinion or editorial of your own. Maybe you have noticed that recycling programs need more community support. Perhaps the city is planning to close your favorite park. An editorial lets you give your opinion about things going on around you.

You'll also get to try your hand at other forms of persuasive writing, and even prepare for writing persuasively on a test.

Mini Index

- **Science**: Writing an Editorial
- **Social Studies**: Creating a Brochure
- **Practical Writing**: Drafting a Persuasive Letter
- **Assessment**: Writing for Assessment

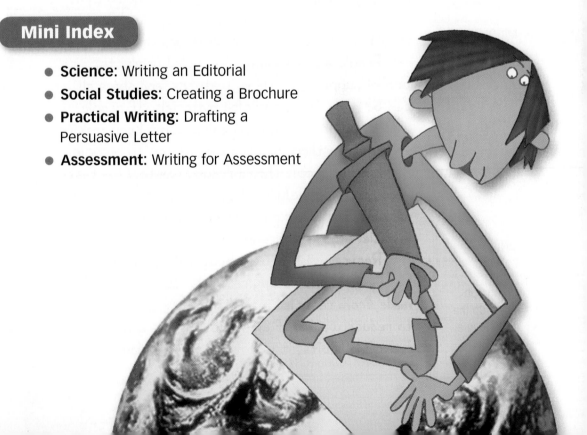

Science: Writing an Editorial

An editorial expresses an opinion about a current issue. The following editorial was written by Akeem and published in his local newspaper.

BEGINNING

The issue is introduced, and the opinion statement (underlined) is given.

MIDDLE

The middle paragraphs support the writer's opinion.

ENDING

The last paragraph sums up the opinion in a thoughtful way.

Beyond the Bins

Most people in Elmwood recycle. They sort out paper, plastic, metal, and glass and put them in the right bins. However, recycling must not stop with throwing things into recycling containers.

People should help the environment by buying reusable items. For example, if a family of four uses paper napkins twice a day, that equals 2,920 napkins a year! Instead of paper napkins, families should switch to washable cloth napkins.

People also should buy recycled products. School supplies, clothing, watches, and shoes all can be made from recycled materials. If people won't buy products, companies won't keep making them. Then there would be no reason to recycle.

Finally, people should reduce waste. One fast-food meal can include a bag, a box, a cup, a straw, napkins, and other packaging. A home-cooked meal is easier on the environment!

Recycling isn't just about filling the bins. People also have to buy reusable items and products made from recycled materials. They also need to reduce waste. If everyone develops some new recycling habits, it will help save our planet.

Prewriting **Selecting a Topic**

One way to find an editorial topic is to read a newspaper. After finding interesting headlines, Akeem wrote an opinion about each.

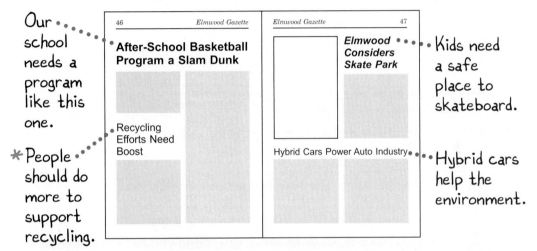

Our school needs a program like this one.

*People should do more to support recycling.

46   *Elmwood Gazette*

After-School Basketball Program a Slam Dunk

Recycling Efforts Need Boost

Elmwood Gazette   47

Elmwood Considers Skate Park

Hybrid Cars Power Auto Industry

Kids need a safe place to skateboard.

Hybrid cars help the environment.

Read headlines. Find four headlines in a local newspaper and write an opinion about each. Choose one to write about.

Gathering Reasons

Freewriting helped Akeem gather reasons for his opinion.

It's really important to recycle. It protects the earth. People put stuff in bins, but that's not enough. So much stuff gets thrown away, like napkins. How many per day? Per year? And what about buying recycled products and using less? There's more than one way to help the environment. . . .

Freewrite. Write freely for 5 to 10 minutes about your topic. Write whatever comes to mind, getting your ideas down on paper.

Prewriting **Researching the Topic**

Akeem had questions about his topic. He wrote down the questions and then checked books, magazines, and Web sites for answers.

<u>What kinds of items are reusable?</u>
People could use cloth napkins, washable towels, and so on.

<u>What things are made from recycled material?</u>
Cans and bottles, but also watches, shoes, clothing, and even school supplies can be made of recycled materials.

<u>What's one way to reduce waste?</u>
Don't buy things with too much packaging—like fast food.

Do your research. Write down questions you have about your topic. Check books, magazines, and Web sites to find answers.

Organizing Your Editorial

To organize his thoughts, Akeem made a table diagram. The "tabletop" gives his opinion, and the "table legs" list reasons that support it.

Opinion

Recycling shouldn't stop at the recycling bins.

Supporting Reasons

reuse products | buy recycled products | avoid waste

Create a table diagram. Write your opinion in a box and your supporting reasons underneath. Find at least three reasons.

Writing **Creating Your First Draft**

The following tips can help you write your first draft. Your first paragraph should include your opinion statement. Each middle paragraph should focus on and discuss one supporting reason. The ending paragraph should summarize your opinion and leave readers with an interesting final thought.

Write your first draft. Using the guidelines above, write a first draft of your editorial.

Revising **Improving Your Writing**

Keep the following traits in mind as you revise your first draft.

- **Ideas** Do I include an opinion and enough supporting details?
- **Organization** Does each middle paragraph focus on one supporting reason? Do my ideas appear in a logical order?
- **Voice** Does my voice show my interest in my topic?
- **Word Choice** Do I use specific nouns and strong verbs?
- **Sentence Fluency** Do my sentences read smoothly?

Revise your writing. Ask yourself the questions above as you revise your writing.

Editing **Checking for Conventions**

When your revising is done, check your paper for conventions.

- **Conventions** Have I checked for punctuation, capitalization, spelling, and grammar errors?

Edit your work. Edit your essay using the question above. Have someone else check it over, too. Then make a final copy and proofread it.

Social Studies:
Creating a Brochure

Travel brochures use words and pictures to invite others to visit a certain place. One student created the following brochure to convince readers to come to his hometown, Madison, Wisconsin.

The cover uses words and pictures to encourage people to visit the city.

Madison, Wisconsin

A City for Explorers!

The headings help create interest.

Inside, details persuade visitors to come.

CATCH SOME WAVES

Madison is practically surrounded by lakes. In the summer, you can swim, sail, or water-ski. When the lakes are frozen, enormous kites sail and snap overhead.

HEY, SPORTS FANS

If you love sports, don't miss the Wisconsin Badgers! At Camp Randall, you can yell and scream for the football team. Make sure to bring extra money for some crispy nachos and ice-cold soda!

MUSEUM MANIA

For fun on a rainy day, visit the Madison Children's Museum. Exhibits are regularly changed, so there is always something new to discover. Make a rain stick or a miniature suspension bridge. This museum lets you learn with your brain, hands, and feet!

Come and explore for yourself!

WRITING TIPS

Planning your brochure . . .

- **Review tourist information.**
  Find brochures or Web sites that advertise your area or state. Notice how they use pictures and words to convince people to visit.

- **Brainstorm a list of favorite places.**
  Think about all the special places to visit and things to do where you live. List as many as you can. Then pick three or four to focus on.

Writing your brochure . . .

- **Select snappy language.**
  Choose words that will excite the reader. Use a thesaurus. For example, instead of using the word *hot,* try the word *sizzling,* or instead of *delicious,* try *scrumptious.*

- **Use exciting pictures.**
  Draw pictures or include photographs.

Checking your brochure . . .

- **Experiment with your layout.**
  Think about whether you have put each picture, paragraph, and heading in the best place to create a balanced look.

- **Check for conventions.**
  Make sure you have followed the rules of English. Double-check the spellings of all placenames and people's names.

Create a brochure. Make a brochure about a favorite place. Draw pictures or use photos to add interest.

Practical Writing:
Drafting a Persuasive Letter

Sometimes letters are written to express an opinion. The letter that follows was written by Lauren to nominate her favorite teacher for an award.

191 Green Lane
Alton, WY 07892
May 20, 2005

Jim Edwards, Publisher
Alton Press Teacher Contest
693 High Street
Alton, WY 07892

Dear Mr. Edwards:

The **opening** introduces the topic and states the opinion.

I'm writing to nominate my fifth-grade reading teacher, Mr. Marcus, for your Teacher of the Year Contest. More than any teacher I've had, Mr. Marcus makes books come to life!

The **body** provides supporting details.

One hot afternoon, Mr. Marcus shut the windows, pulled the blinds, and turned off the lights. He had the girls stand quietly in one corner and the boys in another. Then he read a book about slaves being taken from Africa on small ships. As we got hotter and more uncomfortable, we imagined how hard it was for the slaves.

Mr. Marcus uses many creative activities to make reading exciting. Students leave his class wanting to read more. Please consider Mr. Marcus for Teacher of the Year.

The **ending** calls for action.

Yours truly,

Lauren Saunders

Lauren Saunders

WRITING TIPS

Before you write . . .

- **Do your research.**
  Make sure you have plenty of information to support your opinion.
- **Organize your thoughts.**
  Write an opinion statement, which will appear in your opening paragraph.

During your writing . . .

- **Use the proper format.**
  See pages **246–247** to format your letter correctly.
- **Share specific details.**
  Choose details that will clearly explain your opinion to the reader.

After you've written a first draft . . .

- **Ask someone to review the letter.**
  Ask several of your classmates to read the letter. Do they understand it? What additional information would they like to know?
- **Check for organization.**
  Review the sentences in your paragraphs to make sure each thought leads naturally to the next.
- **Check for conventions.**
  Make sure your letter is free of careless errors.

Write a letter. Use the tips above as you write a letter to your principal to nominate your favorite teacher for an award.

Parts of a Business Letter

1 The heading includes your address and the date. Write the heading at the left margin, at least one inch from the top.

2 The inside address includes the name, title, and address of the person or organization you are writing to.

- Put short titles on the same line as the name. Put longer titles on the next line.
- If you are writing to an organization, use the organization name.

3 The salutation is the greeting. Put a colon after it.

- If you know the person's name, use it:

  Dear Mr. Jones:

- Otherwise, use a salutation like one of these:

  Dear Store Owner:

  Dear Editor:

  Dear Palo Alto Soccer Club:

4 The body is the main part of the letter. Do not indent your paragraphs; instead, skip a line between them.

5 The closing is placed after the body. Use **Yours truly** or **Sincerely**. Capitalize only the first word and put a comma after the closing.

6 The signature ends the letter. If you are using a computer, leave four spaces after the closing; then type your name. Write your signature between the closing and the typed name.

tip Turn to page 477 for more about writing letters. You can also use the set of guidelines on that page for addressing envelopes properly.

Business-Letter Format

1

2

——— Four to Seven Spaces

3

: ——— One Space

——— One Space

——— One Space

4

——— One Space

5

, ——— One Space

——— Four Spaces

6

(Leave a 1-inch margin on all sides.)

Writing for Assessment

Many writing assessments ask you to state an opinion and support it with strong reasons. Study the following sample prompt and student response. You can use a graphic organizer to help you plan.

Persuasive Prompt

The leaders of your community want to pass a law to make in-line skating safer for everyone. People who do not wear protective gear will not be allowed to skate in city parks or on city sidewalks. Do you agree with the leaders of your community? Write an essay that gives your opinion.

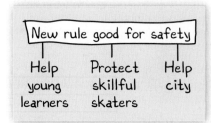

The **beginning** includes the opinion statement (underlined).

 The city of Hamilton wants to require in-line skaters to wear protective gear. Kids without protective gear won't be allowed to skate in city parks. <u>This new law will make in-line skating safer for everyone.</u>

 Protective gear is a must for beginners. Young skaters are still learning how to balance, turn, and stop. They fall often, and their wrists, elbows, and knees can get hurt. The right equipment can keep them safe while they learn the sport.

Even skillful skaters need helmets. In-line skates work best on hard surfaces, and a fall without a helmet could cause a bad head injury. Helmets allow all skaters to be safer.

Each middle paragraph gives a reason and details that support the opinion.

The new law would also help the community. Parents would feel more comfortable about letting their kids skate on city sidewalks. Fewer injuries may set an example for other communities to make the same rule.

The ending summarizes the essay and restates the opinion.

In-line skating is fun, but it should also be safe. The leaders in Hamilton have the right idea. People should be required to grab their safely gear before they get rolling!

Respond to the reading. Answer the questions below to learn more about the student response you just read.

- **Ideas** **(1)** What is the writer's opinion? **(2)** What key words in the prompt also appear in the essay?

- **Organization** **(3)** What group of people is the focus of each middle paragraph?

- **Voice & Word Choice** **(4)** How would you describe the writer's voice (humorous, serious, angry)?

WRITING TIPS

Planning your response . . .

- **Understand the prompt.**
  Make sure to state an opinion that fits the prompt.
- **Use your time wisely.**
  Use a graphic organizer such as a line diagram
  to plan your essay before you write.
- **Form an opinion statement.**
  Write an opinion that you can support.

Writing your response . . .

- **Build your argument.**
  Give strong reasons to support your opinion.
- **End effectively.**
  Summarize your argument and restate your opinion.

Checking your response . . .

- **Check for clear ideas.**
  Rewrite any ideas that sound confusing.
- **Check for conventions.**
  Correct any errors you find in punctuation,
  capitalization, spelling, and grammar.

Persuasive Prompts

- Should children under 12 be allowed to swim at the local pool without an adult? Write an essay expressing your opinion.
- In a letter, convince your teacher to schedule a field trip to a place that truly interests you.

 Write a response. Respond to one of the prompts above. Complete your writing within the period of time your teacher gives you.

Persuasive Writing in Review

In persuasive writing, you try to *convince* people to agree with you.

Prewrite

Select a topic that you feel strongly about and one that will interest your reader. (See page **204**.)

Gather and organize reasons to support your opinion statement. You may use a graphic organizer. (See pages **205–206** and **208**.)

Write an opinion statement that identifies your cause and your feeling about it. (See page **207**.)

Write

In the beginning part, get your reader's attention and state your opinion. (See page **211**.)

In the middle part, each paragraph should list one reason with the facts and examples to support it. (See pages **212–213**.)

In the ending part, repeat your opinion and give a call to action. (See page **214**.)

Revise

Review your ideas, organization, and **voice** first. Then review for **word choice** and **sentence fluency**. Make other changes to improve your first draft. (See pages **216–226**.)

Edit

Check your writing for conventions. Also have a trusted classmate edit your writing. (See pages **227–230**.)

Publish

Make a final copy and proofread it for errors before sharing it. (See page **231**.)

Use the persuasive rubric to assess your finished writing. (See pages **232–233**.)

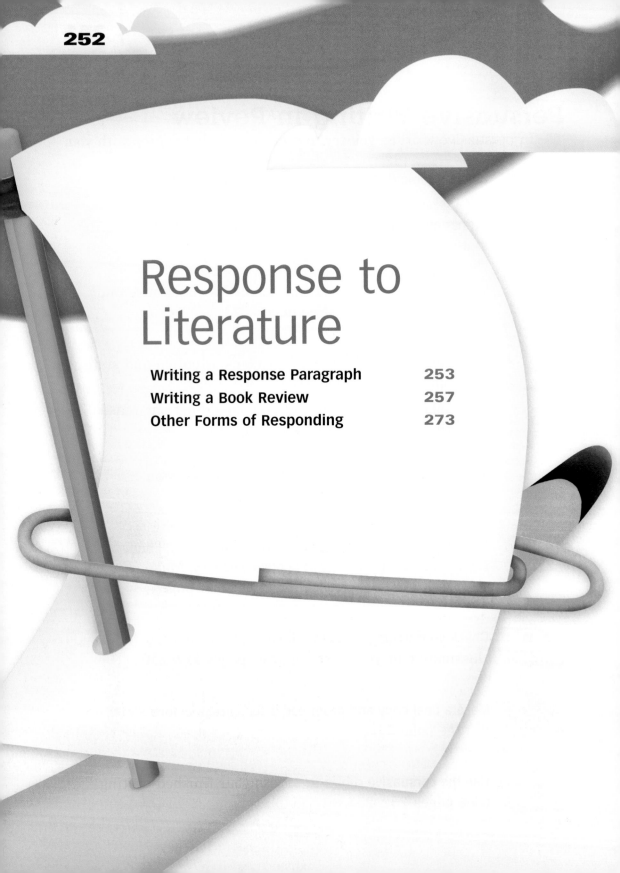

Response to Literature

Response to Literature

Response Paragraph

When your friends ask you about a story you've read, they don't want to know everything—especially the ending! In fact, they just want the story "in a nutshell."

In a response paragraph, you want to encourage others to read the story themselves. Much like the blurb on the back cover of a book jacket, you can do this by highlighting some of the important parts without giving away the whole story.

Writing Guidelines

Subject:	Key parts of a novel
Form:	A paragraph
Purpose:	To preview a novel
Audience:	Classmates

Response Paragraph

Your response paragraph should begin with a **topic sentence** that names the novel and the author. The **body sentences** share key parts of the novel, and the **closing sentence** includes the author's message, or theme.

Topic sentence

Body

Closing sentence

Keeper of the Doves

Keeper of the Doves is a novel by Betsy Byars. The story is told by eight-year-old Amen McBee, who loves writing. Amen lives with her parents and her four sisters in Kentucky in the late 1800s. Mr. Tominski lives on their property in an old chapel in the woods, and he takes care of some doves. He scares the McBee sisters, and they tease him and call him names. Amen notices little things about people, and she decides that Mr. Tominski is a gentle, caring person. When something unexpected happens, Amen must decide if Mr. Tominski is to blame. This story is about accepting people who are different.

Respond to the reading. On your own paper, answer each of the following questions.

- **Ideas** (1) Which sentence explains the message, or the theme, of the novel?
- **Organization** (2) How does the writer organize the paragraph (time order, logical order, or order of importance)?
- **Voice & Word Choice** (3) What words or phrases show that the writer really understands the characters' personalities and actions? Name two.

Prewriting **Selecting a Topic**

Your first step in writing a response to literature is to choose a novel to write about. Brainstorm to come up with ideas.

Ideas List

> ### Novels I Have Read and Liked
> Bud, Not Buddy   Keeper of the Doves*
> Island of the Blue Dolphins   The Castle in the Attic

Prewrite
Choose a novel. Brainstorm a list of novels you know and like. Think of novels you have read recently. Place a star (*) next to the one that interests you the most.

Summarizing the Plot

In any novel, there are characters in a certain place and time (the setting) who are dealing with a problem. To summarize the plot, you must tell *who* the main characters are, *where* and *when* the story takes place, and *what* the problem is.

Collection Sheet

Characters	Setting (where and when)	Problem
McBee family Mr. Tominski	Kentucky in the late 1800s	The McBee girls are scared of Mr. Tominski.

Prewrite
Make a collection sheet. Fill it in with the information for the novel you have chosen.

Writing Creating Your First Draft

A response paragraph contains the following ideas. The topic sentence gives the book title and the author's name. The body tells about the novel's characters, setting, and problem. Finally, the closing sentence explains the author's main message.

Write the first draft of your response paragraph. Use the tips above to guide you as you write your paragraph.

Revising Improving Your Paragraph

The next step is to make changes in the first draft to improve your *ideas, organization, voice, word choice,* and *sentence fluency.*

Revise your paragraph. Use the questions below as you revise your first draft.

1 Do I include enough information about the main action?
2 Do I organize the details clearly?
3 Do I sound interested in the book?
4 Do my sentences flow smoothly?

Editing Checking for Conventions

Now it's time to check your paragraph for *conventions.*

Edit and proofread your work. Use the questions below as you edit. Then make a neat copy and give it a final proofreading.

1 Have I checked my punctuation, grammar, and spelling?
2 Have I underlined the title?
3 Have I used the right words, such as *to, two, too?*

Response to Literature

Writing a Book Review

When you read a new novel, you're like an explorer sailing uncharted oceans. When you write a review of a novel, you're like a mapmaker, sharing your journey with other explorers.

In this chapter, you will write a review of a novel you have read. A book review explores important parts of a novel (without giving away the ending) and tells what you like about it.

Writing Guidelines

Subject:	Review of a novel
Form:	An essay
Purpose:	To show your understanding
Audience:	Classmates

Writing a Book Review

The beginning paragraph in a review names the novel's title and author and includes a sentence or two to introduce the novel. The two middle paragraphs tell what the novel is about and explain the novel's theme or message. The ending paragraph explains why the writer likes the novel.

Treasure Island

BEGINNING
The writer introduces the novel.

Treasure Island was written by Robert Louis Stevenson way back in 1883. The novel is very old, but that doesn't mean that it isn't good. It is one of the best pirate adventures you will ever read.

MIDDLE
The first middle paragraph tells what the novel is about.

A 12-year-old boy named Jim Hawkins tells the story. At his parents' inn, Jim meets a mysterious, old pirate. When introducing himself, the pirate says, "You mought call me Captain." Jim discovers that Captain has a map of an island that shows exactly where a valuable treasure is buried. A bunch of bad guys are after Captain because they want the map and the treasure, too. Jim and some men from his town sail to the island to search for the treasure. They are surprised to learn that some of the men traveling with them are really evil pirates. The pirates will do anything to get the treasure.

MIDDLE
The second middle paragraph explains the book's theme, or message.

ENDING
The final paragraph tells what the writer likes about the book.

Treasure Island may be an adventure story, but it also teaches something. The good guys do win out. Many times it looks like Jim and his friends will be killed by the pirates. Then something surprising happens, and the good guys are back in charge.

I like Treasure Island because it is filled with action and adventure. Almost every chapter ends with a surprise that makes you want to keep reading. Robert Louis Stevenson describes the characters so well that it seems like you are right there with Jim. Here is how Stevenson has Jim describe some sailors: "I saw besides, many old sailors, with rings in their ears, and whiskers curled in ringlets and tarry pig-tails, and their swaggering, clumsy sea-walk." Your parents, your grandparents, and even your great-grandparents probably read Treasure Island. Now it's your turn

Respond to the reading. **Answer the following questions about the sample response.**

- Ideas **(1) What main idea or feeling about the book does the writer share in the first paragraph?**

- Organization **(2) What is the purpose of each middle paragraph?**

- Voice & Word Choice **(3) What words and phrases will make others want to read this book?**

Prewriting Selecting a Topic

For your review, select a novel that you like and know well. You should be able to summarize the story and explain why you enjoyed it. Completing sentence starters is one way to record your ideas.

 Complete sentence starters. Read the sample below. Then complete sentence starters for two books you have read recently.

Sentence Starters

BOOK 1: The Birchbark House

The story is about . . . a Native American girl in Minnesota during the pioneer days.
I like this book because . . . I like reading about pioneer times and Native American customs.

✓ BOOK 2: In the Year of the Boar and Jackie Robinson

The story is about . . . a Chinese girl who moves from China to New York.
I like this book because . . . my family has moved a lot, so I understand how the character feels.

 Choose your topic. Review your sentence completions for both books. Put a check mark by the book you want to write about.

Gathering and Organizing Details

The events you include in your review should be in time order. A time line, like the one below for *In the Year of the Boar and Jackie Robinson,* will help you.

Time Line

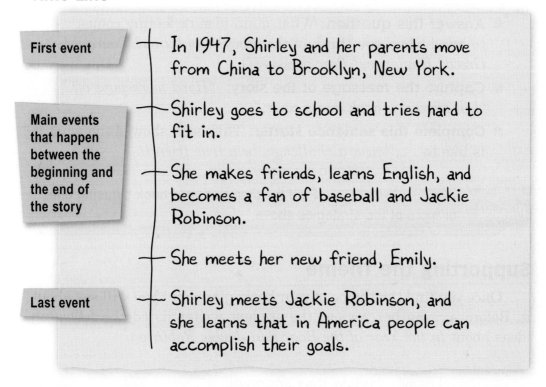

First event

In 1947, Shirley and her parents move from China to Brooklyn, New York.

Main events that happen between the beginning and the end of the story

Shirley goes to school and tries hard to fit in.

She makes friends, learns English, and becomes a fan of baseball and Jackie Robinson.

She meets her new friend, Emily.

Last event

Shirley meets Jackie Robinson, and she learns that in America people can accomplish their goals.

tip Use present-tense verbs in your book review to bring life to your writing. Notice the verbs in the time line above *(move, goes, tries, makes, learns, becomes, meets).*

Prewrite

Create your time line. Make a time line like the one above. Write the main events of your story in the order in which they happen from beginning to end. Be sure to use the present tense. Try to include at least five events.

Prewriting **Thinking About the Theme**

All novels have a theme, the author's message or idea about life. To identify the theme of your novel, try one of these strategies.

Strategies for Identifying the Theme

- **Answer this question:** What main idea or feeling comes to mind when you think of the story? *(Ambition? Courage? Greed? Happiness? Peer pressure?)*

- **Capture the message of the story:** *("Hard work pays off." "Don't judge a book by its cover.")*

- **Complete this sentence starter:** This book showed me what it is like to . . . *(meet a challenge, be a true friend).*

Identify the theme. Find the theme of your book by using one or more of the strategies above.

Supporting the Theme

Once you find the theme of your book, plan what you will say about it. Before writing her review, the student writer listed the following ideas about *In the Year of the Boar and Jackie Robinson.*

> Theme: People can accomplish their goals.
> Supporting Ideas:
>   —Shirley learned English and made a friend.
>   —Jackie Robinson became the first black
>   major-league baseball player.

Support the theme. List details from your book that support the theme you have chosen.

Writing **Starting Your Book Review**

The beginning paragraph of your book review should name the book's title and the author. It should also include details that catch the reader's interest. (Remember to underline the title of your book.)

Beginning

Middle

Ending

Knowing Your Book

Find interesting or unusual facts about your book and its author.

1. Has your book won any awards? The Newbery and Coretta Scott King awards are given each year.

2. Many authors have Web pages. If your author has one, try to find out what inspired him or her to write the book.

Beginning Paragraph

Try using the kinds of facts shown above to grab the reader's interest in your beginning paragraph. (Review the following opening paragraph as well as the one on page 258.)

The beginning paragraph introduces the story and its author.

> Bette Bao Lord wrote the book <u>In the Year of the Boar and Jackie Robinson</u>. It is the story of one year in the life of a Chinese girl who moves to America with her family. The author was born in Shanghai, China. She moved to the United States with her family in 1947. This story is really about her own life!

Write your beginning. Write the first paragraph of your book review. Be sure to include some interesting information that will make the reader want to learn more about the story.

Writing Developing the Middle Part

The middle paragraphs should tell what the book is about and explain the story's theme or message. Your prewriting and planning will help you write these paragraphs.

Beginning

Middle

Ending

First Middle Paragraph

Summarize the story in the first middle paragraph. It should highlight key events without telling everything.

> **The first middle paragraph summarizes the story.**
>
> The story begins with Shirley Temple Wong in China in the Year of the Boar, 1947. That January, she and her parents move from Chungking to Brooklyn, New York. At first, the 10-year-old girl feels sad, lonely, and bored. The author describes Shirley in this way: "She hardly spoke, not even in Chinese, to her mother." But little by little, Shirley makes friends and learns to speak English and play baseball. That summer, she becomes a fan of the Brooklyn Dodgers and Jackie Robinson. He is the first black man to play baseball in the major leagues. By the end of the year, Shirley learns that America is a land of opportunity.

Second Middle Paragraph

The next middle paragraph should tell about the book's theme. Compare the paragraph below with the second middle paragraph in the review on pages 258–259. As you will see, they both name the theme in the topic sentence. The other sentences in the paragraph support or explain the book's theme.

Beginning

Middle

Ending

The second middle paragraph explains the book's message.

> The message of this book is that anything is possible, if you take advantage of an opportunity. Learning about Jackie Robinson gives Shirley confidence. As the author says, "Shirley felt as if she had the power of ten tigers, as if she had grown as tall as the Statue of Liberty." Shirley realizes she can learn English and make friends in America.

Write

Write the middle part of your review. Use your prewriting notes to guide your writing. Also remember to use present-tense verbs.

Adding direct quotations can make your book review come alive.

Writing Ending Your Book Review

In the closing paragraph, you should tell why you like the novel and why you would recommend it to your friends. Your answers to the following questions will help you write this paragraph.

- What did I learn from the story?
- What personal connection do I have with a character?
- Why should my classmates read this book?

Ending Paragraph

Read the ending paragraph below. The writer shares an experience that helped her identify with the main character of the book.

> **The writer gives reasons for liking the book.**
>
> I like <u>In the Year of the Boar and Jackie Robinson</u> because my family has moved a lot, and I know what it's like to be the new kid in school. Shirley has some funny experiences learning English. If you enjoy baseball and learning about Chinese traditions and customs, I think you will like this book.

Write your ending. Use the questions at the top of this page as a guide for writing your closing paragraph.

Form a complete first draft. If necessary, write a complete copy of your first draft. Write on every other line to make room for changes.

Revising **Using a Checklist**

Revise your first draft. Number your own paper from 1 to 9. If you can answer "yes" to a question, put a check mark after that number. If not, work with that part of your essay.

Ideas

_____ **1.** Do I name the book and the author in paragraph one?

_____ **2.** Do I include the main events in the next paragraph?

_____ **3.** Do I tell about the theme in the paragraph after that?

Organization

_____ **4.** Do I have a beginning, a middle, and an ending?

_____ **5.** Is my summary of events in time order?

Voice

_____ **6.** Do I sound interested in and knowledgeable about the book?

Word Choice

_____ **7.** Have I used specific nouns and present-tense verbs?

Sentence Fluency

_____ **8.** Do I use a variety of sentence lengths?

_____ **9.** Are my sentences clear and easy to understand?

Make a clean copy. After revising your review, make a clean copy for editing.

Editing **Using a Checklist**

Edit your revised copy. Number your own paper from 1 to 9. If you can answer "yes" to a question, put a check mark after that number. If not, edit for that convention.

Conventions

PUNCTUATION

_____ **1.** Do I use end punctuation after all my sentences?

_____ **2.** Do I use commas after introductory word groups?

_____ **3.** Do I use commas between items in a series?

CAPITALIZATION

_____ **4.** Do I start all my sentences with capital letters?

_____ **5.** Do I capitalize proper nouns and words in titles?

SPELLING

_____ **6.** Have I spelled all my words correctly?

_____ **7.** Have I double-checked the words my spell-checker may have missed?

GRAMMAR

_____ **8.** Do I use correct verb forms (*had gone*, not *had went*)?

_____ **9.** Do I use the right words (*to, too, two*)?

Three Ways to Create a Title

- Use the title of the book: ***In the Year of the Boar and Jackie Robinson***
- Share the theme of the story: **Opportunity at Bat**
- Be creative: **Not a Boring Year**

Make a clean final copy. Check your paper one last time.

Reflecting on Your Writing

Now that you've finished your book review, take a moment to reflect on it. Complete each sentence starter below on your own paper.

Your thoughts will help you prepare for your next writing assignment.

My Book Review

1. The prewriting activity that worked best for me was . . .

2. The best part of my review is . . .

3. The part that still needs work is . . .

4. The main thing I learned about writing a book review is . . .

5. In my next book review, I would like to . . .

Additional Ideas for Book Reviews

Listed below are additional ideas for book reviews. You can focus on one or two of these ideas in your writing.

Plot (the action of the story)

- The story includes several surprising events.
- The climax (the most important event) of the story is interesting, believable, or unbelievable.
- Several important events lead to the outcome or ending of the story.
- The ending is surprising, predictable, or unbelievable.

Characters (the people—and sometimes animals—in the story)

- A main character changes from _____ to _____ by the end of the story.
- Certain people, settings, events, or ideas affect how the main character or characters act.
- _____ is the main character's outstanding personality trait. (You may point out more than one outstanding trait.)

Setting (the time and place of the story)

- The setting has an important effect on the main character.
- The setting (in a historical novel) increased my knowledge of a certain time in history.
- The setting (in a science-fiction novel) creates a different world.

Theme (the author's statement or lesson about life)

- *Ambition . . . courage . . . greed . . . happiness . . . jealousy . . .* is clearly a theme in (title of book).
- The moral, "Look before you leap" . . . "Haste makes waste" . . . "Pride comes before a fall," is developed in (title of book).
- This book showed me what it is like to be . . .

Writing in a Response Journal

There are many ways to respond to the books you read. One of the best ways is to keep a **response journal**. In your journal, you may write about the main character, try to guess what will happen next in the story, or relate some part of the story to your own life. The choice is yours.

How to Respond

Try to write in your journal at least three times for every book you read—four or five times for long books. Your journal ideas will come in handy when you write book reviews. Use the following questions to help you respond as you read. (Also refer to the additional questions on page 272.)

First Feelings

What did you like best about the first few chapters? How do you feel about the characters?

On Your Way

Are the events in the story clear? Do you still feel the same way about the characters? What do you think will happen next?

The Second Half

What seems to be important now? Is the book still interesting? How do you think it will end?

Summing Up

How do you feel about the ending? How has the main character changed? What do you like most about the book? What do you like least? Why?

Reflections

How does the book connect with today's world? How does the book relate to your own life?

Additional Questions for Responding

Whenever you need a starting point for writing in your response journal, check this page for ideas.

Before and After

- What happens in the first part of the book? What were your feelings after reading this part?
- What important things happen in the middle of the book? (Name two or three.) Why were they important?
- How does this book end? What were your overall feelings about this book?

Favorites

- What was the best part of this book? Explain.
- Which illustration in the book was your favorite? Describe it in detail.

Making Changes

- Are there any parts you would like to change? Explain.
- Could you write a new ending for this book? What would it be?
- Do you think the title of the book is a good one? Why? Can you think of a better title? What is it?

Author! Author!

- What do you think the author wants you to learn from this story?
- What would you say in a short, friendly letter to the author?

Cast of Characters

- What is the main character in the story like? Write about him, her, or it.
- Are you like any of the characters in the book? Explain your answer by telling a story about how you and the character are alike.
- Do any of the characters remind you of friends or family members? Explain by writing a comparison.
- Which character in the book would you like to write a letter to? Write it!
- Would you like having one of the characters in the story as a friend? Explain why.
- What would you say in a poem about one character, scene, or event in the story?

Response to Literature

Other Forms of Responding

Think about the literature you come across every day. There are novels, short stories, articles, poems, plays, and reports. And that's just the beginning of the list! It is safe to say that literature takes many different forms.

In this section, you will learn how to respond to four forms of literature: a quotation, a poem, an article, and an anecdote. These forms are often included on writing assessments.

Mini Index

- **Responding to a Quotation**
- **Responding to a Poem**
- **Responding to a Nonfiction Article**
- **Responding to an Anecdote**

Responding to a Quotation

A **quotation** is a passage from a piece of literature that can make you think. One way to respond to a quotation is to relate it to an experience in your own life. In the sample below, the student writer related a personal experience to this quotation: *"It is far easier to start something than it is to finish it."*

The **beginning** introduces the quotation.

A few years ago, when my family moved to Lansing, I got into soap-box racing. That's when I discovered that "it is far easier to start something than it is to finish it."

The **middle** relates the quotation to an experience the writer had.

Dad bought a kit to make a sleek race car. I was very impatient to get it done. One day, while Dad was at work, I decided to get going on my car. I looked at the plans, and I said to myself, "Dude, you can do this." I got out Dad's toolbox, and I started building. Part A easily fit into Part B. Part C was a little harder to connect to Part D. By the time I got to Part G, I'd made a real mess of things. It took Dad and me two hours to undo what I had done.

The **ending** explains what the quotation means to the writer.

What did I learn from this experience? I was lucky I didn't ruin my race car. Now I know that before I start something, I better be sure I know how to finish it.

Prewriting **Planning Your Response**

To plan a response to a quotation, follow these three steps.

1 **Select a quotation.** Your teacher may have examples for you to choose from. If not, look for one in a book of quotations.

2 **Think about the quotation.** Once you select a quotation, restate it in your own words. This rewriting will show if you really understand the quotation.

> *"It is far easier to start something than it is to finish it."*

> When you start something, you should have a good idea of what it will take to finish it.

3 **List personal experiences related to the quotation.** Then choose the one that you think will work best.

> * Last year I ran in an eight-mile race with my dad. I didn't train very hard because I thought the run would be easy. I didn't make it to the finish line.
>
> * I thought it would take a few hours to clean my room. Once I got started, it took the whole weekend.

Prewrite

Plan your response to a quotation. Use the information above as your planning guide. If you have trouble finding a quotation, use one of these:

● *"Full effort is full victory."*
● *"Honesty is the best policy."*

Writing Developing Your Response

In the **beginning** part, capture the reader's interest and restate the quotation.

> I admit it. My room barely had a path from the door to my bed. One day, I decided to straighten it up. That's when I found out that "it is far easier to start something than it is to finish it."

In the **middle** part, show the details of your experience.

> After piling, sorting, and putting away things all day, my room was still full of books, magazines, and clothing. Some of this stuff had to go. It took a whole weekend for me to decide what to keep, what to give away, and what to throw out. I finally got rid of two boxes of stuff.

In the **ending**, explain what the quotation means to you. Do this by relating the quotation to the experience you described in the middle part.

> When I started cleaning my room, I had no idea it would take a whole weekend to finish the job. I learned that I should have thought more about the neatness and order of my room all along. For me, there'll be no more living like a pack rat in a cluttered room.

 Write a first draft. Write the beginning, the middle, and the ending of your response based on the guidelines above.

Revising and Editing Checklist

Once you finish your first draft, use the following checklist to revise and edit your response.

Ideas

_____ **1.** Do I relate the quotation to one experience?
_____ **2.** Do I use interesting details to share the experience?

Organization

_____ **3.** Does my first paragraph introduce the quotation?
_____ **4.** Do I use time order to organize the middle part?
_____ **5.** Does the ending explain the meaning of the quotation?

Voice

_____ **6.** Do I sound interested in my quotation?

Word Choice

_____ **7.** Do I use specific nouns and strong action verbs?

Sentence Fluency

_____ **8.** Do I use a variety of sentence lengths and beginnings?

Conventions

_____ **9.** Have I checked capitalization, spelling, and punctuation?

Revise

Revise and edit your response. Make the necessary changes in your response. Proofread your final copy before sharing it.

Writing for Assessment

You may be asked to think about and respond to a quotation for a writing assessment. Study the following prompt and student response.

Prompt: *Think about the quotation* "No act of kindness, no matter how small, is ever wasted." *Relate this quotation to an experience in your own life.*

Topics Cluster

The **beginning** introduces the quotation.	Returning a lost letter might seem like a small kindness. But it taught me that "no act of kindness, no matter how small, is ever wasted."
The **middle** shares the experience.	One windy afternoon, I found an envelope blowing down the street. According to the return address, the sender lived five blocks away. I didn't feel like walking that far, but I did anyway. The lady who answered the door was so happy that I brought her the letter. It was a letter to her son, who is a soldier in the army. The letter had blown away when she went to mail it.
The **ending** gives the writer's final thoughts.	The lady gave me a dollar for returning the letter. The best reward was feeling good about myself. I was glad that I had not missed the chance to do this small act of kindness.

WRITING TIPS

Before you write . . .

- **Read the quotation and the prompt.**
  Make sure you understand each one.
- **Make a graphic organizer.**
  Create a cluster of personal experiences that relate to the quotation. Choose the best one.

Topics Cluster

During your writing . . .

- **Introduce the quotation.**
  State the quotation in the first paragraph.
- **Develop the middle part.**
  Share the experience that relates to the quotation.
- **Explain the meaning of the quotation.**
  In the last paragraph, explain what the experience means to you and how it connects to the quotation.

After you've written a first draft . . .

- **Review your writing for ideas and organization.**
  Make sure your ideas are clear.
- **Edit and proofread.**
  Check for errors in spelling, punctuation, and grammar.

Choose a quotation. Apply one of the quotations below to an experience in your life.

- *"All that glitters is not gold."*
- *"The truth of the matter is that you always know the right thing to do. The hard part is doing it."*

Responding to a Poem

A **poem** is a special type of literature that uses only a few words to express an idea or an emotion. To respond to a poem, you should think about its form, the special words that the poet uses, and the main idea or message of the poem. In the essay below, the writer responds to the poem "Fireball."

Fireball
Superior star
Warms the earth
Melting icicles, creating deserts
Sun

The **beginning** introduces the subject and names the form of the poem.

"Fireball" is a word cinquain poem. The poem has five lines that follow this pattern: one word, two words, three words, four words, and one word. The last line is a synonym of the first line.

The **middle** explains how the words are used.

Each line shares different ideas about the topic. The words "Superior star" in line two say that this ball of fire is better than the other stars. In line three, "Warms the earth" describes the value of this star. Line four, "Melting icicles, creating deserts," describes its power.

The **ending** explains the message of the poem.

The main message of this poem is that the sun is both helpful and harmful. This poem describes the sun as the most powerful star in our sky.

Prewriting Planning Your Response

1 **Choose a poem.** Make sure to select a poem that you truly enjoy and understand.

2 **Read the poem several times.**

> **Silence**
> Faithful trees stand guard
> as the forest sleeps under
> a blanket of snow.

3 **Decide what form the poem takes** (*free verse, limerick, haiku, cinquain*). If you're not sure of the form, note the number of lines in the poem, if rhyme is used, and if the poem follows a pattern of some type.

4 **List ideas for your response.** Use a graphic organizer like the one below to gather ideas.

Gathering Chart

form	haiku–nature poem line 1–five syllables; line 2–seven syllables line 3–five syllables
special words	trees "stand guard" like people "forest sleeps"–everything quiet
main message	In winter the trees look like they protect the forest.

Plan your response. Use the information above as your planning guide. If you have trouble finding a poem, consider this one:

> **Full Moon**
> Wakes when darkness comes
> climbs a tall starry ladder
> lights the earth below.

Writing **Developing Your Response**

In the **beginning** paragraph, discuss the form of the poem and explain how the poem is put together. (Refer to page **281** for ideas.)

> "Silence" is a haiku. Haiku poems are about nature. They are three lines long. The first line has five syllables, the second line has seven, and the third line has five.

In the **middle**, explain how the poet uses special words in the poem. Refer to at least two or three specific parts of the poem.

> This poem is about a forest in winter. In the first line, the trees seem like real people "standing guard" over the forest. In the second and third lines, "forest sleeps" tells us that everything is quiet "under a blanket of snow."

In the **ending** paragraph, explain the poem's main message.

> I think that the poet's message in "Silence" is that even though the trees are bare, they still protect the forest. Even in the winter, they shelter everything on the forest floor.

Write a first draft. Write the beginning, the middle, and the ending of your response based on the guidelines and examples above.

Revising and Editing Checklist

Once you finish your first draft, use the following checklist to revise and edit your response.

Ideas

_____ **1.** Do my ideas show that I understand the poem?

_____ **2.** Do I include specific words from the poem in my response?

Organization

_____ **3.** Do I include beginning, middle, and ending parts?

Voice

_____ **4.** Do I sound like I understand and enjoy the poem?

Word Choice

_____ **5.** Do I use specific nouns and verbs?

Sentence Fluency

_____ **6.** Do my sentences read smoothly?

Conventions

_____ **7.** Do I use correct capitalization and punctuation?

_____ **8.** Do I spell all my words correctly?

Revise

Revise and edit your response. Make the necessary changes in your response. Proofread your final copy before sharing it.

Writing for Assessment

You may be asked to respond to a poem for a writing assessment. Study the following prompt and student response.

Prompt: *Respond to the following poem. In your essay, write about the form of the poem, the special words the poet uses, and the poem's message.*

The Bee
There once was a boy in a tree,
Who was bugged by an annoying bee.
When asked, "What's the buzz?"
He said, "That's all it does!
I'll zap it before it zaps me."

The **beginning** describes the form of the poem.

    "The Bee" is a limerick. A limerick is a humorous poem that is five lines long. Lines one, two, and five rhyme. Lines three and four also rhyme. The rhyming makes the poem fun to read.

The **middle** tells how words create images in the reader's mind.

    When I read this poem, I can see the boy in the tree. Words like "bugged" and "annoying" describe how the boy feels about the bee. "Buzz" reminds me of the sound a bee makes. I like the sound of the repeated word "zap" in the last line.

The **ending** explains the poem's message.

    "The Bee" reminds me of how annoying it is to hear the constant buzzing of a bee or a mosquito. I'll be ready to zap the next one that "bugs" me.

WRITING TIPS

Before you write . . .

- **Read the poem several times.**
  Think about its form and how the words are used.
- **Make a graphic organizer.**
  Use a simple gathering chart to gather ideas for your response.

Gathering Chart

Form	
Special Words	
Message	

During your writing . . .

- **Name and describe the form of the poem.**
  Discuss the form of the poem (haiku, cinquain, limerick), and explain how it is put together.
- **Develop the middle part.**
  Tell how the poet uses special words in the poem.
- **Share the meaning of the poem.**
  In the last paragraph, explain the poem's message.

After you've written a first draft . . .

- **Review your writing for ideas and organization.**
  Make sure your ideas are clear.
- **Edit and proofread.**
  Check for errors in capitalization, spelling, punctuation, and grammar.

Respond to a poem. Respond to the following poem or to a poem selected by your teacher.

Dandelion
Yellow dots scattered
across the blanket of green
like the eyes of spring.

Responding to a Nonfiction Article

A **nonfiction article** often shares important information about a real person or a place. One way to respond to a nonfiction article is to point out interesting things that you learned about the subject as well as any questions you still have about the person or the place.

Mr. Kahn Joins Our School!

By Anna Hernandez

Have you noticed there's a new teacher in school? If you have met him already, you know he is an interesting person. His name is Mr. Kahn, and he teaches fifth grade in Room 23.

You will notice that Mr. Kahn has an accent. He was born in Kenya, Africa, but he spent most of his life in England. Six years ago, he and his wife moved to the United States. Since then, they have become big Boston Red Sox fans. Mr. and Mrs. Kahn have two children, a four-year-old son Isaac and a baby daughter named Kia. The family has a Great Dane called Mr. Big. He weighs 130 pounds. When he stands on his hind legs, he is as tall as Mr. Kahn!

Mr. Kahn loves talking with students. So when you see him, introduce yourself. Welcome to Cedar Hills, Mr. Kahn!

The **beginning** names important facts from the article.

This article is about Mr. Kahn, a new teacher in our school. I was excited to learn that Mr. Kahn was born in Kenya, Africa. It was neat to know that he lived in England, too. He must have a lot of different stories to share.

The **middle** names more facts.

Even though Mr. Kahn and his family have only been here six years, they are already big Red Sox fans. I sure would like to meet Mr. Big. A 130-pound dog is huge!

The **ending** tells what the writer still wants to know.

I know that Swahili is the national language of Uganda and Kenya. I wonder if Mr. Kahn knows how to speak this language. If he does, maybe he could teach it to students in our school. We could have an after-school club.

Prewriting Planning Your Response

Follow these steps when you plan a response to an article.

1 Select an interesting article to read, like the one below.

Captain Mecha Lives History

By David Reynolds

On May 3, Captain Bill Mecha spoke to our fifth-grade class. We had been studying early American history. Mr. Mecha is the captain of a tall ship!

Captain Mecha's ship is a copy of one that fought in the War of 1812 against Britain. It is made of wood, and it has sails 118 feet high. The crew dresses in uniforms that sailors would have worn back then. Captain Mecha's crew has 60 officers and men.

People can sail on the ship, help with the rigging, and tour the sleeping quarters, galley, and storage rooms. They can even watch the crew fire the ship's cannons.

The captain gave each student three tickets to sail on the tall ship this summer. He said it will be a great way for kids and their parents to learn all about the War of 1812 and an earlier time in this nation's history.

2 List the most important facts in the article.

Facts List

—Mr. Mecha, captain of a tall ship
—ship is a copy of one used in War of 1812 . . .

3 Think of any questions that you have about the article.

My questions

What kinds of foods did they eat on the ship?
How do the cannons work?

Prewrite

Plan your response. Use the information above as a guide. If you have trouble finding an article, ask your teacher for help.

Writing **Developing Your Response**

In the **beginning** paragraph, name the important things that you learned in the first part of the article.

> Mr. Bill Mecha has a cool job. He captains a tall sailing ship. This ship is a copy of one that fought in the War of 1812. The ship is made of wood, and the sails are 118 feet high! The crew even wears realistic uniforms.

In the **middle** part, identify additional things that you learned in the rest of the article.

> What would it be like to sail on such a ship? Mr. Mecha takes people on board so they can find out. They learn about rigging the sails, and they see how the sailors lived at that time.

In the **ending** paragraph, state any key question that you have after reading the article.

> The cannons interest me the most. I would really like to ask the captain "How are they fired?" Better yet, I would like to be on the ship and watch them being fired. Maybe I will sail on the ship this summer to learn about the cannons.

 Write a first draft. Write the beginning, the middle, and the ending of your response using the information above as a guide.

Revising and Editing Checklist

Once you finish your first draft, use the following checklist to revise and edit your response.

Ideas

_____ **1.** Does my response show that I understand the article?

Organization

_____ **2.** Does my beginning name important information from the first part of the article?

_____ **3.** In the middle part, do I give more information?

_____ **4.** In the ending, do I ask a question related to the article?

Voice

_____ **5.** Do I sound interested in my response?

Word Choice

_____ **6.** Do I use specific words to keep the reader's interest?

Sentence Fluency

_____ **7.** Do my sentences flow smoothly?

Conventions

_____ **8.** Do I use correct capitalization and punctuation?

_____ **9.** Have I corrected spelling or grammar errors?

Revise

Revise and edit your response. Make the necessary changes in your response. Proofread your final copy before sharing it.

Writing for Assessment

You may be asked to respond to a nonfiction article for a writing assessment. Study the following prompt and student response.

Prompt: *Read the article below about a college basketball player. Then write a friendly letter to Mr. Turner. Share something that you learned from the article. Also ask him a question.*

Sports Hero Returns

By Christina Sung

Yesterday, Jahmal Turner visited our school. He plays college basketball in Tennessee. Jahmal graduated from Cedar Hills Elementary School.

Jahmal talked about when he was a student at Cedar Hills and played basketball here. Back then, he liked basketball more than school, but later he learned that it was important to be a good student. Jahmal works very hard in school and plans to be a doctor in the future. But before he does that, his goal is to play professional basketball.

The students at Cedar Hills enjoyed meeting Jahmal Turner. Many of us have seen him on TV. He gave each of us a basketball poster to take home.

The opening names a main thing the writer learned.

In the body the writer asks a question.

The ending adds a final thought.

Dear Mr. Turner,

Thank you for visiting my school. One main thing I learned from your talk is how important it is to stay in school and get an education. I really admire you because you are a great basketball player and a good student.

I try to follow all the rules for making good jump shots, but I miss a lot of them. If you come to Cedar Hills again, could you give me some shooting pointers?

I know if I learned how to shoot from you, I could improve my game.

Sincerely,
Ty Greene

WRITING TIPS

Before you write . . .

- **Read the prompt and the article.**
  Be sure you know what the prompt is asking you to do.

Cluster

I learned . . .   I learned . . .
            article
I learned . . .   a question. . .

- **Make a graphic organizer.**
  Create a cluster about the article to collect details for your response.

During your writing . . .

- **Organize your response.**
  In the first paragraph, explain what you learned from the article. In the second paragraph, ask your question. In the last paragraph, share a final thought.

After you've written a first draft . . .

- **Review your writing for ideas and organization.**
  Make sure that your response refers directly to the article. You can check that by looking for specific references in your writing.
- **Edit and proofread.**
  Check for errors in capitalization, spelling, punctuation, and grammar.

Respond to the following prompt. Read a brief nonfiction article about a person. In a friendly letter to the person, explain something you learned and ask her or him a question.

Responding to an Anecdote

An **anecdote** is a brief story used to make a point. Anecdotes are written about real people and about characters in literature. The following anecdote is about a real person, Oprah Winfrey.

Oprah's Letter

On Oprah Winfrey's first day of kindergarten, her teacher got a letter insisting that Oprah belonged in the first grade. After reading the letter, the teacher agreed. Oprah skipped kindergarten and went right to first grade. Do you know who wrote the letter? Oprah did! At five years old, she knew how to read and write.

In the essay below, a student responds to this prompt: *Read the anecdote "Oprah's Letter." What word or phrase do you think best describes the person being written about? Write an essay using information from the anecdote to support your choice.*

The **beginning** statement identifies the key word about the person.

The **middle** details support the opening statement.

The **ending** gives the reader something to think about.

I think Oprah Winfrey is very clever. She wanted to get a good education even when she was very little. When she was only five years old, Oprah thought she should skip kindergarten.

On the first day of kindergarten, Oprah gave her teacher a letter. She already knew how to read and write. It was a smart idea to write the letter to prove that she should be moved up to first grade.

Today, Oprah Winfrey is one of the most famous women in the world. She always knew how important a good education was. At age five she decided to always do her best.

Prewriting **Gathering Details**

Your teacher may ask you to write a brief essay in response to an anecdote. The following ideas will help you get started.

1 Read the anecdote and the prompt carefully.

> ### Jim's Dream
> Jim Abbott wanted to play Little League baseball. However, he was born with his right arm missing just below the elbow. Yet Jim spent hours throwing tennis balls against a wall. He learned to throw left-handed by holding his glove under his right arm. Then he quickly switched the glove to his left hand so he could catch. Before long, Jim's dream came true. He made a Little League team as a pitcher.

2 Based on this story, what word or phrase would best describe the person's character or personality?

3 Write a statement that identifies the topic of your response. (Include the word or phrase that would best describe the person in your statement.) Then think of three reasons from the anecdote to explain your statement.

> I think Jim Abbott was very determined.
> REASONS:
> 1. He wanted to play baseball, even though he had a birth defect.
> 2. He spent hours throwing a tennis ball.
> 3. He learned to throw and catch with his left hand.

Prewrite   **Respond to an anecdote.** Plan a response to an anecdote provided by your teacher.

Writing Developing Your Response

To respond to an anecdote about a person, focus on a key word that describes something about his or her character.

In the **beginning** part, include a strong statement that best describes the person.

> I think Jim Abbott was very determined. He was born missing his right arm below the elbow, but he found a way to overcome his disability.

Write a **middle** paragraph that supports your opening statement.

> Jim dreamed of playing Little League baseball. He spent a lot of time throwing tennis balls against a wall. He threw and caught a ball left-handed. He would hold his glove under his right arm whenever he threw. Then he switched the glove to his left hand to catch. Because of his hard work, Jim made a team as a pitcher.

Write an **ending** that re-emphasizes the character trait.

> Jim Abbott showed what a determined person can do. His goal was to play baseball, and through hard work, he reached that goal.

Write a first draft. Write the beginning, the middle, and the ending of your response based on the guidelines above.

Revising and Editing Checklist

Use the following checklist to revise and edit your response.

Ideas

_____ **1.** Do I use one key word or phrase to describe the person?

_____ **2.** Do I refer to details in the anecdote?

Organization

_____ **3.** Does my beginning describe the person's character?

_____ **4.** Does the middle support the opening statement?

_____ **5.** Does the ending give the reader one final thought?

Voice

_____ **6.** Do I sound interested in my topic?

Word Choice

_____ **7.** Have I used specific nouns and verbs?

Sentence Fluency

_____ **8.** Do I use a variety of sentence lengths?

Conventions

_____ **9.** Do I use correct capitalization and punctuation?

_____ **10.** Have I checked for errors in spelling and grammar?

Revise

Revise and edit your response. Make the necessary changes in your response. Proofread your final copy before sharing it.

Writing for Assessment

You may be asked to respond to an interesting anecdote for a writing assessment. Study the following prompt and student response.

Prompt: *Read this anecdote based on an event in* 20,000 Leagues Under the Sea. *In an essay, identify something about Captain Nemo's character that is illustrated in the anecdote. Use information in the anecdote to explain your ideas.*

The Shark

We put on our diving suits. Captain Nemo gave us daggers to use as protection against sharks. Then, slowly, we plunged under the waves. Soon we saw an Indian pearl fisherman diving nearby. We saw a look of horror on the man's face as an enormous shark swam toward him with its jaws wide open! Captain Nemo rushed toward the shark with amazing quickness and sank his dagger into its belly. We helped the captain pull the fisherman back to his boat.

Table Diagram

Captain Nemo, brave
- dived in ocean with sharks
- attacked a shark
- saved a man

The beginning names a key character trait.

The middle explains the trait.

The ending gives a final thought.

Captain Nemo was obviously a very brave man. Nothing frightened him, not even sharks.

Captain Nemo wasn't afraid to dive in the ocean, even though he knew there were sharks nearby. He carried a dagger for protection. When he saw a shark about to attack a pearl fisherman, the captain took action. He risked his life by stabbing the shark and rescuing the man. He even helped pull the frightened man back to his boat.

Imagine a big shark with its jaws wide open! Would you want to attack it? Only a brave person like Captain Nemo would fight a huge, hungry shark.

WRITING TIPS

Before you write . . .

- **Read the anecdote and prompt.**
  Make sure that you understand each one.
- **Make a graphic organizer.**
  Use a table diagram to identify a character trait and give some examples or reasons to explain it.

Table Diagram

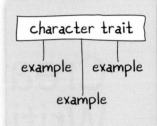

During your writing . . .

- **State your opinion.**
  Begin your essay with a paragraph that catches the reader's interest and identifies a main character trait of the subject.
- **Use strong examples to explain the trait.**
  Find information in the anecdote to illustrate or explain the character trait.
- **Be creative with your ending.**
  Share a thought about the person and his or her actions.

After you've written a first draft . . .

- **Review your writing for ideas and organization.**
  Make sure all of your ideas are clear and easy to follow.
- **Edit and proofread.**
  Check for errors in capitalization, spelling, punctuation, and grammar.

Respond to an anecdote. Write an essay based on an anecdote and prompt supplied by your teacher.

Creative Writing

Creative Writing

Writing Stories

Try to imagine living long ago, at some other time in history. What would it have been like to sail on the *Mayflower* or to travel with Harriet Tubman on the Underground Railroad to freedom? What would it have been like to help Ben Franklin discover electricity or invent bifocals?

Fictional stories set in another time and place allow the writer and the reader to have adventures in history. This chapter will help you write a believable historical fiction story. Afterward you can create a tall tale or even a play!

Writing Guidelines

Subject:	Historical fiction story
Form:	Short story, tall tale, play
Purpose:	To entertain
Audience:	Classmates

Historical Fiction Story

In the following story, Clayton imagines being the best friend of a young Benjamin Franklin. He uses action, dialogue, and sensory details to bring his story to life.

My Best Friend, Ben

BEGINNING

The beginning introduces the setting and the main characters.

The summer of 1716 was a hot one in Boston. Almost every afternoon, I went swimming in Fresh Pond with my best friend, Ben Franklin. We loved those long, hot days.

On one particular afternoon, Ben was late. I went to his house and climbed the stairs to his cluttered bedroom. He was sitting there messing with a kite.

RISING ACTION

A conflict between the characters creates tension.

"What's with the kite?" I said. "I thought we were going swimming."

Ben smiled at me as he tied one more knot in the kite string. "We need the kite for swimming."

"Who goes swimming with a kite?" I asked.

"I do," Ben said. His blue eyes twinkled.

When you're the friend of a genius, you get used to hearing crazy ideas. I just shook my head. "I'd like to see you do it."

Half an hour later, we were standing on the shore of Fresh Pond. Ben held his crazy kite in one hand and an old log in the other. He sat on the muddy shore, slipped off his shoes, and tied the end of the kite string to one big toe. Then he flipped the kite into the air and let a breeze catch it. The kite rose over Fresh Pond.

HIGH POINT
The conflict is resolved when the main character understands the mystery.

"This is ridiculous," I said.

My friend Ben grinned at me and hopped into the pond. He threw one arm over his log, leaned back, and let the kite pull him across the pond.

"Oh, I get it!" I cried as Ben drifted away. "It's a flying sail!"

"Meet you on the other side!" he called back.

ENDING

The ending reflects on the events of the story.

Sure enough, I did! That was my friend Ben's first famous kite trick, and I was there to see it. I only wish I'd been with him years later when he used another kite to discover electricity!

Respond to the reading. On your own paper, answer the following questions about the story.

■ **Ideas** (1) What does the narrator expect when he goes to Ben Franklin's home? (2) What does he discover instead?

■ **Organization** (3) Why are there so many short paragraphs in this story?

■ **Voice & Word Choice** (4) Find three specific action verbs and tell how they strengthen the voice of the story.

Prewriting Selecting a Topic

One way to find a topic is to list historical people and events. Clayton paged through his social studies book to create the list below.

Topic List

> ### Historical People and Events
> Paul Revere riding to warn of the British attack
> Pocahontas saving John Smith from execution
> Ben Franklin using a kite to cross a lake ✻

List topic ideas. Use a history book or the Internet to find some topic ideas. Star (✻) the one you want to write about.

Mixing Fact and Fiction

Since your story will be part fact and part fiction, you can gather details with a fact-fiction chart. Clayton used his history book to fill in the "Fact" column and his imagination to fill in the "Fiction" column.

5 W's Fact-Fiction Chart

5 W's	Fact	Fiction
Who?	Ben Franklin	Me (Ben's best friend)
What?	crossed a lake by kite	I wanted to go swimming
When?	when Franklin was 10	on a summer day
Where?	in Boston	Fresh Pond
Why?	he was smart	it was hot

Create a fact-fiction chart. Use a history book and your imagination to create a chart like the one above for your topic.

Creating a Plot

The actions that take place during a story make up the plot line. Each part of the plot plays an important role in the story.

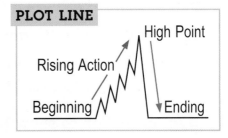

- The **beginning** introduces the characters and the setting.

- The **rising action** develops the conflict—a problem or challenge for the characters.

- The **high point** is the most exciting part.

- The **ending** tells how the conflict worked out.

Clayton used a plot chart to help him think about what would happen during each part of his story.

Plot Chart

Beginning	Rising Action	High Point	Ending
I show up at Ben's house to go swimming. He's building a kite instead.	Ben says the kite is for swimming. I dare him to show me.	Ben ties the kite to his big toe and floats across Fresh Pond.	I laugh at my friend and think of other things he would do with kites.

Prewrite

Create a plot chart. In each column, write what will happen in the beginning, in the rising action, at the high point, and in the ending of your story.

Writing Creating Your First Draft

You are now ready to begin writing your story. The tips below can guide you.

1 **Set the scene by answering *when* and *where*.**

Instead of . . . **Ben and I were going to go swimming.**

Write . . . The summer of 1716 was a hot one in Boston.

2 **Use action to show the reader what is happening.**

Instead of . . . **Ben wasn't ready to go swimming.**

Write . . . Ben was sitting there messing with a kite.

3 **Use dialogue to let characters speak for themselves.**

Instead of . . . **I didn't know why he had a kite.**

Write . . . "What's with the kite?"

4 **Use sensory details to make the story come alive.**

Instead of . . . **He got ready for his experiment.**

Write . . . He sat on the muddy shore, slipped off his shoes, and tied the end of the kite string to one big toe.

5 **Build to a high point.**

Instead of . . . **Ben Franklin went into the pond.**

Write . . . "This is ridiculous," I said. My friend Ben grinned at me and hopped into the pond.

Write your first draft. Use your prewriting charts and the five tips shown above as you create the first draft of your historical fiction story.

Revising Improving Your Writing

Once you finish your first draft, set it aside for a while. When you are ready to revise, the following questions can help.

- **Ideas** Have I included facts and fiction?
- **Organization** Do I follow my plot chart?
- **Voice** Is my storytelling voice engaging or entertaining?
- **Word Choice** Have I used strong verbs?
- **Sentence Fluency** Do my sentences read smoothly?

Revise your writing. Use the questions above as a guide when you revise your first draft.

Editing Checking for Conventions

The following questions can help you edit your story.

- **Conventions** Have I corrected spelling and capitalization errors? Have I included end punctuation for each sentence? Have I checked for easily confused words *(to, too, two)*?

Edit your story. Use the questions above to guide your editing. When you finish, use the tips below to write a title. Then create a clean final copy and proofread it.

Creating a Title

- Use a repeated sound: **My Best Friend, Ben**
- Be playful: **Towed by a Flying Sail**
- Use a line from the story: **Swimming with a Kite**

Creating a Tall Tale

Another type of historical story is a tall tale. When you write a tall tale, you begin with facts, but you include so many exaggerations that the story becomes wild and wacky. Here are the steps for creating a tall tale about a historical figure.

1 Make your hero larger than life.

Pick one idea or trait about your main character and then exaggerate it until it is unbelievable.

Betsy Ross, famous flag maker, designed a flag big enough to be seen by all the original 13 states at once.

2 Give your hero a powerful challenge.

Come up with a villain, a monster, or a natural event that the hero must fight against.

While traveling the Missouri River, Lewis and Clark had to fight a 50-foot killer sturgeon that had just swallowed three canoes.

3 Exaggerate.

Make your story as wild as it can be.

Because one of her plane's engines was damaged, Amelia Earhart overinflated her tires and bounced her way across the country.

Write a tall tale. Exaggerate one of your main character's traits. Then give him or her a great challenge. Use exaggeration to tell the story of how your character succeeds.

Creating a Play

Another creative way to share a story is to write it as a play. A play depends on dialogue to tell a story. Actions are stated in parentheses. Here is the beginning of a play that Clayton wrote based on his Ben Franklin story.

Franklin, the Flying Fish

Characters: Clayton Jones, 10 years old
Ben Franklin, 10 years old

Setting: The shore of a pond

ACT I

(Ben Franklin sits under a tree and ties the last bit of string onto a kite he has just made. Clayton, in a swimsuit, rushes up.)

Clayton: Sorry I'm late.

Ben: No problem. It gave me time to finish my kite.

Clayton: (scratching his head) What's with the kite? I thought we were going swimming.

Ben: (tying the kite string onto his big toe) We are . . . with a kite.

Clayton: Who swims with a kite?

Ben: (standing up and grinning) I do. . . .

 Write your story as a play. Use the sample play above as a guide. List your characters, set the scene, and then write dialogue to tell your story.

Story Patterns

Stories often follow patterns. Here are five popular story patterns that you could try.

The Rescue

In a *rescue* story, a character is either the rescuer or someone who needs to be rescued.

> A boy and his dog are trapped on the roof of a house in a flood.

The Quest

In a *quest* story, a character travels into unknown places to achieve a goal.

> Daniel Boone searches for a pass through the mountains.

The Mystery

In a *mystery* story, a character must answer a puzzling question.

> A girl who finds a ring with strange markings tries to find out where the ring came from and what the markings mean.

The Underdog

In an *underdog* story, a character overcomes real difficulty to succeed.

> A boy faces his fear of water and learns to swim.

The Rivalry

In a *rivalry* story, two characters compete for a single object or goal.

> Al and Jamal try to outdo each other to win the position of starting quarterback.

 Check the story pattern. Think of a favorite story. Does one of the story patterns above fit it? If not, how would you describe the story pattern?

Elements of Fiction

Writers use specific terms to talk about the parts of a story. In the following list, you'll find words that will help you talk about the stories you write and read.

Action The **action** is everything that happens in a story.

Antagonist An **antagonist** (sometimes called a villain) is a person or thing that fights against the hero.

The wolf is the antagonist of the three little pigs.

Character A **character** is a person or humanlike animal in a story.

Conflict **Conflict** is a problem or challenge for the characters. There are five basic types of conflict:

- **Person vs. Person:**
  Two characters have opposite goals.

  A supervillain wants to sink a ship, but a superhero wants to save it.

- **Person vs. Society:**
  A character has a problem with a group of people.

  A student has trouble fitting in at a new school.

- **Person vs. Himself or Herself:**
  A character has an inner struggle.

  A young detective wonders what to do when the clues in his current case point toward his best friend.

- **Person vs. Nature:**
  A character has to battle an element of nature.

  A mountain climber gets caught in a blizzard.

- **Person vs. Fate:**
  A character faces something he or she can't control.

  After falling from a horse, an injured man fights to walk again.

Dialogue   **Dialogue** refers to the words characters speak to each other in a story.

Mood   **Mood** is the feeling a reader gets from a story—happy, sad, frightened, peaceful.

Moral   A **moral** is a lesson the writer wants readers to learn from a story. The moral of "The Boy Who Cried Wolf" is that if you tell lies, no one will believe you even when you tell the truth.

Narrator   The **narrator** is the one who tells the story. Harold the dog tells the story in the book *Bunnicula*, so Harold is the narrator (even though he is a dog!).

Plot   The **plot** is the action or series of events that make up the story. Most plots follow a plot line with four parts: beginning, rising action, high point, and ending. (See page **303**.)

Point of View   **Point of view** is the angle from which a story is told.

- A story about the writer uses *first-person point of view.*

   I went swimming in Fresh Pond with my best friend, Ben Franklin.

- A story about other people uses *third-person point of view.*

   Clayton and Ben went swimming in Fresh Pond.

Protagonist   The **protagonist** is the hero of the story.

Setting   The **setting** is the time and place of a story.

Theme   The **theme** is the main idea or message of a story. The theme of *Charlotte's Web* is the importance of friendship.

Tone   The **tone** is the feeling the author creates in a story. For example, the tone of a story may be serious, funny, or angry.

Creative Writing

Writing Poems

Think of a special place, somewhere you love to be. Then think of how exciting it is to tell someone about it.

A poem is a great way to tell someone about a favorite place. Poems focus on sights, sounds, and feelings. In this unit, you will write a poem about your own favorite place, inviting readers to join you in this special spot.

Writing Guidelines

Subject: A favorite place
Form: Free-verse poem
Purpose: To entertain
Audience: Classmates and family

Free-Verse Poem

Many people think poetry has to rhyme, but not all poems do. What is true is that all poems use language in a special way. Dina Lazeric wrote the following free-verse (nonrhyming) poem about her favorite part of the local zoo.

Aviary

Glass dome above,
like an eggshell
filled with green branches

where rainbow-colored birds
flutter, squawk, and fly!

Stone path leading
through the trees,
crossing a blue pool

where rainbow-colored fish
chase bird reflections.

Respond to the reading. On your own paper, answer the following questions about the poem "Aviary."

- **Ideas** (1) What details do you like best in this poem? List at least three.

- **Organization** (2) Which two similar lines tie the poem together?

- **Word Choice** (3) Why do you think the poet named this poem "Aviary"?

Prewriting Selecting a Topic

To write a poem, first you need a topic. Dina brainstormed ideas by writing a list of her favorite places.

Brainstorming List

my room on rainy days	the playground on Elm Street
✓ the aviary at the zoo	swimming pool in Ash Park

Make a list. List some of your own favorite places. Check (✓) the one that you are most interested in writing about.

Gathering Details

Poems use sensory details to create pictures for the reader. Dina gathered details about the aviary in a sensory chart.

Sensory Chart

See	Hear	Smell	Taste	Touch
Stone path	Birds chattering, singing, squawking	Dirt	none	Damp air
Green leaves and branches		Plants		Cold cement bench
Blue pool	Wings fluttering			Soft flowers and ferns
Bright-colored birds and fish	Water splashing			
Clear glass dome				

Gather sensory details. Make a chart like the one above and list details about your topic.

Prewriting Using Poetry Techniques

Poets use special techniques in their writing. Dina used a *simile* and *onomatopoeia* in her poem.

- A **simile** *(sĭm´ ə-lē)* uses the word *like* or *as* to compare two things.

  Glass dome above,

  like **an eggshell**

- **Onomatopoeia** *(ŏn´ə-măt´ə-pē´ə)* uses words that sound like the noises they name.

  where rainbow-colored birds

  flutter, squawk, **and fly!**

Use poetry techniques. Try to think of one simile to use in your poem. List two words that use onomatopoeia. (Check your sensory chart from page 313 for ideas.)

Writing Developing Your First Draft

Now it's time to write your poem! Follow these tips.

- **Imagine being in your favorite place.** Review your sensory chart for details.
- **Write whatever comes to mind.** If you're not sure how to start, begin with the most important detail.
- **Play with words.** Capture the sights, sounds, and feelings. Experiment. Have fun!

Write the first draft of your poem. Describe your favorite place so the reader can experience being there, too.

Revising Improving Your Poem

Revise your draft by answering these questions about the traits.

- **Ideas** Do I use the best sensory details? Do I share my feelings?
- **Organization** Do I arrange my ideas in an interesting way? (The poem on page 312 is divided into phrases.)
- **Voice** Does my poem show originality?
- **Word Choice** Do I use a simile and onomatopoeia?
- **Fluency** Does my poem read smoothly?

Revise your writing. Keep working with your poem until you're happy with every word.

Editing Fine-Tuning Your Poem

You want your poem to flow smoothly and be easy to read.

- **Conventions** Are my words spelled correctly? Have I used the right words (*there, they're, their*)?

Edit your work. Correct any errors in your poem.

Publishing Sharing Your Poem

Here are a few ways to share your poetry.

- **Perform it.** Read it aloud to friends and family.
- **Post it.** Display it on a bulletin board or on your refrigerator.
- **Send it out.** Submit your poem to a newspaper, magazine, or Web site.

Present your work. Make sure to share your poem. Use one of the ideas above or come up with an idea of your own.

Writing a Diamanté

A diamanté *(dē´ə-män-tā´)* is a five-line poem written in a diamond shape. The lines follow a specific formula, as shown below.

Outside
bright, breezy
running, shouting, jumping
loud, excited, calm, quiet
sitting, whispering, giggling,
warm, cozy
inside

Title: One noun
Two adjectives about the first noun
Three *-ing* words about the first noun
Two words about the first noun and two
about the final noun
Three *-ing* words about the final noun
Two adjectives about the final noun
Ending: One noun (the title's opposite)

WRITING TIPS

- **Select a topic.** Think of an interesting place or idea and its opposite (attic and basement, summer and winter).
- **Gather details.** List contrasting details about these two places or ideas. Make a chart like the one below.
- **Follow the pattern.** Fill in your diamanté. Make sure your poem flows smoothly from the title to the ending.

Planning Chart

1 noun	2 adjectives	3 -ing words	2 more adjectives
Outside	bright, breezy	running, shouting, jumping	loud, excited
inside	warm, cozy	sitting, whispering, giggling	quiet, calm

Create your diamanté. Choose two opposite ideas and write your diamanté using the writing tips above.

Writing Other Forms of Poetry

You can create poems in many ways. Here are two more types of poems for you to try.

Tercet

For a short rhyming poem, try a tercet. It has only three lines. Usually the first and last lines rhyme.

Saturday Mornings

On Saturdays, I wake to kitchen sounds.
Dad making biscuits. Mom making coffee.
Mom and Dad talking while the sausage browns.

List Poem

If you like making lists, you may have the beginning of a list poem. Each item in the list helps build a word picture.

Waiting

Buttery popcorn
Giant drink
Cushiony seats
Dim lights
High ceiling
Hushed talking
Let's start the show!

Write a poem. Choose a favorite time or activity and write your own tercet or list poem.

Using Special Poetry Techniques

The next two pages explain the special techniques that poets use. Try using some of these in your poems.

Figures of Speech

■ A **simile** *(sĭm′ə-lē)* compares two different things using the word *like* or *as*.

> A dresser like a sunken treasure chest

■ A **metaphor** *(mĕt′ə-fôr)* compares two different things without using *like* or *as*.

> My closet is a time machine.

■ **Personification** *(pər-sŏn′ə -fĭ-kā′shən)* makes something seem human that isn't.

> The breeze whispers through the porch screens.

■ **Hyperbole** *(hī-pûr′bə-lē)* is an exaggeration.

> Their lunchroom stretches to another county.

Sounds of Poetry

Poets use the following techniques to add interesting sounds to their work. (Also see page 314.)

■ **Alliteration** *(ə-lĭt′ə-rā′shən)* means repeating beginning consonant sounds.

> flutter, squawk, and fly

■ **Assonance** *(ăs′ə-nəns)* is the repetition of vowel sounds in words.

> On Saturdays, I wake to kitchen sounds.

■ **Consonance** *(kŏn′sə-nəns)* is the repetition of consonant sounds anywhere within words.

> On Saturdays, I wake to kitchen sounds.

- **Line breaks** help slow down the reader, focusing attention on individual words and phrases.

  **Stone path leading
  through the trees**

- **Onomatopoeia** *(ŏn´ə-măt´ə-pē´ə)* means using words that sound like the noise they name.

  flutter, squawk, and fly

- **Repetition** means using the same word, idea, or phrase for rhythm or emphasis.

  Dad making biscuits. Mom making coffee.

- **Rhyme** *(rīm)* means using words whose endings sound alike.

  End rhyme happens at the ends of lines.

  **Janice sings
  while she swings.**

  Internal rhyme happens within lines.

  Teachers left the bleachers.

- **Rhythm** *(rĭth´əm)* is the way a poem flows from one idea to the next. In free-verse poetry, the rhythm follows the poet's natural voice.

  Ă dréssĕr likĕ ă sŭnkĕn tréasurĕ chést

Write a poem. Write about a favorite time or place. Use one figure of speech and at least one sound technique.

Research Writing

Research Writing

Building Skills

Good research combines information from a variety of sources. Because there is so much information available to you today, knowing how to use it is more important than ever before.

The key to effective research is to know where and how to find the best information. This chapter gives you tips for gathering information and helps you use the Internet and the library. The skills and strategies that you learn here will help you write effective research reports.

Mini Index

- **Gathering Information**
- **Researching on the Internet**
- **Using the Library**
- **Using Reference Materials**

Gathering Information

When you are researching a topic, don't rely on one source. Instead, gather information from many different sources.

Reading . . . Learn facts and details by reading about your topic in books, encyclopedias, and magazines.

Surfing . . . Explore the Internet for information.

Viewing and Listening . . . Watch TV programs and videos about your topic.

Interviewing . . . Ask an expert questions about your topic. (See below.)

Guidelines for Interviewing

Use the following tips as a guide when you conduct an interview.

■ Write a list of questions to ask during the interview. (Be sure the questions ask for more than a "yes" or "no" answer.)

What is dyslexia?

What causes dyslexia?

How is dyslexia treated?

■ As you take notes, politely say, "I want to write that down." The person will stop talking so you can write. But don't try to write down too much.

■ Ask the person to spell any words that you are unsure of.

Evaluating Sources

Before you use information in your writing, ask yourself these questions.

● Is the source someone who knows a lot about the subject?
● Is the information current or posted recently?
● Is the information complete and dependable?
● Is the source unbiased? Does it tell both sides of the story?

Researching on the Internet

The easiest way to find out about a topic on the Internet is to use a special Web site known as a **search engine**. Common search engines like Google.com and Yahoo.com are easy to use. Just type in your topic, and links to many sites will appear.

> Check the Write Source Web site for a list of search engines to use.
> **www.thewritesource.com**

Helpful Hints

- **Use the Web carefully.** Find Web sites that will give you trustworthy information. Look for sites that have *.edu, .org,* or *.gov* in the address. These are educational, nonprofit, or government Web sites. If you are not sure about a site, check with your teacher or librarian.

- **Look for links.** Web pages often include links to other pages about your topic. Use these links to find even more information.

- **Be patient.** Searches can get complicated. Sometimes a search engine will list sites that have little, if anything, to do with your topic. If this happens, try the search again using different keywords about your topic.

- **Know your school's Internet policy.** Be sure to follow your school's Internet policy. Also follow the guidelines that your parents may have set up for you.

Practice

Use a search engine to find information about an occupation that you find interesting. Write down the addresses of at least two Web sites that tell you about the training required.

Using the Library

In order to make the best use of your school or public library, you should know where everything is located. Below is a map of a library with its sections labeled. Your library might be arranged differently, but it probably contains these same sections.

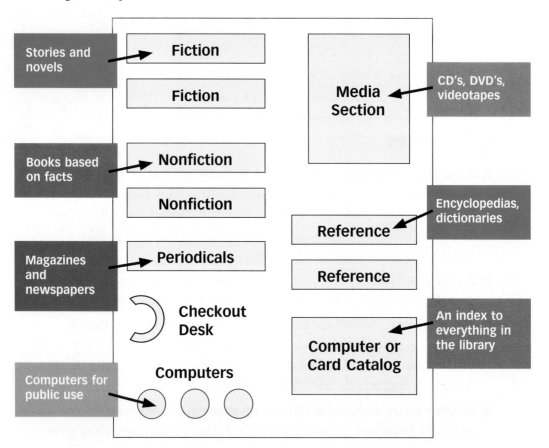

Practice

Study the layout of your school or public library. Then make a map of it, noting where each main section is located.

Searching a Computer Catalog

In a **computer catalog**, you can find information about the same book in three ways:

1 If you know the book's title, enter the title.

2 If you know the book's author, enter the author's name. (When the library has more than one book by the same author, there will be more than one title listed.)

3 Finally, if you know only the subject you want to learn about, enter either the subject or a keyword. (A *keyword* is a word or phrase that is related to the subject.)

Using Keywords

If your subject is . . .	your keywords might be . . .
dyslexia	dyslexia, learning disabilities, ADHD

Computer Catalog Screen

Author:	Landau, Elaine
Title:	Dyslexia (Life Balance)
Published:	Franklin Watts, 2004
Subjects:	Dyslexia, learning disabilities, ADHD
STATUS: Available	**CALL NUMBER:** 616.855LAN
LOCATION: Juvenile collection Nonfiction	

Practice

Create a computer catalog screen like the one above for a book you have read.

Searching a Card Catalog

The **card catalog** is usually found in a cabinet of drawers with title, author, and subject cards arranged alphabetically.

1 If you know the book's **title**, look up the first word of the title. Ignore a beginning *A, An,* or *The* and look under the next word.

2 If you know the book's **author**, look up the author's last name. (There may be more than one card with the author's name at the top.)

3 If you don't know a title or an author, look up the **subject** to learn about a topic.

Sample Catalog Cards

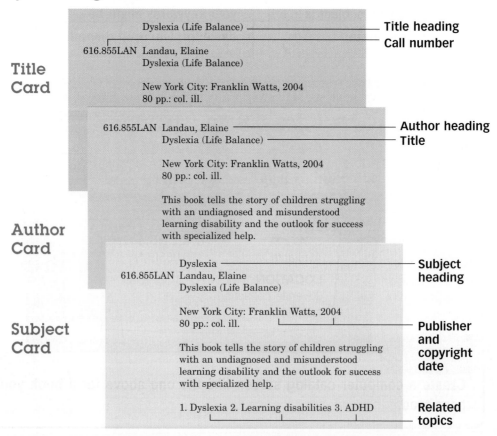

Title Card

Dyslexia (Life Balance) ——————— Title heading
——————— Call number
616.855LAN Landau, Elaine
Dyslexia (Life Balance)

New York City: Franklin Watts, 2004
80 pp.: col. ill.

Author Card

616.855LAN Landau, Elaine ——————— Author heading
Dyslexia (Life Balance) ——————— Title

New York City: Franklin Watts, 2004
80 pp.: col. ill.

This book tells the story of children struggling with an undiagnosed and misunderstood learning disability and the outlook for success with specialized help.

Subject Card

Dyslexia ——————— Subject heading
616.855LAN Landau, Elaine
Dyslexia (Life Balance)

New York City: Franklin Watts, 2004
80 pp.: col. ill. ——————— Publisher and copyright date

This book tells the story of children struggling with an undiagnosed and misunderstood learning disability and the outlook for success with specialized help.

1. Dyslexia 2. Learning disabilities 3. ADHD ——————— Related topics

Finding Books

Nonfiction Books ● Nonfiction books are arranged on library shelves according to **call numbers**.

- **Some call numbers contain decimals.**
  The call number 973.19 is a smaller number than 973.2 (973.2 is really 973.20). The number 973.19 would appear on the shelf before the number 973.20.

- **Some call numbers include letters.**
  The number 973.19D would appear on the shelf before 973.19E.

- **Most call numbers are based on the Dewey decimal system.**

THE TEN CLASSES OF THE DEWEY DECIMAL SYSTEM			
000	General Topics	500	Pure Science
100	Philosophy	600	Technology (Applied Science)
200	Religion	700	The Arts, Recreation
300	The Social Sciences	800	Literature
400	Language	900	Geography and History

Biographies ● Biographies are arranged according to the last name of the person written about. They are shelved in alphabetical order under the call number 921. A biography of astronaut John Glenn would have **921GLENN** on its spine.

Fiction Books ● Fiction books are arranged alphabetically according to the first three letters of the author's last name. A book by Katherine Paterson would have the letters **PAT** on the spine.

Practice

Find the title of your favorite book in the computer catalog or card catalog of your library. Write down the call number of the book and see if you can find it on the shelves.

Understanding the Parts of a Book

Below, you will find a short description of each part of a nonfiction book.

- The **title page** is usually the first page with printing on it. It gives the title of the book, the author's name, the publisher's name, and the city where the book was published.

- The **copyright page** comes next. It gives the year the book was published.

- The **acknowledgement** or **preface** (if the book has one) comes before the table of contents and tells what the book is about. It may also explain why the book was written.

- The **table of contents** tells how the book is organized. It gives the names and page numbers of the sections and chapters.

- The **body** is the main part of the book.

- A **cross-reference** sends the reader to another page for more information. *Example:* (See page 329.)

- The **appendix** has extra information, such as maps, tables, and lists.

- The **glossary** (if there is one) explains special words used in the book. It's like a mini-dictionary.

- The **bibliography** (if there is one) lists books or articles used by the author in writing the book. You can use this list to find more information on the same topic.

- The **index** is an alphabetical list of all the topics in the book. It gives the page numbers where each topic is covered.

Practice

Check for all of the above parts in your science or social studies book.

Using Reference Materials

The reference section in a library contains materials such as encyclopedias and dictionaries.

Using Encyclopedias

An **encyclopedia** is a set of books or a CD with articles on almost every topic. Keep the points below in mind when you use an encyclopedia:

- Articles are written with the most basic information first, followed by more detailed information.
- At the end of an article, you may find a list of related topics. Look them up to learn more about your topic.
- The index volume lists all the places in the encyclopedia where you will find more information about your topic.

Encyclopedia Index

Here in a sample index entry for the topic *dyslexia,* taken from an encyclopedia index.

The capital letter tells which volume.

Page number

More information is available elsewhere.

> **Dyslexia D:358** *with diagram*
> Aphasia **A:511**
> Learning Disabilities
> (Types) **L:235**
> Special Education
> (Reading) **S:604**
> *See also the list of related articles in the* Learning Disabilities *article.*

Practice

Use the index entry above to find the volume and page where you might find the following information.

1. A diagram about dyslexia
2. How schools teach reading to dyslexic students
3. Is aphasia the same thing as dyslexia?

Checking a Dictionary

A **dictionary** is the fastest way to find the meaning of a word. Dictionaries provide the following aids and information.

- **Guide words** These words are listed at the top of each page. They tell the first and last words on that page.

- **Entry words** The entry words are defined on the dictionary page. The most commonly used meaning is usually listed first.

- **Stress marks** A stress (or accent) mark (´) shows which syllable should be stressed when you say a word.

- **Word history** Some words have stories about their origins or how their meanings have changed through the years.

- **Spelling and capital letters** If you don't know how to spell a word, try looking it up by how it sounds. If a word is capitalized, capitalize it in your writing.

- **Pronunciation** A dictionary respells each word phonetically (as it sounds). Special markings are linked to a *pronunciation key*.

- **Synonyms** Synonyms (words with the same or similar meanings) are listed. Antonyms (words with opposite meanings) may also be listed.

- **Parts of speech** A dictionary tells how a word can be used (*noun, verb, adjective*).

- **Syllable division** A dictionary shows where to divide a word.

Practice

Open a dictionary to any page and do the following:

1. Write the guide words on that page.
2. Write a word that has more than one meaning.
3. Find a word with more than one syllable. Write the word's pronunciation.

Dictionary Page

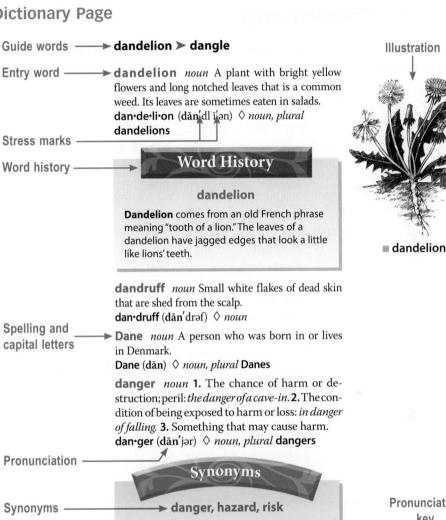

Guide words ⟶ **dandelion ➤ dangle**

Entry word ⟶ **dandelion** *noun* A plant with bright yellow flowers and long notched leaves that is a common weed. Its leaves are sometimes eaten in salads.
dan·de·li·on (dăn′dl ī ən) ◊ *noun, plural* **dandelions**

Stress marks

Word history

Word History

dandelion

Dandelion comes from an old French phrase meaning "tooth of a lion." The leaves of a dandelion have jagged edges that look a little like lions' teeth.

■ **dandelion**

Illustration

dandruff *noun* Small white flakes of dead skin that are shed from the scalp.
dan·druff (dăn′drəf) ◊ *noun*

Spelling and capital letters ⟶ **Dane** *noun* A person who was born in or lives in Denmark.
Dane (dān) ◊ *noun, plural* **Danes**

danger *noun* **1.** The chance of harm or destruction; peril: *the danger of a cave-in.* **2.** The condition of being exposed to harm or loss: *in danger of falling.* **3.** Something that may cause harm.
dan·ger (dān′jər) ◊ *noun, plural* **dangers**

Pronunciation

Synonyms

Synonyms ⟶ **danger, hazard, risk**

The explorer faced many *dangers* in the jungle. ▶ People who live near active volcanoes face certain *hazards*. ▶ It is a *risk* to swim so far, but if you succeed, you will win a prize.

Part of speech ⟶ **dangerous** *adjective* **1.** Full of danger; risky. **2.** Able or likely to cause harm.
dan·ger·ous (dān′jər əs) ◊ *adjective*

dangle *verb* To swing or cause to swing loosely: *A key dangled from the chain.*
Syllable division ⟶ **dan·gle** (dăng′gəl) ◊ *verb* **dangled, dangling**

Pronunciation key

ă	pat	ĭ	pit
ā	pay	ī	ride
â	care	î	fierce
ä	father	ŏ	pot
ĕ	pet	ō	go
ē	be	ô	paw, for
oi	oil	th	bath
ŏŏ	book	*th*	bathe
ōō	boot	ə	ago, item
ou	out		pencil
ŭ	cut		atom
û	fur		circus

Using a Thesaurus

A **thesaurus** is a book of synonyms (words with similar meanings). A thesaurus also lists antonyms (words with opposite meanings). You can use a thesaurus to improve your writing and to expand your vocabulary. A thesaurus helps you . . .

- find just the right word for a specific sentence and
- keep from using the same words again and again.

Thesaurus Entry

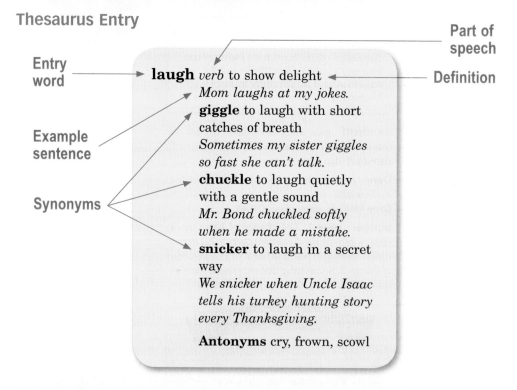

Part of speech

Entry word

laugh *verb* to show delight ◄—— Definition
Mom laughs at my jokes.
giggle to laugh with short catches of breath
Sometimes my sister giggles so fast she can't talk.
chuckle to laugh quietly with a gentle sound
Mr. Bond chuckled softly when he made a mistake.
snicker to laugh in a secret way
We snicker when Uncle Isaac tells his turkey hunting story every Thanksgiving.

Antonyms cry, frown, scowl

Example sentence

Synonyms

Practice

Use the thesaurus entry above to find the right synonym for *laughed* in the sentence below.

I asked the doorman where the Bronx Hotel was, and he <u>laughed</u> as he politely told me, "You're standing in front of it, son."

Research Writing

Summary Paragraph

A road map highlights the key roads and cities in a certain area. In much the same way, a summary highlights the main idea and key details in a longer piece of writing.

In this chapter, you will write a summary of an article you have read. You will need to identify the main idea and the most important supporting details. Then you will summarize the article in your own words, so that other people get the point without having to read it themselves.

Writing Guidelines

Subject: A research article
Form: Summary paragraph
Purpose: To express the main idea
Audience: Classmates

Summary Paragraph

Lon Maddox, a student researching Daniel Boone, summarized the following article in the paragraph "The Wilderness Road."

Crossing the Appalachians, a Barrier to Early Settlement

Look at a physical map of North America, and the Rocky Mountains immediately grab your attention. They stretch from Alaska to Panama. By comparison, the Appalachian Mountains of the East seem insignificant. However, the Appalachians create a natural barrier that affected the settlement of America.

The Appalachians stretch 1,600 miles, from Canada to Georgia. Their average height is 3,000 feet. These mountains include many individual ranges. For example, the Notre Dame Mountains lie at the northern end near Quebec, while the Allegheny Mountains reach from Pennsylvania to Virginia. The Blue Ridge Mountains—the easternmost and highest range—run from southern Pennsylvania to northern Georgia.

Before the United States became a nation, this barrier kept colonists near the coastline. As populations increased, however, so did pressure to move west. In 1775, Daniel Boone led a party of 30 settlers into Kentucky through a natural break in the Appalachians. This pass is known as the Cumberland Gap, and the path the settlers blazed became the Wilderness Road. From 1775 to 1810, roughly a quarter million people traveled that road to begin settling the Central Plains.

Topic sentence (underlined)

Body

Closing sentence

The Wilderness Road

<u>During the early days of this country's history, the Appalachian Mountains kept colonists near the East Coast.</u> The Appalachians form a natural barrier down the east side of the continent from Canada to Georgia. In 1775, Daniel Boone blazed a trail across the Appalachians, through the Cumberland Gap. This trail became the Wilderness Road, which was used by about a quarter of a million settlers to go west. The Appalachians no longer kept them from settling the Central Plains.

Respond to the reading. Answer the following questions.

- **Ideas (1)** What is the main idea of this summary?
- **Organization (2)** How is the paragraph organized?
- **Word Choice (3)** Compare the wording of the summary to the wording of the original. Which is simpler?

Prewriting Selecting an Article

For this assignment, you must find a newspaper or magazine article to read and summarize. Choose one that relates to a subject you are studying. It should be fairly short.

Choose an article. Look through magazines and newspapers for an article (about three to five paragraphs) to summarize.

Reading the Article

If possible, make a photocopy of the article so you can underline important facts as you read. (See the model to the right.)

Before the United States became a nation, this barrier kept colonists near the coastline. As populations increased, however, so did pressure to move west. In 1775, Daniel Boone led a party of 30 settlers into Kentucky through a natural break in the Appalachians. This pass is known as the Cumberland Gap, and the path the settlers blazed became the Wilderness Road. From 1775 to 1810, roughly a quarter million people traveled that road to begin settling the Central Plains.

Read your article. Read carefully to be sure you understand the article. Then read it again to identify the key facts.

Finding the Main Idea

The key to summarizing is finding the main idea of the article. Once you've found it, you need to write it out in the form of a topic sentence. (See the sample summary on page 334.)

Write the main idea. Review the key facts. What main idea do they suggest? Write the main idea as a topic sentence.

Writing Developing the First Draft

In a first draft, you should get all your ideas down on paper. First, state the main idea of the article in a topic sentence. Then, in your own words, include just enough important information to support or explain the main idea. Finally, in the closing sentence, restate or respond to the main idea in a different way.

Write your first draft. Use the suggestions above to write a topic sentence, body sentences, and a closing sentence.

Revising Reviewing Your Writing

It is important to revise your summary for the following traits.

- **Ideas** Does the topic sentence give the main idea of the article? Do I include necessary information to support the main idea?

- **Organization** Is all the information in a logical order?

- **Voice** Does my voice sound interested and informative?

- **Word Choice** Do I explain things in my own words?

- **Sentence Fluency** Do I use a variety of sentence types?

Revise your summary. Read the article and your summary again. Use the questions above to help revise your writing.

Editing Checking for Conventions

Editing means checking your writing for errors.

- **Conventions** Do I have any errors in punctuation, spelling, word usage, or grammar?

Edit your work. Use the question above as a guide when you edit. Then write a clean final copy and proofread it again.

Research Writing
Research Report

Writing a research report is an adventure of sorts. By searching sources like books, magazines, and Web sites, you can discover new and interesting facts about a topic. Are you interested in early explorers, Native American tribes, past presidents?

In this chapter, you will choose an important person and go about the task of learning how he or she affected history. Then you will organize your facts and ideas into an informative and interesting report, one you can share with your classmates and others.

Writing Guidelines

Subject: An important person from history

Form: Research report

Purpose: To find and share information about a historical person's life

Audience: Classmates and parents

Research Report

In this report, student Lon Maddox tells how Daniel Boone's life helped shape early America. As you read Lon's report, notice how the important ideas are arranged. The side notes point out how the report is organized and presented.

The entire report is double-spaced.

↑
1"
↓

1/2" ↑↓

Maddox 1 ← 1" →

← 1" →

Lon Maddox

Ms. Alvarez

Social Studies

December 12, 2005

BEGINNING

The opening leads up to the main idea or thesis statement of the report. (underlined).

Daniel Boone, the Explorer

Daniel Boone loved the wilderness. When he was young, he spent lots of time with Native Americans. Like them, he loved to hunt and live with nature. He also loved to explore. Daniel Boone's exploration helped early Americans go west.

MIDDLE
The first body paragraph tells about Boone's early life and how he got interested in Kentucky.

Boone's early years were adventurous. He was born in 1734 in the Pennsylvania colony, but when he was 15, his family moved to North Carolina. At 19, he fought in the French and Indian War. During the war, he met a man who had hunted in the area called Kentucky. Boone became interested in exploring that land (Chinn).

↑
1"
↓

Maddox 2

The next body paragraphs explain Boone's activities, beginning with the most important.

Boone is famous for exploring Kentucky. "More than any other man, Daniel Boone was responsible for the exploration and settlement of Kentucky" (Chinn). He made several trips there to hunt and explore. In 1775, Boone led 30 settlers over the Appalachian Mountains through the Cumberland Gap. There they started the settlement of Boonesborough. The trail they made became known as the Wilderness Road (Goldman).

Information sources are shown in parentheses.

Daniel Boone and his family soon learned that Kentucky was a beautiful but dangerous land. Not only was it Native American hunting grounds, but also tribal war grounds. The settlers had to defend their families while trying to settle Kentucky. More than once the native people captured Boone, but he always escaped (Salas 16–24).

ENDING

The ending summarizes the last days of Boone's life and reminds readers of the thesis statement.

In 1792, Kentucky became a state, and many more people moved there. Daniel Boone said it was "too crowded," so he moved his family to West Virginia. Then he moved to the Missouri region, where he died and was buried in 1820. Later, the citizens requested that Boone's body be moved back to Kentucky because he was their most important explorer (Chinn).

Maddox 3

The writer's name and page number appear on every page.

Works Cited

Chinn, Col. George M. "Daniel Boone." 1996. 8 Oct. 2004

<http://www.americanwest.com/pages/boone.htm>.

Goldman, Lisa. "Going West: The Cumberland Gap."

Monkeyshines on America Apr. 1999: 26.

Salas, Laura Purdie. The Wilderness Road, 1775.

Mankato: Bridgestone, 2003.

Sources are listed alphabetically by author.

Respond to the reading. After reading Lon's research report, answer the following questions about important traits of writing.

- **Ideas** (1) What did you learn from the report? List at least two facts.

- **Organization** (2) In your own words, what is the main point of each middle paragraph?

- **Voice** (3) Find a sentence that shows the writer is knowledgeable about the topic.

Prewriting

Before you start writing your report, you'll need to choose a topic, gather information about it, and make a writing plan. That's what prewriting is all about.

Keys to Prewriting

1. **Choose** an important person from history to write about.

2. **Make** a list of questions you want to answer about this person.

3. **Use** a gathering grid and note cards to collect information.

4. **Write** a thesis or focus statement that clearly gives the main idea.

5. **Create** an organized list of details.

Prewriting Selecting a Topic

One way to decide on a topic is to create a cluster. After reading about people from colonial times, Lon made the following cluster.

Cluster

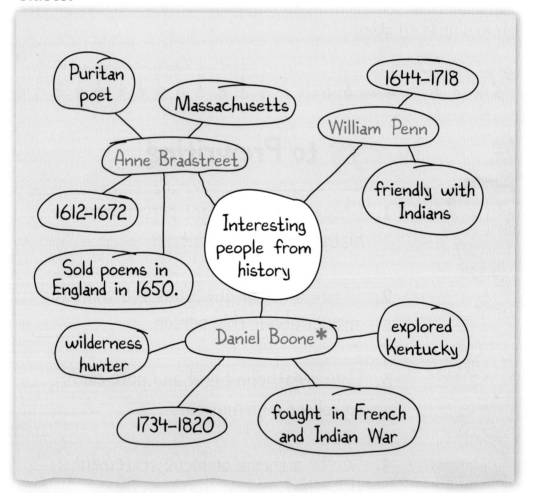

Prewrite

Create your cluster. Write "Interesting people from history" in the middle of a sheet of paper and circle it. Then add names of historical figures around it. List a few details about each person. Put a star (✳) next to the one who interests you the most.

Sizing Up Your Topic

You'll need information to write a report. You can begin by writing a list of questions you want to answer. If you can think of only one or two questions, your topic is too narrow. If you can think of lots of questions, your topic may be too broad. A topic with four or five key questions to answer is probably just right.

Too Broad

Daniel Boone

- Who was Daniel Boone?
- As a boy, how did he make friends with the Native Americans?
- What did he do in the French and Indian War?
- Why did he want to explore Kentucky?
- How did he start the Wilderness Road?
- Who did he marry, and who were his children?
- How did he help shape America?

Too Narrow

Boone and the Wilderness Road

- How did Boone start the Wilderness Road?
- How did that help shape America?

Just Right (Focused)

Boone's Kentucky Exploration

- Who was Daniel Boone?
- Why is he famous?
- Why did he explore Kentucky?
- What problems did he face?
- How did he help shape America?

Prewrite

Size up your topic. Write a list of questions you want to answer about your topic. Do you have the right number of questions for a research report?

Prewriting Using a Gathering Grid

Filling in a gathering grid is one way to collect and organize information for a report. Lon gathered details from three sources.

Gathering Grid

Daniel Boone	The Wilderness Road, 1775 (book)	"Going West: The Cumberland Gap" (magazine article)	"Daniel Boone" (Internet article)
Who was Daniel Boone?	Hunter and explorer who knew native ways		At 19, fought in the French and Indian War
Why is he famous?	Established Boonesborough	Blazed the Wilderness Road	See card 1.
Why did he explore Kentucky?	Loved the wilderness		Heard about it from a hunter
What problems did he face?	Many problems (See card 2.)		
How did he shape America?	Helped early Americans go west		
Other interesting facts		Wilderness Road crosses the Appalachians	Lived from 1734–1820; died in Missouri

Prewrite

Create a gathering grid. List your research questions (from page 343) on the left. Across the top, list your sources. Fill in the blocks with answers to your questions.

Creating Note Cards

If you have answers that are too long to fit on your gathering grid, you may write them on note cards. Number each card and write the research question at the top. Then write your answer. Your answer may be the exact words (a quotation) or information put into your own words (a paraphrase). At the bottom of the card, name your source. (Write the number of the card on your gathering grid.)

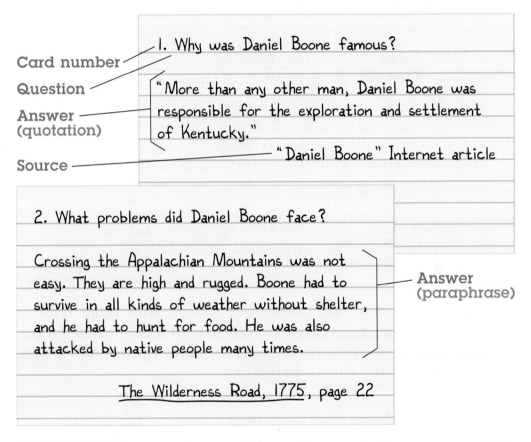

Card number — 1. Why was Daniel Boone famous?

Question

Answer (quotation) — "More than any other man, Daniel Boone was responsible for the exploration and settlement of Kentucky."

Source — "Daniel Boone" Internet article

2. What problems did Daniel Boone face?

Crossing the Appalachian Mountains was not easy. They are high and rugged. Boone had to survive in all kinds of weather without shelter, and he had to hunt for food. He was also attacked by native people many times. — Answer (paraphrase)

The Wilderness Road, 1775, page 22

 tip You must not copy any ideas and pretend they are yours. This is called *plagiarism,* and it is stealing.

 Prewrite **Create note cards.** Make note cards for answers that are too long to fit on your gathering grid.

Prewriting **Keeping Track of Your Sources**

It is important to give authors credit for information you use from their works. As you read and take notes, write down the publication information about each of your sources.

Books

Author (last name, first name). **Title** (underlined). **City** where the book was published: **Publisher, copyright date**.

> Salas, Laura Purdie. The Wilderness Road, 1775.
>   Mankato: Bridgestone, 2003.

Magazines

Author (last name, first name). **Article title** (in quotation marks). **Magazine title** (underlined) **Date** (day, month, year): **Page numbers** of the article.

> Goldman, Lisa. "Going West: The Cumberland Gap."
>   Monkeyshines on America Apr. 1999: 26.

Internet

Author, if available, (last name, first name). **Web page title**, if available, (in quotation marks). **Site title**, if known, (underlined). **Date posted**, or **updated**, (if available). **Date visited** (day, month, year). **<http://(as shown below)>**.

> Chinn, Col. George M. "Daniel Boone." 1996. 8 Oct. 2004
>   <http://www.americanwest.com/pages/boone.htm>.

Keep track of your sources. When you take notes from a source, write down the publication information for your works-cited page.

Organizing Ideas

Now that you've done your research, it's time to organize your ideas. Start by writing a thesis statement. Then arrange your details into an outline.

Writing Your Thesis Statement

Your thesis statement tells what your report is all about. A good thesis statement starts with an interesting topic and then focuses on an important detail about the topic.

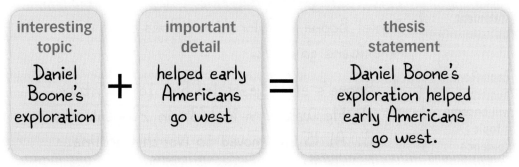

interesting topic		important detail		thesis statement
Daniel Boone's exploration	**+**	helped early Americans go west	**=**	Daniel Boone's exploration helped early Americans go west.

Thesis Statements

The English Quaker William Penn (an interesting topic) founded the Pennsylvania colony to provide religious and political freedom (an important detail).

Anne Bradstreet was a poet in the 1600s (an interesting topic) who wrote poems about family, women in those days, faith, and politics in Massachusetts (an important detail).

Prewrite

Create your thesis statement. Review your notes and write a thesis statement about the most important accomplishment of the person you will write about.

Prewriting **Making an Outline**

An outline is an organized list of the ideas in your report. Below is the first part of Lon's sentence outline. Notice how answers to his research questions are Roman numerals I. and II. and will become topic sentences in his report.

Sentence Outline

Thesis statement

THESIS STATEMENT:
Daniel Boone's exploration helped early Americans go west.

Each Roman numeral will become a topic sentence for a middle paragraph.

I. Boone's early years led him to adventure.
  A. He was born in 1734 in Pennsylvania.
  B. At 15, he moved to North Carolina.
  C. At 19, he fought in the French and Indian War.
  D. In the war, he met a hunter who told him about Kentucky.

The A. B. C. D. sentences will provide supporting details in each paragraph.

II. Boone is famous for exploring Kentucky.
  A. He hunted there.
  B. He led settlers through Cumberland Gap.
  C. They started Boonesborough.
  D. Their trail became the Wilderness Road.

Prewrite

Write your outline. Review your thesis statement. Then look at the details you've gathered and organize them into an outline. Each topic sentence should relate to your thesis statement.

Writing

Prewrite Revise Publish
Write Edit

Your planning is finished, and now you're ready to start writing! When you write your first draft, you put all your ideas on paper (or key them into the computer).

Keys to Writing

1. **Write** a strong first paragraph that gives your thesis statement.

2. **Start** each middle paragraph with an effective topic sentence.

3. **Organize** the supporting details in each middle paragraph.

4. **Write** a thoughtful ending paragraph that reminds the reader of your thesis.

5. **Cite** your sources on a works-cited page.

Writing **Starting Your Research Report**

The opening paragraph of your report should grab your reader's attention, introduce your topic, and present your thesis statement. Below are two possible ways to start a report about Daniel Boone.

Beginning

Middle

Ending

Beginning Paragraph

> **This paragraph begins with an interesting detail. It ends with the thesis statement.**
>
> Daniel Boone loved the wilderness. When he was young, he spent lots of time with Native Americans. Like them, he loved to hunt and live with nature. He also loved to explore. <u>Daniel Boone's exploration helped early Americans go west.</u>

> **This paragraph starts with a question. It ends with the thesis statement.**
>
> Would you like to live like Daniel Boone? Boone loved to live in the great outdoors. He spent a lot of time in the woods, hunting and exploring. <u>Daniel Boone's exploration helped early Americans go west.</u>

Write your opening paragraph. Write a beginning paragraph for your report. Use one of the examples above as a guide, or try an idea of your own.

Developing the Middle Part

Each of your middle paragraphs should have a topic sentence followed by details, facts, and examples that support the topic sentence.

Beginning

▶ Middle

Ending

Middle Paragraphs

The details in each paragraph support the topic sentences (underlined).

<u>Boone's early years were adventurous.</u> He was born in 1734 in the Pennsylvania colony, but when he was 15, his family moved to North Carolina. At 19, he fought in the French and Indian War. During the war, he met a man who had hunted in the area called Kentucky. Boone became interested in exploring that land (Chinn).

An exact quotation is put in quotation marks.

<u>Boone is famous for exploring Kentucky.</u> "More than any other man, Daniel Boone was responsible for the exploration and settlement of Kentucky" (Chinn). He made several trips there to hunt and explore. In 1775, Boone led 30 settlers over the Appalachian Mountains through the Cumberland Gap. There they started the settlement of Boonesborough. The trail they

Each source is cited (in parentheses).

made became known as the Wilderness Road (Goldman).

Final Middle Paragraph

> **Sentences lead naturally from one idea to the next.**

<u>Daniel Boone and his family soon learned that Kentucky was a beautiful but dangerous land.</u> Not only was it Native American hunting grounds, but also tribal war grounds. The settlers had to defend their families while trying to settle Kentucky. More than once the native people captured Boone, but he always escaped (Salas 16–24).

> **A specific example adds interest to the report.**

Citing Your Sources

You must always give credit for other people's ideas. As you write your research paper, be sure to do the following:

- **Set off exact words with quotation marks.**
  (See the second paragraph in the model on page 351.)

- **Add your sources in parentheses as you write your report.**
  (See author names in parentheses on page 351.)

- **List page numbers for information, if possible.**
  (See the last sentence in the paragraph above.)

- **Give the publication details on your works-cited page.**
  (See pages 340, 346, and 354.)

Write

Write your middle paragraphs. Use your outline as a guide when you write. Don't worry about getting everything perfect right now. Just get your main ideas down in writing.

Writing **Ending Your Report**

The ending paragraph should remind your reader about your thesis and bring your report to a close. To do this, try one or more of the following ideas.

- **Tell about the person's final years.**
- **Tell one last interesting fact about the person.**
- **Summarize the person's accomplishment or overall importance.**

Ending Paragraph

The ending sums up the person's final years.

The reader is reminded of the thesis (underlined).

> In 1792, Kentucky became a state, and many more people moved there. Daniel Boone said it was "too crowded," so he moved his family to West Virginia. Then he moved to the Missouri region, where he died and was buried in 1820. Later, the citizens requested that Boone's body be moved back to Kentucky <u>because he was their most important explorer</u> (Chinn).

Write your final paragraph. Use one of the three strategies above to write your ending paragraph.

Look over your draft. Read through your entire first draft. Did you include all the necessary details? Is your report well organized and easy to read? Review your notes and outline and write down changes you might want to make.

Writing **Creating Your Works-Cited Page**

While you were doing your research, you wrote down the important publication details of your sources. As you wrote your paper, you added source notes in parentheses. Now you can arrange all your sources in alphabetical order on a works-cited page at the end of your paper.

> **The title "Works Cited" is centered at the top of the page.**

> **Sources are listed alphabetically by author.**

Works Cited

Chinn, Col. George M. "Daniel Boone."
    1996. 8 Oct. 2004 <http://
    www.americanwest.com/pages/
    boone.htm>.
Goldman, Lisa. "Going West: The
    Cumberland Gap." Monkeyshines on
    America Apr. 1999: 26.
Salas, Laura Purdie. The Wilderness Road,
    1775. Mankato: Bridgestone, 2003.

Create your works-cited page. List the sources you used (in alphabetical order) on a separate page at the end of your report. Remember to center the title, "Works Cited," at the top. Indent the second, third, and fourth lines in each entry.

Revising

Revising may be the most important step in the writing process. When you revise, you check your report for *ideas*, *organization*, *voice*, *word choice*, and *sentence fluency*.

Keys to Revising

1. **Read** through your first draft to get an overall sense of your report.

2. **Review** each part carefully—the beginning, the middle, and the ending.

3. **Check** that your thesis statement contains the main idea.

4. **Be sure** the middle paragraphs contain details that support your main idea.

5. **Change** any parts that need improving.

Revising for Ideas

A research report should be based on facts. When revising, watch for general statements and unsupported opinions. Either remove them or replace them with strong, factual statements. In the example below, Lon made changes to make his report more factual.

Revising in Action

When Lon revised for ideas, he replaced a general sentence with a more detailed one. He also deleted an unsupported opinion.

Boone is famous for ~~helping to settle~~ exploring Kentucky. "More than any other man, Daniel Boone was responsible for the exploration and settlement of Kentucky" (Chinn). He made several trips there to hunt and explore. ~~He spent a lot of time there.~~ In 1775, Boone led 30 settlers over the Appalachian Mountains through the Cumberland Gap. There they started the settlement of Boonesborough. ~~I think they called it that because Boone wanted to be famous.~~ The trail they made . . .

Revise

Check for strong, factual statements. Could more facts be added to support your points? Should any opinions be deleted? Make changes to improve your paper.

Revising for Organization

Sometimes when you read your first draft, you realize that a sentence or two may be out of place. Sometimes an entire paragraph may need to be moved. When revising, you can move ideas or details to improve the organization of your report. That's what Lon did in the sample paragraph below.

Revising in Action

When Lon revised for organization, he moved several sentences and reworded several others to improve his report.

> In 1792, Kentucky became a state, and many more people moved there. ~~Boone went~~ to West Virginia. Daniel Boone said it was "too crowded," so he moved his family. Then he moved to the Missouri region, where he died and was buried in 1820. Later, the citizens requested that Boone's body be moved back to Kentucky because he was their most important explorer (Chinn).

Revise

Check your organization. Read your report for overall sense, and look for ideas and details that may need to be moved. Make any needed changes to improve the organization.

Revising **Using a Checklist**

Check your revising. Number a piece of paper from 1 to 8. If you can answer "yes" to a question, put a check mark after that number. If not, continue to work on that part of your report.

Ideas

_____ **1.** Have I written a clear thesis statement?

_____ **2.** Do my facts and details support my main points?

Organization

_____ **3.** Do I have a beginning, a middle, and an ending?

_____ **4.** Do I have a topic sentence for each paragraph?

Voice

_____ **5.** Do I sound knowledgeable and interested in the topic?

Word Choice

_____ **6.** Have I defined or explained any unfamiliar words?

Sentence Fluency

_____ **7.** Have I varied my sentence lengths?

_____ **8.** Have I varied my sentence beginnings?

Make a clean copy. When you have finished revising your report, make a clean copy for editing.

Editing

Editing becomes important after you've revised your first draft. When you edit, you make sure you have followed all punctuation, capitalization, spelling, and grammar rules.

Keys to Editing

1. **Use** a dictionary and the "Proofreader's Guide" in the back of this book for help.

2. **Edit** on a printed copy if you use a computer. Then make your changes on the computer.

3. **Double-check** your spelling, grammar, punctuation, and capitalization.

4. **Check** your report for proper formatting. (See pages 338–340)

Editing **Using a Checklist**

Edit

Check your editing. Number a piece of paper from 1 to 9. If you can answer "yes" to a question, put a check mark after that number. If not, continue to edit for that convention.

Conventions

PUNCTUATION

_____ **1.** Have I used the correct end punctuation after all my sentences?

_____ **2.** Have I used quotation marks correctly?

_____ **3.** Have I correctly punctuated my works-cited page?

CAPITALIZATION

_____ **4.** Have I started sentences with capital letters?

_____ **5.** Have I capitalized proper nouns and titles?

SPELLING

_____ **6.** Have I spelled all words correctly?

_____ **7.** Have I double-checked the spelling of all names?

GRAMMAR

_____ **8.** Have I used correct verb forms (*had gone*, not *had went*)?

_____ **9.** Do my subjects and verbs agree in number? (People were settling, not People was settling.)

Adding a Title

- Describe the main idea: **Leading Americans West**
- Be creative: **A Boone to America's Growth**
- Borrow words from the paper: **Daniel Boone, the Explorer**

Publishing

Prewrite • Write • Revise • Edit • Publish ✓

You worked hard on your report. Be sure to share the results with family and friends.

Presentation

- Use black or blue ink and double-space the entire paper.
- Leave a one-inch margin on all four sides of your paper.
- Write your name, your teacher's name, the class, and the date in the upper left corner of page 1.
- Skip a line and center your title. Skip another line and start your report.
- Write your last name and the page number in the upper right corner of every page of your report.

Prepare an Electronic Presentation

Create a computer slide show of your report. (See "Multimedia Presentations" on pages 363–367 for more information.)

Develop an Illustrated Report

Draw a picture to illustrate the main point or make a time line that shows important dates.

Go Online

Visit **www.thewritesource.com** for information about publishing your writing online.

Publish

Make a final copy. Follow your teacher's instructions or use the guidelines above. (If you are using a computer, see pages 44–46.) Prepare a clean final copy of your research report.

Reflecting on Your Writing

After your research report is finished, complete the starter sentences below.

When you think about your writing, you will see how you are growing as a writer.

My Research Report

1. The best part of my research report is . . .

2. The most challenging part of writing the report was . . .

3. The main thing I learned about writing a report is . . .

4. The next time I write a research report, I would like to . . .

Research Writing
Multimedia Presentations

What is a multimedia presentation? Since *multimedia* means "more than one form of communication," this kind of report shares information in several different ways. With the help of a computer, you can prepare a multimedia report using your voice, pictures, sounds, and the printed word. Think of it as a speech with a slide show on the side.

In this chapter, you will learn how to prepare a multimedia presentation using a report you have already written.

Mini Index

- **Getting Started**
- **Presentation Checklist**

Getting Started

For your multimedia presentation, use an essay, speech, or report you've already written. Then you can focus on finding the right words to say and the best pictures and graphics to use as slides.

Some computer programs allow you to make slides. If you need help figuring out how to do it, ask a friend or your teacher.

Get organized. Make sure the computer you use has the right software. Then select an essay, speech, or report to present.

Creating the Slides

1 **Find the main ideas in your report.**

Each main idea should have its own slide. Make up a storyboard plan for your presentation, as shown on page 366.

2 **Find pictures and sounds for each slide.**

Look for pictures and sounds in your software program or on the Internet. (You can also create your own pictures and sounds.)

Gather your thoughts. Make a cluster like the one below for each slide. Write the main idea in the middle and add your picture and sound ideas around it.

3 Design your slides.

Select fonts that are easy to read. Use the same fonts and some of the same colors on all your slides to tie your presentation together.

4 Build your slides one by one.

Arrange the words and pictures so that each slide is attractive and easy to understand.

Improving Your Presentation

When you make your presentation, you will read your report aloud and use the computer at the same time. Practice moving from slide to slide until you can do it smoothly.

Rehearse your presentation. Practice your presentation in front of friends and family. Ask for suggestions to make it better. Change any parts that are unclear.

It is also important that your slides are free of careless errors. You may ask an adult or a classmate to help you check your slides.

Make corrections. Check each slide for spelling, punctuation, grammar, and capitalization errors. Practice going through your presentation a few times to make sure it runs smoothly.

Giving a Multimedia Presentation

Reading your report and showing your slides to the class will be like giving a speech. See the chapter on "Giving Speeches" (pages 373–378) for valuable information about speaking to groups.

Present your report. Before you begin, take a deep breath and relax. Enjoy giving the presentation you've worked so hard to prepare.

Multimedia Presentation Storyboard

This is a storyboard plan for the report "Daniel Boone, the Explorer" on pages **338–340**. Each box stands for one slide in the presentation.

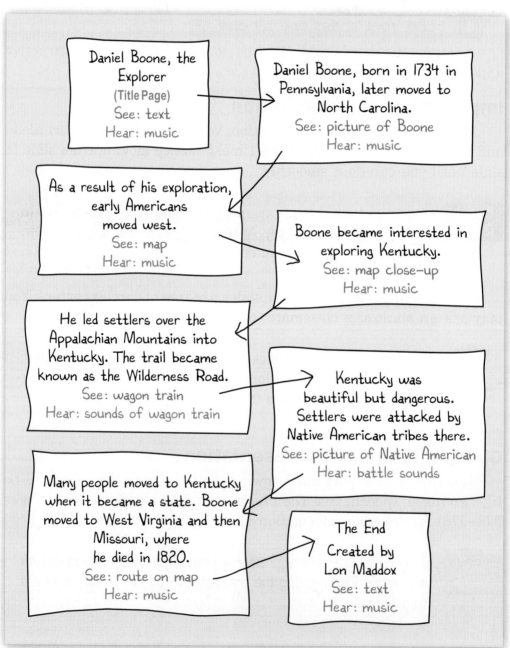

Daniel Boone, the Explorer
(Title Page)
See: text
Hear: music

Daniel Boone, born in 1734 in Pennsylvania, later moved to North Carolina.
See: picture of Boone
Hear: music

As a result of his exploration, early Americans moved west.
See: map
Hear: music

Boone became interested in exploring Kentucky.
See: map close-up
Hear: music

He led settlers over the Appalachian Mountains into Kentucky. The trail became known as the Wilderness Road.
See: wagon train
Hear: sounds of wagon train

Kentucky was beautiful but dangerous. Settlers were attacked by Native American tribes there.
See: picture of Native American
Hear: battle sounds

Many people moved to Kentucky when it became a state. Boone moved to West Virginia and then Missouri, where he died in 1820.
See: route on map
Hear: music

The End
Created by Lon Maddox
See: text
Hear: music

Presentation Checklist

Use the following checklist to make sure your presentation is the best it can be. When you can answer all ten of the questions with a "yes," you're ready to present!

Ideas

_____ **1.** Have I chosen an interesting speech or report for my presentation?

Organization

_____ **2.** Have I introduced my topic clearly in the beginning?
_____ **3.** Have I included the main points in the middle part?
_____ **4.** Have I ended with a summary or final thought?

Voice

_____ **5.** Do I show interest in my topic?
_____ **6.** Does my voice fit my audience and topic?

Word and Multimedia Choices

_____ **7.** Are the words on my slides accurate and easy to read?
_____ **8.** Have I chosen interesting pictures and sounds?

Presentation Fluency

_____ **9.** Does my presentation move smoothly from one slide to the next?

Conventions

_____ **10.** Is my presentation free of punctuation, capitalization, spelling, and grammar errors?

Speaking and Writing to Learn

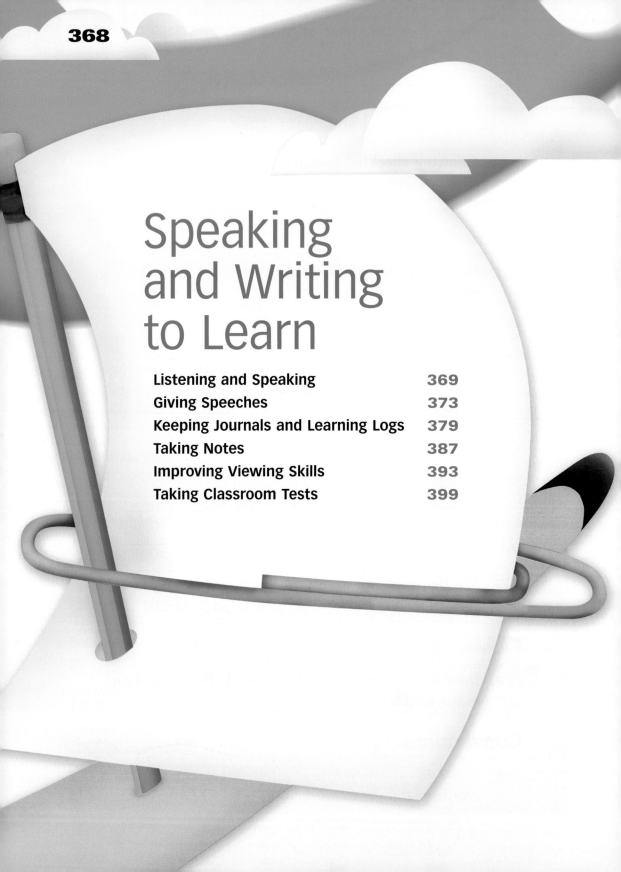

Listening and Speaking

Did you know that listening and hearing are not the same? You can hear someone without really listening to the person. When you listen, you think about what is being said. Listening is essential to doing well in school.

Speaking is also important. In school, you must ask and answer questions, give reports, and work in groups. This chapter can help you improve your listening and speaking skills.

Mini Index

Listening in Class

Listening is more than just hearing someone talk. It's also thinking about what is being said. In fact, listening is one of the best ways to learn. The following tips will help you become a better listener.

1 **Know your purpose for listening.** Are you getting directions for a science project? Are you learning about an important time in history? Are you reviewing for a test?

2 **Take notes.** Think about what the speaker is saying. List key ideas in your notebook. Write down questions about things you don't understand.

3 **Ask questions.** Ask questions about specific ideas or concepts. But wait until the speaker is finished before you ask your questions.

Note Taking in Action

When you take notes, write down the main ideas in your own words. See pages **387–392** for more information.

Sample Notes

Kitchen Science   Mar. 8

What does the salt in our ice-cream maker do?
- Salt lowers the freezing point of water to about 28°.
- The mixture of water and ice stays colder than 32° so milk and cream can freeze.

How much salt is needed?

Participating in a Group

When you work in a group, you must cooperate with others to solve a problem or reach a goal. Two important parts of cooperation are respecting yourself and respecting others.

Skills for Cooperating

In a group, you respect yourself when you . . .

- know that your own ideas are important.
- share your ideas with the group.
- ask questions if you don't understand something.

In a group, you respect others when you . . .

- listen carefully.
- pay attention to others' opinions.
- take turns speaking or asking questions.
- avoid personal criticism.
- praise the ideas of others.
- encourage everyone to participate.

Listening and cooperating are key people skills.

Practice

Read the following situations. For each one, decide which of the skills listed above would help the group work together more effectively.

Situation 1

Someone else in the group said something that you didn't understand. Now others are discussing it, and you're totally lost.

Situation 2

One member of your group sits quietly and listens to the others. She never says what she thinks or asks a question.

Speaking in Class

Speaking in class is an important classroom activity. The guidelines listed below will help you and your classmates become better classroom speakers.

Pay attention. Listen to what others are saying and stay on the topic being discussed.

Be respectful. Respond politely to what others say.

Make eye contact. Look at the person you are speaking to.

Wait your turn. Show respect for others by not interrupting.

Get to the point. State your ideas briefly and clearly.

> Hey, mates! Think before you speak so you're sure that you have something important to say.

Play "Pass It On." The following game requires you to listen and speak carefully.

1 The class is divided into rows containing the same number of students. Then the teacher whispers a sentence to the first person in each row.

2 When the teacher says, "Start," the first person in each row whispers the sentence to the next person in the row. That person whispers the sentence to the next person until it reaches the last person in the row.

3 The last person in the row goes to the board and writes the sentence the way that he or she heard it.

4 The first row to write the sentence exactly as the teacher whispered it, wins.

Giving Speeches

When you get really excited about something, you probably want to tell someone about it. Your latest interest—the secret lives of frogs, the mysterious Russian princess Anastasia, or the wonders of cyberspace—is a great topic for a speech. Your enthusiasm will capture your listeners and take them into the world of your favorite subject.

In this chapter, you will learn how to give an informative speech. You will find tips on how to plan your speech, use visual aids, and keep your listeners' attention.

Mini Index

- **Preparing Your Speech**
- **Organizing an Informative Speech**
- **Giving Your Speech**

Preparing Your Speech

If you want to give an informative speech that will interest your audience, choose a topic that you know something about. You could use an expository essay that you've already written as a starting point for your speech. Here's how to rewrite your essay into a speech.

Rewriting in Action

Below is the opening of the original essay "Food for Everybody" (pages 145–146). Notice that the new beginning (on gold paper) adds drama and a surprising twist to grab the audience's attention.

Original Essay

Kids are always saying, "I'm starving!" They probably hope to get some potato chips or oatmeal cookies. Mom may give them apples or oranges. All of these foods come from plants, but where do plants get their food? Plants actually make their own food through a process called photosynthesis.

Speech

Have you ever walked into your house yelling, "I'm starving"? Does your mom jump up and get you a bowl of chips or a plate of chocolate-chip cookies? Or does she bring out something good for you, like fruit or carrot sticks? Worse yet, does she tell you to wait for supper? If you were a plant, you could do something about it. You could make your own food.

Photosynthesis is the amazing process in plants . . .

Rework your beginning. Choose an essay that you would like to present as an informative speech. Rewrite your opening to add drama and grab your audience's attention.

Organizing an Informative Speech

The next step is to select interesting details from your essay and prepare a set of note cards for your speech. Note cards are easy to handle and will help you stay organized as you are speaking. It's also a good idea to write out your beginning and ending word for word. For the details in between, use sentences or short phrases.

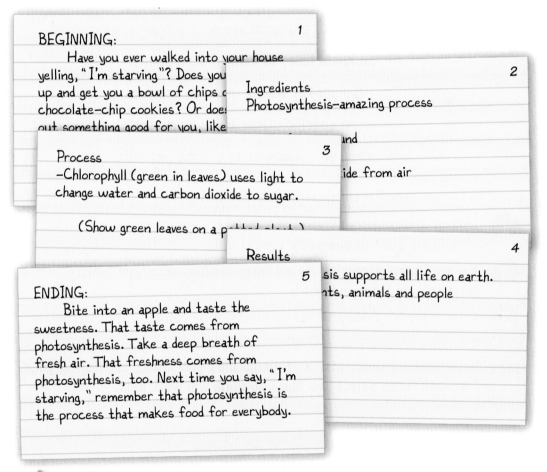

1

BEGINNING:
Have you ever walked into your house yelling, "I'm starving"? Does you up and get you a bowl of chips c chocolate-chip cookies? Or doe: out something good for you, like

2

Ingredients
Photosynthesis—amazing process

3

Process
—Chlorophyll (green in leaves) uses light to change water and carbon dioxide to sugar.

(Show green leaves on a p

nd

ide from air

4

Results

sis supports all life on earth.
nts, animals and people

5

ENDING:
Bite into an apple and taste the sweetness. That taste comes from photosynthesis. Take a deep breath of fresh air. That freshness comes from photosynthesis, too. Next time you say, "I'm starving," remember that photosynthesis is the process that makes food for everybody.

Create your note cards. Look over the note cards on this page. Then create a note card for each step in your speech. Include a beginning and an ending that your listeners will remember. (Be sure to add notes to yourself about visual aids.)

Using Visual Aids

You have written the beginning and prepared your note cards from your essay. Now you are ready to plan a few visual aids for your speech. Visual aids, like the ones listed below, will help your listeners *see* what you're talking about.

Posters	show words, pictures, or both.
Photographs	help your audience see what you are talking about.
Charts	compare ideas or explain main points.
Transparencies	highlight key words, ideas, or graphics.
Maps	show specific places being discussed.
Objects	allow your audience to see the real thing.

Here are some tips for preparing your visual aids.

1. **Make them big.** The people in the back of the room should be able to see your visual aids.

2. **Keep them simple.** Avoid long sentences. Short labels, pictures, and graphs work best.

3. **Use a good design.** Make visual aids colorful and attractive.

 List visual aids. List four visual aids you could use during your speech. Then select two that you think will work best.

Potted plant	to point out green leaves
Poster	diagram of the process of photosynthesis
Drawing	a leaf cell

Giving Your Speech

After you have planned your whole speech and outlined it on note cards, there are just two things left to do: Practice your speech and present it.

Practicing Your Delivery

Practice your speech several times, using the following tips and the checklist at the bottom of the page.

- Find a quiet place where you can listen to your own voice.
- Practice in front of friends or parents. Ask for suggestions.
- If possible, videotape or tape-record yourself.

Presenting Your Speech

When you give your speech, remember the following:

- Take a deep breath and relax.
- Look at your audience, or just over their heads.
- Stand up straight.
- Speak loudly, clearly, and slowly.

Using a Checklist

Use the following checklist as a guide when you practice your speech. Others can also use this list to give you comments.

_____ **1.** I have good posture, and I look relaxed.

_____ **2.** I look at my audience as I speak.

_____ **3.** My voice can be heard at the back of the room.

_____ **4.** I sound interested in my topic.

_____ **5.** I am not speaking too fast.

_____ **6.** I avoid "stalling" words like *um, er,* and *like.*

_____ **7.** My visual aids are large and easy to understand.

_____ **8.** I point out information on my visual aids.

SPEAKING TIPS

Before your speech . . .

- **Get everything organized.**
  Put the main points of your speech on note cards and make your visual aids.
- **Time your speech.**
  Read your note cards out loud. If your speech is too short or too long, add or remove details to adjust the length.
- **Practice.**
  The more you remember without looking at your notes, the easier it will be to give your speech.

During your speech . . .

- **Speak loudly.** Be sure that everyone can hear you.
- **Speak clearly and slowly.**
  Don't hurry through your speech.
- **Look at your audience.** Connect with your listeners.
- **Put visual aids where everyone can see them.**
  Point out the things that you are talking about.

After your speech . . .

- **Answer questions.**
  Ask if anyone has questions about your topic.
- **Collect materials.**
  Gather your visual aids and note cards and return to your seat.

Practice and present. Practice your speech one more time with a friend or family member. After you present your speech in the classroom, listen for suggestions from your teacher or classmates.

Keeping Journals and Learning Logs

When you *surf* through the channels on your TV, does it ever remind you of the way your brain works? If you're like most students, ideas jump around in your head all day. At the end of the day, it's sometimes hard to remember all the things you've thought about.

Writing regularly in a personal journal can be a good way to explore and sort out your personal thoughts. In the same way, writing in a learning log can be a good way to make sense of your schoolwork. The following activities will help you sharpen your mind and become a better writer.

Mini Index

- **Keeping a Personal Journal**
- **Writing in Other Journals**
- **Writing in a Learning Log**
- **Writing-to-Learn Activities**

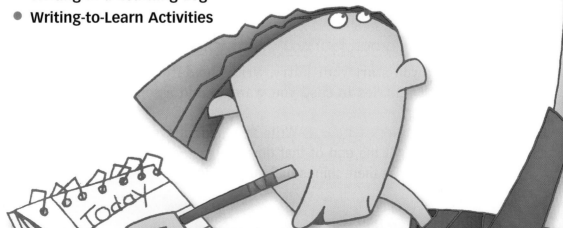

Keeping a Personal Journal

A personal journal is a place to explore your thoughts, feelings, and experiences. In your journal, you become the author of your own life story. You can write about your adventures, surprises, disappointments, friendships, and other personal experiences.

Getting Started

Follow these steps to get started with your own personal journal.

1 Collect the right tools.

All you really need is a notebook and a pen or pencil. You could also keep a file for your journal on a computer or print out pages to make into a book.

2 Choose a special place and time to write.

Write early in the morning if you have time before school. Or find a quiet corner where you can write after dinner. Set aside a time that works for you.

3 Write for at least 5 to 10 minutes every day.

Stay in the habit of writing every day, even if you sometimes write only a sentence or two.

4 Write about your day.

Write about what happened during the day or whatever you think is important—little things or big things.

5 Keep your journal organized.

Before you start your entry, write the date. Skip a line or two between the entries in case you want to add a comment later.

 Start your journal. Write in a journal every day for at least two weeks. At the end of that time, go back and read through what you wrote. Are there things that surprise you?

Journal Entries

In the journal entries below, a student wrote about his first two days in a new school. At one point, he went back to an earlier entry and added a comment in parentheses.

Wed., Sept. 1

Mom dropped me off at Lincoln School this morning. I was scared because I didn't know anyone. My classroom was near the school office, so at least I didn't get lost.

A boy named Manny asked about my soccer jersey. I told him I wasn't really a fan of that team, but I collect soccer shirts because it's my favorite sport.

(I didn't have to be scared about not knowing anyone—I think Manny will be my friend.)

Thurs., Sept. 2

Today, a few kids on the bus asked where I came from. When I said Minnesota, they asked if it is cold there now. Some of them have never seen snow except in the mountains.

I learned that my science teacher trained as an astronaut. I think I'm going to like his class.

Sometimes it helps to ask yourself questions when you write. What did I learn at that time? How do I feel now?

Writing in Other Journals

Writing in a personal journal and other types of journals is a good way to explore your thoughts and experiences. Here are three more journals you can try.

Specialized Journal

A specialized journal is a place to write about an ongoing event or experience, like participating in a sport or working on a group project. Write about your thoughts as you face new challenges or learn new skills.

Travel Journal

In a travel journal, you can write about your impressions as you travel from one place to another. Or you can make entries at the end of each day.

Reader-Response Journal

In a reader-response journal, you write about how you feel about the books you are reading. Answer the following questions to help you write about literature.

1. How do you feel about the book after reading the beginning? The middle? The ending?

2. Do you think the book is funny? Sad? Surprising?

3. Have you learned anything new? Does the story connect with your life?

4. What do you like about the way the book is written?

5. Would you recommend this book to others? Why? Why not?

Write in a reader-response journal. The next time you read a story or a book, write your thoughts in a journal. You can use the five questions above and add some of your own.

Writing in a Learning Log

In a learning log, you write down your thoughts and questions about the subjects you are studying, like math, science, social studies, and language arts. Here are some tips.

1   **Set up a learning log for any subject.**
Learning logs can help you better understand all your subjects, especially those that are hardest for you.

2   **Keep your logs organized.**
Use a separate notebook for each subject. Date each entry and leave room for information that you may add later (shown in red below).

3   **Make drawings and charts.**
Diagrams and pictures can help you understand ideas.

4   **Write freely about these types of ideas:**
- an assignment or class presentation
- questions about things you don't understand
- new information

Math Class   Sept. 13

   Estimating the Sum of Large Numbers
Steps:
     1. Round the numbers
     2. Add the rounded numbers
Here's how I would estimate the sum of 245,592 and 638,340.
   The first number would round up to 246,000, and the second would round down to 638,000. The rounded sum would be 884,000.

Social Studies Log

Learning logs work for any subject. In the sample below, a student wrote about an idea introduced in her social studies class. Writing about it helped the student explore her thoughts and feelings about this idea.

Social Studies   Sept. 17

Pre-Columbian America

Today we talked about the Native Americans who lived in America before the Europeans came. Movies I've seen about Indians always showed them riding horses and living in tepees. In the winter, it must've gotten really cold if the fire went out, and the cold air came in the hole in the top of the tepee. I guess only tribes on the Great Plains lived that way.

Some Native Americans of the Southwest lived in cliffs and adobe houses. Living in places you could only get to by ropes or ladders would be like living on an island and having to get there by boat.

Tribes in the Northwest and east of the Mississippi River built shelters, like wigwams, that stayed in one place.

Wigwam

Log on in math or social studies. On your own paper, name the subject of the unit you are now studying in social studies. Then write a learning-log entry about something in the unit that you find interesting, surprising, or confusing.

Writing-to-Learn Activities

There are many ways to write in a learning log. Three basic ways are described below, and three other ways are listed on the next page.

The Basic Three

Freewriting Writing freely in your learning log allows your ideas to flow from your mind to the paper. You don't have to worry about correct spelling and punctuation—just keep writing until you run out of information.

Clustering Making a cluster helps you see how all your ideas fit together. Place the name of the subject you are studying in the middle of a page and circle it. Around the subject, write words and phrases about it. Circle each word or phrase and draw a line connecting it to the closest related idea. (See page **456**.)

Listing Listing shows how ideas relate to each other. As you think about a subject, make a list of your ideas, feelings, and questions.

Health Class   Oct. 4

Avoiding In-Line Skating Injuries
- wrist, elbow, knee, head injuries
  (from most common to least common)
- Why are wrist injuries more common than elbow injuries?
- Rigid wrist guards protect from scrapes, sprains, and breaks.
- Padded guards protect knees and elbows.
- Helmets protect from head injuries.

Practice

Make a list like the one above for a subject you are studying in one of your classes. *Remember:* Write the subject and date at the top of your list. Keep listing until you run out of ideas.

More Writing-to-Learn Activities

Here are three more ways to write in your learning log. Each one can be used to help you learn by writing.

Nutshelling When you put something *in a nutshell,* you say it in the fewest words possible. After a lesson, demonstration, or experiment is over, try to write the main idea in one sentence.

> The heart pumps all the blood in the body through a big circle of arteries, capillaries, and veins.

Predicting Stop at a key point in a book or lesson and write what you think will happen next. This is a good learning-log activity for a science lesson.

Dialoguing In this writing-to-learn activity, you write an imaginary conversation between yourself and a person from history. In the following entry, Tanya created a conversation between herself and the English doctor William Harvey.

Tanya: Dr. Harvey, did you discover blood circulation all by yourself?

Dr. Harvey: No, Tanya, I knew that a Muslim doctor named Ibn Nafis had the idea almost 400 years ago. I simply used science to prove it.

Tanya: Why did it take so long to find the truth?

Dr. Harvey: Doctors thought that the dark blood in the veins came from the liver and the bright red blood came from the heart. Now we know that the same blood moves in a circle through the body. It changes color as it moves.

Practice

Write a dialogue between you and a person you have learned about recently. In your writing, ask some questions about the important ideas or events this person has experienced.

Taking Notes

Think about the new ideas and information that you hear every day in school. Teachers tell you how to write clearly, how to make graphs, and how to stay healthy. Wouldn't it be nice if you could put all that knowledge into your backpack and take it home?

If you take good notes in your classes, you can do just that. As you move up through the grades, taking notes will become more and more important.

Mini Index

- **Taking Classroom Notes**
- **Taking Reading Notes**

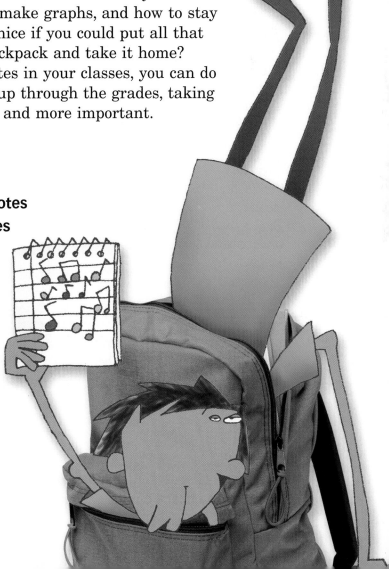

Taking Classroom Notes

Taking good notes in your classes will make you a better student. It will help you in three ways:

- Taking notes helps you pay attention.
- Reading over notes helps you understand information.
- Studying notes helps you remember information.

Guidelines for Taking Good Notes

These guidelines will help you improve your note-taking skills.

Listen carefully!
1. Pay close attention.
2. Write down information that the teacher puts on the board or on an overhead projector.

Summarize!
1. Write down only the important ideas.
2. Draw pictures if they help you understand the ideas.

Get organized!
1. Write the subject and date at the top of each page of notes.
2. Use numbers to organize your notes (1, 2, 3).
3. Check your notes and recopy anything that is hard to read.

Take class notes. Use the guidelines above the next time you take notes. Also check out the sample set of notes on the next page.

Setting Up Your Notes

Taking notes in two columns can help you organize information. Draw a line down the page that makes the left column narrower than the right column. Write key ideas on the left and related details on the right. You can also add illustrations, questions, or comments.

Science   Water   March 5

vapor	– evaporated water – moves in air (clouds, fog)

liquid	– freshwater (rain)
	   • limited resource
	   • valuable
	– salt water
	   • most of earth's water
	   • covers 70% of earth

solid	– ice (hail, snow)

cloud   condensation: when vapor
                turns to a liquid
↑ evaporation ↓ precipitation
(vapor)   (rain, snow, sleet, hail)

water

Review your notes. After you take notes, check them to be sure that they are clear and complete. Add any comments or drawings that will help you understand the material, like the diagram shown above.

Taking Reading Notes

Taking notes will help you understand what you read. Keep your notebook handy whenever you read an assignment so you can write down key ideas and details. Here are some tips to follow.

Preview the Assignment

Skim the assignment to see what it is about. You can get clues from . . .

- **titles,**
- **headings,** and
- **graphics.**

Take Notes

As you read, write down . . .

- **key ideas** and headings,
- **details** about the key ideas,
- **information** shown on charts and other graphics,
- **new words** that you may have to look up later, and
- **questions** about things that you don't understand.

Organize Your Thoughts

Add visual aids to your notes by drawing . . .

- **diagrams,**
- **charts,** or
- **graphic organizers** (see pages 456–457).

Practice

Select a chapter that you haven't studied yet in one of your textbooks. Skim the chapter, using the "Preview the Assignment" guidelines above. Then read the first two pages and take notes.

Using a 5 W's Organizer

Many reading assignments are about important people and events in history. You can take notes on this type of information by making a **5 W's organizer**. The 5 W's *(who? what? when? where? why?)* are listed across the top of the chart so that the details can be written below.

Read the following paragraph. Then look at the 5 W's chart to see how the information is listed.

Francisco Vásquez de Coronado

In 1540, the Spanish government sent the explorer Coronado on a mission from Mexico to the area that is now Arizona and New Mexico. He was supposed to find the Seven Golden Cities of Cibola. After exploring the area for many months, he returned to Mexico in 1542.

---

5 W's Chart

Who?	What?	When?	Where?	Why?
– Coronado – explorer	– sent on a mission by Spanish government	– 1540 to 1542	– area that is now Arizona and New Mexico	– to find the Seven Golden Cities of Cibola

Practice

Read the following paragraph. Then create a 5 W's organizer for the information in the paragraph.

Tecumseh

Tecumseh was the chief of the Shawnee Indian tribes. He wanted to stop the white settlers from taking Native American land east of the Mississippi River. To gain power, he joined his tribes to the British forces in the War of 1812.

Using a Venn Diagram

A **Venn diagram** is a graphic organizer you can use to take notes on the similarities and differences between two subjects. To make the diagram, draw two circles side by side that overlap in the center.

Read the following comparison-contrast paragraph about paper wasps and honeybees. Then look at how the similarities and differences are listed in the Venn diagram below.

> The slender paper wasp is often brown with yellow markings and can sting many times. It kills many garden pests to feed its young. The plump honeybee is yellow with black stripes and can sting only once. It gathers nectar for its young and pollinates flowers, which helps gardeners.

Venn Diagram

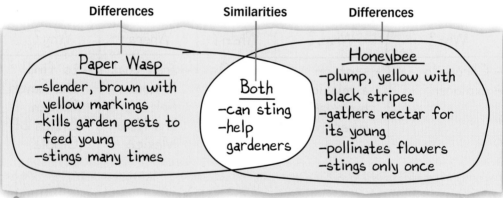

Differences   **Similarities**   **Differences**

Paper Wasp
- slender, brown with yellow markings
- kills garden pests to feed young
- stings many times

Both
- can sting
- help gardeners

Honeybee
- plump, yellow with black stripes
- gathers nectar for its young
- pollinates flowers
- stings only once

Create a Venn diagram. Take notes on the following paragraph, using a Venn diagram like the one above.

People say that you can't compare apples to oranges because they are two different types of fruit. Still, they are interesting to compare. Apples usually have smooth, shiny skin that is red, yellow, or green in color. Oranges have bumpy orange skin. Apple seeds are in the core of the apple, while orange seeds are in the segments. Apples grow in temperate climates, but oranges need tropical weather. Both apples and oranges are crushed to make fruit juice.

Improving Viewing Skills

Health officials are worried that television is turning everyone into *couch potatoes*—people who sit around without exercising their bodies. However, it may be just as harmful for people to watch television without exercising their minds. What you see on television affects what you know, what you believe, and what you buy.

Viewing is *listening* with your eyes. Like listening, viewing isn't complete until your brain becomes part of the process. This chapter will help you become a better viewer.

Mini Index

- **Watching the News**
- **Watching Television Specials**
- **Being Aware of Commercials**
- **Viewing Web Sites**

Watching the News

Remember that you are seeing the news on television through someone else's eyes. The people who put together the news program decide what you will hear and see. When you watch the news, pay attention to completeness, correctness, and balance.

1 Completeness: Are you getting enough information?

A news story should answer the 5 W's and H about an event.

Who?   *Why?*   *When?*

Astronomers searching for other worlds recently

What?   *Where?*

have found 125 planets in other solar systems.

How?

The astronomers used improved telescopes to conduct their search.

2 Correctness: Are you sure of the facts?

When reporters aren't sure they have all the facts, they may use wording like the blue part of this sentence:

According to some sources in Washington, the United States has been selected to host the 2016 Olympics.

3 Balance: Are both sides of the story fairly represented?

A newscast should tell the whole story, not just one side of it.

According to one city alderperson, we don't really need a new stoplight at the corner of Fifth and Main. He says that intersection just isn't that busy.

(The camera shows very little traffic at 2:00 p.m. But what about just before or after school?)

Respond to a newscast. The next time you watch a newscast, write down phrases that tell you the reporters don't have all the facts. (See number 2 above.)

Watching Television Specials

A television special is a program that gives information about one topic. Here is a plan to help you learn from television specials.

Before Viewing . . .
- Think about what you already know about the topic.
- Write down questions about it.

During Viewing . . .
- Watch and listen for the answers to your questions.
- Take a few notes. Write down key facts.
- Watch for completeness, correctness, and balance. (See page 394.)

After Viewing . . .
- Compare notes with someone else who saw the special.
- Write about the program in your learning log.

Notes from TV special about aardvarks   Dec. 17

All I knew about aardvarks was from my old coloring book, "A is for . . ." Now I know they look like giant rats with anteater faces. The name aardvark means "earth pig." Aardvarks live in Africa and can grow to more than seven feet long. They have thick skin, weak eyes, and good hearing. They claw insect mounds open and get the termites out with their 12-inch-long, sticky tongues.

Respond to a TV special. Write a learning-log entry about a television special. Write about what you find most surprising or most interesting.

Thinking About What You Watch

Watching television can be fun and relaxing. But it is also important to think about what you're watching.

Is it fact or opinion? A newsperson, an actor, or an athlete may present an opinion on television as if it were a fact. He or she may say, "This is the best deodorant on the market." Don't assume that this person is an expert just because he or she is famous.

Is it real or staged? Documentaries show you what *may* have happened during an event such as the sinking of the *Titanic*. Film taken during an actual event will be used if it's available. Otherwise, scenes are created. Pay careful attention. Try to tell what is real and what is re-created.

Is it exaggerated? Remember that television shows are meant to entertain you. Even serious shows may exaggerate emergencies or car chases. Although those look real, they often aren't. For example, you may have seen a car jumping a river. In real life, the car would have crashed and injured the driver.

Is it showing a stereotype? A stereotype is a kind of prejudice. It is saying that what is true for one person in a group is true for all. Here is an example of a stereotype:

Girls can't throw a ball very well, so they shouldn't play softball.

While some girls may not throw a ball very well, most girls have strong throwing arms. Watch out for stereotypes on television. Don't judge anyone or anything based on a stereotype.

 Log your viewing. Make entries in your learning log the next time you watch TV. Try to record one example of each of the following:

1 An opinion that is stated as a fact
2 A situation that is staged so that it looks real
3 A situation that is exaggerated
4 A character that is stereotyped

Being Aware of Commercials

Television commercials have only one purpose—to get you to buy things. Here are five common selling methods:

Selling Methods	On Television	In Real Life
1 Slice of Life looks like everyday life.	A happy family is having breakfast. They're all eating Chocobits cereal.	Actors are being paid to look happy. They may never eat Chocobits cereal.
2 Famous Faces shows a celebrity using a product.	Your favorite athlete is shown drinking Energy Aid during the big game.	This person gets paid and may never really use the product.
3 Just the Facts focuses on a fact about the product.	Big Red apples are cholesterol free. (or) These cookies are fat free!	All fruit is cholesterol free. The cookies are high in sugar.
4 Problem-Solution shows a product solving a problem.	A student hates homework until she gets a new computer program.	Very few problems can be fixed just by buying something.
5 Infomercial looks like a talk show or documentary.	One kitchen gadget does everything.	The gadget may not do anything very well.

Create a commercial. Invent a product that you would like to sell. Using one of the techniques above, write a television commercial for your product. Read it aloud to a classmate.

Viewing Web Sites

People are spending more and more time on the Web or Internet. Like watching television, viewing the Internet requires some thinking. To be a smart viewer, you should think about the following questions:

Is the information balanced or biased?

Let's say that you want to compare a fast-food diet to a vegetarian diet. You could get balanced information from government and university Web sites. But information from fast-food companies or vegetarian organizations may be biased (presenting just one side of the issue).

Is the information from an expert source?

If you're writing a report on hurricanes, a Web site published by the National Weather Service will have information that you can trust. A personal Web site containing a story about a hurricane would probably not be so dependable.

Is the site up-to-date?

Information changes. Many Web sites are updated daily or weekly. Other sites have information that is too old to be useful. Look for sites that tell you when information was updated.

How does the information compare to other sources?

When you search the Web, look at several sites and at information in a book or magazine. Comparing these sources helps you check for accuracy. Give credit to any sources you use. (See page 346.)

Check out the Web. Find out about a place you would like to visit by searching the Web. Look for sites that seem to be good sources of information. How do you know these sites are reliable?

Taking Classroom Tests

How is taking a test like climbing a mountain? They are both easier if you prepare ahead of time. Experienced climbers know that they must prepare their bodies and gather their supplies long before they head up the mountain. The same thing is true for taking a classroom test.

The first step in preparing for a test is to keep up with your daily work. Then, if you remember some helpful tips, you'll do your very best!

Mini Index

- Preparing for a Test
- Taking Objective Tests
- Responding to Writing Prompts

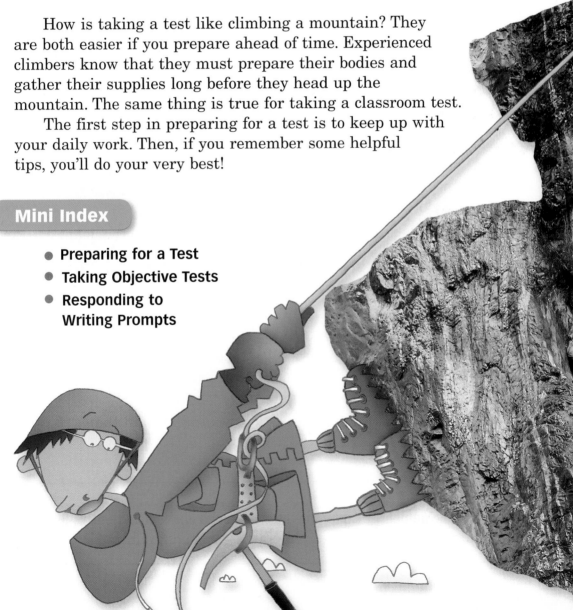

Preparing for a Test

When your teacher announces a test, prepare for it by using the guidelines below:

Ask questions. Ask your teacher . . .
- What will be covered on the test?
- What kind of test will it be? (Multiple-choice? True/False? Writing prompts?)

Review. Use your time wisely . . .
- Begin reviewing as soon as your teacher announces the test.
- Look over your notes and your textbook. List the things that you think are the most difficult.
- Be sure that you understand everything. Get extra help with anything that is still unclear to you.

Study. Use several ways to study . . .
- Write the main ideas and important vocabulary words on note cards.
- Say the information out loud and explain it in your own words.
- Study with someone else and explain the information to each other.

Practice

Review the guidelines under the three headings above. List three of these guidelines that you will try as you prepare for your next test.

TEST-TAKING TIPS

Before You Start . . .

- **Pay close attention** to all of the directions. Can you use notes, a dictionary, or your textbook?

- **Have a couple of sharpened pencils** and an eraser ready.

- **Write your full name** on the test.

- **Look over the entire test** so that you can plan your time.

During the Test . . .

- **Read the directions** and follow them carefully. Ask the teacher about any questions that confuse you.

- **Study each question** by looking for key words like *always, only, all,* and *never.*

- **Answer the questions** you are sure of first. Don't spend too much time on any one question.

- **Go back to any questions** that you skipped.

After the Test . . .

- **Be sure** you answered all the questions.

- **Check your answers** if you have time.

Taking Objective Tests

The four basic kinds of questions on objective tests are *multiple-choice, true/false, matching,* and *fill-in-the-blanks.*

Multiple-Choice Test

■ **READ** all the choices carefully before marking an answer. If there is more than one correct answer, look for a choice like *all of the above* or *both a and b.*

> **Question:** Blood flows through which parts of the body?
>
> **a.** heart   **b.** lungs   **c.** hair   **(d.)** both a and b

■ **RECOGNIZE** that a question may ask you to find a mistake. If no mistake can be found, look for the choice *no mistake.*

> **Question:** Which sentence needs to be corrected?
>
> **a.** Plants and animals breathe.
> **b.** Teeth are part of an animal's digestive system.
> **c.** Plants use carbon dioxide to help them make food.
> **(d.)** No mistake.

■ **LOOK FOR** negative words like *not, never, except,* and *unless.* Pay attention to any numbers.

> **Question:** Which two things are not released during photosynthesis?
>
> **(a.)** carbon dioxide   **b.** oxygen   **(c.)** sugar

■ **THINK ABOUT** what the question is asking. It may ask you to mark the choice that matches a sample sentence.

> **Question:** Which sentence below uses the word <u>waste</u> in the same way as the following sentence?
>
> **Both plant and animal cells get rid of <u>waste</u> material.**
>
> **a.** She tries not to <u>waste</u> time.
> **b.** Muscles <u>waste</u> away while you are on crutches.
> **(c.)** Carbon dioxide is a <u>waste</u> product of respiration.

True/False Test

- **READ** the entire question carefully before answering. For a statement to be true, the entire statement must be true.

- **WATCH** for words like *all, every, always, never.* Statements with these words in them are often false.

   Direction: Mark each statement "T" for True or "F" for False.

   _____ **1.** Every word has either a Latin or a Greek root.

   _____ **2.** A word's root always comes at its beginning.

   _____ **3.** A root word can never stand alone as a word.

   Answers: All three are false. 1. Not *every* word is based on Latin or Greek. 2. A root doesn't *always* come at the beginning of a word. 3. To make the sentence true, the word *never* should be replaced by *sometimes.*

Matching Test

- **REVIEW** both lists before you make any matches.

- **CHECK OFF** each answer you use.

   Direction: Match the word pairs on the left to the terms on the right.

   _____ fast, speedy   **a.** antonyms

   _____ interesting, dull   **b.** homonyms

   _____ lie (recline), lie (deceive)   **c.** synonyms

   Answers: _c._ fast, speedy; _a._ interesting, dull; _b._ lie, lie

Fill-in-the-Blanks Test

- **READ** each sentence completely before filling in the blank.

   Direction: Fill in the blanks below with the correct answers.

   1. A prefix comes at the _____ of a word.

   2. The root *bio,* used in words like *biology* and *biography,* means _____.

   Answers: 1. beginning 2. life

Responding to Writing Prompts

Sometimes test directions ask you to write about topics that you've been studying. To respond correctly, you must first understand the test prompt. Here are two sample prompts:

- Explain how a rainbow forms.
- Describe a rainbow.

Both prompts have the same topic: a rainbow. But each prompt tells you to write about the topic in a different way. The first one tells you to *explain,* and the second one tells you to *describe.*

1 Find the key word in the writing prompt.

It is important to understand the key words used in writing prompts. Here are some common ones:

Compare/Contrast • To **compare**, tell how two things are alike. To **contrast**, tell how things are different. A prompt may tell you to compare, contrast, or both. *(Example: Compare how the Plains Indians and the Southwest Desert Indians lived.)*

Define • To **define** something, tell what it means, what it is, or what it does. *(Example: Define ultraviolet light.)*

Describe • To **describe** something, tell how it looks, sounds, smells, tastes, and/or feels. *(Example: Describe your favorite childhood toy or game.)*

Explain • To **explain** something, tell how it works or how it happens. *(Example: Explain how a thunderstorm forms.)*

List • To **list**, give a number of facts, ideas, reasons, or other details about the topic. *(Example: List three causes of the American Revolution.)*

Persuade • To **persuade**, give facts and reasons that would make someone agree with your opinion. *(Example: Do you think that students your age need eight hours of sleep per night? Write a paragraph to convince someone else of your opinion.)*

2 Plan your answer.

Here are the steps in responding to a writing prompt:

1 **Listen** carefully to all directions.

2 **Find out** how much time you have for the test.

3 **Pay attention** to the key words in the prompt.

4 **Write** a topic sentence or a focus statement for your answer. Include key words in your topic sentence or focus statement.

5 **List** your supporting points in a simple graphic organizer.

6 **Write** your response and check it for errors.

Sample Responses

The two responses below are completely different, even though they are about the same topic. The first response *explains;* the second one *describes.*

Explain how a rainbow forms. (The response gives a scientific explanation.)

A rainbow forms when raindrops act as tiny prisms. The sun's rays hit the water drops, which break the sunlight into bands of red, orange, yellow, green, blue, indigo, and violet. Because the drops are round, the rainbow arches in a half circle.

Describe a rainbow. (The response tells about a rainbow using several senses.)

Seeing a rainbow is awesome. Beautiful colors—red, orange, yellow, green, blue, indigo, and violet—form a giant arch in the sky. I have also seen rainbows in the mist of a thundering waterfall and in the spray of a garden hose.

Practice

For each prompt below, write the key word and tell what you need to do.

1. Compare and contrast two forms of precipitation.

2. Describe a tepee.

3. Persuade someone to read a particular book.

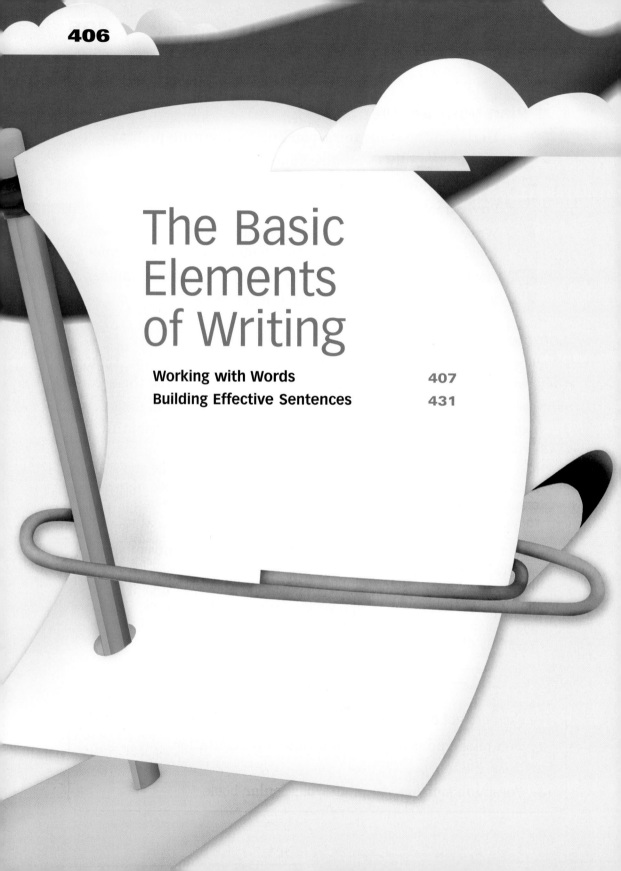

The Basic Elements of Writing

Working with Words

Do you look for something to do on a rainy afternoon? Try working on a crossword puzzle. Every day, thousands of people exercise their brains by working on these word puzzles.

Our language includes eight types of words called the parts of speech. The parts of speech are *nouns, pronouns, verbs, adjectives, adverbs, prepositions, conjunctions,* and *interjections.* This chapter will help you learn about the parts of speech and how to use words effectively in your writing.

Mini Index

Using Nouns

A **noun** is a word that names a person, a place, a thing, or an idea. (Also see page 570.)

Kinds of Nouns

There are two kinds of nouns. A **proper noun** names someone or something specific. Proper nouns are capitalized. A **common noun** does not name someone or something specific. Common nouns are not capitalized.

PROPER NOUNS	COMMON NOUNS
Josie, Echo Park, Labor Day	girl, park, holiday

Number of Nouns

The number of a noun tells whether the noun is singular or plural. A **singular noun** names one person, place, thing, or idea. A **plural noun** names more than one person, place, thing, or idea.

SINGULAR NOUNS	PLURAL NOUNS
president, child, airport	presidents, children, airports

Practice

Number your paper from 1 to 4 and copy the nouns in each sentence. Write each noun and label it as "C" for common or "P" for proper. Also label each common noun as "S" for singular or "PL" for plural.

■ *Treasure Island* contains exciting adventures.
  Treasure Island P,   adventures C, PL

1. Many books are filled with wonderful journeys.
2. My favorite story is about a girl growing up in Canada.
3. Doris lived with her mother and two sisters.
4. Life was hard, but the children had fun times.

Possessive Nouns

A **possessive noun** shows ownership. An apostrophe is used to show that a noun is possessive. If the noun is singular, an apostrophe and the letter -*s* are added to the end of the word. For plural nouns ending in -*s*, an apostrophe is placed after the -*s*. The possessive form for plurals like *women* or *children* is created by adding an apostrophe and -*s*. (See page **492** for more information.)

SINGULAR POSSESSIVE NOUNS	PLURAL POSSESSIVE NOUNS
boy's father (one boy)	**boys' father** (more than one boy)
child's game (one child)	**children's games** (more than one child)

Practice

Number your paper from 1 to 5. For each of the sentences below, choose the correct possessive in parentheses and write it on your paper.

■ Four *(girl's, girls')* bicycles were parked by a giant pine tree.
girls'

1. The friends had decided to hike along the *(river's, rivers')* edge.

2. The *(dolphin's, dolphins')* tails splashed when they jumped out of the water.

3. My *(grandfather's, grandfathers')* car is spotless.

4. The *(wrestler's, wrestlers')* families cheered them on.

5. In the science contest, my *(friend's, friends')* report won an award for best individual project.

 Write three or four sentences about a sport that you like. Try to use a possessive noun in each one of your sentences.

How can I improve my writing with nouns?

Use Specific Nouns

Your writing will be more interesting if you use **specific nouns**. The chart below can help you understand the difference between general and specific nouns.

GENERAL NOUNS	SPECIFIC NOUNS
woman	Harriet Tubman
country	Thailand
car	convertible
emotion	joy

> Specific nouns make your writing clear and precise.

Practice

Rewrite sentences 1 through 5 two times. Each time replace the underlined general noun with a more specific one. See the difference specific nouns can make!

- The <u>man</u> turned and walked away.
  The police officer turned and walked away.
  Our coach turned and walked away.

1. Later that day, Alice walked down the <u>road</u>.
2. I enjoyed the <u>show</u> very much.
3. At recess, Carley got mud on her <u>clothes</u>.
4. Darren studied the <u>material</u> before the test.
5. After school we met at our favorite <u>place</u>.

Write NOW Check the nouns in a piece of your writing. Make any general nouns more specific.

Use Nouns with the Right Feeling

The nouns you include in your writing should have the right feeling, or **connotation**. Suppose you are writing about a dream that really scared you. The word *dream* may not have a strong enough feeling for this situation.

You could look in a thesaurus and find synonyms for *dream* like *fantasy, illusion,* and *nightmare*. The word with the right feeling is *nightmare* because it means "a frightening dream."

Don't settle for any word. Find the word with the right feeling.

Practice

Number your paper from 1 to 4. There are three synonyms listed after each underlined noun below. Choose the synonym that best fits the feeling of the situation and explain why that word is best. Use a dictionary if you need help making your choices.

■ Our class had disappointed our teacher. The look *(frown, smile, surprise)* on her face told us that everyone was in big trouble.

A "frown" usually shows disapproval.

1. Our family visited San Simeon, a huge, showy house *(cottage, mansion, building)* where a rich family lived.

2. My dad wears special steel-toed shoes *(sneakers, boots, clogs)* when he works at dangerous construction sites.

3. I have thought about being a doctor, a job *(profession, trade, position)* that would require years of training.

4. Because of the severe rain *(drizzle, downpour, shower),* the baseball game was canceled.

Using Pronouns

A **pronoun** is a word used in place of a noun. The noun it replaces or refers to is called the pronoun's **antecedent**. (Also see **576.1**.)

The phoenix **is an imaginary beast, but** it **has become a symbol of hope.**

(*Phoenix* is the antecedent of the pronoun *it*.)

Personal Pronouns

Personal pronouns are the most common types of pronouns. (See page **578** for a complete list.)

PERSONAL PRONOUNS						
I	you	he	she	it	we	they
me		him	her		us	them

Person and Number of a Pronoun

Pronouns can vary in person (*first, second,* or *third*) and in number (*singular* or *plural*).

	SINGULAR	PLURAL
First person (*the person speaking*)	I ride.	We ride.
Second person (*the person spoken to*)	You ride.	You ride.
Third person (*the person spoken about*)	He/She/It rides.	They ride.

Practice

Number your paper from 1 to 4. Write a sentence using each pronoun given below as the subject. Underline the pronoun that is the subject.

■ second-person singular.
  You should sit next to me.

1. third-person singular

2. first-person plural

3. third-person plural

4. first-person singular

Indefinite Pronouns

An **indefinite pronoun** refers to people or things that are not named or known. The chart below lists the common indefinite pronouns. As you will see, some indefinite pronouns are singular, some are plural, and some can be either singular or plural.

INDEFINITE PRONOUNS	
Singular	another, something, nobody, neither, either, everybody, everyone, anybody, anyone, no one, somebody, anything, someone, one, each, everything, nothing
Plural	both, few, many, several
Singular or Plural	all, any, most, none, some

When you use an indefinite pronoun as a subject, the verb must agree with it in number.

Singular: Nobody wants the special lunch today.

Plural: Few of us eat breakfast at 6:00 a.m.

However, when the indefinite pronoun is singular or plural and comes before a prepositional phrase, the noun in that phrase must agree in number with the verb.

Singular or Plural:

All of the pizza disappears. All of my friends like pizza.

Practice

Number your paper from 1 to 9. Write a sentence using each indefinite pronoun below as a subject. Underline the pronoun and the verb.

■ everyone
   Everyone wants an easy math assignment.

1. some	**4.** something	**7.** nobody
2. many	**5.** both	**8.** none
3. all	**6.** few	**9.** someone

How can I use pronouns properly?

Forming the Possessive of Pronouns

Special forms of **personal pronouns** are used to show ownership. Some of these pronouns can stand alone. Others are used before a noun and function as adjectives.

You found your coat. Where is mine? (*Your* comes before the noun *coat* and functions as an adjective. *Mine* can stand alone.)

My coat is bright red. (*My* functions as an adjective before *coat*.)

> **POSSESSIVE FORMS OF PERSONAL PRONOUNS**
>
> my, mine, your, yours, his, her, hers, its, our, ours, their, theirs

Possessive **indefinite pronouns** are formed by simply adding an apostrophe and -*s* to the word.

No one's project is graded yet.

I can't remember everybody's name!

Practice

Number your paper from 2 to 6. Each possessive pronoun below is numbered. If the pronoun is correct, write "C" after the number. If it is incorrect, write the possessive in its correct form.

1. hers

I went to Mrs. Lee's house to see if the gray kitten was **(1)** her's. She said that her family loves cats, but this one wasn't **(2)** theirs. I really wanted to help the kitten find **(3)** it's home, so I took it to the next house. The people in the house said that the kitten wasn't **(4)** their's either. Then I checked with Mrs. Brown. She would know if **(5)** someone's cat was missing. She said, "That kitten is **(6)** our's!"

How can pronouns improve my writing?

Avoid Repeating Nouns

Use pronouns so that you don't repeat the same nouns over and over again. This will make your sentences flow more smoothly. Read the sample paragraph below. The writer improved his sentences by replacing nouns with pronouns.

> John Alden was one of the settlers who came to Cape Cod
>
> on the Mayflower in 1620. ~~John Alden~~ *He* was hired as a barrel maker
>
> for the voyage. After the ship landed, ~~Alden's~~ *his* decision was to stay
>
> rather than return to England. Priscilla Mullens was a young woman
>
> who also settled in Plymouth Colony. In about 1622, ~~Priscilla~~ *she* and
>
> Alden were married. ~~John Alden and Priscilla~~ *They* had 10 children, and
>
> they became one of Plymouth's most important families.

Practice

Rewrite the paragraph below. Change some of the underlined nouns to pronouns so the paragraph will read more smoothly.

William Bradford was one of the many people who came to Plymouth for religious freedom. Bradford and his wife, Dorothy, were on the *Mayflower*. Tragically, Dorothy died in Cape Cod Bay. Bradford was selected as a replacement for the colony's first leader. From that point on, Bradford's life was linked with Plymouth Colony. Bradford married his second wife, Anne, at Plymouth.

Choosing Verbs

The main **verb** either shows action or links the subject to another word in the sentence. There are three types of verbs: action verbs, linking verbs, and helping verbs. (Also see page **582**.)

Action Verbs

An **action verb** tells what the subject is doing. Always try to use action verbs that are specific because they bring life to your writing.

GENERAL ACTION VERBS	SPECIFIC ACTION VERBS
Paul left.	Paul disappeared.
Hungry dogs eat food.	Hungry dogs gobble food.
Grandma always gives us hugs.	Grandma always hugs us.

A thesaurus and dictionary will help you find specific action verbs. Be sure you know the exact meaning of a verb before using it.

Practice

Number your paper from 1 to 5. Verbs are underlined in the following sentences. Rewrite each sentence, replacing the general verb with a more specific one. You may need to change the wording of some of your new sentences.

■ The mountain <u>stood</u> before Kit.
    The mountain <u>towered</u> before Kit.

1. She <u>walked</u> through the deep snow.
2. The bitter wind <u>hurt</u> her face.
3. The snow <u>moved</u> all around her.
4. The temperature <u>dropped</u> very quickly.
5. Kit <u>looked</u> at her map of the trail.

Linking and Helping Verbs

A **linking verb** connects a subject to a noun or an adjective in the predicate.

Artichokes are unusual vegetables.

(The linking verb *are* connects the subject *artichokes* to the noun *vegetables*.)

> **LINKING VERBS**
>
> Forms of the verb *be*—is, are, was, were, being, been, am
>
> Other linking verbs—appear, become, feel, grow, look, remain, seem, smell, sound, taste

A **helping verb** comes before the main verb and helps to form some of the tenses.

We will eat the artichokes tomorrow.

(The helping verb *will* expresses future time.)

> **HELPING VERBS**
>
> Forms of the verb *be*—is, are, was, were, being, been, am
>
> Other helping verbs—shall, will, should, would, could, must, can, may, have, had, has, do, did, does

Practice

Write five sentences using the following linking verbs.

1. is   **2.** were   **3.** become   **4.** look   **5.** smell

Also write five sentences using the following helping verbs before main verbs of your choice.

1. are   **2.** will   **3.** would   **4.** have   **5.** did

Tenses of Verbs

The **tense** of a verb tells when the action takes place. Verb tenses may be either simple or perfect. (Also see page 584.)

Simple Tenses

The **simple** tenses include **present, past,** and **future**.

The **present tense** of a verb states an action that is *happening now* or that *happens regularly*.

I practice **multiplication.**   I study **for my tests.**

The **past tense** of a verb states an action or a state of being that *happened at a specific time in the past*.

I practiced **multiplication.**   I studied **for my tests.**

The **future tense** of a verb states an action that *will take place*. It needs a helping verb such as *will* or *shall* before the main verb.

I will practice **multiplication.**   I shall study **for my tests.**

Form the past tense of irregular verbs, like "give," by changing the spelling: "gave."
(See pages 586 and 588.)

Practice

Number your paper from 1 to 5. Identify the tense of each underlined verb below.

■ I <u>like</u> to visit my uncle in Arizona.
  present

1. He <u>invites</u> us every year.

2. Next summer we <u>will spend</u> an entire week with him.

3. Last time we <u>visited</u> the Hopi Reservation near Flagstaff.

4. Huge, flat mountains, called mesas, <u>rise</u> above the flat land.

5. Someday I <u>will study</u> to become an archaeologist.

Perfect Tenses

The **perfect tenses** include **present perfect**, **past perfect**, and **future perfect**. (See page **584** for more information.)

The **present perfect tense** states an action that *began in the past but is still happening*. The helping verb *has* or *have* is added before the past-participle form of the main verb.

Derek has practiced **his cello a lot.**

The **past perfect tense** states an action that *began and was completed in the past*. The helping verb *had* is added before *practiced*, the past-participle form of the main verb.

He had practiced **for an hour.**

The **future perfect tense** states an action that *will begin in the future and end at a specific time*. The helping verbs *will have* are added before *practiced*, the past-participle form of the main verb.

By concert time, he will have practiced **enough.**

Practice

Number your paper from 1 to 5. Identify the tense of each underlined verb below.

■ Our band teacher, Mr. Huan, has planned this concert for months.

present perfect

1. We have practiced the music for "Peter and the Wolf."

2. A month ago, we had asked our principal to read the narration.

3. She has performed the spoken part many times.

4. After this concert, she will have narrated the piece five times.

5. She had been an actor before becoming a principal.

How can I use verbs correctly?

Number of a Verb

Make sure that the subjects and verbs in your sentences agree in number. If you use a singular subject, use a singular verb. If you use a plural subject, use a plural verb. (See **586.3**.)

Subject-Verb Agreement

The chart below shows how subject-verb agreement works.

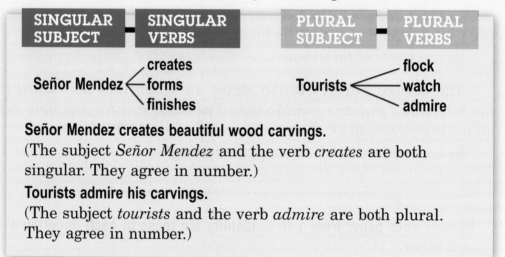

SINGULAR SUBJECT	SINGULAR VERBS	PLURAL SUBJECT	PLURAL VERBS
Señor Mendez	creates forms finishes	Tourists	flock watch admire

Señor Mendez creates beautiful wood carvings.
(The subject *Señor Mendez* and the verb *creates* are both singular. They agree in number.)

Tourists admire his carvings.
(The subject *tourists* and the verb *admire* are both plural. They agree in number.)

Practice

Match each subject below with the best verb. (Make sure that each subject and verb agree in number.) Then write a sentence for each subject-verb pair.

Subjects: cats   Lila   coach   vegetables
Verbs: complains   sleep   contain   instructs

Write NOW Write a paragraph (at least five sentences) about a craft or hobby that interests you. Make sure all your verbs agree in number with their subjects.

Agreement in Sentences with Compound Subjects

In sentences with compound subjects connected by *and,* the verb should be plural.

Latrelle, Michael, and Jason sing well together.
(*Latrelle, Michael, and Jason* is a compound subject connected by *and.* The subject agrees in number with the plural verb *sing.*)

Spaghetti and tacos are my favorite foods.
(*Spaghetti and tacos* is a compound subject connected by *and.* The subject agrees in number with the plural verb *are.*)

In sentences with compound subjects connected by *or,* the verb should agree in number with the subject nearer to it.

Either the cats or the dog pounces on me every morning.
(The subject *dog* is nearer to the verb *pounces.* They are both singular and agree in number.)

Anna or her brothers feed the pets each evening.
(The subject *brothers* is nearer to the verb *feed.* They are both plural and agree in number.)

Practice

Match each compound subject below with the best verb. (Each subject and verb should agree.) Then write a sentence for each subject-verb pair.

Compound Subjects	*Verbs*
Rosa and Pasha	plans
diet and exercise	make
assistants or the head coach	eat
brother or sisters	improve

Write NOW Check the sentences in a piece of your writing. In each sentence, make sure the subjects and verbs agree in number. Pay special attention to any sentences that contain compound subjects.

How can I improve my writing with verbs?

Share the Right Feeling

Strong action verbs create clear word pictures for the reader. The feeling, or connotation, of a verb should fit the picture you want to create. For example, in the sentence below, the verb *walks* suggests "moving at a normal pace." Notice how the feeling in the sentence changes each time you substitute a different synonym from the chart.

John walks through the park.

SYNONYM	DEFINITIONS
strolls	to walk slowly, in a relaxed way
strides	to walk briskly, with long steps
trudges	to walk very slowly, with effort
struts	to walk in a very confident, showy way
stomps	to walk with heavy, aggressive steps
hobbles	to walk haltingly and with difficulty

Make sure the connotation, or feeling, of a word clearly matches the picture you want to create for your reader.

Practice

Write a sentence using the verb *smile.* Then rewrite the sentence twice, using a new synonym for *smile* in each sentence. Each synonym should have a different connotation. Repeat the exercise with the verbs *run* and *see.* (Use a thesaurus or dictionary to find your synonyms.)

Describing with Adjectives

An **adjective** is a word that describes a noun or a pronoun. An adjective answers *what kind? how much? how many?* or *which one?* about the word it describes. Other adjectives called **articles** include the words *a, an,* and *the*. (See page 590.)

EXAMPLE ADJECTIVES			
What kind?	wooly **socks**	blue **eyes**	Chinese **cabbage**
How much? How many?	six **eggs**	few **books**	many **days**
Which one?	that **girl**	these **notes**	this **problem**

Proper and Common Adjectives

Proper adjectives (in red) are formed from proper nouns and are always capitalized. **Common adjectives** (in blue) are any adjectives that are not proper.

A Chicago **pizza has a** thick **crust and** spicy **sausage.**

Practice

Number your paper from 1 to 7. List any adjectives, including articles, that you find in each line. If there are no adjectives in the line, write "none." There are 24 adjectives in all.

1   This city has a conservatory, which is a living greenhouse of
2   unusual trees and plants. The conservatory has three sections.
3   One section has a tropical climate, one has a desert environment,
4   and one has a temperate climate. I love the tropical exhibit
5   because it has gorgeous birds. I always enjoy seeing those birds.
6   The desert section is an awesome place, too. It contains unusual
7   cactuses and desert animals.

Forms of Adjectives

Use the **comparative form** of an adjective when comparing two things. For most one-syllable adjectives, add -er to make the comparative form. Use the **superlative form** to compare three or more things. For most one-syllable adjectives, add -est. (See page 592.)

POSITIVE	COMPARATIVE	SUPERLATIVE
hot	hotter	hottest

Comparative: It's hotter today than yesterday.
Superlative: Tomorrow is predicted to be the hottest day of the week.

tip Place *more* or *most* in front of most multisyllable adjectives to form the comparative and superlative forms.

POSITIVE	COMPARATIVE	SUPERLATIVE
amazing	more amazing	most amazing

Comparative: This week's episode of "Shark Life" was more amazing than last week's episode.
Superlative: Ants are the most amazing insects on earth.

Practice

On your own paper, write the correct form of each adjective.

1. youngest

I took my three cousins to their baseball game. My (**1.** young) cousin, Kyle, wore a mitt that was (**2.** big) than he was. He also wore a smile that was even (**3.** wide). The star player on the other team came up to bat. He is the (**4.** strong) hitter in the league. He slammed the first pitch. It was (**5.** loud) than thunder. The ball soared into left field, and Kyle caught it to make the last out in the inning. Kyle's catch was the (**6.** exciting) part of the game up to that point. When Kevin, one of my other cousins, came to bat, he drove in two runs. His double was the (**7.** important) hit in the inning.

How can I improve my writing with adjectives?

Use Specific Adjectives

Adjectives need to be specific in order to create interesting and clear word pictures for the reader. Some adjectives like *good* and *neat* should be avoided because they are overused.

>*Overused adjectives:* **good, neat, big, pretty, small, cute, fun, bad, nice, dumb, great**

>**I get a good feeling when I think of my grandmother's house.**
>(*Good* is an overused adjective.)

>**I get a cozy feeling when I think of my grandmother's house.**
>(The adjective *cozy* presents a clearer picture than *good*.)

Practice

Rewrite each of the following sentences twice. Each time, replace the overused adjective (underlined) with an adjective that is more specific.

That was a good lunch!   The poster looks bad.
My mom makes nice sweaters.

Include Sensory Details

Effective adjectives often appeal to the senses. Each underlined adjective below helps you *see, hear, smell,* and *feel* an autumn day.

>The October sky was framed by the glowing, golden leaves. The air smelled musty from the powdery leaves that crunched beneath my feet. Swirling winds blew in gusts, and the crackling chatter of the dry leaves drowned out any other sound.

Practice

Describe your favorite kind of day. Use sensory details that help the reader see, hear, smell, and feel the experience.

Describing with Adverbs

An **adverb** is a word that describes a verb, an adjective, or another adverb. An adverb usually answers *how? when? where? how often?* or *how much?* in a sentence. (For more information, see page **594**.)

Erin left the game early.

(The adverb *early* answers *when?* in the sentence.)

Kim runs daily **to get into shape.**

(The adverb *daily* tells *how often?* in the sentence.)

Forms of Adverbs

Adverbs come in three different forms: **positive, comparative, and superlative.** For most one-syllable adverbs, add *-er* to make the comparative form and *-est* to make the superlative form.

POSITIVE	COMPARATIVE	SUPERLATIVE
late	later	latest

Comparative: **Pepe goes to bed** later **than his sister does.**
Superlative: **He goes to bed** latest **on Saturday night.**

In most cases, when an adverb has more than one syllable, place the word *more* or *most* in front of the adverb to form the comparative and superlative forms.

POSITIVE	COMPARATIVE	SUPERLATIVE
often	more often	most often

Comparative: **Jordan wins races** more often **than Ellie does.**
Superlative: **He races** most often **in 100-yard dashes.**

On your own paper, write a paragraph about an enjoyable weekend activity. Use some comparative and superlative forms of adverbs in your writing.

How can I improve my writing with adverbs?

Describe Actions

Use adverbs to help describe the action in a sentence. Remember that adverbs often end in *-ly*.

Sentence without an adverb:
We squeezed through the subway door before it closed.

Sentence with an adverb:
We barely squeezed through the subway door before it closed.

(The adverb *barely* makes the action clearer.)

Practice

Write four interesting sentences using the adverbs listed below. Each adverb should help describe the action in the sentence.

■ **gladly** I gladly gave Steve some of my sunflower seeds.

1. quickly   **2.** quietly   **3.** smoothly   **4.** carefully

Modify Adjectives

Also use adverbs to make the meaning of adjectives clearer and more exact in a sentence.

Sentence without an adverb: **That writer's stories are scary.**

Sentence with an adverb: **That writer's stories are sometimes scary.**

(The adverb *sometimes* makes the meaning of the adjective *scary* more exact.)

Practice

Write four interesting sentences using the adverbs listed below. Each adverb should make the meaning of an adjective more exact.

■ **often** Little children are often noisy.

1. always   **2.** extremely   **3.** very   **4.** uncomfortably

Connecting with Prepositions

A **preposition** introduces a prepositional phrase. A preposition usually shows direction or position. (See page **598** for a complete list of prepositions.)

> **My dog scampered under the bed.** (The preposition *under* introduces the prepositional phrase *under the bed.*)
>
> **The trees near the school have lost their leaves.** (The preposition *near* introduces the prepositional phrase *near the school.*)

A **prepositional phrase** includes a preposition, the object of the preposition (a noun or a pronoun), and any words that modify the object.

preposition	*object of the preposition*		*preposition*	*object of the preposition*
outside	**my bedroom window**		**around**	**the last turn**

modifiers   *modifiers*

Practice

Identify the prepositional phrases in the sentences below. There may be more than one prepositional phrase in some of the sentences.

■ Thuan broke his leg during the game.
  during the game

1. He was rushed to the emergency room in the hospital.
2. A doctor took X-rays of his leg.
3. Thuan and the doctor waited for the results.
4. A nurse put ice on Thuan's injured leg.
5. With the help of the nurse, the doctor applied a temporary cast on the leg.
6. After a few weeks, the leg will be ready for a more permanent cast.

Connecting with Conjunctions

A **conjunction** connects individual words or groups of words.

The river is wide and deep.

(The conjunction *and* connects the words *wide* and *deep*.)

We can take the ferry or walk across the bridge.

(The conjunction *or* connects the phrases *take the ferry* and *walk across the bridge*.)

Kinds of Conjunctions

The chart below shows the three kinds of conjunctions. (See page 600 for a more complete list of conjunctions.)

COORDINATING

Coordinating conjunctions (and, but, for, nor, so, yet) connect equal words, phrases, or clauses:

Anita cleaned the yard, and Luis washed the car.

CORRELATIVE

Correlative conjunctions are used in pairs (either/or, neither/nor) to connect words or groups of words:

Either they got tired, or they ran out of time.

SUBORDINATING

Subordinating conjunctions (after, although, because, when) introduce the dependent clauses in complex sentences: (Dependent clauses cannot stand alone as sentences.)

After the two stopped, they had something to eat.

Practice

Write interesting sentences using the following conjunctions.

1. but   **2.** either/or   **3.** when   **4.** and   **5.** while

How can I use prepositions and conjunctions?

Add Information

You can use prepositional phrases to add useful information.

Sentence without prepositional phrases:
Ben reads many books.

Sentence with two prepositional phrases:
During study time, Ben reads many books about space exploration.

Practice

Make each of the following sentences more informative by adding one or more prepositional phrases.

1. Justin threw the football.
2. Claudia played her favorite song.
3. The clerk answered my question.

Connect Short Sentences

You can use conjunctions to combine short sentences. Combining short sentences will make your writing read more smoothly.

Two short sentences: **The marching band performed at Rockville. The drill team stayed home.**

The two sentences combined: **The marching band performed at Rockville,** but **the drill team stayed home.**

Practice

Combine each pair of sentences using the *noted* conjunction.

1. *(but)* Jason loves music. Sondra's favorite class is math.
2. *(because)* We can't play hockey. The pond isn't frozen.
3. *(either/or)* You work hard in practice. You may not play in the game.

Building Effective Sentences

A sentence is like a railroad track. If the track is incomplete or damaged, the train can't get through. In the same way, if a sentence is incomplete or incorrect, the idea can't get through—it won't make sense to the reader.

On the other hand, writing complete, correct sentences will put your ideas on the right track. This chapter will show you how to build effective sentences.

Mini Index

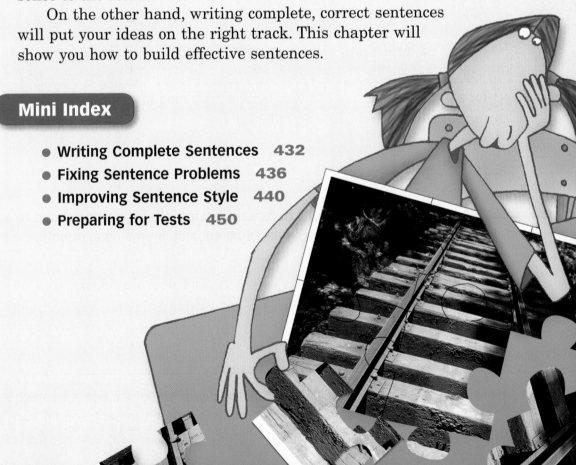

Writing Complete Sentences

A **complete sentence** is a group of words that expresses a complete thought.

How can I make sure my sentences are complete?

A sentence must have a **subject**, which tells who or what is doing something. A sentence must also have a **predicate**, a **verb**, or **verb phrase** that tells what the subject is doing or what is being done to the subject.

INCOMPLETE THOUGHT	COMPLETE SENTENCE
My cousin Jillian *(a predicate is missing)*	**My cousin Jillian runs.**
runs every afternoon *(a subject is missing)*	**She runs every afternoon.**
for a race *(a subject and a predicate are missing)*	**She is training for a race.**

Practice

Number your own paper from 1 to 5. Make each of the following groups of words a complete sentence by adding a subject, a predicate, or both. The first one has been done for you.

■ in the summer
   I play baseball in the summer.
1. run around the yard
2. my little brother

3. the dog next door
4. rides a bicycle
5. at the park

 Write NOW Write five sentences about an activity you enjoy. Include a subject and a predicate and express a complete thought in each sentence.

Complete Subjects and Predicates

The **complete subject** in a sentence includes the simple subject and its modifiers. The **complete predicate** includes the simple predicate (the verb) and its modifiers.

COMPLETE SUBJECT	COMPLETE PREDICATE
Who or what is doing something?	*What is being done?*
Our new bus driver	likes to tell jokes.
Janelle and I	planned the class picnic.
The noise in the background	spoiled the concert.
Mr. Cosford, our neighbor,	is very friendly.

> Read your sentences aloud. Listen for complete thoughts.

Practice

Copy sentences 1 to 5 on your own paper. Then draw a line between the complete subject and the complete predicate in each one.

■ The members of my team visited the hospital yesterday.

The members of my team | visited the hospital yesterday.

1. A volunteer in a blue uniform showed us around.
2. Another person gave each of us a first-aid booklet.
3. The surgery room was the most interesting place.
4. We asked some good questions afterward.
5. My teammates and I learned about sports medicine.

Write NOW Write five sentences about a short trip or a weekend activity. Then draw a line between the complete subject and the complete predicate in each sentence.

Simple Subjects and Predicates

A **simple subject** (shown in orange) is the subject without the words that describe or modify it. A **simple predicate** (shown in blue) is the verb without any of the other words that modify it.

SIMPLE SUBJECT	SIMPLE PREDICATE
My friend Jan	bought her ticket at the door.
The entire audience	waited patiently.
We	cheered.

Sometimes the simple subject or predicate serves as the complete subject or predicate. (We cheered.)

Practice

Copy sentences 1 to 5 on your own paper. Underline the simple subject with one line and the simple predicate with two lines.

■ The school cooks announced a new menu.
   The school <u>cooks</u> <u>announced</u> a new menu.

1. Hungry students choose from a large variety of foods.
2. The school copied the idea from food courts.
3. Most students prefer healthful foods to junk food.
4. Salads are a popular choice.
5. Nutritious snacks give students energy.

Write NOW Write five sentences about your school lunch program (or the lunch you bring to school). In each sentence, underline the simple subject with one line and the simple predicate with two lines.

Compound Subjects and Predicates

A **compound subject** includes two or more simple subjects. A **compound predicate** includes two or more simple predicates. The simple subject (in orange) and the simple predicate (in blue) are shown in each sentence below.

COMPOUND SUBJECT	COMPOUND PREDICATE
Harry and Lana	caught and released three fish.
My cousin	sings and dances in the musical.
Tim and Colin	ran outside and played soccer after dinner.

> Compound subjects are usually joined by the coordinating conjunctions "and," "but," or "or."

Practice

Copy sentences 1 to 5 on your paper. Underline each subject with one line and each predicate with two lines.

■ Jake and Elijah gathered their fishing gear.
  Jake and Elijah gathered their fishing gear.

1. Their uncle took them to Blue Lake and rented a boat.

2. The fish and the mosquitoes always bite.

3. The boys caught the fish and slapped the mosquitoes.

4. The uncle and his nephews joked and laughed a lot.

5. The small boat rocked and rolled in the choppy water.

 Write NOW Write three sentences about an activity you enjoy. Use a compound subject or a compound predicate in each of your sentences.

Fixing Sentence Problems

How can I make sure my sentences are correct?

One way to check your sentences for correctness is to look for **fragments,** or incomplete sentences. A fragment is an incomplete sentence that is missing a subject, a predicate, or both.

FRAGMENT	SENTENCE
Eats chips with dip.	Saul eats chips with dip.
Many people.	Many people like salty chips.
Not a healthful snack.	Salty chips are not a healthful snack.

Practice

Number your paper from 1 to 5. Write "C" for each complete sentence and "F" for each fragment below. Rewrite each fragment to make it a complete sentence.

■ Got back from the skating rink.

   F | We got back from the skating rink.

1. My little sister was ready for dessert.
2. Maurice and his friends after school.
3. Close to the end of class.
4. Ling and her puppy won the grand prize.
5. All the other dogs.

> A fragment is part of a sentence, but it doesn't express a complete thought.

Write NOW   Write five sentences about a favorite snack. Be sure your sentences are complete and punctuated correctly.

Check for Run-On and Rambling Sentences

Run-on sentences are two or more sentences that run together. One type of run-on is called a *comma splice* because the sentences are connected (spliced together) with a comma instead of a period.

Rambling sentences occur when several sentences are connected with coordinating conjunctions such as *and, or,* or *but.*

INCORRECT SENTENCE	CORRECTED
Run-On (Comma Splice): The pet show was fun, the crowd loved Jenn's friendly dog, Brenna.	The pet show was fun. The crowd loved Jenn's friendly dog, Brenna.
Rambling: I knew that Maya's parrot would get an award and I also thought that Lem's cat would win something but I was not so sure that Jenn's dog would do well.	I knew that Maya's parrot would get an award, and I also thought that Lem's cat would win something. I was not so sure that Jenn's dog would do well.

Check your sentences for too many conjunctions.

Practice

Rewrite the following rambling sentence. Keep any necessary *and*'s.

Tara's monkey jumped on David's shoulder and his dog, Kip, started barking and the monkey jumped on Kip's back and Kip began to turn in circles trying to get the monkey off his back.

Write NOW Think of something funny that happened to you. Write at least four sentences about it. Don't write any rambling or run-on sentences.

Watch for Subject-Verb Agreement

You need to make sure that the subjects and the verbs agree in the sentences you write. That means when you use a singular subject, you also need to use a singular verb. When you use a plural subject, you need to use a plural verb. (Also see pages 420–421.)

SINGULAR AGREEMENT	PLURAL AGREEMENT
That girl loves tap dancing.	Those girls love ballet.
My watch ticks softly.	The boys' watches tick loudly.
Anna creates dried flower art.	Anna and Lily create dried flower art.

Most nouns ending in "s" or "es" are plural.
Most verbs ending in "s" are singular.

Practice

Number your paper from 1 to 5. For each sentence below, select the subject or verb in parentheses that fits with the underlined words.

■ My <u>mother</u> (think, thinks) we need an air purifier.
thinks

1. <u>She</u> (say, says) that clean air is important.
2. (We, My brother) <u>agree</u> that it's a good idea.
3. Our <u>dog</u> and <u>cat</u> (raises, raise) a lot of dust.
4. The (window, windows) <u>get</u> very dirty, too.
5. <u>We</u> (needs, need) a machine that cleans windows, too.

Write NOW Write five sentences about the biggest housekeeping job where you live. Use some singular and some plural subjects. Be sure the verbs agree with the subjects.

Avoid Double Negatives

A **double negative** is an error that occurs when you use two negative words in the same sentence. Double negatives change the meaning of your ideas and should be avoided.

NEGATIVE WORDS

barely	hardly	neither	never	nobody
none	not	nothing	nowhere	

Contractions that end in *n't,* meaning "not," are also negative words.

can't	couldn't	didn't	don't
hadn't	shouldn't	won't	wouldn't

> Since a contraction like "can't" is already negative,
> don't use it with another negative word.

Practice

Rewrite the paragraph below, correcting the double negatives you find. (Hint: There are four of them.)

■ Hardly nobody showed up for the party.

Hardly anybody showed up for the party.

> Allie was upset that very few people came to her party. She hadn't never thrown a party before, and she had worked really hard. There wasn't nothing missing, or so she thought. Then she found a pile of invitations in a desk drawer. She hadn't never sent them out. Allie won't never make that mistake again!

 Write NOW **Write a short paragraph about a funny mistake you once made. Be careful to avoid double negatives.**

Improving Sentence Style

How can I add variety to my writing?

Here are five ways to improve your writing by adding variety to your sentences.

1 Try different kinds of sentences.

2 Use different types of sentences.

3 Combine short sentences.

4 Expand sentences by adding words and phrases.

5 Model sentences other writers have created.

SENTENCES LACKING VARIETY

I love going to pick apples. We go to an orchard in autumn. I like Jonathans the best. My brother likes Macintoshes. Mom chooses Granny Smiths. The best part is when we get home. We make apple pies and applesauce. We also make caramel apples. It's a tasty time of year.

SENTENCE VARIETY IMPROVED

I love going to pick apples in an orchard in autumn. My favorite apples are Jonathans, my brother likes Macintoshes, and my mom prefers Granny Smiths. Do you know what's the best part? When we get home we make apple pies, applesauce, and caramel apples. It's a tasty time of year.

Adding variety to your sentences is a simple way to add style to your writing.

Try Different Kinds of Sentences

You can use four kinds of sentences to add variety and punch to your writing.

KINDS OF SENTENCES

Declarative .	Makes a statement about a person, a place, a thing, or an idea	I am looking forward to the movie.	**This is the most common kind of sentence.**
Interrogative ?	Asks a question	Can we get there in time?	**A question gets the reader's attention.**
Imperative . or !	Gives a command	Find your glasses.	**Commands often appear in dialogue or directions.**
Exclamatory !	Shows strong emotion or feeling	Oh no, we'll never get there in time!	**These sentences emphasize a point.**

Practice

Number your paper from 1 to 5. Punctuate each sentence and label it "DEC" for declarative, "INT" for interrogative, "IMP" for imperative, or "EX" for exclamatory.

■ Do you want to see that movie on Saturday night?
INT

1. It should be really funny and our friends will be there
2. Are you listening to the radio
3. Quiet down for one minute until the song ends
4. We'll leave in an hour if everyone is ready
5. You are so sure about the answer

 On your paper, write a paragraph describing a movie. Use at least one example of each kind of sentence.

Use Different Types of Sentences

There are three types of sentences: **simple, compound,** and **complex.** Use all three types to add variety and help your writing flow more smoothly. (For more about sentence patterns, see page **470**.)

Use Simple Sentences

A **simple sentence** is one independent clause. An independent clause has a subject and a predicate and expresses a complete thought.

SIMPLE SENTENCES	
Simple subject with single predicate	Mount Saint Helens **erupted violently in 1980.**
Simple subject with compound predicate	**The** volcano **rumbled and** spewed **ash.**
Compound subject and compound predicate	Scientists **and** photographers watched **and** snapped **pictures.**

Practice

Copy sentences 1 to 4 on your own paper. In each sentence, underline the simple subject once and the simple predicate twice.

■ The United States and Canada boast a number of volcanoes.
   The <u>United States</u> and <u>Canada</u> <u>boast</u> a number of volcanoes.

1. Volcanoes tell us about the earth.
2. However, they seldom erupt.
3. Mount Saint Helens presents a different story.
4. Geologists and other scientists measure volcanic activity.

 Write NOW Write four simple sentences about a storm or flood that happened in your area. Vary your sentences using examples from this page.

Form Compound Sentences

A **compound sentence** is made up of two or more simple sentences joined together. One way to join simple sentences is by using a comma and a coordinating conjunction *(and, but, or)*.

> At the zoo, my sister Wanda rode a camel, **and** I took her picture.
>
> My brother fed the seals, **but** I preferred just to watch.
>
> Next, we can go to the lion house, **or** we can watch the monkeys.

In a compound sentence, the coordinating conjunction often shows two different ideas.

Practice

On your paper, combine the pairs of sentences in numbers 1 to 4 below. Use the coordinating conjunction given in parentheses. Add a comma before the connecting word (conjunction).

■ My parents planned a trip. They asked us for ideas. *(and)*
  My parents planned a trip, and they asked us for ideas.

1. Wanda wanted to go to the desert. I'm not fond of hot weather. *(but)*

2. Nevada is beautiful. It is one day's drive from home. *(and)*

3. We could hike up Mount Washington. We could reach the top by car. *(or)*

4. Dad said we could see for miles from the peak. The top of the mountain was covered with clouds. *(but)*

Write NOW

Write three compound sentences about a place you have visited (or would like to visit). Be sure to punctuate your compound sentences correctly. (See 482.3 for more information.)

Create Complex Sentences

A **complex sentence** contains one independent clause and one or more dependent clauses. A dependent clause contains a subject and a verb, but it does not express a complete thought. A dependent clause often begins with a subordinating conjunction like *because* or *although*. (See page 600 for more on subordinating conjunctions.)

COMPLEX SENTENCE =		
A DEPENDENT CLAUSE	+	**AN INDEPENDENT CLAUSE**
After the rain stopped,		the air smelled fresh and clean.
AN INDEPENDENT CLAUSE	+	**A DEPENDENT CLAUSE**
We were amazed at the rainbow		when the sun came out.

> Practice rewriting your sentences to improve their style.

Practice

Number your paper from 1 to 5. Find the dependent clause in each of the following sentences, and write it on your paper.

■ Because the storm brought strong winds, damage was heavy.
  Because the storm brought strong winds

1. We walked to the park after it was dark.
2. Since the power went out, the streetlights haven't worked.
3. City workers tried to clean up, although it was hard to see.
4. When we saw branches on the ground, we picked them up.
5. We became very hot while we worked.

Write NOW Write a short paragraph about a time when you experienced the power of nature. Use at least two complex sentences to help you explain your experience.

Combine Short Sentences
Use Key Words and Phrases

One way you can combine short, choppy sentences is by moving a key word or phrase from one sentence to another.

SHORT SENTENCES	COMBINED SENTENCES
My shoes are red. They are <u>new</u>. *(The key word is underlined.)*	My new shoes are red. *(The adjective* new *has been moved to the first sentence.)*
We play volleyball. We play <u>on sand courts</u>. *(The prepositional phrase is underlined.)*	We play volleyball on sand courts. *(The prepositional phrase has been moved to the first sentence.)*

Practice

On your own paper, combine the pairs of short sentences in numbers 1 to 5 below. Move a key word or phrase from one sentence to the other.

■ Alberto hit a long drive. He hit it to left field.
  Alberto hit a long drive to left field.

1. Anne got a new sweater. The sweater is made of wool.
2. Dimitri's jacket is new. His jacket is leather.
3. Our cat curls up. He curls up on our couch.
4. Jerome cleans his bedroom. He cleans it on Saturdays.
5. The child slid down the slope on an inner tube. The child was squealing.

Write **NOW** Write a paragraph that describes a favorite item of clothing. Next, combine any short, choppy sentences you may have written by moving a key word or phrase from one sentence to another.

Use a Series of Words or Phrases

Sentences can be combined using a key word or phrase. Sentences can also be combined using a **series of words or phrases**. All the words or phrases in a series should be parallel—stated in the same way. (See **482.1**.)

SHORT SENTENCES	COMBINED SENTENCES
Children like to ride bicycles. They ride skateboards, too. Other children ride scooters.	Children like to ride bicycles, skateboards, and scooters.
Ellie had paint in her hair. She had it on her clothes. She had it under her fingernails.	Ellie had paint in her hair, on her clothes, and under her fingernails.

Practice

Combine each group of sentences with a series of words or phrases. (Some words may need to be changed to make the sentences work.)

■ The fifth-grade boys get exercise by climbing the monkey bars. They play kickball. They run around the school yard.

   The fifth-grade boys get exercise by climbing the monkey bars, playing kickball, and running around the school yard.

1. The fourth-grade girls play volleyball at recess. The fifth-grade girls play volleyball at recess. The sixth-grade girls play volleyball, too.

2. When it rains, we enjoy working on jigsaw puzzles. We read books. Some of us do art projects.

3. The huge green gumball rolled out of Breanne's pocket. It rolled down the aisle. It went under the teacher's desk.

Write NOW Write three sentences for a classmate to combine. Make sure your sentences can be combined using a series of words or phrases.

Combine Sentences with Compound Subjects and Predicates

Sometimes you can combine two sentences by moving a subject or a predicate from one sentence to another. This creates a **compound subject** or a **compound predicate**. (See page 435.)

SHORT SENTENCES	COMBINED SENTENCES
I raked the leaves. I piled them high.	I raked the leaves and piled them high. (a compound predicate)
Conall jumps in the leaves. Kaleigh jumps in the leaves, too.	Conall and Kaleigh jump in the leaves. (a compound subject)

Combining short sentences can make your writing smoother and easier to read!

Practice

Number your paper from 1 to 5. Write down the compound subjects and compound predicates from these sentences.

■ The gym filled quickly and rang with excitement.
  filled and rang

1. The coach and players laughed and joked as they changed.
2. Coach blew his whistle and told the team to go into the gym.
3. The crowd cheered and yelled for their team.
4. Referees and cheerleaders added to the noise.
5. Our team played well and won the game.

Expand Sentences with Prepositional Phrases

A **prepositional phrase** can add important information to a sentence. A prepositional phrase begins with words like *on, in, above, at, with, for, until,* and *under.* (See page **598** for more prepositions.)

PREPOSITIONAL PHRASES

I **looked** for my glasses. (Where did I look?)

I **looked** for my glasses on Dad's desk **and** under my bed.

> Prepositional phrases can add details to your sentences.

Number your paper from 1 to 4. Write down the prepositional phrases you find in each of the following sentences.

■ I left my permission slip on the table in the hall.
   on the table, in the hall

1. We will hike through the forest.

2. The lake lies at the bottom of the valley.

3. We have reservations at the campground.

4. We sleep on cots in the cabins.

Use one or two prepositional phrases to add information to each of the sentences below.

1 Luc will join the camping trip.

2 He brought a sleeping bag.

3 We're leaving.

Model Sentences

Artists learn to paint by studying the works of other artists. You can learn to write good sentences by studying or modeling the work of professional writers. Modeling is following a writer's use of words, phrases, and punctuation in sentences of your own.

PROFESSIONAL MODEL	STUDENT MODEL
Walking through the woods, I listened to the wind, and I pulled my coat tighter around my body.	Rushing toward school, I heard the call of my friends, and I shifted my backpack more comfortably across my shoulders.

Guidelines for Modeling

- **Varying Sentence Beginnings**
  Try starting sentences with a dependent clause or a phrase.
  Perhaps if people talked less, animals would talk more.
  —*Charlotte's Web* by E. B. White

- **Moving Adjectives**
  Sometimes you can vary a sentence by placing an adjective or two after the noun it modifies.
  And because it was autumn, the leaves were lovely colors, orange-red, reddish-orange, deep yellow.
  —*Afternoon of the Elves* by Janet Taylor Lisle

- **Repeating a Word**
  You can repeat a word to emphasize a particular idea or feeling.
  The baying of the hounds grew nearer, then still nearer, nearer, ever nearer.
  —*The Most Dangerous Game* by Richard Connell

Practice

Write three sentences of your own, modeled after the examples above. Follow the pattern of the original sentence as closely as you can.

Preparing for Tests

How can I check my sentence knowledge?

Read the following questions. For each one select the correct answer.

1. Which sentence is complete?
   a. He saw the doctor and took the medicine.
   b. The cough and the runny nose and sneeze.
   c. Missed school for one week.
   d. His teacher and the principal and his parents.

2. Choose the punctuation mark that goes at the end of the sentence below.
   What was the final score of the game___
   a. period (.)   **c.** comma (,)
   b. question mark (?)   **d.** exclamation point (!)

3. Which sentence has the comma in the correct place?
   a. What is the first, thing you will do?
   b. Next, the cat will have to be fed.
   c. He didn't, eat all the food in his dish.
   d. I think that the cat, was ill.

4. You are writing about getting a new pet. Which sentence helps the reader picture your pet?
   a. On the way to the pet store, the traffic was horrible.
   b. There were puppies, kittens, and birds in the first room.
   c. Our kitten looks like a little tiger with white paws.
   d. We could hardly wait to get home with our pet.

5. Which sentence is correct?
   a. Climbed the hill, ran all the way down, and got on her bike.
   b. Laughed at the ending and read it again.
   c. The fifth graders finished the project before it was due.
   d. Was the time for everyone to try their best.

6. **Which sentence is punctuated correctly?**
   a. At the park Conall, ran and played ball.
   b. He liked the swings, but I was tired of pushing him.
   c. Then he wanted, to slide, and teeter-totter.
   d. Finally, it was time, to go home.

7. **In which sentence does the subject agree with the verb?**
   a. Those classes joins the team every year.
   b. Mrs. Smith like her students to participate.
   c. She encourage her entire class to sign up for an event.
   d. They always win a ribbon for best student participation.

8. **Your friend is meeting Matt, another one of your friends, at the park. Since they do not know each other, which information about Matt would be most helpful?**
   a. His favorite sport is baseball, and he plays very well.
   b. He lives in the house on the corner, near the park entrance.
   c. Matt will be wearing a red cap and carrying a baseball.
   d. His family moved to the neighborhood in June.

9. **Which sentence should end with an exclamation point?**
   a. What time did our teacher say that the concert would start
   b. Our parents will bring snacks for the offstage time
   c. Mrs. Erdman told us to bring a book along
   d. Get away from that shaky old ladder

10. **Choose the sentence that belongs in a paragraph with this topic sentence: Our student council voted to have a pet day.**
   a. The student council meets once a month.
   b. The tulips on our playground bloom in spring.
   c. Students will bring their pets and parade around the gym.
   d. The student council is made up of six girls and seven boys.

A Writer's Resource

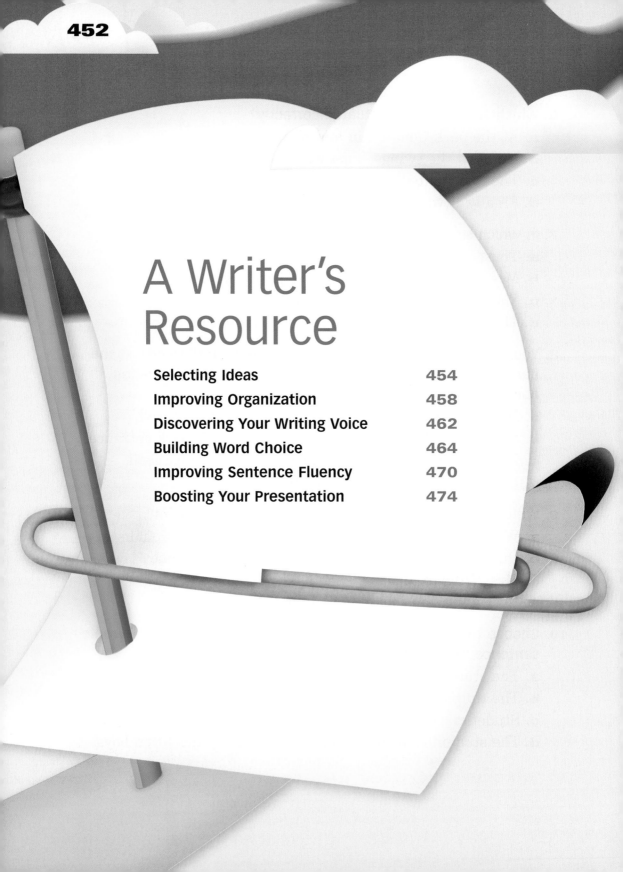

A Writer's Resource

Writers sometimes get stuck and need a little help. Finding a good topic to write about or looking for just the right word can be challenging. If you're in class when questions come up, you can ask your teacher for help. What happens, though, when you're somewhere else, like home?

This chapter is a great place to find answers to your questions! When you can't find a topic, aren't sure how to organize your details, or your sentences sound boring—be sure to look in "A Writer's Resource" for help.

Mini Index

You will learn how to . . .

How can I find a good topic to write about?

Try a Topic-Selecting Activity

Here are some topic-selecting strategies you can try.

Clustering Begin a cluster by writing a word connected with your assignment in the middle of a piece of paper. Then write related words around it. Circle and connect the words. (See the cluster on page **456**.)

Freewriting With your general topic in mind, write freely for 3 to 5 minutes. Do not stop to make corrections or look up facts—just write. As you freewrite, you may find one or two topics you could use.

Listing As you think about your assignment, make a list of related ideas and key words. After you have listed as many as you can, check for ideas or words you feel would make good writing topics.

Sentence Completion Another way to develop ideas is to complete a sentence starter in as many ways as you can. Make sure that your sentence starter relates to your assignment. Here are some samples:

I remember when . . .   I wonder how . . .
One thing I know about . . .   I just learned . . .

"Basics-of-Life" List

Look at the list below for possible topic areas. Here's how to use the "Basics-of-Life" list: (Also see page **148**.)

1. Choose a topic category. *(environment)*
2. Decide what part of this subject fits your assignment. *(report on oceans)*
3. List possible subjects. *(farming algae and pearls)*

animals	school	clothing	sports	food
friends	community	family	faith	environment
health	computers	games	rules	books
movies	science	exercise	money	television

What else can I do to get started?

Use a List of Writing Topics

The following topics are organized according to the four basic forms of writing. Depending on your assignment, look through these lists to find ideas.

Descriptive Writing

People: a relative, a teacher, a friend, a neighbor, yourself, someone you spend time with, someone you admire, someone from history

Places: a room, a garage, a basement, an attic, a rooftop, the alley, the gym, the library, a museum, a lake, the zoo, a barn, a park

Things: a pet, a cartoon, a video game, a junk drawer, a photograph, a favorite possession, a Web site, a stuffed animal

Narrative Writing

Tell about . . . getting caught, getting lost, making a mistake, helping someone, being surprised, making the news, learning to do something

Expository Writing

How to . . . make a burrito, care for a pet, organize your life, earn money, get in shape, be a good friend, eat a balanced diet, saddle a horse

The causes of . . . pollution, rust, hurricanes, infections, success in school, happiness, accidents, volcanoes

Kinds of . . . music, commercials, clouds, heroes, clothes, restaurants, fun, books, games, animals, houses, vehicles

The definition of . . . friendship, courage, a hero, geology, rap, freedom, love, a team, family

Persuasive Writing

Issues: school rules, homework, recycling, helmets (bicycle, skateboard), things that need to be improved, favorite causes, pet peeves, something that deserves support, a need for more or less of something

How can I collect details for my writing?

Try Graphic Organizers

A graphic organizer is a good way to gather and organize details for writing. Use a **5 W's chart** (page **93**) for a personal narrative or a news story and a **Venn diagram** (page **392**) for comparison-contrast writing. Four more graphic organizers are shown on these two pages. See which one works best for you.

Cluster A cluster or web will help you gather facts and ideas for reports, narratives, and poems. Begin by writing the subject in the middle of the page. Then list related words around it. Circle and connect your words.

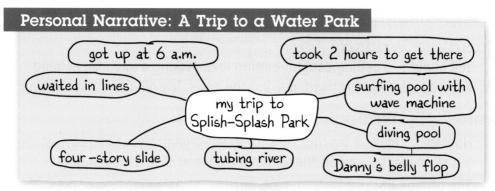

Personal Narrative: A Trip to a Water Park

- got up at 6 a.m.
- took 2 hours to get there
- waited in lines
- surfing pool with wave machine
- my trip to Splish-Splash Park
- diving pool
- four-story slide
- tubing river
- Danny's belly flop

Sensory Chart This organizer will help you collect details for observation reports and descriptions. Make a chart with five columns— one for each sense. Under each sense, list your details.

Observation Report: Growing Baker's Yeast

Sight	Sound	Smell	Taste	Touch
–tan –thick and puffy –bubbles pop slowly	–little "poof-poof" sounds	–like bread baking –a bit like vinegar	–sour, not sweet	–cold –wet

Time Line Time lines organize events in chronological (time) order. Personal narratives and how-to essays often follow this pattern. Write the topic at the top of your time line. Then list the events or steps in order, from first to last.

How-To Essay: Feeding a Cat

1 ⊥ Buy two heavy bowls—one for water, one for food.
2 ┼ Buy cat food that is dry and nutritious.
3 ┼ Place food and water away from litter pan.
4 ┼ Fill each bowl twice a day.

Process Diagram Science-related writing often tells how events are connected. To make a process diagram, start with the first event in the process. Then write the second event, the third event, and so on. Connect the events with arrows.

Science Report: How Water Boils

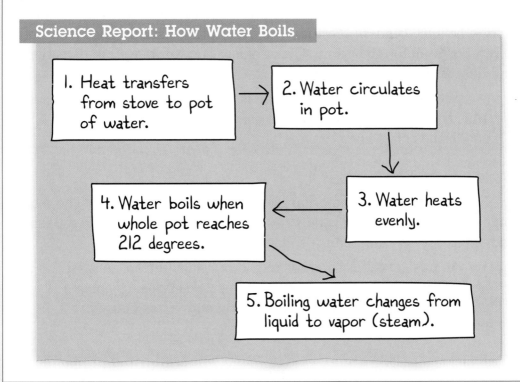

1. Heat transfers from stove to pot of water.

2. Water circulates in pot.

3. Water heats evenly.

4. Water boils when whole pot reaches 212 degrees.

5. Boiling water changes from liquid to vapor (steam).

How can I organize my details effectively?

Put Ideas in Order

After you choose your topic and collect your details, you need to organize your information. First, decide on an order and then make an outline. Here are three ways to put your information in order.

Time Order

It's easy to follow ideas when the facts or events are explained in the order in which they happened (*before, during, after*). Time order works for stories, explanations, directions, and reports.

> First, we used a rope to raise the wood up into the tree. Next, our parents helped us make a frame for the floor. After we nailed boards to the frame, we put up the walls and roof.

Order of Location

When details are described in the order in which they are located (*above, behind, beneath, beside*), the description usually goes from left to right or from top to bottom. Order of location works well in directions and descriptions.

> The trunk of our tree-house tree is so wide that I can't reach my arms around it. The patterns in the bark seem to crawl up the tree, and the tips of its branches reach for the sky.

Order of Importance

News stories are often organized by order of importance. The most important detail usually comes *first,* but it may come *last.* Persuasive and expository writing can also be organized in this way.

> All kids need a place to call their own, and a tree house is the perfect place. It is a place to get away from televisions, computers, and little brothers and sisters. Most importantly, a tree house is a place to just hang out with your friends.

Build a Topic Outline

After you have decided how to organize your details, you can write an outline. First, you need to select the main points that support your topic. Then, under each main point, list the details that help explain it. A *topic outline* contains only words and phrases, but if you want to express your ideas in complete sentences, you can write a *sentence outline.*

Topic Outline

    I. Daniel Boone's early adventures
        A. Moved often
        B. Fought in French and Indian War
        C. Got interested in Kentucky
   II. Famous as Kentucky explorer
        A. Several trips from 1767 to 1774
        B. Blazed the Wilderness Trail
        C. Started Boonesborough
  III. Kentucky beautiful but dangerous
        A. Hunting and warring ground
        B. French and British opposition
        C. Settlers often attacked

Sentence Outline

    I. Daniel Boone had many adventures.
        A. He moved often when he was young.
        B. He fought in the French and Indian War.
        C. He became interested in Kentucky.
   II. Boone became a famous Kentucky explorer.

How can I write effective topic sentences?

Try a Special Strategy

A **topic sentence** gives the main idea of a paragraph. A good topic sentence (1) names the topic and (2) states a detail or feeling about it. The following strategies will help you write terrific topic sentences.

Use a Number

Use number words to tell what the paragraph will be about.

> Here are three reasons why our class should serve a meal at the homeless shelter.

> I'm having several problems training our new puppy.

Create a List

Create a list of the things that the paragraph will include.

> Trees add beauty to nature, give shelter to wildlife, and make shade for people and plants.

> The setting of a story is the time and the place it happens.

Use Word Pairs

Use conjunctions that come in pairs to connect ideas in a topic sentence.

> Either keep dogs on a leash or keep them in fenced yards.

> My doctor said that both a balanced diet and regular exercise are needed to stay healthy.

Word Pairs
- either . . . or
- not only . . . but also
- both . . . and
- whether . . . or

Quote an Expert

Quote someone who knows something about your topic.

> Walt Disney once said, "All our dreams can come true."

> Amelia Earhart said, "It is easier to start something than it is to finish it."

What forms can I use for my writing?

Try These Forms of Writing

Finding the right form for your writing is very important. When you choose a form, think about *who* you're writing for (your *audience*) and *why* you're writing (your *purpose*). Listed below are a few different forms of descriptive, narrative, expository, and persuasive writing.

Anecdote	A little story used to make a point (See pages 292–297.)
Autobiography	The story of the writer's own life (See pages 83–124.)
Biography	The story of someone else's life (See pages 63–74.)
Book Review	Writing that shares your thoughts and feelings about a book (See pages 257–272.)
Cartoon	A simple drawing with a humorous message
Character Sketch	A description of one character in a story
Editorial	Newspaper letters or articles that give opinions
Fable	A short story that often uses talking animals as characters to teach a lesson
News Release	An explanation of a newsworthy event using the 5 W's *(who, what, where, when,* and *why)*
Pet Peeve	A personal feeling about something that bugs you
Proposal	Writing that asks for approval of an idea, a report, or a schedule
Tall Tale	A humorous, exaggerated story about a character that does impossible things (See page 306.)
Travelogue	Writing that describes a trip or travel pictures

How can I create an effective voice?

Make Your Voice Fit Your Purpose

Your writing will have an effective voice if it fits your purpose.

Descriptive Voice

A good descriptive voice sounds *interested*. One way to improve your descriptive voice is to follow this rule: "*show,* don't *tell.*"

- **Telling:** Here a writer tells what a mongoose is like.

    He was a mongoose, and he looked sort of like a cat and sort of like a weasel. He ran around a lot and made a strange noise.

- **Showing:** Here the author Rudyard Kipling describes a mongoose in a story from *The Jungle Book*:

    He was a mongoose, like a little cat in his fur and his tail but like a weasel in his head and his habits. He could scratch himself anywhere he pleased with any leg. . . . His war cry as he scuttled through the long grass was *Rikk-tikk-tikki-tikki-tchk!*

Narrative Voice

A good narrative voice sounds *natural* and *personal*. Your narrative writing should sound as if you are telling a story to a friend.

- **Unnatural and Impersonal:** This narrative sounds too dull.

    Last Saturday I couldn't find Moses, my pet ferret. I finally gave up looking and went to bed. Later I woke up because Moses was hiding in my bed.

- **Natural and Personal:** Here is the same story told in a more personal voice.

    Last Saturday I couldn't find Moses, my pet ferret. I was afraid he had run out the back door, so I looked for him for hours. Finally, I gave up and went to bed. At about midnight, I woke up because something was licking my toe. I screamed and threw off the covers! You guessed it—Moses had found a warm place to hide in my bed.

Expository Voice

An expository voice should sound *well-informed* and *enthusiastic*. Use interesting facts and specific details to get and hold your reader's attention.

- **Uninterested:** This writer simply presents the facts.

    Seaweed is sometimes served as a vegetable. Seaweed is also used in many foods. Some of the foods are ice cream, hot fudge, and stir-fry.

- **Well-informed and enthusiastic:** This writer sounds truly interested.

    Have you ever had a long strand of seaweed wrap around your leg at the beach? Don't panic—it's not going to eat you! You have probably eaten several forms of seaweed, however. Some kinds of ice cream and hot fudge use seaweed to make them creamy. Seaweed is also served as a vegetable. Your favorite stir-fried food may contain some of the delicious green stuff!

Persuasive Voice

A persuasive voice should sound *convincing* and *positive*. Support your opinion with good reasons and positive solutions.

- **Unconvincing and negative:** This writer simply complains and offers no solutions.

    Monday mornings are awful. My brother and I have to get up early and go to school while we're still sleepy. The teachers aren't very happy, either. Why doesn't someone do something about Monday mornings?

- **Convincing and positive:** This writer has a more positive attitude and proposes a solution.

    Wouldn't it be great if our class did something that was fun every Monday? I think our class should have a Monday Morning Talent Show. That would be one way to put the teachers and students in a good mood for the rest of the week.

How can I spice up my writing style?

Use Some Writing Techniques

You can develop a lively writing style by using some special effects. For example, you can add dialogue to your stories to make them sound more natural and seem more real. (See pages 96 and 116–117.) Below are additional techniques you can experiment with in your own writing.

Exaggeration Overstating the truth to make a point

Gramps is the funniest man in the world.

Idiom Using a word or phrase in a way that is different from its usual or dictionary meaning

Maha and Jake ironed out **their problems.**
(In this sentence, *ironed out* means "solved.")
My sister and I don't see eye to eye **about how to clean our room.**
(In this sentence, *see eye to eye* means "agree.")

Metaphor Comparing two different things without using the word *like* or *as*

That player **in the red jersey is a regular** roadrunner.
Mom's chicken soup **was the best** medicine **for my cold.**

Personification Giving human qualities to nonhuman things, such as an idea, an object, or an animal

That stubborn **rock** refused to move.

Sensory Details Details that help the reader *hear, see, smell, taste,* or *feel* what is being described

When the book crashed **to the floor, our cat** jumped three feet straight up, **giving me** the chills.

Simile Comparing two things using the words *like* or *as*

The new hamburgers at Brute Burger are as big around as a pizza.
The ice was as smooth as glass **before the skaters arrived.**

How can I learn to talk about my writing?

Study Some Writing Terms

This glossary includes terms that name important parts of the writing process.

Audience	The people who read or hear your writing
Dialogue	Written conversation between two or more people
Focus Statement	The specific part of a topic that a writer chooses to concentrate or "focus" on (See page 23.)
Point of View	The angle or viewpoint from which a story is told (See page 310.)
Purpose	The main reason for writing a certain piece to describe to narrate to explain to persuade
Style	The way a writer puts words, phrases, and sentences together
Supporting Details	Specific details used to develop a topic or bring a story to life
Theme	The main idea or message in a piece of writing
Topic	The specific subject of a piece of writing
Topic Sentence	The sentence that expresses the main idea of a paragraph (See page 460.)
Transition	A word or phrase that ties ideas together in essays, paragraphs, and sentences (See pages 472–473.)
Voice	The tone or feeling a writer uses to express ideas

How can I increase my vocabulary skills?

Try Vocabulary-Building Techniques

Use context.

When you are reading and you come to a word you don't know, check the words around it to see if you can figure out its meaning. (See the next page.) Here is an example:

The situation looked perilous, **but Bob's friend told him that it wasn't as** dangerous **as it appeared.** (You can figure out what *perilous* means by looking at how the word *dangerous* is used.)

Look up words in the dictionary.

When you come to a word you don't know, look it up in the dictionary. (See page 331.) This example shows how a dictionary can help you understand a word:

You could see by the horse's musculature **that he was strong.**

> **mus•cu•la•ture** (mŭs´kyə lə cho͞or´) *n.* The system of muscles of an animal or of a body part.

Learn about word parts.

You can figure out the meanings of new words by learning about prefixes, suffixes, and roots. (See pages 468–469.) The following sentence contains two examples:

A car's antifreeze **should be checked** annually.
(*Anti-* is a prefix meaning "against" **freezing**.
Annu is a root meaning "year": **once a year**.)

Use Context

You can often figure out an unfamiliar word by looking at the words surrounding it. Here are some strategies you can use:

- Study the sentence containing the unfamiliar word, as well as the sentences that come before and after it.

  > On his first day at the mine, Harold took an elevator deep into the earth. He never knew subterranean spaces were so dark. Working underground would be an adventure. (*Subterranean* means "under the earth.")

- Search for **synonyms** (words with the same meaning).

  > Because I plan to be a lawyer, Dad calls me a barrister. (A *barrister* is a "lawyer.")

- Search for **antonyms** (words with the opposite meaning).

  > Dad says that fishing is tedious, but I think it's exciting. (*Tedious* means "boring," the opposite of "exciting.")

- Search for a **definition** of the word.

  > We saw yuccas, common desert plants, on our drive to the Grand Canyon. (*Yuccas* are common desert plants.)

- Search for **familiar words in a series** with the new word.

  > In the South, many houses have a veranda, porch, or patio. (A *veranda* is a large, open porch.)

- Watch for **idioms** (words that have different uses from their most typical dictionary meanings).

  > My cell phone is cutting out. (The dictionary meaning of this phrase could be "removing something using scissors," but here it means "disconnecting.")

Learn About Word Parts

Beginning with Prefixes

Prefixes are word parts that come before the root or base word (*Pre-* means "before"). Prefixes can change the meaning of a word. *Kind* means "gentle." Add the prefix *un-*, meaning "not," and the resulting word, *unkind*, means "not gentle." Here are some other common prefixes:

ex *(out)*
  expel (to drive out)

non *(absence of, not)*
  nonfat (without fat)

inter *(among, between)*
  international (between two or more nations)

pre *(before)*
  preview (to show something before the regular time)

mal *(bad, poor)*
  malnutrition (poor nutrition)

re *(again, back)*
  rewrite (to write again)

Ending with Suffixes

Suffixes are word parts that come at the end of a word. Sometimes a suffix will tell you what part of speech a word is. For example, many adverbs end in the suffix *-ly*. Add the suffix *-able*, which means "able to," to the word *agree*, and the resulting word, *agreeable*, means "able or willing to agree." Here are some other suffixes:

ion *(state of)*
  infection (state of being infected)

ness *(state of)*
  carelessness (state of being careless)

less *(without)*
  careless (without care)

ology *(study, science)*
  biology (study of living things)

ly *(in some manner)*
  bashfully (in a bashful manner)

y *(tending to)*
  itchy (tending to itch)

Knowing Your Roots

A **root** is the main part of a word. If you know the root of a difficult word, you may be able to figure out the word's meaning.

Suppose that you hear your friend say, "I couldn't understand what the speaker said because his voice wasn't *audible*." If you know that the root *aud* means "hear or listen," you will know that your friend couldn't hear the speaker's voice. Here are some other roots:

alter *(other)*
  alternate (another choice)

bio *(life)*
  biography (book about a person's life)

chron *(time)*
  chronological (in time order)

cise *(cut)*
  incision (a thin, clean cut)

dem *(people)*
  democracy (ruled by the people)

equi *(equal)*
  equinox (a day and night of equal length)

fin *(end)*
  final (the last or end of something)

flex *(bend)*
  flexible (able to bend)

fract, frag *(break)*
  fracture (to break)
  fragment (a small piece)

geo *(earth)*
  geography (the study of the earth's surface)

graph *(write)*
  autograph (writing one's name)

multi *(many, much)*
  multicultural (including many cultures)

port *(carry)*
  export (to carry out)

scope *(see, watch)*
  microscope (an instrument used for viewing objects too small to be seen with the naked eye)

tele *(over a long distance)*
  telephone (machine used to speak over a distance)

therm *(heat)*
  thermostat (a device for controlling heat)

voc *(call)*
  vocalize (to use the voice; sing)

How can I vary my sentences?

Study Sentence Patterns

Use a combination of sentence patterns to make your writing more interesting. Some basic sentence patterns are shown below.

1 Subject + Action Verb

    S   AV
Samantha smiled. (Some action verbs, like *smiled,* do not need a direct object to make a complete thought.)

2 Subject + Action Verb + Direct Object

    S   AV   DO
Stan threw the ball. (Some action verbs, like *threw,* need a direct object, like *ball,* to make a complete thought.

3 Subject + Action Verb + Indirect Object + Direct Object

    S   AV IO   DO
Latesha gave me a penny.

4 Subject + Action Verb + Direct Object + Object Complement

       S   AV   DO   OC
Coach Allison named Rodney captain.

5 Subject + Linking Verb + Predicate Noun

    S   LV   PN
Frogs are amphibians.

6 Subject + Linking Verb + Predicate Adjective

    S   LV   PA
Toads are bumpy.

(In the patterns above, the subject comes before the verb. In the patterns below, the verb comes before the subject.)

    LV   S   PN
7 **Is Lanette your sister?** (A question)

       LV   S
8 **Here is my jacket.** (A sentence beginning with *there* or *here*)

Practice Sentence Diagramming

Diagramming a sentence can give you a "picture" of how the parts fit together. Below are diagrams of the sentences from page 470.

1 Samantha smiled.

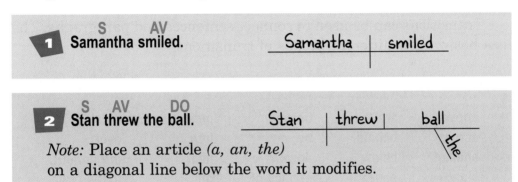

2 Stan threw the ball.

Note: Place an article *(a, an, the)* on a diagonal line below the word it modifies.

3 Latesha gave me a penny.

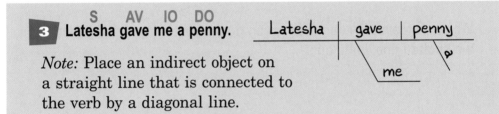

Note: Place an indirect object on a straight line that is connected to the verb by a diagonal line.

4 Coach Allison named Rodney captain.

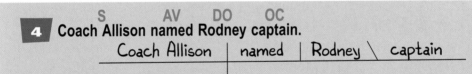

Note: Place a vertical line between a verb and its direct object. Use a diagonal line before the object compliment.

5 Frogs are amphibians.

Note: Place a diagonal line between a linking verb and the predicate noun or adjective.

6 Toads are bumpy.

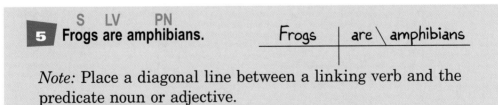

How can I connect my ideas?

Use Transitions

Transitions can be used to connect sentences and paragraphs. The lists below show different groups of transitions.

Words that show location:

above	around	between	inside	outside
across	behind	by	into	over
against	below	down	near	throughout
along	beneath	in back of	off	to the right
among	beside	in front of	on top of	under

> We saw at least five hundred green ducks yesterday. Among them we spotted one white one.

Words that show time:

about	during	until	yesterday	finally
after	first	meanwhile	next	then
at	second	today	soon	as soon as
before	third	tomorrow	later	when

> On the day that I was supposed to meet Robbie at 9:00 a.m., I didn't wake up until 9:15. Meanwhile, Robbie had slept late, too.

Words that show comparisons (similarities):

in the same way	likewise	as	while
similarly	like	also	

> You should always wear protective gear at the skate park. Similarly, you should always wear a helmet when you ride a bike.

Words that show contrast (differences):

on the other hand	otherwise	but	although
even though	however	still	yet

Dogs that play and exercise on grassy yards must have their toenails trimmed regularly. On the other hand, dogs that are walked on pavement seldom need to have their toenails trimmed.

Words that emphasize a point:

again	truly	especially	for this reason
to repeat	in fact	to emphasize	

The coach might announce a last-minute change in a play. For this reason, it's important to listen carefully to his calls.

Words that add information:

again	for instance	and	as well
also	besides	next	along with
another	for example	finally	in addition

The best reason for saving energy is to make resources last longer. Another important reason is to cut down on pollution.

Words that summarize:

as a result	finally	in conclusion
therefore	lastly	because

During her serve, the judges said Sela stepped over the line. As a result, Sela's opponent was given the point that won the match.

How can I make my final copy look better?

Add Diagrams and Graphs

Diagrams are simple drawings that include labels.

■ **Picture diagrams** show how something is put together, how the parts relate to each other, or how the object works.

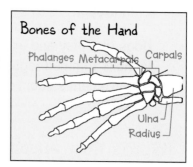

Bones of the Hand

Phalanges Metacarpals Carpals

Ulna
Radius

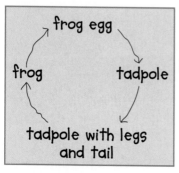

frog egg

frog

tadpole

tadpole with legs and tail

■ A **cycle diagram** shows how something happens over time. The process always leads back to the starting point.

Graphs show information about how things compare to each other. They help show information that includes numbers.

■ A **circle graph** shows what part (or percentage) of the total number each portion contains.

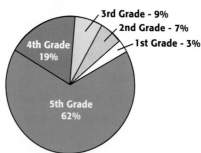

Percentage of Guppies in Each Grade

3rd Grade - 9%
2nd Grade - 7%
1st Grade - 3%
4th Grade 19%
5th Grade 62%

■ A **bar graph** compares two or more things at one point in time—like a snapshot. Bars on a graph can go up and down or sideways.

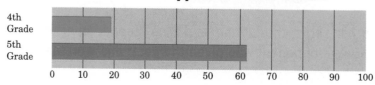

Number of Guppies in Grades 4 and 5

4th Grade
5th Grade

0   10   20   30   40   50   60   70   80   90   100

Add Pictures

Pictures will help make your final copy clear and interesting. Use photos from magazines or newspapers or download them from the Internet. (*Note:* Web sites often have rules for using their pictures. Check with your teacher first.)

■ **To Inform** . . . Pictures can help the reader understand your topic. They can add color and interesting details in the body of a report or an essay or decorate a report cover. You can wrap your text around a picture, as shown in this example from a how-to essay:

If you've never used a computer, just looking at one can make you ask lots of questions. How do I get the screen to light up? What are all the buttons for? Do I have to know how to type? What does the mouse do? Don't worry; computers are easy to use. If you can use the remote for a TV, you can use a computer. There are three basic things you should know.

■ **To Set the Tone** . . . Pictures can show the reader how you feel about your topic. The photo below, included in a report on occupations, says that being a chef is fun. The words and the picture work together.

Have you ever thought about being a chef? There are many jobs available for cooks. Even if you don't know how to cook, you can go to school to learn. The pay is good, and you can move around the country because there are restaurants everywhere. The best part of the job is that good food makes people happy. Being a chef could be fun.

How should I set up my practical writing?

Follow Guidelines for Letters

Friendly letters and **business letters** have the same basic parts—*heading, salutation, body, closing,* and *signature*. In addition, a business letter has an *inside address*.

Friendly Letter

In a friendly letter, the paragraphs are indented. The side notes below explain the parts.

Heading
Sender's address and date

Salutation
A greeting followed by a comma

Body
Paragraphs indented; no space between them

Closing
First word capitalized and a comma at end
Signature
Written signature

1040 Tolman Street
Williamsburg, VA 23185
January 8, 2005

Dear Phillipe,

My name is Michael, and I am your new pen pal. I'm in fifth grade at Page Elementary School in Williamsburg, Virginia.

I just started taking swimming lessons at the local YMCA. My parents got me the lessons for Christmas. I still need to practice keeping my head down and breathing between strokes. My instructor says I'm getting better though, and the classes are a lot of fun!

My family is my parents and my little brother, Danny, who is only six. We also have a dog named Ginger. My family lives in a duplex. Danny and I take Ginger to the park nearby to play catch.

Please write back and tell me about yourself.

Your pen pal,
Michael Fritz

Business Letter

All the parts of a business letter start at the left margin in block style. Check the side notes below for more details.

Heading
Sender's address and date

4824 Park Street
Richland Center, WI 53581
January 20, 2005

Inside Address
Name and address of person or company

Mr. David Shore
Box 168
Yellowstone Park, WY 82190

Salutation
A greeting followed by a colon

Dear Mr. Shore:

We're having a contest in my family to see who can plan the best summer vacation. I want to convince everyone that a trip to Yellowstone National Park would be better than going to the seashore for a week.

Body
No indentations and double-spaced between paragraphs

I would appreciate any help you could give me. I am interested in brochures with photos and maps of the park. I will also need some information about where we can stay and what special activities we can do in the park.

Thank you for your help. Maybe I'll see you next summer.

Closing
First word capitalized and a comma at end

Sincerely yours,

Luke Johnson

Signature
Written signature before the typed or printed name

Luke Johnson

Envelope

Address envelopes for business and friendly letters the same way: Use all capital letters and no punctuation.

LUKE JOHNSON
4824 PARK STREET
RICHLAND CENTER WI 53581

MR DAVID SHORE
BOX 168
YELLOWSTONE PARK WY 82190

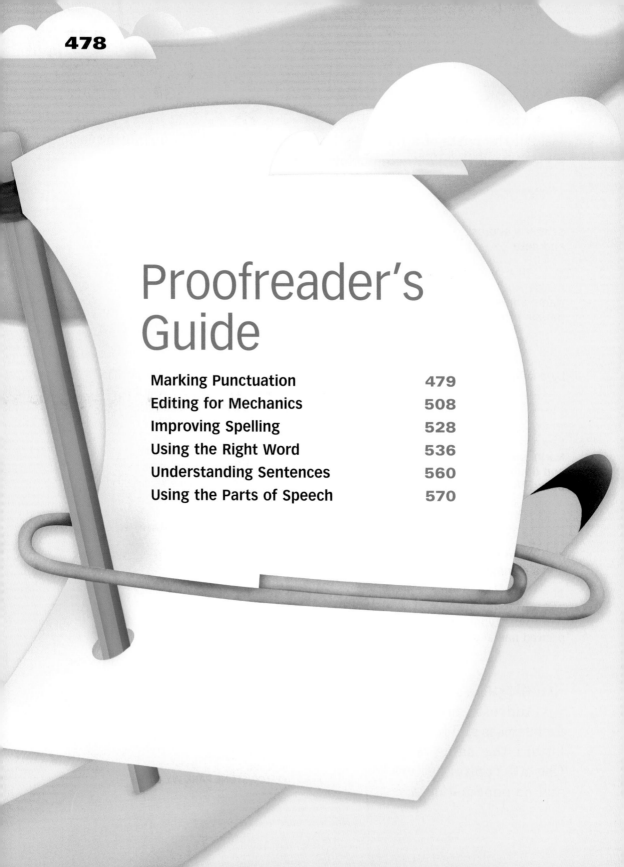

Proofreader's Guide

Marking Punctuation

Periods

A **period** is used to end a sentence. It is also used after initials, after abbreviations, and as a decimal point.

479.1

At the End of a Sentence

Use a period to end a sentence that is a statement, a command, or a request.

> **Taro won the pitching contest.** (statement)
>
> **Take his picture.** (command)
>
> **Please loan me your baseball cap.** (request)

479.2

After an Initial

Use a period after an initial in a person's name. (An initial is the first letter of a name.)

> **B. B. King** (blues musician)
>
> **A. A. Milne** (writer)

479.3

As a Decimal Point

Use a period as a decimal point and to separate dollars and cents.

> **Robert is 99.9 percent sure that the bus pass costs $2.50.**

479.4

In Abbreviations

Use a period after an abbreviation. (See page **520** for more about abbreviations.)

> **Mr. Mrs. Jr. Dr. B.C.E. U.S.A.**

Use only one period when an abbreviation is the last word in a sentence.

> **A library has books, CD's, DVD's, magazines, etc.**

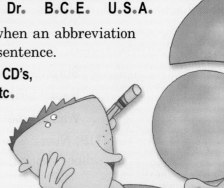

Question Marks

A **question mark** is used after a direct question (an interrogative sentence). Sometimes it is used to show doubt about the correctness of a detail.

480.1

In Direct Questions

Place a question mark at the end of a direct question.

Do air bags make cars safer?

No question mark is used after an indirect question. (In an indirect question, you tell about the question you or someone else asked.)

I asked if air bags make cars safer.

480.2

In Tag Questions

A question mark is used when you add a short question to the end of a statement. (This type of statement is called a *tag question*.)

The end of this century is the year 2099, isn't it?

480.3

To Show Doubt

Place a question mark in parentheses to show that you aren't sure a fact is correct.

The ship arrived in Boston on July 23(?), 1652.

Exclamation Points

An **exclamation point** is used to express strong feeling. It may be placed after a word, a phrase, or a sentence.

480.4

To Show Strong Feeling

Surprise! (word)

Happy birthday! (phrase)

Wait for me! (sentence)

TIP: Never use extra exclamation points (Hooray!!!) in school writing assignments or in business letters.

End Punctuation

For each of the following sentences, write the correct end-punctuation mark (a period, a question mark, or an exclamation point).

Example: Do you know what the capital of Ohio is?

1. Ooh, I know, I know—it's O

2. No, I'm not asking about capital letters

3. Darla, you tell me the answer

4. The state capital of Ohio is Columbus

5. What city is South Carolina's capital

6. I'll give you a hint

7. It starts the same way as Ohio's capital

8. It sounds like the name of a South American country

9. Is it Columbia

10. Yes, you're right

Next Step: Write a question about a state capital. Then write another sentence that answers it. Make sure that you use the correct end punctuation.

Commas

Commas keep words and ideas from running together. They tell your reader where to pause, which makes your writing easier to read.

482.1 Between Items in a Series

Place commas between words, phrases, or clauses in a series. (A series is three items or more in a row.)

Hanae likes pepperoni, pineapple, and olives on her pizza. (words)

During the summer I read mysteries, ride my bike, and play basketball. (phrases)

482.2 To Set Off Dialogue

Use a comma to set off the words of the speaker from rest of the sentence.

The stranded frog replied, "I'm just waiting for the toad truck."

If you are telling what someone has said but are not using the person's exact words, do *not* use commas or quotation marks.

The stranded frog told me that he was just waiting for the toad truck.

482.3 In Compound Sentences

Use a comma between two independent clauses that are joined by the coordinating conjunction *and, but, or, nor, for, so,* or *yet.*

Aunt Carrie offered to pay my way, so I am going to the amusement park with her.

We'll try to get on all the rides, and we'll see one of the stage shows.

TIP: Do not connect two independent clauses with a comma only. That is called a comma splice. (See **564.2** for more information about independent clauses.)

Commas 1

■ Between Items in a Series
■ To Set Off Dialogue

For each sentence below, write the word or words that should be followed by a comma. Write the commas, too.

Example: Gloria said "I have a dentist
appointment today."

said,

1. The dentist says to make sure
you get enough calcium vitamin
D and vitamin C.

2. "These vitamins and minerals are important for
healthy teeth" Dr. Green said.

3. Gloria asked "Doesn't milk have calcium and
vitamin D?"

4. "Yes, and so does cheese" said the dentist.

5. Other foods with calcium include fish almonds and
yogurt.

6. Good sources of vitamin C are oranges green peppers
and strawberries.

Next Step: Write two sentences of dialogue between a dentist
and a patient. Make sure that you place commas
correctly.

Commas . . .

484.1
To Separate Introductory Phrases and Clauses

Use a comma to separate a long phrase or clause that comes before the main part of the sentence.

> After checking my knee pads, I started off. (phrase)
>
> If you practice often, skating is easy. (clause)

You usually do not need a comma when the phrase or the clause comes after the main part of the sentence.

> Skating is easy if you practice often.

Also, a comma is usually unnecessary after a short opening phrase.

> In time you'll find yourself looking forward to practice.
> (No comma is needed after *In time*.)

484.2
In Dates and Addresses

Commas are used to set off the different parts in addresses and dates. (Do *not* use a comma between the state and ZIP code.)

> My family's address is 2463 Bell Street, Atlanta, Georgia 30200.
>
> I will be 21 years old on January 15, 2015.

Do not use a comma if only the month and year are written (January 2015).

484.3
To Keep Numbers Clear

Place commas between hundreds, thousands, millions, and billions.

> Junji's car has 200,000 miles on it. He's trying to sell it for $1,000.

When a number refers to a year, street address, or ZIP code, no comma is used. Also, write numbers in the millions and billions this way: 7.5 million, 16 billion. (See 524.2.)

> Brazil is a country of 184 million people.

Commas 2

■ To Separate Introductory Phrases and Clauses
■ In Dates and Addresses

 ▶ **Rewrite the paragraph below. Be sure to add commas to dates, address parts, and introductory word groups that should be followed by a comma.**

Example: When Dad was young he
played soccer.
When Dad was young,

1   The International Children's Games began on July 30

2   2004. During the five-day event in Ohio more than 2,000

3   kids from 12 to 15 years old competed in 10 different

4   sports. Contestants played table tennis and baseball at

5   John Carroll University 20700 North Park Boulevard

6   University Heights Ohio. They played basketball at

7   Cleveland State University 2121 Euclid Avenue Cleveland

8   Ohio. When the Games return on July 6 2005 kids from

9   150 cities around the world will meet in Coventry, England.

Next Step: Write two sentences about a friend who enjoys athletics. Tell when your friend was born and give his or her address.

Commas . . .

486.1
To Set Off Interruptions

Use commas to set off a word, phrase, or clause that interrupts the main thought of a sentence.

> **You could, for example, take the dog for a walk instead of watching TV.**

Here is a list of words and phrases that you can use to interrupt main thoughts.

for example	to be sure	moreover
however	as a matter of fact	in fact

TESTS: Try one of these tests to see if a word or phrase interrupts a main thought:

1. Take out the word or phrase. The meaning of the sentence should not change.
2. Move the word or phrase to another place in the sentence. The meaning should not change.

486.2
To Set Off Interjections

Use a comma to separate an interjection or a weak exclamation from the rest of the sentence.

> **Wow, look at that sunrise!**
>
> **Hey, we're up early!**

If an interjection shows very strong feeling, an exclamation point (!) may be used after it.

> **Whoa! Let's slow down.**

The following words are often used as interjections.

Hello	Hey	Ah
Oh my	No kidding	Hmm
Really	Wow	Well

486.3
In Direct Address

Use commas to separate a noun of direct address (the person being spoken to) from the rest of the sentence.

> **Yuri, some computers do not need keyboards.**
>
> **I know that, Maria. They respond to voice commands.**

Commas 3

■ To Set Off Interruptions
■ To Set Off Interjections

▶ **For each sentence below, write the word or words that should be followed by a comma. Write the commas, too.**

Example: Wow did you know that the seasons in the United States are the opposite of Australia's seasons?

Wow,

1. Well it's true!

2. In Australia for example winter is from June to August.

3. In most areas of Australia however even winter temperatures don't fall below 50 degrees Fahrenheit.

4. In the southern part of Argentina on the other hand it gets quite cold in July and August.

5. No kidding you can ski down a mountain then!

6. Hmm that would be different.

Next Step: Write two sentences about your favorite season. Use an interruption in one and an interjection in the other. Use commas correctly.

Commas . . .

488.1
To Separate Equal Adjectives

Use commas to separate two or more adjectives that equally modify a noun.

> **There are plenty of nutritious, edible plants in the world.** (*Nutritious* and *edible* are separated by a comma because they modify *plants* equally.)

> **We may eat many unusual plants in the years to come.** (*Many* and *unusual* do *not* modify *plants* equally. No comma is needed.)

TESTS: Use one of the tests below to help you decide if adjectives modify equally:

1. Switch the order of the adjectives. If the sentence is still clear, the adjectives modify equally.
2. Put the word *and* between the adjectives. If the sentence sounds clear, the adjectives modify equally.

Remember: Do not use a comma to separate the last adjective from the noun.

488.2
To Set Off Explanatory Phrases and Appositives

Use a comma to set off an explanatory phrase from the rest of the sentence. (*Explanatory* means "helping to explain.")

> **Sonja, back from a visit to Florida, showed us some seashells.**

Use commas to set off appositives. An appositive is a word or phrase that is another way of saying the noun or pronoun before it. (See 566.5.)

> **Mrs. Chinn, our science teacher, says that the sun is an important source of energy.**

> **Solar power and wind power, two very clean sources of energy, should be used more.**

488.3
In Letter Writing

Place a comma after the salutation, or greeting, in a friendly letter and after the closing in all letters.

> **Dear Uncle Jim,** (greeting)   **Love,** (closing)

Commas 4

- ■ To Separate Equal Adjectives
- ■ To Set Off Appositives

▶ **For each sentence below, write the word or words that should be followed by a comma. Write the commas, too.**

Example: Clyde my youngest brother was at the fair.

Clyde, my youngest brother,

1. He saw a round red-haired clown selling helium balloons.

2. The clown had tied about 30 colorful balloons to an old rusty fence post.

3. Suddenly Mrs. Flanders our neighbor shouted, "The balloons are getting away!"

4. Clyde ran as fast as he could, trying to reach the bright weightless bundle of color.

5. As Clyde grabbed the strings, Ricky our older cousin yelled, "No, Clyde! Let go!"

6. But Clyde a fearless boy was thrilled as the balloons lifted him into the air.

Next Step: Write an ending to this story. If you use an appositive or two equal adjectives, use commas correctly with them.

Apostrophes

An **apostrophe** is used to form contractions, to show possession, to form some plurals, or to show that letters have been left out of a word.

490.1
In Contractions

Use an apostrophe to show that one or more letters have been left out of a word, forming a contraction. The list below shows some common contractions.

Common Contractions

couldn't (could not)	**it's** (it is; it has)
didn't (did not)	**I've** (I have)
doesn't (does not)	**she's** (she is)
don't (do not)	**they'll** (they will)
hasn't (has not)	**they're** (they are)
haven't (have not)	**we've** (we have)
I'll (I will)	**wouldn't** (would not)
isn't (is not)	**you'd** (you would)

490.2
To Form Singular Possessives

Form the possessive of most singular nouns by adding an apostrophe and -s.

My sister's hobby is jazz dancing.

When a singular noun ends with an s or a z sound, the possessive may be formed by adding just an apostrophe.

Carlos' weather chart is very detailed.
(or) **Carlos's chart**

If the singular noun is a one-syllable word, form the possessive by adding both an apostrophe and -s.

Chris's lab report is incomplete.

TIP: An apostrophe is never used with a possessive pronoun (*its, hers, yours*).

The horse had its hooves trimmed.

Apostrophes 1

■ In Contractions
■ To Form Singular Possessives

Find the words in the following sentences that should have apostrophes but don't. Write these words correctly.

Example: Lately Ive been wondering who invented the compact disc (CD).
I've

1. The CD was James Russells invention.

2. He didnt like the hiss and the scratches that he heard on his records.

3. To play a record, youd put a stylus, or "needle," right on the vinyl disk.

4. This wasnt very good for the record, which would become more worn with each play.

5. In the late 1960s, Russell asked for his employers permission to work at his idea.

6. He recorded code onto a discs special surface; then a laser light beam "read" it without touching the CD.

7. Russell figured out that a recording wouldnt wear out this way.

Apostrophes . . .

492.1
To Form Plural Possessives

Add just an apostrophe to make the possessive form of plural nouns ending in *s*.

> **The visitors' ideas were helpful.**
>
> **The girls' washroom should be expanded.**

For plural nouns not ending in *s*, add an apostrophe and an *-s*.

> **The children's team practices today, and the men's league starts this weekend.**

Remember: The word before the apostrophe is the owner.

> **Justin's CD** (The CD belongs to Justin.)
>
> **the boys' shoes** (The shoes belong to the boys.)

492.2
To Form Possessives with Indefinite Pronouns

Form the possessive of an indefinite pronoun (*someone, everyone, no one, both, anyone*) by adding an apostrophe and *-s*.

> **everyone's idea**   **no one's fault**
>
> **somebody's book**   **another's suggestion**

492.3
To Form Shared Possessives

When possession is shared by more than one noun, add an apostrophe and *-s* to the last noun only.

> **Danetta, Sasha, and Olga's science project deals with electricity.**

492.4
To Form Some Plurals

An apostrophe and *s* are used to form the plural of a letter, a number, or a sign.

> **A's   B's   3's   10's   +'s   &'s**

492.5
In Place of Omitted Letters or Numbers

Use an apostrophe to show that one or more letters or numbers have been left out.

> **class of '15** (*20* is left out)
>
> **fixin' to go** (*g* is left out)

Apostrophes 2

■ To Form Plural Possessives
■ To Form Shared Possessives

▶ **Find the words in the following sentences that should have apostrophes but don't. Write these words correctly.**

Hello . . .

Example: Someone rang the
Lombards doorbell.
Lombards'

1. Roderick and Antoines dog barked when the doorbell rang.

2. A teenager said, "I have the Hoffmans pizza here."

3. "They live down the street," Roderick said, "next to the Singers house."

4. "That must be Leanna and Kaleys pizza," Antoine said.

5. Roderick said to the delivery boy, "Look for their parents car, a green minivan, in the driveway."

6. But there were green minivans parked in both the Singers and the Hoffmans driveways!

7. The pizza became Sovann and Howies dinner.

Next Step: Write a sentence about two of your neighbors who share possession of something. Place the apostrophe correctly.

Quotation Marks

Quotation marks are used to enclose the exact words of the speaker, to show that words are used in a special way, and to punctuate some titles.

494.1 To Set Off Dialogue

Place quotation marks before and after the spoken words in dialogue.

> Martha asked, "How long did you live in Mexico?"

494.2 Placement of Punctuation

Put periods and commas *inside* quotation marks.

> Trev said, "Let's make tuna sandwiches."
> "Sounds good," said Rich.

Place question marks or exclamation points *inside* the quotation marks when they punctuate the quotation.

> "Do we have any apples?" asked Trev.
> "Yes!" replied Mom.

Place them *outside* the quotation marks when they punctuate the main sentence.

> Did you hear Rich say, "We're out of pickles"?

494.3 To Punctuate Titles

Place quotation marks around titles of songs, poems, short stories, book chapters, and titles of articles in encyclopedias, magazines, or electronic sources. (See 502.1 for information on other kinds of titles.)

> "Oh! Susanna" (song) "Casey at the Bat" (poem)
> "McBroom Tells the Truth" (short story)
> "Local Boy Wins Competition" (newspaper article)

(See 514.2 for information on capitalization of titles.)

494.4 For Special Words

Quotation marks may be used to set apart a word that is being discussed or that is used in a special way.

> The word "scrumptious" is hard to spell.
> The queen wanted to sell the royal chairs rather than see them "throne" away.

Quotation Marks

■ **To Set Off Dialogue**
■ **To Punctuate Titles**

▶ **For each sentence, write the words, including any periods or commas, that should be enclosed in quotation marks.**

Example: Tyra said, I love to dance.
"I love to dance."

1. She wrote a poem about it called Dance Cake.

2. She especially likes dancing to the song Georgia Express.

3. That song rocks! said Ahmad.

4. Do you dance? asked Tyra.

5. He replied, I am just learning.

6. He had read Learn Basic Dance Steps, an article in a magazine.

7. Let's dance together sometime, Tyra suggested.

8. Ahmad hinted that he could dance only to an easy song like Hokey Pokey.

Next Step: Write a few lines of dialogue between two friends. Use quotation marks correctly.

Hyphens

A **hyphen** is used to divide a word at the end of a line. Hyphens are also used to join or create new words.

To Divide a Word

Use a hyphen to divide a word when you run out of room at the end of a line. A word may be divided only between syllables *(ex-plor-er)*. Always refer to a dictionary if you're not sure how to divide a word. Here are some guidelines for hyphenating words:

- Never divide a one-syllable word (*act, large, school*).
- Try not to divide a word of five or fewer letters (*older, habit, loyal*).
- Never divide a one-letter syllable from the rest of the word (*apart-ment*, not *a-partment*).
- Never divide abbreviations or contractions (*Mrs., Dr., don't, haven't*).

In Compound Words

Use a hyphen in certain compound words.

> **the two-year-old**   **sister-in-law**

In Fractions

Use a hyphen between the numbers in a fraction.

> **one-half (1/2)**   **five-tenths (5/10)**

To Create New Words

Use a hyphen to form new words beginning with the prefixes *all-, self-, ex-,* or *great-*. A hyphen is also used with suffixes such as *-elect* and *-free*.

> **all-star team**   **self-respect**   **president-elect**
> **great-grandmother**   **ex-hero**   **smoke-free**

Use a hyphen to join two or more words that work together to form a single adjective *before* a noun.

> **school-age children**   **lightning-fast skating**

To Join Letters and Words

A hyphen is often used to join a letter to a word.

> **T-shirt**   **X-ray**   **e-mail**   **U-turn**

Hyphens

■ To Divide a Word
■ In Compound Words

If a word at the end of a sentence is hyphenated incorrectly, or if a compound word needs a hyphen, write the word correctly on your paper.

Example: Uncle Jay, who is Mom's brother in law, is an artist.
          brother–in–law

1. She asked him to paint a mural in a room that does-n't have a window.

2. Uncle Jay said he would paint a couple of fake wi-ndows along with the scene outside them.

3. It turned out to be a time consuming project.

4. First, Mom painted the whole room in a medium bei-ge color.

5. Uncle Jay sketched the outline using a felt tip pen.

6. Then he used a many colored palette of paints to complete the mural.

7. He said, "Since the paint won't dry for a while, do-n't touch it!"

8. Mom will invite her friends to a get together to show them the mural.

Colons

A **colon** may be used to introduce a list or a quotation. Colons are also used in business letters and between the numbers expressing time.

498.1
To Introduce a List

Use a colon to introduce a list that follows a complete sentence.

The following materials can be used to build houses: plants, shells, sod, and sand.

When introducing a list, the colon often comes after summary words like *the following* or *these things*.

On cleaning day, I do these things: sweep the floor, clean the bathroom mirror, and take out the garbage.

TIP: It is incorrect to use a colon after a verb or after a preposition.

498.2
As a Formal Introduction

Use a colon to introduce an important quotation in a serious report, essay, or news story.

President Lincoln concluded the Gettysburg Address with these famous words: " . . . government of the people, by the people, for the people, shall not perish from the earth."

498.3
In Business Letters

A colon is used after the greeting in a business letter.

Dear Ms. Kununga: Dear Sir:
Dear Dr. Watts:

498.4
Between Numbers in Time

Place a colon between the parts of a number that shows time.

7:30 a.m.   1:00 p.m.   12:00 noon

Colons

■ To Introduce a List
■ Between Numbers in Time

For each sentence, write the numbers that need a colon or the word that should be followed by a colon. Write the colon, too.

Example: We're leaving the house to go river tubing at 800 tomorrow morning.
8:00

1. Before you go tubing, make sure you have these things a swimsuit, a T-shirt, a hat, and some shoes.

2. You may also want to bring the following lip balm, sunglasses, and sunscreen.

3. The sun can be quite strong between the hours of 1100 a.m. and 200 p.m.

4. Here are some words that describe river tubing cool, relaxing, and scenic.

5. We will probably be back home by about 600 p.m.

Next Step: Write a sentence that includes a list of things you'd bring on a long car trip. Use a colon to introduce your list.

Semicolons

A **semicolon** sometimes works in the same way that a comma does. At other times, it works like a period and indicates a stronger pause.

500.1

To Join Two Independent Clauses

You can join two independent clauses with a semicolon when there is no coordinating conjunction (like *and* or *but*) between them. (See **564.2** for more information about independent clauses.)

> **In the future, some cities may rest on the ocean floor; other cities may float like islands.**

> **Floating cities sound great; however, I get seasick.**

TIP: Independent clauses can stand alone as separate sentences.

500.2

To Separate Groups in a Series with Commas

Use a semicolon to separate a series of phrases that already contain commas.

> **We crossed the stream; unpacked our lunches, cameras, and journals; and finally took time to rest.**

(The second phrase contains commas.)

Ellipses

An **ellipsis** (three periods with a space before, between, and after) is used to show omitted words or sentences and to show a pause in dialogue.

500.3

To Show Omitted Words

Use an ellipsis to show that one or more words have been left out of a quotation.

> **"Give me liberty or give me death."**
> **"Give me liberty or . . . death."**

500.4

To Show a Pause

Use an ellipsis to indicate a pause in dialogue.

> **"That's . . . incredible!" I cried.**

Semicolons

▶ **For the sentences below, write the words that should be separated by a semicolon. Write the semicolon, too.**

Example: Troy's family went on a
unique trip they went to
Iqaluit (pronounced
ĭ-kăl´ōō-ĭt).
trip; they

1. Iqaluit is the capital city of Nunavut this Canadian territory was created in 1999.

2. Troy visited a museum and a theater exercised at an ice arena, a health club, and a swimming pool and ate at some great restaurants.

3. Iqaluit is located north of Quebec its Arctic climate means there is snow nine months of the year.

4. Birds and animals living there include the snow bunting, Arctic tern, and snowy owl caribou, lemming, and Arctic fox and even some polar bears.

5. Most of Iqaluit's people are Inuit they are one of the native peoples of the far north.

Next Step: Write a compound sentence about an unusual place. Use a semicolon to join the independent clauses.

Italics and Underlining

Italics is a style of type that is slightly slanted, like this: *girl*. It is used for some titles and special words. If you use a computer, you should use italics. In handwritten material, underline words that should be in italics.

502.1
In Titles

Use italics (or underlining) for the titles of books, plays, very long poems, magazines, and newspapers; the titles of television programs, movies (videos and DVD's), and albums of music (cassettes and CD's); and the names of ships and aircraft. (See **494.3** for information on other kinds of titles.)

> *The Giver* OR The Giver (book)
> *National Geographic* OR National Geographic (magazine)
> *Air Bud* OR Air Bud (movie)
> *Dance on a Moonbeam* OR Dance on a Moonbeam (CD)
> *Los Angeles Times* OR Los Angeles Times (newspaper)
> *Titanic* OR Titanic (ship)
> *Discovery* OR Discovery (spacecraft)

502.2
For Special Words

Use italics (or underlining) for scientific names and for words or letters being discussed or used in a special way.

> The marigold's scientific name is *Tagetes*.
> The word *friend* has different meanings to different people.

Punctuation Marks

'	Apostrophe	...	Ellipsis	.	Period
:	Colon	!	Exclamation point	?	Question mark
,	Comma	-	Hyphen	" "	Quotation marks
–	Dash	( )	Parentheses	;	Semicolon

Italics and Underlining

▶ **For each sentence, write the words that should be italicized and underline them.**

Example: Consuela read the book The
          Polar Express.
          <u>The Polar Express</u>

1. She said that it was muy bien,
   and I know that means "very
   good."

2. Tom Hanks is in the movie based on the book; he was
   also in the movie Cast Away.

3. Mom read a review of the movie in the Miami Herald,
   the newspaper she usually gets.

4. She told me that the movie is not about Ursus
   maritimus, the polar bear.

5. "I know," I said. "It's the name of a train, just as
   Queen Elizabeth 2 is the name of a ship."

6. "Oh, have you been reading my Cruising the World
   magazine?" she said.

Next Step: Write a sentence that includes the name of your
            favorite book or movie. Remember to underline
            the title.

Dashes

A **dash** is used to show a break in a sentence, to emphasize certain words, or to show that a speaker has been interrupted.

504.1
To Show a Sentence Break

A dash can show a sudden break in a sentence.

> Because of computers, our world—and the way we describe it—has changed greatly.

> With a computer—or a cell phone—people can connect to the Internet.

504.2
For Emphasis

Use a dash to emphasize a word, a series of words, a phrase, or a clause.

> You can learn about customs, careers, sports, weather—just about anything—on the Internet.

504.3
To Show Interrupted Speech

Use a dash to show that someone's speech is being interrupted by another person.

> Well, hello—yes, I—that's right—yes, I—sure, I'd love—I'll be there!

Parentheses

Parentheses are used around words that add extra information to a sentence or make an idea clearer.

504.4
To Add Information

Use parentheses when adding information or making an idea clearer.

> I accidentally left the keys to Mom's car (a blue Osprey) on the front seat.

> Five of the students provided background music (very quiet humming) for the singer.

Dashes and Parentheses

▶ **For each sentence, write whether you would use parentheses or a dash (or dashes) to set off the underlined words.**

Example: A real taco is a corn tortilla filled with meat, onions, and spice <u>nothing else.</u>
dash

1. People make different kinds of sauces with *chipotle* <u>smoked jalapeño pepper</u>.

2. Although lima beans first came from Guatemala, their name came from <u>you guessed it</u> Lima, Peru.

3. People in Costa Rica eat *gallo pinto* <u>a rice and bean dish</u> for breakfast, lunch, or dinner.

4. Mango <u>a fruit native to India</u> is used in many Latino dishes.

5. *Gazpacho* is a soup made of tomatoes, cucumbers, and garlic <u>and it's served cold!</u>

6. In Spain, a tortilla is an egg omelet <u>not a flat, thin bread as it is known in the United States</u>.

Next Step: Write a sentence about an unusual food. Add some extra information and enclose it in parentheses.

Test Prep

▶ **Number your paper from 1 to 10. For each underlined part of the paragraphs below, write the letter (from the answer choices on the next page) of the best way to punctuate it.**

Can a sign send a message without using <u>words</u> The
_{**1**}
answer is "yes." Symbols make reading signs easier. Since
people around the world recognize these symbols, <u>theyre</u> on
_{**2**}
signs everywhere!

Some signs warn of danger. A sign with a skull and <u>crossb-</u>
_{**3**}
<u>ones</u> warns of poison. A fire inside a triangle warns that
something is flammable.

Other signs show where something is located. A drawing
of a telephone says, <u>"A</u> phone is here." The message of a
_{**4**}
red cross is "first aid." The familiar symbols for men and
women point out where restrooms <u>are, and</u> a sign with a
_{**5**}
jet points to an airport.

Signs also tell people the rules for a certain area. People
know what the <u>red yellow and green</u> colors on a traffic light
_{**6**}
mean. Speed-limit signs and stop signs give rules. Also
consider the sign of a cigarette with a slash through it. Can
you figure it <u>out</u>
_{**7**}

People who <u>cant</u> read words, such as young children or
8
<u>foreign visitors</u> can understand signs without words. Imagine
9
what a sign would look like if its message had to be in 10

different <u>languages?</u> The use of symbols on signs lets everyone
10
"get the picture."

1. A words.
    B words?
    C words!
    D correct as is

6. A red, yellow and green
    B red, yellow, and green,
    C red, yellow, and green
    D correct as is

2. A theyr'e
    B they're
    C theyre'
    D correct as is

7. A out.
    B out!
    C out?
    D correct as is

3. A cross-bones
    B cros-sbones
    C crossbon-es
    D correct as is

8. A can't
    B ca'nt
    C cant'
    D correct as is

4. A "a
    B a
    C A
    D correct as is

9. A Foreign visitors
    B foreign visitors,
    C foreign, visitors
    D correct as is

5. A are. and
    B are and
    C are? And
    D correct as is

10. A languages,
    B languages'
    C languages!
    D correct as is

Editing for Mechanics

Capitalization

508.1
Proper Nouns and Adjectives

Capitalize all proper nouns and proper adjectives. A proper noun names a specific person, place, thing, or idea. A proper adjective is formed from a proper noun.

Proper Nouns:

Beverly Cleary	Golden Gate Bridge
Utah Jazz	Thanksgiving Day

Proper Adjectives:

American citizen	Chicago skyline
New Jersey shore	Belgian waffle

508.2
Names of People

Capitalize the names of people as well as the initials or abbreviations that stand for those names.

John Steptoe	Harriet Tubman
C. S. Lewis	Sacagawea

508.3
Titles Used with Names

Capitalize titles used with names of persons.

President Carter   Dr. Li Tam   Mayor Rita Gonzales

TIP: Do not capitalize titles when they are used alone: *the president, the doctor, the mayor.*

508.4
Abbreviations

Capitalize abbreviations of titles and organizations.

M.D. (doctor of medicine)   **Mr. Martin Lopez**
ADA (American Dental Association)

508.5
Organizations

Capitalize the name of an organization, an association, or a team, as well as its members.

Girl Scouts	the Democratic Party
Chicago Bulls	Republicans

Capitalization 1

- Proper Adjectives
- Titles Used with Names

▶ **For each sentence, correctly write any word that is not properly capitalized.**

Example: Arthur Conan Doyle was a scottish author at the turn of the twentieth century.
Scottish

1. Scotland is part of the british nation.

2. Queen Victoria ruled Great Britain until she died in 1901; then king Edward took over.

3. The King knighted Mr. Doyle in 1902.

4. From then on, he was known as sir Arthur Conan Doyle.

5. Doyle wrote stories about Sherlock Holmes and his companion, doctor Watson.

6. Holmes and Watson solved mysteries that took them across the english countryside.

7. Doyle's books are still popular, even among american readers.

Next Step: Write a sentence about a favorite book. Include a title that is used with a name or a proper adjective (or both).

Capitalization . . .

510.1
Words Used as Names

Capitalize words such as *mother, father, aunt,* and *uncle,* when these words are used as names.

Ask Mother what we're having for lunch.

(*Mother* is used as a name; you could use her first name in its place.)

Words such as *dad, uncle, mother,* and *grandma* are not usually capitalized if they come after a possessive pronoun *(my, his, our).*

Ask my mother what we're having for lunch.

(In this sentence, *mother* refers to someone but is not used as a name.)

510.2
Days, Months, and Holidays

Capitalize the names of days of the week, months of the year, and holidays.

Wednesday	**March**	**Easter**
Arbor Day	**Passover**	**Juneteenth Day**

TIP: Do not capitalize the seasons.

winter   spring   summer   fall (or **autumn**)

510.3
Names of Religions, Nationalities, and Languages

Capitalize the names of religions, nationalities, and languages.

Christianity, Hinduism, Islam (religions)

Australian, Somalian, Chinese (nationalities)

English, Spanish, Hebrew (languages)

510.4
Official Names

Capitalize the names of businesses and official product names. (These are called trade names.)

Budget Mart   Crispy Crunch cereal   Smile toothpaste

TIP: Do not capitalize a general word like *toothpaste* when it follows the product name.

Capitalization 2

- Names of Religions, Nationalities, and Languages
- Official Names

▶ **Write the word or words in each sentence that require capitalization.**

Example: This ad for mountain man boots claims they'll protect you from snake bites.
Mountain Man

1. The zippy boot company makes them.

2. It is a canadian company.

3. Nayeli's favorite kind of car is the newmobile fastcar.

4. Her puerto rican grandparents have one.

5. Her grandfather used to work for island electric.

6. The people of Chile speak spanish.

7. Some young jewish people study the hebrew language.

8. Many europeans immigrating to the United States in the late 1800s were catholics.

Next Step: Write a sentence about a product you enjoy using. Capitalize its name correctly.

Capitalization . . .

512.1
Names of Places

Capitalize the names of places that are either proper nouns or proper adjectives.

Planets and heavenly bodies	**Earth, Jupiter, Milky Way**
Continents	**Europe, Asia, South America, Australia**
Countries	**Chad, Haiti, Greece, Chile, Jordan**
States	**New Mexico, West Virginia, Delaware**
Provinces	**Alberta, British Columbia, Quebec, Ontario**
Cities	**Montreal, Portland**
Counties	**Wayne County, Dade County**
Bodies of water	**Hudson Bay, North Sea, Lake Geneva, Saskatchewan River, Gulf of Mexico**
Landforms	**Appalachian Mountains, Bitterroot Range**
Public areas	**Vietnam Memorial**
Roads and highways	**New Jersey Turnpike, Interstate 80, Central Avenue**
Buildings	**Pentagon, Oriental Theater, Empire State Building**
Monuments	**Eiffel Tower, Statue of Liberty**

512.2
Sections of the Country

Capitalize words that name particular sections of the country. (Also capitalize proper adjectives formed from these words.)

A large part of the United States population lives on the East Coast. (*East Coast* is a section of the country.)

Southern **cooking** out West

Do *not* capitalize words that simply show direction.

If you keep driving west**, you will end up in the Pacific Ocean.** (direction)

western **Brazil** northeasterly **wind**

Capitalization 3

■ Names of Places

▶ **For each sentence, write the word or words that should be capitalized.**

Example: A group of people had
         gathered at villa road and
         30th street.
         Villa Road, Street

1. They waited in line to buy
   tickets for a ride across lake
   erie.

2. They would take a restful trip from the united states
   to canada.

3. The ferry would take passengers from cleveland, ohio,
   to port stanley, ontario.

4. Winding through the town, kettle creek empties into
   the lake at pierside beach.

5. Canadians making the trip to cleveland might like to
   visit the rock 'n' roll hall of fame.

6. The 125-foot-tall soldiers and sailors monument is
   located in public square.

7. There is also a lot to do at cleveland lakefront state
   park.

Next Step: Write a sentence or two about a trip, stating
           where you started and where you ended up.

Capitalization . . .

514.1
Historical Events

Capitalize the names of historical events, documents, and periods of time.

> **Boston Tea Party**
>
> **Emancipation Proclamation**
>
> **Stone Age**

514.2
Titles

Capitalize the first word of a title, the last word, and every word in between except short prepositions, coordinating conjunctions, and articles *(a, an, the).*

> *National Geographic World* (magazine)
>
> **"The Star-Spangled Banner"** (song)
>
> *Beauty and the Beast* (movie)
>
> *In My Pocket* (book)

514.3
First Words

Capitalize the first word of every sentence.

> **We play our first basketball game tomorrow.**

Capitalize the first word of a direct quotation.

> **Jamir shouted, "Keep that ball moving!"**

Capitalize	Do Not Capitalize
January, March	winter, spring
Grandpa (as a name)	my grandpa
Mayor Sayles-Belton	the mayor
President Washington	our first president
Ida B. Wells Elementary School	the local elementary school
Lake Ontario	the lake area
the South (section of the country)	south (a direction)
planet Earth	a mound of earth (dirt)

Capitalization 4

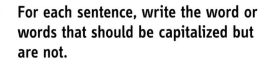

■ Historical Events
■ Titles

For each sentence, write the word or words that should be capitalized but are not.

Example: A good book about space
journeys is *Our space
program.*
Space Program

1. In a way, astronauts are like the explorers on the lewis and clark expedition.

2. Some missiles built during world war II became the first spaceships.

3. The United Nations created the outer space treaty of 1967, which encouraged peaceful space exploration.

4. An article in the magazine *National geographic* explains the many dangers that astronauts face.

5. The movie *apollo 13* also showed how risky space travel can be.

6. Millions still watch the old TV show *star trek.*

7. The book *The martian chronicles* is about people moving to Mars.

Next Step: List some magazines in your home, books you have read, and important historical events you have learned about. Capitalize them correctly.

Plurals

516.1
Most Nouns

Form the **plurals** of most nouns by adding -s.

    balloon—balloons   **shoe**—shoes

516.2
Nouns Ending in *sh*, *ch*, *x*, *s*, and *z*

Form the plurals of nouns ending in *sh*, *ch*, *x*, *s*, and *z* by adding -es to the singular.

    brush—brushes   **bunch**—bunches   **box**—boxes
    dress—dresses   **buzz**—buzzes

516.3
Nouns Ending in *o*

Form the plurals of most words that end in *o* by adding -s.

    patio—patios   **rodeo**—rodeos

For most nouns ending in *o* with a consonant letter just before the *o*, add -es.

    echo—echoes   **hero**—heroes

However, musical terms and words of Spanish origin form plurals by adding -s; check your dictionary for other words of this type.

    piano—pianos   **solo**—solos
    taco—tacos   **burrito**—burritos

516.4
Nouns Ending in *-ful*

Form the plurals of nouns that end with *-ful* by adding an -s at the end of the word.

    two spoonfuls   **three** tankfuls
    four bowlfuls   **five** cupfuls

516.5
Nouns Ending in *f* or *fe*

Form the plurals of nouns that end in *f* or *fe* in one of two ways.

1. If the final *f* is still heard in the plural form of the word, simply add -s.

    goof—goofs   **chief**—chiefs   **safe**—safes

2. If the final *f* has the sound of *v* in the plural form, change the *f* to *v* and add -es.

    calf—calves   **loaf**—loaves   **knife**—knives

Plurals 1

- ■ Nouns Ending in *sh*, *ch*, *x*, *s*, and *z*
- ■ Nouns Ending in *-ful*

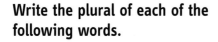 **Write the plural of each of the following words.**

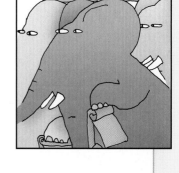

Example: lunch
           lunches

1. tax

2. class

3. forkful

4. ash

5. mix

6. eyelash

7. batch

8. mouthful

9. rush

10. handful

11. fax

12. fox

13. dish

14. bus

15. six

16. ditch

17. plateful

18. mess

19. watch

Next Step: Make a list of four or five other nouns that end in *sh*, *ch*, or *-ful*. Then write their plurals.

Plurals . . .

518.1
Nouns Ending in y

When a common noun ends in a consonant + *y*, form its plural by changing the *y* to *i* and adding *-es*.

sky—skies   bunny—bunnies
story—stories   musky—muskies

For proper nouns, do *not* change the letters—just add *-s*.

area Bargain Citys   the Berrys   two Timmys

For nouns that end in a vowel + *y*, add only *-s*.

donkey—donkeys   monkey—monkeys   day—days

518.2
Compound Nouns

Form the plurals of most compound nouns by changing the most important word in the compound to its plural form.

sisters-in-law   maids of honor   life jackets
secretaries of state   houses of assembly

518.3
Irregular Nouns

Some nouns form plurals using an irregular spelling.

child—children   goose—geese   foot—feet
man—men   woman—women   tooth—teeth
ox—oxen   mouse—mice
cactus—cacti or cactuses

A few words have the same singular and plural forms.

Singular:	Plural:
That sheep wanders away.	The other sheep follow it.
I caught one trout.	Dad caught three trout.

Others: deer, moose, buffalo, fish, aircraft

518.4
Adding an 's

The plurals of symbols, letters, numerals, and words discussed as words are formed by adding an apostrophe and *-s*.

two ?'s and two !'s   five 7's   *x*'s and *y*'s

TIP: For more information on forming plurals and plural possessives, see page **492**.

Plurals 2

- Compound Nouns
- Irregular Nouns

For each of the following sentences, write the correct plural form of the underlined word.

Example: Grandpa counted 68 <u>sheep</u> before falling asleep.

sheep

1. Moose have bigger <u>foot</u> than deer.

2. Park rangers say there are more <u>deer</u> in the United States now than there were 400 years ago.

3. Wild <u>goose</u> will not fly south for the winter if they can find open water and food.

4. Hikers in Glacier National Park sometimes see many <u>mountain goat</u>.

5. Did you know that <u>mouse</u> are wild animals?

6. Some fish have very sharp <u>tooth</u>.

7. My mother's two <u>brother-in-law</u> like to photograph sandhill cranes.

Next Step: Write one or two sentences using the correct plural forms of *child* and *vice president*.

Abbreviations

An **abbreviation** is the shortened form of a word or phrase.

520.1
Common Abbreviations

Most abbreviations begin with a capital letter and end with a period. In formal writing, do *not* abbreviate the names of states, countries, months, days, or units of measure. Also do *not* use symbols (%, &) in place of words.

TIP: The following abbreviations are always acceptable in both formal and informal writing:

Mr.	Mrs.	Ms.	Dr.	Jr., Sr.
M.D.	B.C.E.	C.E.	a.m., p.m. (A.M., P.M.)	

520.2
Acronyms

An **acronym** is made up of the first letter or letters of words in a phrase. An acronym is pronounced as a word, and it does not have any periods.

SADD (**S**tudents **A**gainst **D**estructive **D**ecisions)

PIN (**p**ersonal **i**dentification **n**umber)

520.3
Initialisms

An **initialism** is like an acronym except the letters that form the abbreviation are pronounced individually (not as a word).

TV (**t**ele**v**ision)   DA (**d**istrict **a**ttorney)

CD (**c**ompact **d**isc)   PO (**p**ost **o**ffice)

Common Abbreviations

a.m.	ante meridiem (before noon)	**Inc.**	incorporated	**oz.**	ounce
ATM	automatic teller machine	**kg**	kilogram	**pd.**	paid
B.C.E.	before the Common Era	**km**	kilometer	**p.**	page
C.E.	the Common Era	**lb.**	pound	**p.m.**	post meridiem (after noon)
etc.	and so forth	**M.D.**	doctor of medicine		
FYI	for your information	**mpg**	miles per gallon	**qt.**	quart
		mph	miles per hour		

Abbreviations 1

- Common Abbreviations
- Acronyms
- Initialisms

▶ **For each sentence, write the word or words that the underlined abbreviation stands for.**

Example: <u>Mr.</u> Al E. Gator met some pals in the swamp.
Mister

1. They had a meeting every Friday at 2:30 <u>p.m.</u>

2. A speedboat went by, going about 60 <u>mph</u>.

3. "Those boats get only 6 <u>mpg</u> of fuel," Al said.

4. "Did you know that a gallon is about the same as eight <u>lbs.</u>?" asked C. Rocky Dile.

5. "I learned that fact on a <u>TV</u> program," he said.

6. Then little Green Tree Frog, <u>Jr.</u>, piped up, "Would anyone like to hear some music?"

7. "I have a new <u>CD</u>," he said.

8. "It's called *Horns in the <u>U.S.A.</u>*"

9. "<u>FYI</u>, the CD is a fund-raiser for school bands," he added.

Next Step: Write a silly sentence that includes an acronym or initialism you make up. Write what the abbreviation stands for.

Abbreviations . . .

You may use a state or an address abbreviation when it is part of an address at the top of a letter or on an envelope. (Also see pages 476–477.) Remember, do not use these abbreviations in sentences.

On a letter:

2323 N. Kipp St.
Cleveland, OH 52133

On an envelope:

7828 E FIRST AVE
ORONO ME 04403

In sentences:

Jasper lives at 2323 North Kipp Street, Cleveland, Ohio.

His old address was 7828 East First Avenue, Orono, Maine 04403.

State Postal Abbreviations

Alabama	AL	Idaho	ID	Missouri	MO	Pennsylvania	PA
Alaska	AK	Illinois	IL	Montana	MT	Rhode Island	RI
Arizona	AZ	Indiana	IN	Nebraska	NE	South Carolina	SC
Arkansas	AR	Iowa	IA	Nevada	NV	South Dakota	SD
California	CA	Kansas	KS	New Hampshire	NH	Tennessee	TN
Colorado	CO	Kentucky	KY	New Jersey	NJ	Texas	TX
Connecticut	CT	Louisiana	LA	New Mexico	NM	Utah	UT
Delaware	DE	Maine	ME	New York	NY	Vermont	VT
District of		Maryland	MD	North Carolina	NC	Virginia	VA
Columbia	DC	Massachusetts	MA	North Dakota	ND	Washington	WA
Florida	FL	Michigan	MI	Ohio	OH	West Virginia	WV
Georgia	GA	Minnesota	MN	Oklahoma	OK	Wisconsin	WI
Hawaii	HI	Mississippi	MS	Oregon	OR	Wyoming	WY

Address Abbreviations

Apartment	Apt.	Expressway	Expy.	Parkway	Pkwy.	Square	Sq.
Avenue	Ave.	Heights	Hts.	Place	Pl.	Station	Sta.
Boulevard	Blvd.	Highway	Hwy.	Road	Rd.	Street	St.
Court	Ct.	Lane	Ln.	Route	Rte.	Terrace	Terr.
Drive	Dr.	North	N.	Rural	R.	Turnpike	Tpke.
East	E.	Park	Pk.	South	S.	West	W.

Abbreviations 2

■ State and Address Abbreviations

Imagine that you are addressing
envelopes. Write each of the following
addresses using the correct abbreviations.

Example: 3999 West Fourman Court,
Waukegan, Illinois 60085

3999 W FOURMAN CT
WAUKEGAN IL 60085

1. 620 South Highway 187, Dallas,
   Texas 75019

2. 161 Saturn Parkway North,
   Dayton, New Jersey 08810

3. 950 Splice Heights, Eagan,
   Minnesota 55121

4. 2256 Benton Harbor Road, Route
   44, Duluth, Georgia 30096

5. 26123 East Francis Lane, Lake
   Forest, California 92630

Next Step: Write your own address as if you were addressing
an envelope.

Numbers

524.1
Numbers from 1 to 9

Numbers from one to nine are usually written as words. (Most of the time, numbers 10 and higher are written as numerals.)

one   three   nine   10   115   2,000

Keep any numbers that are being compared in the same style, either words or numerals.

Students from 8 to 11 years old are invited.

Students from eight to eleven years old are invited.

524.2
Very Large Numbers

You may use a combination of numbers and words for very large numbers.

15 million   1.2 billion

You may spell out large numbers that can be written as two words, but if you need more than two words to spell out a number, write it as a numeral.

three million   fifteen thousand   3,275,100   7,418

524.3
Sentence Beginnings

Use words, not numerals, to begin a sentence.

Fourteen new students joined the jazz band.

Fifty-two cards make up a deck.

524.4
Numerals Only

Use numerals for numbers in the following forms:

decimals **25.5**

with dollar signs **$3.97**

percentages . . . . **6 percent**

chapters . . . . **chapter 8**

pages . . . . **pages 17–20**

addresses . . . . **445 E. Acorn Dr.**

dates . . . . **June 19, 2005**

times with a.m. or p.m. . . . . **1:30 p.m.**

statistics . . . . **a vote of 5 to 2**

Numbers

■ Sentence Beginnings
■ Numerals Only

 **For each sentence, write the number the correct way. (If it is already correct, write "C.")**

Example: 26 chickens got loose from the Jones farm yesterday.
Twenty-six

1. The date was May thirty.

2. Some of the chickens actually crossed Highway 9.

3. Some of them hid in the bushes near the house at fifty National Road.

4. By one p.m., I was tired of chasing chickens.

5. 11 chickens were still missing.

6. Farmer Jones wouldn't be happy until one hundred percent of the birds were found.

7. Twenty-five chickens were back in the coop by sunset.

8. The last chicken didn't turn up until June six, but it was fine.

Next Step: Write a short paragraph about a time when you lost something. Include one sentence that begins with a number.

Test Prep

For each sentence below, write the letter of the line that contains a capitalization error. If there is no error, choose "D."

1. **A** Many european countries
    B use the same kind of
    C paper money and coins.
    D correct as is

2. **A** Aunt Gertrude brought
    B a big bag of cheetos
    C snacks to the picnic.
    D correct as is

3. **A** My friend Alicia
    B goes to a Lutheran
    C church on Sundays.
    D correct as is

4. **A** One of Abe Lincoln's
    B most famous speeches
    C was the gettysburg address.
    D correct as is

5. **A** Hector got the book
    B *Charlie and the chocolate Factory*
    C at the library.
    D correct as is

6. **A** do you want to come
    B to a party with Lupe
    C and me?
    D correct as is

7. **A** We walked over to
    B mrs. bosworth's house
    C to see her new kitten.
    D correct as is

8. **A** "Have you ever read
    B *Bud, Not Buddy*?"
    C asked Devon.
    D correct as is

9. **A** Many visitors go to
    B Washington, D.C.,
         to visit
    C the jefferson
         memorial.
    D correct as is

10. **A** Antoine showed me
         where
    B the helix galaxy is
    C with his telescope.
    D correct as is

11. **A** When I go to high
         school,
    B I want to learn how
    C to speak the german
         language.
    D correct as is

12. **A** As we hiked along
    B the ice age trail, we
    C saw many animal
         tracks.
    D correct as is

13. **A** Cho said, "it's already
    B time to get the cattle
    C back in the barn!"
    D correct as is

14. **A** Did you know that
    B Thanksgiving is
         always
    C on a thursday?
    D correct as is

15. **A** My favorite meal is
    B Maine lobster with
    C lots of napkins!
    D correct as is

Improving Spelling

528.1
i* before *e

Write *i* before *e*—except after *c* or when rhyming with *say* as in *neighbor* and *weigh*.

believe   chief   receive   freight

Exceptions to the *i* before *e* rule include the following:

either   neither   heir   leisure   species
foreign   height   seize   weird

528.2
Silent *e*

If a word ends with a silent *e*, drop the *e* before adding a suffix (ending) that begins with a vowel.

judge—judging   **continue**—continual
create—creative—creation   **relate**—relating—relative

528.3
Words Ending in *y*

When a word ends in a consonant + *y*, change the *y* to *i* before adding a suffix. Do not, however, change the *y* when adding the *-ing* suffix.

happy—happiness   **try**—tries—trying
lady—ladies   **cry**—cried—crying

When forming the plural of a word that ends in *y* with a vowel just before it, add *-s*.

holiday—holidays   **key**—keys   **boy**—boys

528.4
Words Ending in a Consonant

When a one-syllable word ends in a consonant that has a single vowel before it, double the final consonant before adding a suffix that begins with a vowel.

beg—begging   **hop**—hopped   **sit**—sitting

When a word with more than one syllable ends with a vowel + consonant, double the final consonant only if the accent is on the last syllable and the suffix begins with a vowel.

admit—admitting   **occur**—occurrence

Spelling 1

- *i* before *e*
- Silent *e*

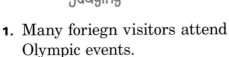

For each sentence, write any misspelled words correctly.

Example: In the Olympics, judgeing is an important part of each sport.

judging

1. Many foriegn visitors attend Olympic events.

2. Each athlete beleives that he or she can win a gold medal.

3. An athlete's hieght is not important in most of the sports.

4. Figure skateing is a crowd favorite in the Winter Olympics.

5. The top three athletes in each sport recieve medals.

6. You'll see the winners raiseing their medals above their heads for everyone to see.

Next Step: Write a list of five words that are spelled with *i* before *e*. Then write a list of five words that end with a silent *e*; add a suffix to each of the five words, spelling the new words correctly.

Spelling 2

■ Words Ending in **y**
■ Words Ending in a Consonant

▶ **For each sentence, write the correct spelling of the underlined word or words.**

Example: Pirates left <u>buryed</u> treasure on Cat Island.

buried

1. Nate imagined his family's <u>happyness</u> if he were to find a chest of jewels.

2. He <u>grined</u> from ear to ear.

3. It would be the <u>begining</u> of the good life!

4. Nate <u>grabed</u> a shovel and started <u>diging</u>.

5. The <u>dustyness</u> of the dry sand bothered his eyes.

6. He grunted as he <u>jabed</u> the shovel into the hard ground.

7. He was not <u>enjoing</u> this work.

8. The shovel wasn't <u>hiting</u> anything hard.

9. <u>Worryed</u> that he was wasting his time, Nate <u>faned</u> himself for a minute.

10. Then he <u>droped</u> the shovel and <u>hurryed</u> home to dinner.

Spelling Review

▶ **For each sentence, write the correct spelling of the underlined word.**

1. Dwight had books from two <u>librarys</u>.

2. He <u>carryed</u> the books to the study area of the second library.

3. After almost an hour of <u>writeing</u>, he finished his essay.

4. He looked up at the <u>cieling</u> and sighed.

5. "Oh, my <u>acheing</u> hand!" Dwight moaned.

6. He had a <u>breif</u> cramp in his right hand.

7. He <u>rubed</u> it to ease the cramp.

8. All of a sudden, he realized that it was <u>geting</u> late.

9. He <u>journied</u> home before it got dark.

10. His mom was a bit <u>exciteable</u>, and Dwight did not want her to worry.

11. She had a <u>feirce</u> need to protect her child (as many mothers do).

12. When Dwight got home, he discovered he had <u>forgoten</u> his essay at the library.

Proofreader's Guide to Improved Spelling

Be patient. Becoming a good speller takes time and practice. Learn the basic spelling rules.

Check your spelling by using a dictionary or a list of commonly misspelled words.

Check a dictionary for the correct pronunciation of each word you are trying to spell. Knowing how to pronounce a word will help you remember how to spell it.

Look up the meaning of each word. Knowing its meaning will help you to use it and spell it correctly.

Study the word in the dictionary. Then look away from the dictionary page and picture the word in your mind's eye. Next, write the word on a piece of paper. Finally, check its spelling in the dictionary. Repeat these steps until you can spell the word correctly.

Make a spelling dictionary. Include any words you frequently misspell in a special notebook.

A

	adjust	already	another	architect
	admire	although	answer	arctic
abbreviate	adventure	altogether	antarctic	aren't
aboard	advertisement	aluminum	anxious	argument
above	advise	always	anybody	arithmetic
absence	afraid	ambulance	anyone	around
absent	afterward	amendment	anything	arrange
absolute	again	American	anyway	arrival
accept	against	among	anywhere	article
accident	agreeable	amount	apartment	artificial
according	agreement	ancient	apologize	asleep
account	aisle	angel	appearance	assign
ache	alley	anger	appetite	assist
achieve	allowance	angle	appointment	associate
acre	all right	angry	appreciate	association
across	almost	animal	approach	assume
actual	alone	anniversary	approval	athlete
addition	along	announce	approximate	athletic
address	a lot	annual	April	attach

attack
attempt
attendance
attention
attitude
attractive
audience
August
author
authority
automobile
autumn
available
avenue
average
awful
awkward

B

baggage
baking
balance
balloon
banana
bandage
barber
bargain
barrel
basement
battery
beautiful
beauty
because
becoming
been
before
beginning
behave
behavior
behind
belief
believe

belong
beneath
between
bicycle
blizzard
bother
bottom
bought
bounce
boundary
breakfast
breath
breathe
breeze
bridge
brief
bright
brilliant
brother
brought
buckle
budget
build
built
burglar
bury
business
busy

C

cafeteria
calendar
cancel
candidate
candle
canoe
canyon
captain
cardboard
career
carpenter
carriage

casual
catalog
catcher
caught
ceiling
celebration
cemetery
century
certain
certificate
challenge
champion
change
channel
character
chief
chocolate
choice
choir
choose
chorus
church
circle
citizen
city
clear
climate
climb
closet
clothes
coach
cocoa
cocoon
college
color
column
comedy
coming
commercial
commit
committed
committee
communicate
community

company
comparison
competitive
complain
complete
concern
concert
concrete
condition
conference
confidence
congratulate
connect
continue
continuous
convenient
convince
cooperate
cough
could
country
county
courage
courageous
cousin
coverage
cozy
crawl
cried
criticize
cruel
crumb
curiosity
curious
current
customer

D

daily
damage
danger
dangerous

daughter
December
decide
decision
decorate
definite
definition
delicious
describe
description
design
develop
dictionary
difference
different
difficulty
disappear
disastrous
discipline
discover
discuss
discussion
disease
distance
divide
division
doctor
doesn't
dollar
doubt

E

eager
early
easily
easy
edge
eight
eighth
either
electricity
elephant

embarrass
emergency
encourage
enormous
enough
entertain
entrance
environment
equal
equipment
escape
especially
every
everybody
exactly
excellent
excited
exercise
exhausted
expensive
experience
experiment
explain
explanation
extinct
extreme
eyes

F

face
familiar
family
famous
fashion
favorite
February
field
fierce
fifty
finally
foreign
fortunate

forty
forward
fountain
fragile
Friday
friend
frighten
fuel

G

gadget
gauge
general
generous
genius
gentle
genuine
geography
ghost
gnaw
goes
government
governor
graduation
grammar
grateful
great
grief
grocery
group
guarantee
guard
guess
guilty
gymnasium

H

half
handsome
happen

happiness
hazardous
headache
health
heavy
height
history
holiday
honor
horrible
hospital
humorous
hundreds
hygiene

I

icicle
ideal
identical
illustrate
imaginary
imagine
imitate
imitation
immediately
immigrant
impatient
important
impossible
incredible
independence
independent
individual
initial
innocent
instead
intelligence
intelligent
interest
interrupt
invitation
island

J

January
jealous
jewelry
journal
journey
judgment
July
June

K

knew
knife
knives
knowledge

L

label
language
laugh
lawyer
league
leave
leisure
length
library
license
lightning
liquid
listen
loose
lovable

M

machine
magazine
manufacture

March
marriage
material
mathematics
May
mayor
meant
measure
medicine
message
millions
miniature
minute
mirror
mischief
misspell
Monday
morning
mountain
multiplication
muscle
music
musician
mysterious

N

national
natural
necessary
neighbor
neither
nephew
nervous
nickel
niece
nineteen
ninth
noisy
no one
nothing
November
nuclear

O

obey
occasion
occur
occurred
o'clock
October
office
official
often
once
operate
opinion
opportunity
opposite
ordinary
original

P

package
paid
paragraph
parallel
participate
particular
patience
people
perfect
permanent
personal
persuade
physical
picture
pleasant
please
point
poison
popular
possess
possible
practical
practice
precious
preparation
president
pretty
privilege
probably
problem
produce
protein

Q

quarter
quickly
quiet
quit
quite
quotient

R

raise
ready
realize
really
reason
receive
recipe
recognize
recommend
relieve
remember
responsibility
restaurant
review
rhyme
rhythm
ridiculous
right
rough
route

S

safety
said
salary
Saturday
says
scared
scene
schedule
science
scissors
secretary
seize
sentence
separate
September
serious
several
similar
since
sincerely
skiing
soldier
spaghetti
special
statue
stomach
straight
strength
stretch
studying
subtraction
succeed
success
suddenly
sugar
Sunday
suppose
sure
surprise
surround
symptom
system

T

table
teacher
tear
temperature
terrible
Thanksgiving
theater
thief
though
thought
thousand
through
Thursday
tired
together
tomorrow
tongue
touch
toward
treasure
tried
trouble
truly
Tuesday

U

unconscious
unfortunately
unique
universe
until
unusual
usually

V

vacation
vacuum
valuable
various
vegetable
vehicle
violence
visitor
voice
volume
volunteer

W

wander
weather
Wednesday
weight
weird
welcome
what
when
where
which
while
whole
women
write
wrong
wrote

Y

yellow
yesterday
young
yourself

Using the Right Word

You need to use "the right words" in your writing and speaking, and this section will help you do that. First, look over the commonly misused words on the next 21 pages. Then, whenever you have a question about which word is the right word, come back to this section for help. (Remember to look for your word in a dictionary if you don't find it here.)

536.1
a, an

We took a ride to look for wildlife.
(Use *a* before words beginning with a consonant sound.)
José saw an eagle and an antelope.
(Use *an* before words beginning with a vowel sound.)

536.2
accept, except

Zachary walked up to accept his award.
(*Accept* means "to receive" or "approve of.")
Except for his sister, the whole family was there.
(*Except* means "other than.")

536.3
allowed, aloud

We are allowed to read to partners in class.
(*Allowed* means "permitted.")
We may not read aloud in the library, however.
(*Aloud* is an adverb meaning "out loud" or "clearly heard.")

536.4
a lot

A lot of my friends like chips and salsa.
(*A lot* is always two words.)

536.5
**already,
all ready**

I already finished my homework.
(*Already* is an adverb telling when.)
Now I'm all ready to shoot some buckets.
(*All ready* is a phrase meaning "completely ready.")

536.6
ant, aunt

A large black ant crawled across the picnic blanket.
Aunt Lucinda, my mom's sister, got out of its way.

Using the Right Word 1

■ accept, except; allowed, aloud; a lot; already, all ready

▶ **For each of the following sentences, write the correct word or words from the pair in parentheses.**

Example: At the start of every school day, we say the Pledge of Allegiance *(aloud, allowed)*.
aloud

1. Our teacher wants us to read *(alot, a lot)* of books this year.

2. I guess I have a head start because I often read *(aloud, allowed)* to my little sister.

3. My teachers do not always *(accept, except)* late homework.

4. Our new classmate will be *(aloud, allowed)* to hand in his book report next week.

5. Zed volunteered to help clean the blackboard, but Sherman had *(already, all ready)* washed it.

6. Everyone in the class *(accept, except)* Bria takes the bus home.

7. Sean says he is *(already, all ready)* to go fishing after school.

Next Step: Use the words *accept* and *except* in sentences.

538.1
ate, eight

I ate a bowl of popcorn.

He had eight pieces of candy.

538.2
bare, bear

She put her bare feet into the cool stream.

She didn't see the bear fishing on the other side.

538.3
blew, blue

I blew on my cold hands.

The tips of my fingers looked almost blue.

538.4
board, bored

One board in the wooden floor was loose.

With nothing to do, I felt bored.

538.5
borrow, lend

It's so cold—could I borrow a sweater?
(*Borrow* means "receive.")

It's so cold—could you lend me a sweater?
(*Lend* means "give.")

538.6
brake, break

Pump the brake to slow down.

You could break a bone if you skateboard without protection.

538.7
breath, breathe

Take a deep breath and calm down. (*Breath* is a noun.)

My nose is so stuffed up that it's hard to breathe.
(*Breathe* is a verb.)

538.8
bring, take

Please bring me my glasses.
(*Bring* means "to move toward the speaker.")

Take your dishes to the kitchen.
(*Take* means "to carry away.")

538.9
by, buy

Chuck stopped by the store window.

He wanted to buy a new baseball glove.

Using the Right Word 2

■ bare, bear; board, bored; borrow, lend; brake, break;
breath, breathe; bring, take

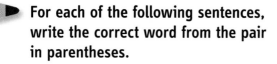

▶ **For each of the following sentences,
write the correct word from the pair
in parentheses.**

Example: Kelvin was feeling a little
(board, bored) during his
family camping trip.
bored

1. He was surprised to see a *(bare, bear)*
helping itself to a peanut butter sandwich.

2. He whispered, "Tamela—quick! May I *(borrow, lend)*
your camera?"

3. Tamela said, "Okay, but don't *(brake, break)* it."

4. "And *(bring, take)* it back to me when you're done,"
she added.

5. Kelvin held his *(breath, breathe)* as he clicked the
shutter.

6. He asked Tamela if he could *(bring, take)* the roll of
film to the store for developing.

7. She asked, "Will you *(borrow, lend)* me that picture
of the bear to show my friends?"

Next Step: Write one or two sentences that use two of these
words: *bare, board, brake,* and *breathe.*

540.1
can, may

Do you think I can go off the high dive?
(I am asking if I have the *ability* to do it.)
May I go off the high dive?
(I am asking for *permission* to do something.)

540.2
capital, capitol

The capital city of Texas is Austin.
Be sure to begin Austin with a capital letter.
My uncle works in the capitol building.
(*Capitol*, with an *ol*, refers to a government building.)

540.3
cent, scent, sent

Each rose cost one cent less than a dollar.
The scent of the flowers is sweet.
Dad sent Mom a dozen roses.

540.4
choose, chose

David must choose a different instrument this year.
Last year he chose to take drum lessons.
(*Chose* [chōz] is the past tense of the verb *choose* [cho͞oz].)

540.5
close, clothes

Please close the window.
Do you have all your clothes packed for your trip?

540.6
coarse, course

A cat's tongue feels coarse, like sandpaper.
I took a course called "Caring for Cats."

540.7
creak, creek

Old houses creak when the wind blows hard.
The water in the nearby creek is clear and cold.

540.8
dear, deer

Amber is my dear friend.
The deer enjoyed the sweet corn in her garden.

Using the Right Word 3

■ can, may; capital, capitol; cent, scent, sent; close, clothes; coarse, course

▶ **Look at the underlined word in each of the following sentences. Write a "C" if it is used correctly. If it is not, write the right word.**

Example: <u>May</u> you eat five pieces of chicken?

Can

1. The fox caught the <u>cent</u> of the chicken farm.

2. We're not going anywhere until you <u>close</u> the car door!

3. My older brother wants to take a <u>coarse</u> in car mechanics.

4. The state <u>capitol</u> of Alaska is Juneau.

5. Jill says she <u>sent</u> the package last Friday.

6. Tai asked the coach, "<u>Can</u> we play softball instead of running today?"

7. The <u>capitol</u> building of North Dakota is designed to look like a giant grain elevator.

8. Chandra's hair is thick and <u>course</u>.

9. Mom took lots of old <u>close</u> to the school's rummage sale.

10. This book cost only one <u>scent</u> at last year's sale!

542.1
desert,
dessert

Cactuses grow in the desert near our house.

My favorite dessert is strawberry pie.

542.2
dew, do, due

The dew on the grass got my new shoes wet.

I will do my research after school since the report is due on Wednesday.

542.3
die, dye

The plant will die if it isn't watered.

The red dye in the sweatshirt turned everything in the wash pink.

542.4
doesn't, don't

She doesn't like green bananas.
(*Doesn't* is the contraction of "does not.")

I don't either.
(*Don't* is the contraction of "do not.")

542.5
fewer, less

We had fewer snow days this winter than we did last year.
(*Fewer* refers to something you can count.)

That meant less time for ice-skating.
(*Less* refers to an amount that you cannot count.)

542.6
flower, flour

A tulip is a spring flower.

Flour is the main ingredient in bread.

542.7
for, four

The friends looked for a snack.

They found four apples on the table.

542.8
forth, fourth

We set forth on our journey through the forest.

Reggie was the fourth player to get hurt during the game.

542.9
good, well

Ling looks good in that outfit. (*Good* is an adjective modifying *Ling*.)

It fits her well. (*Well* is an adverb modifying "fits.")

Using the Right Word 4

■ desert, dessert; dew, do, due; die, dye; doesn't, don't; fewer, less; forth, fourth; good, well

▶ **For each of the following sentences, write the correct word from each pair of choices in parentheses.**

Example: A baby crocodile named Liz was the *(forth, fourth)* animal born at the zoo this spring.

fourth

1. Crocodiles *(doesn't, don't)* give birth to live young.

2. They *(do, due)* lay eggs, from which the babies hatch.

3. Since they feed on fish and other small water animals, they would *(die, dye)* in a *(desert, dessert)*.

4. A croc's *(good, well)* hearing allows it to hear prey.

5. A frog *(doesn't, don't)* have a chance against a croc.

6. Swamps and riverbanks with lots to eat serve crocodiles *(good, well)*.

7. Their bellies are *(fewer, less)* scaly than their backs.

8. They use their powerful tails to charge *(forth, fourth)*.

9. There are *(fewer, less)* crocodiles than alligators in Florida.

Next Step: Write one or two sentences that use two of these words correctly: *dessert, dew, due,* and *dye.*

544.1
hair, hare

Celia's hair is short and curly.

A hare looks like a large rabbit.

544.2
heal, heel

Most scrapes and cuts heal quickly.

Gracie has a blister on her heel.

544.3
hear, here

I couldn't hear your directions.

I was over here, and you were way over there.

544.4
heard, herd

We heard the noise, all right!

It sounded like a herd of charging elephants.

544.5
hi, high

Say hi to the pilot for me.

How high is this plane flying?

544.6
hole, whole

A donut has a hole in the middle of it.

Montel ate a whole donut.

544.7
hour, our

It takes one hour to ride to the beach.

Let's pack our lunches and go.

544.8
its, it's

This backpack is no good; its zipper is stuck.
(*Its* shows possession and never has an apostrophe.)

It's also ripped. (*It's* is the contraction of "it is.")

544.9
knew, new

I knew it was going to rain.

I still wanted to wear my new shoes.

544.10
knot, not

I have a knot in my shoelaces.

I am not able to untie the tangled mess.

544.11
knows, nose

Mr. Beck knows at least a billion historical facts.

His nose is always in a book.

Using the Right Word 5

■ heal, heel; hear, here; hole, whole; hour, our; its, it's; knew, new; knot, not

▶ **For the following sentences, write the correct word from each pair of choices in parentheses.**

Example: Adrian did *(knot, not)* feel well; he *(knew, new)* he had to get some rest.
not, knew

1. The train would not leave for an *(hour, our)*, but Ebony wanted to *(hear, here)* the train whistle.

2. Tera dug a *(hole, whole)* in the garden to plant a *(knew, new)* rose bush.

3. Gretchen cut her *(heal, heel)* on some broken glass when she dropped a *(hole, whole)* bottle of juice.

4. Wesley ties a *(knot, not)* so tight that *(its, it's)* impossible to untie!

5. This is *(hour, our)* cat right *(hear, here)*; that one does *(knot, not)* belong to us.

6. When Ira's gerbil got a sore on *(its, it's)* back, Ira's mom assured him that it would *(heal, heel)* just fine.

Next Step: Write two sentences using the words *its* and *it's* correctly.

546.1
lay, lie

Just lay the sleeping bags on the floor.
(*Lay* means "to place.")

After the hike, we'll lie down and rest.
(*Lie* means "to recline.")

546.2
lead, led

Today I will lead (lēd) the ponies around the show ring.
Yesterday I led (lĕd) them, too.
(*Led* is the past tense of the verb *lead*.)

Some old paint contains the metal lead (lĕd).

546.3
learn, teach

I need to learn these facts about the moon.
(*Learn* means "to get information.")

Tomorrow I have to teach the science lesson.
(*Teach* means "to give information.")

546.4
loose, lose

Lee's pet tarantula is loose!
(*Loose* [lo͞os] means "free or untied.")

No one but Lee could lose a big, fat spider.
(*Lose* [lo͞oz] means "to misplace" or "fail to win.")

546.5
made, maid

Yes, I have made a big mess.

I need a maid to help me clean it up!

546.6
mail, male

Many people get more mail on their computers than in their mailboxes.

Men are male; women are female.

546.7
meat, meet

I think meat can be a part of a healthful diet.

We were so excited to finally meet the senator.

546.8
metal, medal

Gold is a precious metal.

Is the Olympic first-place medal actually made of gold?

Using the Right Word 6

■ lay, lie; lead, led; learn, teach; loose, lose; metal, medal

For each pair of words in parentheses below, write the line number and the correct choice.

Example: 1 The teacher *(lead, led)*
2 the first graders to
3 the drinking fountain.

Answer: l. led

1   Larry was ready to *(learn, teach)* us

2 how to pan for gold. He said that early gold miners used

3 *(lead, led)* pans. Today most pans are made of plastic, not

4 *(metal, medal)*.

5   "The first thing a prospector should *(learn, teach)*,"

6 Larry said, "is which streams have gold." Then he

7 *(lead, led)* the following demonstration.

8   He put a few handfuls of *(loose, lose)* gravel from a

9 stream into a pan. He submerged the pan just under some

10 water. He shook the pan gently and removed bigger rocks.

11   "After repeating the process a few times," he

12 explained, "only a bit of black sand should *(lay, lie)* in the

13 pan. You may see little nuggets or flakes of gold, too!"

14   Larry said to pick out the gold and *(lay, lie)* the

15 pieces aside. "Don't *(loose, lose)* sight of them. Start all

16 over again, and soon you may have enough gold for a

17 *(metal, medal)*!"

548.1
miner, minor

A coal miner may one day get black lung disease.

A minor is a young person who is not legally an adult.

A minor problem is one of no great importance.

548.2
oar, or, ore

Row the boat with an oar in each hand.

Either Kim or Mike will give a report on the iron ore mines near Lake Superior.

548.3
one, won

Markus bought one raffle ticket.

He won the bike with that single ticket.

548.4
pain, pane

Injuries like cuts and scrapes cause pain.

After cleaning the dirty window, we could see through the pane of glass.

548.5
pair, pare, pear

A pair of pigeons (two) roosted on our windowsill.

To pare an apple means to peel it.

A ripe pear is sweet and juicy.

548.6
passed, past

The school bus passed a stalled truck.

In the past, most children walked to school.

548.7
peace, piece

Ms. Brown likes peace and quiet in her room.

Would you like a piece of cake, Jake?

548.8
peak, peek

The whipped topping formed a peak on my pudding.

Alex stood on a footstool to peek inside the cookie jar.

548.9
pedal, petal

Even though one pedal on the bike was broken, I was still able to pedal to school.

Chantal plucked one petal after another from the daisy.

Using the Right Word 7

■ miner, minor; oar, or, ore; pain, pane; passed, past;
peace, piece; pedal, petal

For each of the following sentences, write the correct word from each pair in parentheses.

Example: Someone put an *(oar, ore)* through a *(pain, pane)* of the boathouse window.

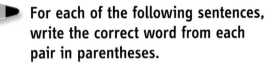

oar, pane

1. Then my brother Richard stepped on a *(peace, piece)* of glass.

2. The doctor recommended either aspirin *(ore, or)* bigger shoes for his foot *(pain, pane)*.

3. In the *(passed, past)*, he would moan and groan at every *(miner, minor)* ache.

4. He always complained about having to *(pedal, petal)* his bike to school.

5. However, he still *(passed, past)* me up!

6. Perhaps with his new shoes, we'll get some *(peace, piece)* and quiet!

7. In this picture, Richard is bending over to pick up a *(pedal, petal)* that dropped off a tulip.

Next Step: Write one or two sentences that use the words *miner* and *ore* correctly.

550.1
plain, plane

Toni wanted a plain (basic) white top.

The coyote ran across the flat plain.

A stunt plane can fly upside down.

550.2
poor, pore, pour

The poor man had no money at all.

Every pore on my nose is clogged with oil.

Please pour the lemonade.

550.3
principal, principle

Our principal visits the classrooms often.
(The noun *principal* is a school administrator.)

Her principal job is to be sure we are learning.
(The adjective *principal* means "most important.")

She asks students to follow this principle: Respect each other, and I'll respect you.
(*Principle* means "idea" or "belief.")

550.4
quiet, quit, quite

Libraries should be quiet places.

Quit talking, please.

I hear quite a bit of whispering going on.

550.5
raise, rays

Please don't raise (lift) the shades.

The sun's rays are very bright this afternoon.

550.6
read, red

Have you read any books by Betsy Byars?

Why are most barns painted red?

550.7
real, really

Mom gave me a stuffed animal, but I wanted a real dog.
(Use *real* as an adjective.)

I was really disappointed.
(*Really* is an adverb.)

550.8
right, write

Is this the right (correct) place to turn right?

I'll write the directions on a note card.

Using the Right Word 8

■ plain, plane; principal, principle; raise, rays; real, really;
right, write

▶ **Look at each underlined word in the
following sentences. Write a "C" if
it is used correctly. If it is not, write
the right word.**

Example: Sarai will <u>right</u> her uncle a
thank-you note.

write

1. He gave her a present in a
<u>plain</u> cardboard box.

2. She opened it and saw a model jet <u>plain</u>.

3. Sarai <u>really</u> wants to be a pilot someday.

4. She knows one <u>principal</u> of flight: rotating blades
provide lift.

5. It was <u>plane</u> to see she was <u>real</u> happy with her gift.

6. Her name was printed on the <u>right</u> side of the <u>plane</u>.

7. She could <u>rays</u> and lower the landing gear just as a
<u>real</u> pilot would.

8. <u>Rays</u> of light shone from the jet's headlights.

9. Sarai took her gift to school to show her class, and she
could tell that the <u>principle</u> was impressed.

Next Step: Write two sentences about a gift you've received.
Use the words *real* and *really* correctly.

552.1 road, rode, rowed

My house is one block from the main road.

I rode my bike to the pond.

Then I rowed the boat to my favorite fishing spot.

552.2 scene, seen

The movie has a great chase scene.

Have you seen it yet?

552.3 sea, see

A sea is a body of salty water.

I see a tall ship on the horizon.

552.4 seam, seem

The seam in my jacket is ripped.

I seem to always catch my sleeve on the door handle.

552.5 sew, so, sow

Shauna loves to sew her own clothes.

She saves her allowance so she can buy fabric.

I'd rather sow seeds and watch my garden grow.

552.6 sit, set

May I sit on one of those folding chairs?

Yes, if you help me set them up first.

552.7 some, sum

I have some math problems to do.

What is the sum of 58 + 17?

552.8 son, sun

Joe Jackson is the son of Kate Jackson.

The sun is the source of the earth's energy.

552.9 soar, sore

We watched hawks soar above us.

Our feet and legs were sore after the long hike.

552.10 stationary, stationery

A stationary bike stays in place while you pedal it.

Wu designs his own stationery (paper) on the computer.

Using the Right Word 9

■ road, rode, rowed; scene, seen; seam, seem; sew, so, sow;
sit, set; soar, sore; stationary, stationery

For each underlined word below, write "C" if it is correct or the right word if it isn't.

Example: Can a dragon <u>sore</u>
through the sky?

soar

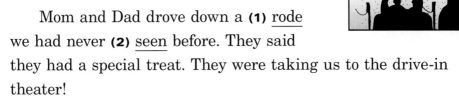

Mom and Dad drove down a **(1)** <u>rode</u> we had never **(2)** <u>seen</u> before. They said they had a special treat. They were taking us to the drive-in theater!

Marla and I **(3)** <u>rowed</u> in the back seat on the way there. A **(4)** <u>stationary</u> car didn't **(5)** <u>seam</u> like the ideal place to watch a movie, **(6)** <u>so</u> Mom said we could **(7)** <u>set</u> on some lawn chairs. Dad **(8)** <u>set</u> them up right next to the car.

This was the best **(9)** <u>seen</u> in the movie: It was dark. The bad guy had just **(10)** <u>rode</u> a small boat across a lake. He was spying on people in a cabin through the torn **(11)** <u>seem</u> of a curtain. (Gosh, too bad no one knew how to **(12)** <u>sow</u>!) Then a dragon breathed fire on the bad guy. I'll bet he was **(13)** <u>soar</u> for a few days!

Next Step: Write two sentences using the words *sow* and
stationery correctly.

554.1
steal, steel

Our cat tries to steal our dog's food.
The food bowl is made of stainless steel.

554.2
tail, tale

A snake uses its tail to move its body.
"Sammy the Spotted Snake" is my favorite tall tale.

554.3
than, then

Jana's card collection is bigger than Erica's.
(*Than* is used in a comparison.)
When Jana is finished, then we can play.
(*Then* tells when.)

554.4
their, there, they're

What should we do with their cards?
(*Their* shows ownership.)
Put them over there for now.
They're going to pick them up later.
(*They're* is a contraction of "they are.")

554.5
threw, through

He threw the ball at the basket.
It swished through the net.

554.6
to, too, two

Josie passed the ball to Maria.
Lea was too tired to guard her. (*Too* means "very.")
Maria made a jump shot and scored two points.
The fans jumped and cheered, too. (*Too* can mean "also.")

554.7
waist, waste

My little sister's waist is tiny.
Do not waste your time trying to fix that bike chain.

554.8
wait, weight

I can't wait for the field trip.
Many students complain about the weight of their bookbags.

554.9
way, weigh

What is the best way to get to the park?
Birds weigh very little because of their hollow bones.

Using the Right Word 10

■ steal, steel; than, then; their, there, they're; threw, through; waist, waste; way, weigh

▶ **For each of the following sentences, write the correct word from the pair in parentheses.**

Example: Only one superhero is the "man of *(steal, steel)*."
steel

1. He is faster *(than, then)* a speeding bullet.

2. He can see right *(threw, through)* brick walls.

3. A big safe might *(way, weigh)* a thousand pounds, but it's easy for him to lift.

4. People trust this hero with *(they're, their)* lives.

5. At lunch, Nina *(threw, through)* her cookies away.

6. Ms. Sabb said, "Nina! Don't *(waist, waste)* food!"

7. *(Than, Then)* Nina's face turned red.

8. "But *(there, they're)* too hard," she complained.

9. "*(There, Their)* must be someone who would like them," Ms. Sabb said.

10. A young boy made his *(way, weigh)* to Ms. Sabb to claim the cookies.

Next Step: Write sentences with the words *steal* and *waist*.

556.1
weak, week

The opposite of strong is weak.

There are seven days in a week.

556.2
wear, where

Finally, it's warm enough to wear shorts.

Where is the sunscreen?

556.3
weather,
whether

I like rainy weather.

My dad goes golfing whether it's nice out or not.

556.4
which, witch

Which book should I read?

You'll like *The Lion, the Witch, and the Wardrobe.*

556.5
who, that,
which

The man who answered the phone had a loud voice.
(*Who* refers to people.)

The puppy that I really wanted was sold already. Its brother, which had not been sold yet, came home with me.
(*That* and *which* refer to animals and things. Use commas around a clause that begins with *which.*)

556.6
who, whom

Who ordered this pizza?

And for whom did you order it?

556.7
who's, whose

Who's that knocking at the door?
(*Who's* is a contraction of "who is.")

Mrs. Lang, whose dog ran into our yard, came to get him.

556.8
wood, would

Some baseball bats are made of wood.

Would you like to play baseball after school?

556.9
your, you're

You'll get your ice cream; be patient.

You're talking to the right person!
(*You're* is a contraction of "you are.")

Using the Right Word 11

■ weather, whether; who, that, which; who, whom;
who's, whose; your, you're

▶ **For the following sentences, write the
correct word from each pair in
parentheses.**

Example: *(You're, Your)* going to get
all wet if you don't take an
umbrella today.
You're

1. This *(weather, whether)* is sure
to bring heavy rain.

2. *(Who, Whom)* knows *(weather, whether)* it will rain
cats and dogs . . . or fish and frogs?

3. Fred Hodgkins, *(who, which)* lives in England, said it
rained fish there in 2000.

4. The fish *(that, who)* rained down in his yard actually
came from the North Sea.

5. A waterspout, *(that, which)* is a tornado over water,
picked the fish up and then dropped them over land.

6. Mr. Hodgkins, *(who's, whose)* garden the fish fell into,
was quite surprised.

7. You would be surprised, too, if fish fell from the sky
into *(you're, your)* garden.

8. *(Who's, Whose)* going to look for fish on the ground
after the next rain?

Test Prep

For each sentence below, write the letter of the line in which the underlined word or words are used incorrectly. If there is no mistake, choose "D."

1. **A** May I use your
   B new colored pencils
   C to right a note?
   D no mistakes

2. **A** After Kwan rode his
   B bike for over an our,
   C he went to lie down.
   D no mistakes

3. **A** Bright rays of warm
   B sunlight really sparkled
   C on the morning do.
   D no mistakes

4. **A** Your probably going
   B to lose that ring if
   C you don't put it away.
   D no mistakes

5. **A** Farrah passed a mime
   B who was making
   C quite a scene on the sidewalk.
   D no mistakes

6. **A** Whose shoes have a
   B not in the shoelaces and
   C a hole by the big toe?
   D no mistakes

7. **A** I am not allowed
   B to have more than
   C one desert after dinner.
   D no mistakes

8. **A** Grandma can't hear
   B very good, so she misses
   C a lot of what we say.
   D no mistakes

9. **A** Eli said that a peace
   B of metal tore the
   C seam of his pants.
   D no mistakes

10. **A** For the fourth time, a
    B bear had been drawn to our site
    C by the sent of food.
    D no mistakes

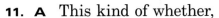

11. A This kind of <u>whether,</u>
    B <u>which</u> is hot and
      windy,
    C could <u>lead</u> to storms.
    D no mistakes

12. A Ms. Walker <u>already</u>
    B told me to <u>bring</u> the
      attendance
    C sheet to the <u>principal.</u>
    D no mistakes

13. A You could <u>dye</u> these
    B <u>clothes</u> so they would
    C not look so <u>plain.</u>
    D no mistakes

14. A <u>It's</u> vital for drivers
    B to <u>learn</u> where the
    C <u>break</u> pedal is in
      a car.
    D no mistakes

15. A If <u>their</u> going to get
    B <u>there</u> in time, they'd
    C better <u>pedal</u> fast!
    D no mistakes

16. A Tanisha will <u>except</u>
    B the third-place <u>medal</u>
    C for the <u>whole</u> class.
    D no mistakes

Understanding Sentences

A **sentence** expresses a complete thought. Usually it has a subject and a predicate. A sentence begins with a capital letter and ends with a period, a question mark, or an exclamation point.

Parts of a Sentence

560.1
Subjects

A **subject** is the part of a sentence—a noun or pronoun—that names who or what is doing something.

Marisha **baked a chocolate cake.**

A subject can also be the part that is talked about.

She **is a marvelous cook.**

560.2
Simple Subjects

A simple subject is the subject without the words that describe or modify it.

Marisha's little sister **likes to help.**

560.3
Complete Subjects

The complete subject is the simple subject along with all the words that describe it.

Marisha's little sister **likes to help.**

560.4
Compound Subjects

A compound subject has two or more simple subjects joined by a conjunction *(and, or)*.

Marisha **and her** sister **worked on the puzzle.**

Parts of a Sentence 1

■ Subjects

Write the complete subject of each sentence and underline the simple subject (or subjects).

Example: Mom and Dad built a small tree house for me.
<u>Mom</u> and <u>Dad</u>

1. My little tree house sits in our cedar tree.

2. Three tree branches support the structure.

3. A homemade wooden ladder leads up to it.

4. Some people build tree houses to live in.

5. They are like playhouses for adults.

6. Those tree houses have electricity and plumbing.

7. Most kids' tree houses have light, too—from the sun and moon!

8. My friends and I read, write, talk, and dream in my tree house.

9. We eat snacks up there, too.

10. This private place gives us space to be ourselves.

Next Step: Write two sentences about your own private place. In each sentence, underline the complete subject. Then circle the simple subject.

Parts of a Sentence . . .

A **predicate** is the part of the sentence that contains the verb. The predicate can show action by telling what the subject is doing.

> **Marisha baked the cake for my birthday.**

A predicate can also say something about the subject.

> **She is a good cook.**

A simple predicate is the verb without any of the other words that modify it.

> **Marisha baked the cake yesterday.**

The complete predicate is the verb along with all the words that modify or complete it.

> **Marisha baked the cake yesterday.**
> **She had made cupcakes, too.**

A compound predicate has two or more verbs.

> **She decorated the cake and hid it in a box in the cupboard.**

A modifier is a word (an adjective or an adverb) or a group of words that describes another word.

> **My family planned a surprise party.** (*My* modifies *family*; *a* and *surprise* modify *party*.)
> **They hid behind the door and waited quietly.** (*Behind the door* modifies *hid*; *quietly* modifies *waited*.)

Parts of a Sentence 2

■ Predicates

▶ Write the complete predicate of each sentence. Then underline the simple predicate (the verb or verbs).

Example: Angelita has made a wish.

 has made a wish

1. She wished for diamonds.

2. A diamond is one of the hardest materials known.

3. A diamond can scratch just about anything else.

4. Diamonds are formed in a hard coal called anthracite.

5. Anthracite is a beautiful, shiny black color.

6. Constant underground pressure and heat may cause a change in the coal.

7. Sometimes it becomes a colorless crystal called a diamond.

8. Most anthracite does not produce diamonds.

9. This type of coal is usually burned for heat or power.

10. It burns very cleanly.

Next Step: Write a sentence about diamonds and exchange it with a partner. Underline the complete predicate in your partner's sentence. Then circle the simple predicate.

Parts of a Sentence . . .

A **clause** is a group of words that has a subject and a predicate. A clause can be independent or dependent.

An independent clause expresses a complete thought and can stand alone as a sentence.

I ride my bike to school.

Bryan gets a ride from his dad.

A dependent clause does not express a complete thought, so it cannot stand alone as a sentence. Dependent clauses often begin with subordinating conjunctions like *when* or *because*. (See **600.2**.)

when the weather is nice

Some dependent clauses begin with relative pronouns like *who* or *which*. (See **580.1**.)

who works near our school

A dependent clause must be joined to an independent clause. The result is a complex sentence.

I ride my bide to school when the weather is nice. Bryan gets a ride from his dad, who works near our school.

Parts of a Sentence 3

■ Clauses

▶ **For each clause below, write an "I" for independent clause or a "D" for dependent clause.**

Example: all of Geeta's friends were
wearing sunglasses

I

1. because her outfit was so bright

2. Geeta often wears colorful clothes

3. once she colored her hair to match her outfit

4. which was a pair of pink polka-dot overalls

5. last spring, if it was a rainy day

6. she wore a neon-yellow rain slicker

7. when we went to the zoo on a field trip

8. Geeta dressed in safari clothes

9. she says she gets her fashion sense from her grandmother

10. who has traveled around the world

Next Step: Choose a dependent clause and an independent clause from the list above. Then combine them into one complex sentence.

Parts of a Sentence . . .

566.1
Phrases

A **phrase** is a group of related words. Phrases cannot stand alone as sentences since they do *not* have both a subject and a predicate.

566.2
Noun Phrases

A noun phrase doesn't have a predicate. A noun and the adjectives that describe it make up a noun phrase.

the new student

566.3
Verb Phrases

A verb phrase doesn't have a subject. It includes a main verb and one or more helping verbs.

could have written

566.4
Prepositional Phrases

A prepositional phrase doesn't have a subject or a predicate. However, it can add important information to a sentence. (See page 598.)

about George Washington

566.5
Appositive Phrases

An appositive phrase is another way of saying or renaming the noun or pronoun before it.

George Washington, our first president

NOTE: When you put these phrases together, they become a sentence.

The new student could have written about George Washington, our first president.

Parts of a Sentence 4

■ Phrases

▶ Identify the underlined phrases. Write "N" for a noun phrase, "V" for a verb phrase, "P" for a prepositional phrase, and "A" for an appositive phrase.

Example: Look at this book showing the flags <u>of the world</u>.

P

1. A flag <u>might have</u> horizontal bars or stripes.

2. I <u>have seen</u> that one many times before!

3. Red, <u>a popular flag color</u>, is in the flags of the three largest North American countries.

4. Our class will have its own flag <u>by the end</u> of the week.

5. <u>Your own family flag</u> can fly in front of your home.

6. You could also hang it <u>on the refrigerator door</u>.

7. George's flag has a Komodo dragon, <u>a monitor lizard</u>, on it.

8. <u>My older brother</u> would like that one.

Next Step: Write a sentence about a flag you would design. Try to include one of each type of phrase (noun, verb, prepositional, and appositive). Then identify the phrases.

Test Prep

▶ **Number your paper from 1 to 10. Read the paragraphs below. Then identify each underlined sentence part. Choose from the answers on the next page.**

Have <u>you</u> ever been stuck in a line of cars at a railroad
    1
crossing? The long wait <u>might feel</u> like several hours.
             2
<u>The average freight train—100 cars, one mile long</u>—actually
        3
takes only two or three minutes to go by. Many trains,
however, are <u>longer than average</u>. As a result, <u>drivers (and
       4   **5**
their passengers)</u> may end up waiting as long as 10 minutes
at a railroad crossing.

<u>Drivers</u> in a hurry <u>must be</u> patient. They should never
  6   **7**
try to cross the tracks before an oncoming train. <u>The train</u>
             8
may look slow moving. However, heavy freight trains <u>must
travel more than a mile</u> before stopping. Until trains <u>can fly,</u>
       9   **10**
the waits at railroad crossings are here to stay.

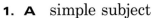

1. **A** simple subject
   B complete subject
   C simple predicate
   D complete predicate

2. **A** simple subject
   B complete subject
   C simple predicate
   D complete predicate

3. **A** simple subject
   B complete subject
   C simple predicate
   D complete predicate

4. **A** simple subject
   B complete subject
   C simple predicate
   D complete predicate

5. **A** simple subject
   B complete subject
   C simple predicate
   D complete predicate

6. **A** simple subject
   B complete subject
   C simple predicate
   D complete predicate

7. **A** simple subject
   B complete subject
   C simple predicate
   D complete predicate

8. **A** simple subject
   B complete subject
   C simple predicate
   D complete predicate

9. **A** simple subject
   B complete subject
   C simple predicate
   D complete predicate

10. **A** simple subject
    B complete subject
    C simple predicate
    D complete predicate

Using the Parts of Speech
Nouns

A **noun** is a word that names a person, a place, a thing, or an idea.

Kinds of Nouns

Proper Nouns

A proper noun names a specific person, place, thing, or idea. Proper nouns are capitalized.

> **Roberta Fischer**   **Millennium Park**   *Shrek*   **Labor Day**

Common Nouns

A common noun does *not* name a specific person, place, thing, or idea. Common nouns are not capitalized.

> **woman   park   movie   holiday**

Concrete Nouns

A concrete noun names a thing that you can experience through one or more of your five senses. Concrete nouns are either common or proper.

> **magazine   rose   Washington Monument   chocolate**

Abstract Nouns

An abstract noun names a thing that you can think about but cannot see, hear, or touch. Abstract nouns are either common or proper.

> **love   democracy   Judaism   Wednesday**

Compound Nouns

A compound noun is made up of two or more words.

> **busboy** (spelled as one word)
> **blue jeans** (spelled as two words)
> **two-wheeler   sister-in-law** (spelled with hyphens)

Collective Nouns

A collective noun names a certain kind of group.

> Persons: **class   team   clan   family**
> Animals: **herd   flock   litter   pack   colony**
> Things: **bunch   batch   collection**

Nouns 1

■ Common, Proper, Concrete, and Abstract Nouns

▶ **For each sentence, write whether the first underlined noun is common or proper.**

Example: What is a fair <u>price</u> for an
          <u>ice cream cone</u>?

          common

1. In the <u>United States</u>, <u>wealth</u> is measured in dollars.

2. The dollar bill has a <u>drawing</u> of <u>George Washington</u> on its face.

3. A picture of <u>Sacagawea</u>, a Native American woman who helped Lewis and Clark, is on the dollar <u>coin</u>.

4. Most <u>bills</u> and coins have little real <u>worth</u> by themselves.

5. For money to have value, <u>people</u> must agree on it as a symbol of fair <u>trade</u>.

6. For instance, <u>Americans</u> agree that the bill with Ben Franklin's <u>picture</u> on it is worth $100.

7. And when you trade it for 50 <u>Super Nutty Fudge Ice Cream Bars</u>, you've determined the <u>value</u> of $100!

Next Step: Write whether the second underlined noun is concrete or abstract.

Nouns . . .

Number of Nouns

572.1
Singular Nouns

A singular noun names just one person, place, thing, or idea.

room   paper   pen pal   hope

572.2
Plural Nouns

A plural noun names more than one person, place, thing, or idea.

rooms   papers   pen pals   hopes

Gender of Nouns

572.3
Noun Gender

The gender of a noun refers to its being *feminine* (female), *masculine* (male), *neuter* (neither male nor female), or *indefinite* (male or female).

Feminine (female): mother, sister, women, cow, hen

Masculine (male): father, brother, men, bull, rooster

Neuter (neither male nor female):
tree, closet, cobweb

Indefinite (male or female):
child, pilot, parent, dentist

Nouns 2

■ Number of Nouns
■ Gender of Nouns

Identify the underlined noun in each sentence as "F" for feminine, "M" for masculine, "N" for neuter, or "I" for indefinite.

HURRAY!

Example: <u>Frank</u> wanted to go fishing.
        M

1. He gathered up fishing <u>rods</u>, hooks, and bait.

2. He walked down to the <u>pier</u>.

3. Before he even got there, he heard his <u>mom</u> calling.

4. He looked at his watch and realized it was time to walk the neighbor's <u>dogs</u>.

5. Frank's neighbor, <u>Mr. Wise</u>, was ill.

6. <u>Mrs. Wise</u> was working and couldn't walk the dogs.

7. Frank put <u>leashes</u> on Skippy and Spot and took them out.

8. Frank saw one of his <u>friends</u> riding a bike.

9. He shouted, "Hey, Sandy! Let's go to the <u>lake</u>!"

10. Sandy said, "Okay! My <u>cousin</u> will come, too."

Next Step: Read the sentences above again and add either "S" for singular or "P" for plural to your answers.

Nouns . . .
Uses of Nouns

Subject Nouns

A noun may be the subject of a sentence. (The subject is the part of the sentence that does something or is being talked about.)

Joe ran away from the bee.

Predicate Nouns

A predicate noun follows a form of the verb *be* (*is*, *are*, *was*, *were*) and renames the subject.

The book is a mystery.

Possessive Nouns

A possessive noun shows ownership. (See **490.2** and **492.1** for information on forming possessives.)

The book's ending is a big surprise.

The books' bindings are torn and weak.

Object Nouns

Direct Object: A direct object is the word that tells *what* or *who* receives the action of the verb. The direct object completes the meaning of the verb.

Nadia spent all her money. (*What* did Nadia spend? The verb *spent* would be unclear without the direct object, *money*.)

Indirect Object: An indirect object names the person *to whom* or *for whom* something is done.

Joe gave Nadia the book. (The book is given *to whom*? The book is given to *Nadia*, the indirect object.)

Object of a Preposition: An object of a preposition is part of a prepositional phrase. (See page **598**.)

Nadia put the book on the shelf. (The noun *shelf* is the object of the preposition *on*.)

Nouns 3

■ Uses of Nouns

▶ **For each sentence below, tell whether the underlined noun is a subject, an object, or a predicate noun.**

Example: People like to look at <u>stars</u>.
object

1. Long ago, <u>people</u> thought certain groups of stars looked like bears, lions, and people.

2. One <u>group</u> of seven stars is known as the Big Dipper.

3. Orion the Hunter is a <u>group</u> of 20 stars.

4. In rural areas, as many as 3,000 stars might be visible to the human <u>eye</u>.

5. People in the <u>city</u> don't see that many stars.

6. One <u>woman</u> in the city painted stars on her house.

7. For the most part, stars are simply great <u>balls</u> of gas.

8. Just like the sun, stars produce <u>energy</u> as a result of nuclear reactions.

Next Step: Copy this sentence and complete it with a predicate noun: *When I looked at the sky, the clouds were _____.* Then underline the object noun in the sentence.

Pronouns

A **pronoun** is a word used in place of a noun.

An antecedent is the noun that a pronoun refers to or replaces. All pronouns have antecedents.

Anju's brother has his own skateboard now.
(*Brother* is the antecedent of the pronoun *his*.)

Number of a Pronoun

Pronouns can be either singular or plural.

I grabbed my skateboard and joined LeRon.
We were going to the skate park.

Person of a Pronoun

The *person* of a pronoun tells whether the antecedent of the pronoun is speaking, being spoken to, or being spoken about.

A first-person pronoun is used in place of the name of the speaker.

Petra said, "I like raspberry ice cream." (*I* replaces the name *Petra*, the person who is speaking.)

A second-person pronoun names the person spoken to.

Su, have you decided on a flavor? (*You* replaces the name *Su*, the person being spoken to.)

A third-person pronoun is used to name the person or thing spoken about.

Jon said that he wants pumpkin ice cream because it is so good. (*He* refers to *Jon*, the person being spoken about, and *it* refers to *ice cream*, the thing being spoken about.)

Pronouns 1

■ Number of a Pronoun
■ Person of a Pronoun

▶ **In the following sentences, write whether the underlined pronoun is first, second, or third person.**

Example: Carey asked Aunt Dulcie, "Will <u>you</u> be picking up Mac at the airport?"
second person

1. "Yes," <u>she</u> replied.

2. "May <u>we</u> join you?" asked Cleo.

3. "Are <u>you</u> both ready?" asked Aunt Dulcie.

4. When <u>they</u> reached the airport, they watched for Mac's plane.

5. Carey said, "<u>I</u> can't wait to see Mac!"

6. "I wonder if <u>he</u> will look different," Cleo said.

7. "Maybe he won't recognize <u>us</u>!" Carey worried.

8. When Mac got off the plane, he went to get <u>his</u> bags.

9. Aunt Dulcie, Carey, and Cleo were waiting there, and Mac immediately waved at <u>them</u>.

10. "Boy, that makes <u>me</u> feel good!" Carey exclaimed.

Next Step: Read each sentence again and add either "S" for singular or "P" for plural to your answers.

Pronouns . . .
Uses of Pronouns

578.1
Subject Pronouns

A subject pronoun is used as the subject of a sentence.

I can tell jokes well.

They really make people laugh.

578.2
Object Pronouns

An object pronoun is used as a direct object, an indirect object, or the object of a preposition.

Mr. Otto encourages me. (direct object)

Mr. Otto gives us help with math. (indirect object)

I made a funny card for him. (object of the preposition)

578.3
Possessive Pronouns

A possessive pronoun shows ownership. It can be used before a noun, or it can stand alone.

Gloria finished writing her story.
(*Her* comes before the noun *story*.)

The idea for the plot was mine. (*Mine* can stand alone.)

Before a noun: *my, your, his, her, its, our, their*

Stand alone: *mine, yours, his, hers, ours, theirs*

Uses of Personal Pronouns

	Singular Pronouns			Plural Pronouns		
	Subject Pronouns	Possessive Pronouns	Object Pronouns	Subject Pronouns	Possessive Pronouns	Object Pronouns
First Person	I	my, mine	me	we	our, ours	us
Second Person	you	your, yours	you	you	your, yours	you
Third Person	he	his	him	they	their, theirs	them
	she	her, hers	her			
	it	its	it			

Pronouns 2

■ Uses of Pronouns

For the underlined pronoun in each sentence below, write "SP" if it is a subject pronoun, "OP" if it is an object pronoun, or "PP" if it is a possessive pronoun.

Example: What is <u>your</u> favorite kind of candy?
PP

1. <u>I</u> like lemon drops.

2. <u>My</u> mom likes chocolate and caramel the best.

3. Dad gave <u>her</u> a whole box of chocolates.

4. <u>She</u> was thrilled!

5. First, she ate all <u>her</u> favorites.

6. Then she shared the rest with <u>us</u>.

7. We finished <u>them</u> all in no time.

8. Boy, <u>they</u> were good!

9. Poor Dad–there were none left for <u>him</u>.

10. Mom said, "Next time I'll get some for <u>you</u>."

Next Step: Write a sentence that answers the question in number 1 above. Underline the pronoun you use and tell how it is used.

Pronouns . . .

Types of Pronouns

Relative Pronouns

A relative pronoun connects a dependent clause to a word in another part of the sentence.

> **Any fifth grader who wants to join our music group should see Carlos.**

Relative pronouns: *who, whose, whom, which, what, that, whoever, whomever, whichever, whatever*

Interrogative Pronouns

An interrogative pronoun asks a question.

> **Who is going to play the keyboard?**

Interrogative pronouns: *who, whose, whom, which, what*

Demonstrative Pronouns

A demonstrative pronoun points out or identifies a noun without naming it. The demonstrative pronouns are *this, that, these,* and *those.*

> **That sounds like a great idea!**

TIP: When *this, that, these,* and *those* are used before nouns, they are adjectives, not pronouns.

Intensive and Reflexive Pronouns

An intensive pronoun stresses the word it refers to. A reflexive pronoun refers back to the subject. These pronouns have *-self* or *-selves* added at the end.

> **Carlos himself taught the group.** (intensive)
>
> **Carlos enjoyed himself.** (reflexive)

Indefinite Pronouns

An indefinite pronoun refers to people or things that are not named or known. (See page 413.)

> **Nobody is here to videotape the practice.**

Indefinite pronouns: *all, another, any, anybody, anyone, anything, both, each, each one, either, everybody, everyone, everything, few, many, most, much, neither, nobody, none, no one, nothing, one, other, several, some, somebody, someone, something, such*

Pronouns 3

■ Relative, Demonstrative, and Indefinite Pronouns

▶ **For each underlined pronoun in the sentences below, write "R" if it is a relative pronoun, "D" if it is demonstrative, or "I" if it is indefinite.**

Example: Giant pandas, <u>whose</u> only natural habitat is central China, can eat 30 pounds of bamboo every day.

R

1. <u>Some</u> can eat more than 80 pounds in a day.

2. <u>That</u> is a lot of food, even for a 300-pound animal!

3. Ask <u>someone</u> what kind of animal a panda is.

4. <u>Many</u> will say a panda is a bear.

5. <u>Others</u> will call it a member of the raccoon family.

6. With such a lean diet, pandas don't build up the fat <u>that</u> is needed for a long winter sleep.

7. <u>This</u> makes them unlike most other bears.

8. They are also active mainly at night, <u>which</u> is when raccoons are active.

9. <u>Everyone</u> was sad when giant pandas were placed on the endangered species list.

Next Step: Use a relative pronoun in a sentence about another unusual animal.

Verbs

A **verb** shows action or links the subject to another word in the sentence. The verb is the main word in the predicate.

Types of Verbs

582.1

Action Verbs

An action verb tells what the subject is doing.

> **The wind** blows. **I** pull **my sweater on.**

582.2

Linking Verbs

A linking verb links a subject to a noun or an adjective in the predicate part of the sentence. (See chart below.)

> **That car** is **a convertible.** (The verb *is* links the subject *car* to the noun *convertible*.)

> **A new car** looks **shiny.** (The verb *looks* links the subject *car* to the adjective *shiny*.)

582.3

Helping Verbs

Helping verbs (also called auxiliary verbs) come before the main verb and give it a more specific meaning.

> **Lee** will **write in his journal.** (The verb *will* helps state a future action.)

> **Lee** has been **writing in his journal.** (The verbs *has* and *been* help state a continuing action.)

Linking Verbs

is, are, was, were, am, being, been, smell, look, taste, remain, feel, appear, sound, seem, become, grow, stand, turn

Helping Verbs

shall, will, should, would, could, must, can, may, have, had, has, do, did, does

The forms of the verb *be (is, are, was, were, am, being, been)* may also be helping verbs.

Verbs 1

■ Types of Verbs

▶ **In the following sentences, write whether the underlined verb is an action verb, a linking verb, or a helping verb.**

Example: My dogs, Butch and Bailey, <u>learned</u> how to "sing."
action verb

1. They <u>can</u> bark several tunes.

2. Butch's deep "woof" <u>supplies</u> the low notes.

3. Bailey <u>is</u> the soprano of the duo.

4. They <u>sound</u> funny!

5. They <u>have</u> performed at local talent shows.

6. They <u>are</u> very popular.

7. The audience <u>cheers</u> for more.

8. Everyone <u>will</u> gather around Butch and Bailey at the end of a show.

9. The dogs just <u>love</u> all the attention!

10. Maybe someday they'll <u>be</u> famous.

Next Step: Wherever you wrote "helping verb" on your paper, write the main verb of that sentence.

Verbs . . .

Simple Verb Tenses

The tense of a verb tells when the action takes place. The simple tenses are *present, past,* and *future.* (See page **418**.)

584.1

Present Tense Verbs

The present tense of a verb states an action (or state of being) that is *happening now* or that *happens regularly.*

I like **soccer.   We** practice **every day.**

584.2

Past Tense Verbs

The past tense of a verb states an action or (state of being) that *happened at a specific time in the past.*

Anne kicked **the soccer ball.   She** was **the goalie.**

584.3

Future Tense Verbs

The future tense of a verb states an action (or state of being) that *will take place.*

I will like **soccer forever.   We** will practice **every day.**

Perfect Verb Tenses

Perfect tense is expressed with certain helping verbs.

584.4

Present Perfect Tense Verbs

The present perfect tense states an action that is *still going on.* Add *has* or *have* before the past participle form of the main verb.

Alexis has slept **for two hours so far.**

TIP: The past participle is the same as the past tense of most verbs.

584.5

Past Perfect Tense Verbs

The past perfect tense states an action that *began and ended in the past.* Add *had* before the past participle.

Jondra had slept **for eight hours before the alarm rang.**

584.6

Future Perfect Tense Verbs

The future perfect tense states an action that *will begin in the future and end at a specific time.* Add *will have* before the past participle form of the main verb.

Riley will have slept **for 12 hours by 9:00 a.m. tomorrow.**

Verbs 2

■ Simple Verb Tenses

▶ **Write the tense—*past*, *present*, or *future*—of the underlined verbs in the following sentences.**

Example: Isabel <u>loves</u> clothes.
present

1. She <u>will show</u> me her new poncho tomorrow.

2. She <u>saw</u> some great new styles in *Latina* magazine.

3. Many of her clothes <u>are</u> quite colorful.

4. She <u>enjoys</u> wearing ruffled skirts in green, purple, orange, and yellow.

5. Designers Carolina Herrera and Oscar de la Renta <u>brought</u> Latin flavor into their styles.

6. They <u>mixed</u> different textures in one outfit.

7. Famous people like Jennifer Lopez and Carlos Santana <u>design</u> their own lines of clothing.

8. Perhaps many people <u>will choose</u> to wear more Latin-flavored items.

Next Step: Write a sentence about your favorite clothes. Write it three ways, using each of the simple verb tenses.

Verbs . . .

Forms of Verbs

An action verb is called a transitive verb if it is followed by a direct object (noun or pronoun). The object makes the meaning of the verb complete.

> Direct Object: **Ann Cameron** writes books **about Julian.**

A transitive verb may also be followed by an indirect object. An indirect object names the person *to whom* or *for whom* something is done.

> Indirect Object: **Books** give children **enjoyment.**
> (*Children* is the indirect object. *Give* is a transitive verb, and *enjoyment* is the direct object.)

A verb that is not followed by a direct object is intransitive.

> **Ann Cameron** writes **about Julian in her books.** (The verb is followed by two prepositional phrases.)

A verb is active if the subject is doing the action.

> **Tia** threw **a ball.** (The subject *Tia* is doing the action.)

A verb is passive if the subject does not do the action.

> **A ball** was thrown **by Tia.** (The subject *ball* is not doing the action.)

A singular verb is used with a singular subject.

> **Ben** likes **cream cheese and olive sandwiches.**

A plural verb is used when the subject is plural. (A plural verb usually does not have an *s* at the end, which is just the opposite of a plural subject.)

> **Black olives** taste **like wax.**

Some verbs in the English language are irregular. Instead of adding *-ed*, the spelling of the word changes in different tenses. See page **588** for a chart of irregular verbs.

> I speak.   **Yesterday I** spoke.   **I have** spoken.

Verbs 3

■ Active and Passive Verbs

▶ **Decide whether the subject (underlined) does or does not do the action in the following sentences. If it does, write "active verb"; if not, write "passive verb."**

Example: A <u>mother mallard duck</u> protects her babies.
active verb

1. <u>She</u> doesn't need an umbrella to protect them, though.

2. <u>Ducklings</u> are protected by their feathers.

3. Their <u>feathers</u> help them stay warm and dry.

4. Within a day of hatching, the <u>babies</u> are led to the water by their mother.

5. The <u>ducklings</u> can already feed themselves!

6. In 50 or 60 days, <u>they</u> fly off to independence.

7. <u>Adult feathers</u> are molted by the ducks every summer.

8. By October, <u>they</u> have all their feathers again and can begin to fly south.

9. Their <u>quacking</u> can be heard by everyone!

Next Step: Choose one of the passive sentences from above and rewrite it as an active sentence.

Verbs . . .
Forms of Verbs

Common Irregular Verbs

The principal parts of some common irregular verbs are listed below. The past participle is used with the helping verbs *has, have,* or *had*.

Present Tense	I hide.		She hides.
Past Tense	Yesterday I hid.		Yesterday she hid.
Past Participle	I have hidden.		She has hidden.

Present Tense	Past Tense	Past Participle	Present Tense	Past Tense	Past Participle	Present Tense	Past Tense	Past Participle
am, is, are	was, were	been	give	gave	given	shrink	shrank	shrunk
begin	began	begun	go	went	gone	sing	sang, sung	sung
bite	bit	bitten	grow	grew	grown	sink	sank, sunk	sunk
blow	blew	blown	hang	hung	hung	sit	sat	sat
break	broke	broken	hide	hid	hidden, hid	sleep	slept	slept
bring	brought	brought	hold	held	held	speak	spoke	spoken
buy	bought	bought	keep	kept	kept	spring	sprang, sprung	sprung
catch	caught	caught	know	knew	known	stand	stood	stood
come	came	come	lay (place)	laid	laid	steal	stole	stolen
dive	dived, dove	dived	lead	led	led	swear	swore	sworn
do	did	done	leave	left	left	swim	swam	swum
draw	drew	drawn	lie (recline)	lay	lain	swing	swung	swung
drink	drank	drunk	make	made	made	take	took	taken
drive	drove	driven	ride	rode	ridden	teach	taught	taught
eat	ate	eaten	ring	rang	rung	tear	tore	torn
fall	fell	fallen	rise	rose	risen	throw	threw	thrown
fight	fought	fought	run	ran	run	wake	woke	woken
fly	flew	flown	see	saw	seen	wear	wore	worn
freeze	froze	frozen	shake	shook	shaken	weave	wove	woven
get	got	gotten	shine (light)	shone	shone	write	wrote	written

* The following verbs are the same in each of the principal parts: *burst, cost, cut, hurt, let, put, set,* and *spread*.

Verbs 4

■ Irregular Verbs

▶ **For each sentence below, write the correct form of the verb or verbs in parentheses.**

Example: I *(sit)* in the park for five
          hours yesterday.
          sat

1. Sarah had *(eat)* a candy bar
   just before supper.

2. Jasmine *(set)* the dictionary on the
   teacher's desk last Friday.

3. Jamal has already *(go)* home.

4. For some reason, Omar *(leave)* eight copies of the
   newspaper in our mailbox.

5. Olive *(swim)* 22 laps during the races last summer.

6. When Yadira's parakeet *(fly)* out of its cage, she *(run)*
   to catch it and *(put)* it back in its cage.

7. When he was little, my dad *(keep)* a squirrel as a pet.

8. The teacher *(lead)* the class to the museum's
   prehistoric exhibit.

9. Grandma had *(fall)* and had *(hurt)* her hip.

Next Step: Use the past tense of the words *bring, write,* and
          speak in sentences.

Adjectives

Adjectives are words that modify (describe) nouns or pronouns. Adjectives tell *what kind, how many,* or *which one.* (Also see pages **423–425**.)

590.1
Articles

The adjectives *a*, *an*, and *the* are called articles.

"Owlet" is the name for a baby owl.

The article *a* comes before singular words that begin with consonant sounds. Also use *a* before singular words that begin with the long *u* sound.

a shooting star   a unique constellation

The article *an* comes before singular words that begin with any vowel sounds except for long *u*.

an astronaut   an inquiring mind   an unusual outfit

590.2
Proper and Common Adjectives

Proper adjectives are formed from proper nouns. They are always capitalized. (See page **423**.)

On a cold Minnesota day, a Hawaiian trip sounds great.

Common adjectives are any that are *not* proper.

I'll pack my big blue suitcase for a weeklong trip.

590.3
Predicate Adjectives

Predicate adjectives follow linking verbs and describe subjects. (See page **470**.)

The apples are juicy. They taste sweet.

590.4
Compound Adjectives

Compound adjectives are made up of more than one word. Some are spelled as one word; others are hyphenated.

white-throated sparrows   evergreen tree

590.5
Demonstrative Adjectives

Demonstrative adjectives point out specific nouns.

This nest has four eggs, and that nest has two.

These eggs will hatch before those eggs will.

TIP: When *this, that, these,* and *those* are not used before nouns, they are pronouns, not adjectives.

Adjectives 1

■ Common and Proper Adjectives
■ Predicate Adjectives

For the sentences below, tell whether each underlined adjective is common or proper. Add a "PA" if it is a predicate adjective.

Example: My dog Ramona makes some noises that are quite <u>unusual</u>.

common, PA

1. I wish I knew what the <u>poor</u> animal is trying to say!

2. She barks a lot, but she's really <u>sweet</u>.

3. She is an <u>Australian</u> cattle dog.

4. She was born in Montana, though, so she is actually <u>American</u>.

5. Cattle dogs are <u>muscular</u> and have a lot of energy.

6. Whenever I throw a ball, Ramona makes some <u>amazing</u> catches.

7. The breed is also very <u>protective</u>.

8. Ramona's <u>low</u> growl alerts us if a stranger approaches our house.

Next Step: Write two sentences about a pet. Use a proper adjective in one sentence and a predicate adjective in the other.

592

Adjectives . . .

592.1 Indefinite Adjectives

Indefinite adjectives tell approximately (not exactly) *how many* or *how much.*

> Most **students love summer.**

> Some **days are rainy, but** few **days are boring.**

Forms of Adjectives

592.2 Positive Adjectives

The positive (base) form of an adjective describes a noun without comparing it to another noun. (See page 424.)

> A hummingbird is small.

592.3 Comparative Adjectives

The comparative form of an adjective compares two people, places, things, or ideas. The comparison is formed by adding *-er* to one-syllable adjectives or the word *more* or *less* before longer adjectives.

> A hummingbird is smaller **than a sparrow.**

> Hummingbirds are more colorful **than sparrows.**

592.4 Superlative Adjectives

The superlative form of an adjective compares three or more people, places, things, or ideas. The superlative is formed by adding *-est* to one-syllable adjectives or the word *most* or *least* before longer adjectives.

> The hummingbird is the smallest **bird I've seen.**

> The parrot is the most colorful **bird in the zoo.**

592.5 Irregular Forms of Adjectives

The comparative and superlative forms of some adjectives are different words. *More* or *most* is not needed with these words.

Positive	Comparative	Superlative
good	better	best
bad	worse	worst
many	more	most
little	less	least

Adjectives 2

■ Indefinite Adjectives
■ Forms of Adjectives

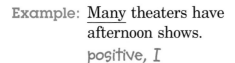 For each underlined adjective below, write whether it is positive, comparative, or superlative. Add an "I" if the adjective is indefinite.

Example: <u>Many</u> theaters have afternoon shows.

positive, I

1. The audience for a matinee is <u>smaller</u> than the audience for a show at night is.

2. Since there are <u>fewer</u> viewers in the afternoon, a good seat is easy to find.

3. <u>Most</u> people who see a movie go on the weekend.

4. That is my <u>least favorite</u> time to see a movie.

5. The <u>best</u> movie I've ever seen is the new version of *Charlie and the Chocolate Factory*.

6. It is <u>more faithful</u> to the book than the old movie is.

7. For instance, the Oompa-Loompas had <u>orange</u> skin in the old movie but not in the book.

8. The new movie's special effects are <u>more impressive</u> than the old one's were.

9. Forty years after Dahl wrote the book, it is still a <u>great</u> story.

Adverbs

Adverbs are words that modify (describe) verbs, adjectives, or other adverbs. (Also see pages **426–427**.)

The softball team practices faithfully.
(*Faithfully* modifies the verb *practices*.)

Yesterday's practice was extra **long.**
(*Extra* modifies the adjective *long*.)

Last night the players slept quite **soundly.**
(*Quite* modifies the adverb *soundly*.)

Types of Adverbs

594.1 **Adverbs of Time**	Adverbs of time tell *when*, *how often*, or *how long*. **Max batted** first. (when) **Katie's team plays** weekly. (how often) **Her team was in first place** briefly. (how long)
594.2 **Adverbs of Place**	Adverbs of place tell *where*. **When the first pitch curved** outside, **the batter leaned** forward. **"Hit it** there!**" urged the coach, pointing to right field.**
594.3 **Adverbs of Manner**	Adverbs of manner tell *how* something is done. **Max waited** eagerly **for the next pitch.** **He swung** powerfully **but missed the ball.**
594.4 **Adverbs of Degree**	Adverbs of degree tell *how much* or *how little*. **The catcher was** totally **surprised.** (how much) **He** scarcely **saw the fastball coming.** (how little) **TIP:** Adverbs often end in *-ly*, but not always. Words like *not*, *never*, *very*, and *always* are common adverbs.

Adverbs 1

■ Types of Adverbs

▶ **Identify the type of each underlined adverb. Write "T" for time, "P" for place, "M" for manner, or "D" for degree.**

Example: My little brother put a peanut butter sandwich in our DVD player <u>yesterday</u>.
T

1. He told Mom he was putting <u>away</u> his sandwich.

2. Karina <u>cleverly</u> solved the puzzle.

3. Nelson had never been to a movie theater <u>before</u>.

4. When we got to Pine Lane, Rae shouted, "Turn <u>here</u>!"

5. Emilio was <u>completely</u> exhausted.

6. <u>Finally</u>, he turned the lights off and went to bed.

7. You need to slide your feet <u>backward</u> to do this dance.

8. I had <u>hardly</u> gotten to sleep when it was time for me to get up again.

9. The coach said, "We'll have something to drink <u>shortly</u>."

Next Step: For the adverbs of time above, write whether they tell *when, how often,* or *how long.*

Adverbs . . .
Forms of Adverbs

596.1
Positive Adverbs

The positive (base) form of an adverb does not make a comparison. (See page **426**.)

> Max plays hard from the first pitch to the last out.

596.2
Comparative Adverbs

The comparative form of an adverb compares how two things are done. The comparison is formed by adding *-er* to one-syllable adverbs or the word *more* or *less* before longer adverbs.

> Max plays harder than his cousin plays, and he plays more often than his cousin does.

596.3
Superlative Adverbs

The superlative form of an adverb compares how three or more things are done. The superlative is formed by adding *-est* to one-syllable adverbs or the word *most* or *least* before longer adverbs.

> Max plays hardest in close games. He plays most often in center field.

596.4
Irregular Forms of Adverbs

The comparative and superlative forms of some adverbs are different words. *More* or *most* is not needed with these words.

Positive	Comparative	Superlative
well	better	best
badly	worse	worst

TIP: Do not confuse *well* and *good*. Good is an adjective and *well* is usually an adverb. (See **592.5**.)

Adverbs 2

■ Forms of Adverbs

▶ **For each sentence, write the comparative or superlative form of the adverb given in the blank.**

Example: My cat could predict the weather ___(well)___ than Channel 29's forecaster can!

better

1. I think Debra Lynch, the forecaster on Channel 6, predicts weather ___(well)___ of all.

2. When we read aloud in class, I thought I was reading ___(quietly)___ of anyone.

3. Then Reuben read after me, and he read ___(quietly)___ than I did.

4. Dan can type ___(fast)___ than my mom can.

5. Of all the secretaries at Bottles Incorporated, Ms. Glass types ___(fast)___.

6. The zoologist told us we could move ___(close)___ to the snake than we were.

7. Rosanna was the bravest; she moved ___(close)___ to it.

8. When Terrence explained the math homework to me, I understood it ___(clearly)___ than I did before.

9. He explains math ___(clearly)___ of anyone in class.

Prepositions

Prepositions are words that introduce prepositional phrases. They can show position or direction, or they can show some other relationship between the words in a sentence. (Also see pages **428** and **430**.)

Our cats do what they please in **our house.**

598.1 **Prepositional Phrases**	Prepositional phrases include a preposition, the object of the preposition (a noun or pronoun that comes after the preposition), and any words that modify the object.

Jo-Jo sneaks toward the gerbil cage. (*Toward* is the preposition, and *cage* is the object of the preposition. *The* and *gerbil* modify *cage*.)

Smacker watches from the desk drawer **and then ducks** inside it. (The noun *drawer* is the object of the preposition *from*, and the pronoun *it* is the object of the preposition *inside*.)

NOTE: If a word found in the list of prepositions has no object in a sentence, then it is not a preposition in that sentence.

Common Prepositions

aboard	around	but	into	over	until
about	at	by	like	past	up
above	before	down	near	since	up to
across	behind	during	of	through	upon
across from	below	except	off	throughout	with
after	beneath	except for	on	till	within
against	beside	for	on top of	to	without
along	besides	from	onto	toward	
along with	between	in	out	under	
among	beyond	inside	outside	underneath	

Prepositions

Write down the prepositional phrase from each sentence. (There are two prepositional phrases in one of the sentences.) Underline the preposition in each phrase.

Example: As you learn about fractions, you might wonder how you'll ever use them.

<u>about</u> fractions

1. Well, suppose you are making a cake for your friend.

2. You must double the cake size so you can share it with everyone.

3. The recipe lists 2 1/4 cups of flour and 2/3 cup of sugar.

4. How do you add one fraction to another?

5. Before your math lessons, you wouldn't have known.

6. Now you know that the numerator is the number before the slash.

7. The denominator is after the slash.

8. As long as there is a common denominator, you add only the numbers in the numerator.

Next Step: Write one or two sentences about some other school subject. Use the following prepositions correctly: *over, by,* and *from.*

Conjunctions

Conjunctions connect individual words or groups of words.

600.1 Coordinating Conjunctions

A coordinating conjunction connects equal parts: two or more words, phrases, or clauses.

> **The river is wide and deep.** (words)
>
> **We can fish in the morning or in the evening.** (phrases)
>
> **The river rushes down the valley, and then it winds through the prairie.** (clauses)

600.2 Subordinating Conjunctions

A subordinating conjunction is often used to introduce the dependent clause in a complex sentence.

> **Our trip was delayed when the snowstorm hit.**
>
> **Until the snow stopped, we had to stay in town.**

TIP: Relative pronouns can also be used to connect clauses. (See **564.3**.)

600.3 Correlative Conjunctions

Correlative conjunctions are used in pairs.

> **Either snow or wind can make the trip dangerous.**

Common Conjunctions

Coordinating Conjunctions
and, but, or, nor, for, so, yet

Correlative Conjunctions
either/or, neither/nor, not only/but also, both/and, whether/or, as/so

Subordinating Conjunctions
after, although, as, as if, as long as, as though, because, before, if, in order that, since, so, so that, that, though, unless, until, when, where, whereas, while

Conjunctions

■ **Coordinating Conjunctions**
■ **Subordinating Conjunctions**

▶ **Write the conjunction from each sentence below. Then write "C" for coordinating conjunction or "S" for subordinating conjunction.**

Example: Rusty and Ahmed went on a camping trip with their scout troop.
and, C

1. The scouts talked around a campfire until it was time to turn in.

2. Ahmed heard some noise, so he crawled back out of the tent.

3. While he was looking around, he saw a flying saucer!

4. Ahmed didn't know what to do, for he had never seen one in the past.

5. As Ahmed stared, Rusty came out of their tent.

6. Before he left home, Rusty put a cell phone in his bag.

7. He found the phone, and he called the police.

8. The police were not happy when they discovered the source of the "spacecraft."

9. Some older boys had been on a nearby hill, where a toy flying saucer now lay on the ground.

Interjections

Interjections are words or phrases that express strong emotion. Commas or exclamation points are used to separate interjections from the rest of the sentence.

Wow, look at those mountains!

Hey! Keep your eyes on the road!

Quick Guide: Parts of Speech

Nouns   Words that name a person, a place, a thing, or an idea (Bill, office, billboard, confusion)

Pronouns   Words used in place of nouns (I, me, her, them, who, which, those, myself, some)

Verbs   Words that express action or state of being (run, jump, is, are)

Adjectives   Words that describe a noun or pronoun (tall, quiet, three, the, neat)

Adverbs   Words that describe a verb, an adjective, or another adverb (gently, easily, fast, very)

Prepositions   Words that show position or direction and introduce prepositional phrases (on, near, over, on top of)

Conjunctions   Words that connect words or groups of words (and, or, because)

Interjections   Words (set off by commas or exclamation points) that show emotion or surprise (Wow, Oh, Yikes!)

Parts of Speech Review

▶ Write down the part of speech for each underlined word or words in the following sentences.

(1) Marcella is dreaming of her summer <u>vacation</u>. **(2)** She knows she <u>will be swimming</u> a lot. **(3)** <u>She</u> will go hiking on nature trails near her home. **(4)** Also, Marcella will not set her <u>dreadful</u> alarm clock for 6:15 a.m.!

(5) <u>If</u> her mom can take some time off work, Marcella's family will go on a trip. **(6)** <u>Oh</u>, how Marcella would like to see the Statue of Liberty! **(7)** However, that would be quite a <u>long</u> drive. **(8)** It is more than a thousand miles <u>from</u> their apartment in New Orleans to New York City. **(9)** Marcella would have to work hard to convince her family to go so <u>far</u>.

(10) Marcella is also looking forward to spending time <u>with</u> her friends. **(11)** They could rent movies <u>and</u> listen to their CD's. **(12)** <u>They</u> could have picnics out in the courtyard. **(13)** Maybe they could go fishing <u>sometimes</u>. **(14)** For sure, they will also go to the <u>library</u> a lot. **(15)** Marcella <u>knows</u> that she'll enjoy this summer.

Test Prep

▶ **Tell the part of speech for each underlined word below by writing the correct letter from the answer choices on the next page.**

What kind of work do <u>you</u> want to do when you are older?
1

<u>Many</u> occupations might interest you. Two of the careers that
2

have been around the longest are farming and <u>construction</u>.
3

People who <u>work</u> with computers have newer kinds of careers.
4

The jobs of tomorrow will be decided by what people need

<u>and</u> want. People who provide health care will probably never
5

have a <u>problem</u> finding work. There will <u>always</u> be a need
6 **7**

for people, such as truck drivers, to transport goods. Most

people who own a car will need it serviced <u>at</u> some time, so
8

mechanics should also be able to find work <u>easily</u>.
9

The best advice about getting a good job is to figure out

what <u>you</u> love doing. Get the required education or training.
10

Then <u>look</u> forward <u>to</u> a rewarding career.
11 **12**

1. **A** noun
   B verb
   C pronoun
   D adjective

2. **A** preposition
   B adjective
   C adverb
   D conjunction

3. **A** noun
   B pronoun
   C conjunction
   D verb

4. **A** noun
   B verb
   C pronoun
   D adverb

5. **A** preposition
   B adjective
   C adverb
   D conjunction

6. **A** pronoun
   B adjective
   C noun
   D adverb

7. **A** preposition
   B adjective
   C noun
   D adverb

8. **A** noun
   B verb
   C preposition
   D adverb

9. **A** pronoun
   B adverb
   C noun
   D adjective

10. **A** pronoun
    B adverb
    C noun
    D verb

11. **A** noun
    B verb
    C preposition
    D adverb

12. **A** noun
    B verb
    C preposition
    D adverb

Credits

Photos:

comstock.com: pages 3, 63, 83, 125, 195, 321, 337, 369, 379, 475

Getty Images: pages iii, 125, 143, 146, 273, 311, 321, 363, 387

Hemera: pages 7, 9, 21, 31, 43, 51, 67, 75, 139, 181, 199, 237, 253, 373, 393, 606

Ulead Systems: pages 87, 143, 146, 257, 299, 399, 431

www.jupiterimages.com: pages 312, 314, 317, 318, 319

Acknowledgements

We're grateful to many people who helped bring *Write Source* to life. First, we must thank all the teachers and students from across the country who contributed writing models and ideas.

In addition, we want to thank our Write Source/Great Source team for all their help:

Steven J. Augustyn, Laura Bachman, Ron Bachman, William Baughn, Heather Bazata, Colleen Belmont, Lisa Bingen, Evelyn Curley, Sandra Easton, Chris Erickson, Mark Fairweather, Jean Fischer, Hillary Gammons, Sherry Gordon, Mariellen Hanrahan, Mary Anne Hoff, Rob King, Lois Krenzke, Joyce Becker Lee, Ellen Leitheusser, Dian Lynch, Kevin Nelson, Douglas Niles, Sue Paro, Pat Reigel, Jason C. Reynolds, Susan Rogalski, Chip Rosenthal, Janae Sebranek, Lester Smith, Richard Spencer, Julie Spicuzza, Thomas Spicuzza, Barbara Stratton, Jean Varley, Sandy Wagner, and Claire Ziffer.

Index

The **index** will help you find specific information in this book. Words that are in italics are from the "Using the Right Word" section. The colored boxes contain information you will use often.